The Book of *Jubilees*

Supplements to the Journal for the Study of Judaism

Editor
John J. Collins
The Divnity School, Yale University

Associate Editor
Florentino García Martínez
Qumran Institute, University of Groningen

Advisory Board
J. Duhaime
A. Hhilhorst
P. W. van der Horst
A. Klostergaard Petersen
M. A. Knibb
H. Najman
J. T. A. G. M. van Ruiten
J. Sievers
G. Stemberger
E. J. C. Tigchelaar
J. Tromp

VOLUME 117

The Book of *Jubilees*

REWRITTEN BIBLE, REDACTION,
IDEOLOGY, AND THEOLOGY

By

Michael Segal

Society of Biblical Literature
Atlanta

Copyright © 2007 by Koninklijke Brill NV, Leiden,
The Netherlands

This edition published under license from Koninklijke Brill NV, Leiden, The Netherlands by the Society of Biblical Literature.

All rights reserved. No part of this work may be reproduced or transmitted in any form or by any means, electronic or mechanical, including photocopying and recording, or by any means of any information storage or retrieval system, except as may be expressly permitted by the 1976 Copyright Act or in writing from the Publisher. Requests for permission should be addressed in writing to the Rights and Permissions Department, Koninklijke Brill NV, Leiden, The Netherlands.

Authorization to photocopy items for internal or personal use is granted by Brill provided that the appropriate fees are paid directly to The Copyright Clearance Center, 222 Rosewood Drive, Suite 910, Danvers, MA 01923, USA. Fees are subject to change.

Library of Congress Cataloging-in-Publication Data
Segal, Michael, 1972-
 [Sefer ha-yovlim. English]
 The Book of Jubilees : rewritten Bible, redaction, ideology, and theology / by Michael Segal.
     pages cm. — (Supplements to the Journal for the study of Judaism ; volume 117)
 Includes bibliographical references and index.
 ISBN 978-1-58983-731-7 (paper binding : alk. paper)
 1. Book of Jubilees—Criticism, interpretation, etc. I. Title.
 BS1830.J8S4615 2012
 229'.911--dc23
                    2012042228

CONTENTS

Preface ix
Introduction 1
The Book and its Contents 2
The Literary Genre 4
Ideology and Theology in Jubilees 5
The State of Scholarship 11
A New Approach to the Study of the Book of Jubilees 21
The Date of Composition 35

PART I

THE EDITORIAL LAYER: REWRITTEN STORIES, LEGAL PASSAGES, AND THE CHRONOLOGICAL FRAMEWORK

Introduction: The Halakhic Redaction 45

Chapter One: The Entry into the Garden of Eden
(*Jubilees* 3) 47
The Connection between the Entry into the Garden of Eden and the Law of Impurity due to Childbirth (3:8–14) 47
The Relationship between the Legal Passage and the Surrounding Story 52
Summary and Conclusions 57

Chapter Two: Judah and Tamar (*Jubilees* 41) 59
The Rewritten Narrative (41:1–21, 27–28) 60
The Legal Passage (41:23–26) 65
Summary and Conclusions 71

Chapter Three: Reuben and Bilhah (*Jubilees* 33) 73
The Rewritten Narrative (33:1–9a) 73
The Legal Passage (33:9b–20) 77
Summary and Conclusions 81

Chapter Four: The Chronological Redaction of the Book of
Jubilees 83
The Births of Jacob's Sons (Jubilees 28) 85
"Let the days allowed him be one hundred and twenty years"
(Genesis 6:3) 91
The Testament of Noah (7:20–39) 93
Summary and Conclusions 94

PART II

THE ORIGIN OF EVIL IN THE WORLD

Introduction 97
The Origin of Evil in the World 98

Chapter Five: The Watchers Story (*Jubilees 5*) 103
The Biblical Background 103
A Comparison Between Jubilees 5 and Genesis 6 105
The Watchers Story in 1 Enoch 6–11 109
The Relationship between Jubilees 5 and 1 Enoch 10–11 115
Exegetical Issues in Jubilees 5 118
The Boundaries of the Story and the New Material 136
YHWH as a Righteous Judge and the Judgment of the World
(5:13–18) 137
Summary 143

Chapter Six: The Testament of Noah (7:20–39) 145
Analysis of the Testament 145
The Arrangement of the Passages Concerning the End of
Noah's Life 158
Did Enoch Die? 164

Chapter Seven: Noah's Prayer (10:1–13) 169
The Relationship Between Jubilees 10 and the Introduction to the
Book of Asaph 170
The Origin of the Demons and the Root of Evil in the World 174

Chapter Eight: The Actions of Noah's Sons 181
The Relationship Between the Description of Noah's Sons' Actions
(11:1–6) and Other Passages in the Book 181
The Sending of Ravens and Birds (11:11–13) 186

Chapter Nine: The Akedah and the Festivals of Passover/
    Unleavened Bread (17:15–18:19) 189
Theological Questions 189
The Akedah Story as a Foreshadowing of the Passover Law 191
The Legal Passage (18:18–19) 198
Summary 202

Chapter Ten: The Exodus (*Jubilees* 48–49) 203
Replacing God with Mastema 203
Who Brought the Plague of the Firstborn? 210
The Continuation of the Struggle Between Mastema and the Angel
    of the Presence 214
The Hardening of Egypt's Heart 217
The Plague of the Firstborn in the Legal Passage (Jubilees 49) 223
The Terminology of the Legal Passage 227

Chapter Eleven: The Commandment of Circumcision and the
    Election of Israel (15:25–34) 229
Israel's Special Relationship with YHWH 229
The Provenance of the Legal Passage 243

Chapter Twelve: The Prayer of Moses (1:19–21) 247
The Spirit of Belial 251

Chapter Thirteen: Abraham's Blessing and Prayer 257
Abraham's Blessing of Jacob (19:26–29) 257
Abraham's Prayer (12:19–20) 259

Summary and Conclusions 263

PART III

THE ORIGIN OF LAW

Chapter Fourteen: The Commandments, the Covenant,
    and the Election of Israel 273
The Transmission of Laws Prior to the Sinaitic Revelation 273
The Meaning of "Torah and Teʿudah" 282
Teʿudah/ʿEdut as Covenant 292
"Torah and Teʿudah"—The Stipulations of the Covenant 299
The Constancy of the Celestial Bodies 301
The "Heavenly Tablets" Containing the "Torah and Teʿudah" 313

Conclusion 317
The Literary Question 317
The Date of the Redactional Layer 319
Ideology and Theology 322

Bibliography 325
Abbreviations 345

Index of Modern Authors 347
Index of Ancient Jewish Sources 350

PREFACE

The current book began as an investigation of the ideology and theology of *Jubilees*. However, I soon expanded its focus to address fundamental philological questions and the broader question of the literary development of the book as a whole, in addition to a variety of topics from the fields of early biblical exegesis, biblical chronology, and the halakhah in the Second Temple period. Although most of this study is devoted to the detailed analysis of selected passages from *Jubilees*, I have attempted when possible to offer a broader perspective regarding the aims of the redaction of the book, and their importance for understanding the worldview of the redactional layer. The combination of these different disciplines has provided me with a richer understanding of *Jubilees*, and with a deeper appreciation of the ancient writers who are responsible for the exemplary literary work that will be studied in the pages to come.

* * *

This book was originally written as a doctoral dissertation under the auspices of the Bible Department of the Hebrew University of Jerusalem (2004). I would like to express my profound gratitude to my many teachers, friends, and family members who assisted and encouraged me throughout a decade of graduate studies, research and writing. During that time, I was fortunate to have the opportunity to study with numerous gifted scholars and teachers at the Hebrew University. First and foremost, my two doctoral advisers, Profs. Menahem Kister and Israel Knohl, invested their time and energies in both me and my work, and labored tirelessly to ensure the quality of this work. Prof. Emanuel Tov served as the advisor of my M.A. thesis on 4QReworked Pentateuch, and was involved in the early stages of this project. Dr. Baruch Schwartz, the chairman of the department, a teacher and a friend, has given of himself time and again to assist me in my academic progress. Mr. Noam Mizrahi edited my dissertation, and offered important remarks on the language and content of that version.

The two additional referees of the dissertation, Prof. Shlomo Naeh of the Hebrew University and Prof. Gary Anderson of the University of Notre Dame, both offered further comments to my work, which helped improve the final product. I was awarded a post-doctoral fellowship by the Rothschild Foundation for the 2004–2005 academic year, during which I studied at Yale University, hosted by Prof. John Collins. While there, I delivered a series of six lectures on the book of *Jubilees*, organized by Prof. Steven Fraade, and the comments that I received there have been incorporated into this work. Prof. Collins, the editor of this series, invited me to submit an English version of my book for publication. Mr. Eli Elias proofread the English manuscript and offered many valuable corrections. The indices for this volume were prepared by Ms. Avigail Wagschal.

During my many years of studies, I benefited from a number of fellowships from the Hebrew University, and I would like to express my appreciation to the university for this significant material support. The Memorial Foundation for Jewish Culture awarded me the Ephraim Urbach Postdoctoral Fellowship in order to assist in the preparation of the English version of this work.

I have already dedicated the Hebrew version of this book to my wife Aliza. She has read and offered critical comments on many passages of this book. For the past thirteen years of marriage, she has brought happiness, love, warmth and caring into my life and into our home. Words cannot describe the debt of gratitude that I feel for her support and for her friendship over the years. She, and our sons, Amichai, Elyashiv, Sariel, and Ori, make every day a joyous occasion.

I am privileged to have been raised in a home in which both the traditional learning of Jewish texts and academic studies were highly valued. It greatly pains me that my mother Susan Segal ז"ל, who was tragically killed by a drunk driver five years ago, is not here to see the fruits of my labors. She constantly encouraged me and my siblings to excel in all of our endeavors, and at the same time forged our family into a cohesive and caring group. She is sorely missed by all who knew her. My father, Dr. Robert Segal, serves for me as a model of personal integrity and intellectual curiosity, in both Jewish and general knowledge. He actively participated in the preparation of this book by translating chapters four and five. This work is dedicated to my parents with respect, admiration, and love.

The quotations of *Jubilees* throughout this book are based when possible upon the Hebrew fragments preserved in Qumran, and the translations provided in the *Discoveries of the Judaean Desert* series. If the passage quoted, or part of it, is not preserved in Hebrew, and this is the case in the vast majority of instances, then the quotations are taken from VanderKam's masterful critical edition (1989), with changes where noted. I want to thank Prof. VanderKam for generously providing me with the English translation from that edition in Word file form, thus sparing both my time in reentering the text, and the potential for error during this process. Biblical quotations have generally been adopted from the NJPS translation, with some adaptations to more closely reflect the Hebrew text.

This book presents an English translation of my Hebrew book of the same name, published by the Magnes Press of the Hebrew University of Jerusalem. Chapters 2 and 3, with minor changes, were already published in "The Relationship Between the Legal and Narrative Passages in *Jubilees*," in *Reworking the Bible: Apocryphal and Related Texts at Qumran* (eds. E. Chazon, D. Dimant and R. Clements; STDJ 58; Leiden: Brill, 2005) 203–228. An earlier version of ch. 1 appeared in Hebrew ("Law and Narrative in Jubilees: The Story of the Entrance into the Garden of Eden Revisited," *Meghillot* 1 [2003] 111–125).

INTRODUCTION

Since the discovery of the Dead Sea Scrolls more than a jubilee ago, the interest in the study of Jewish literature of the Second Temple period has steadily grown. Despite the fact that a wide variety of compositions from antiquity were known before the finding of the Scrolls, the excitement generated by the discovery of texts in their original languages, even in a fragmentary state, inspired the imagination of scholars and the public at large around the world. As the publication project progressed (and it did not always progress), the number of researchers and studies in the field grew. Every piece of leather or papyrus from the Judean desert has received, and continues to receive, detailed analysis from different perspectives that enrich each other. This fertile scholarly discourse has produced many fruits, and our understanding of the scrolls, both as individual compositions and in their entirety, has improved accordingly.

Fifteen (fragmentary) Hebrew copies of the book of *Jubilees*, an extrabiblical book composed in the second century B.C.E. that rewrites the Pentateuch from the beginning until the middle of Exodus, were preserved at Qumran. The rewriting is expressed through additions (sometimes of great length), omissions, and changes in comparison with the Torah itself. It was written originally in Hebrew, translated into Greek, and from Greek into Latin and Geʿez (ancient Ethiopic). Since the first studies of the Dead Sea Scrolls, *Jubilees* has occupied a prominent place within the literature of its time. In light of the parallels in a number of areas between the sectarian literature preserved in Qumran and *Jubilees*, this extrabiblical work has often been cited as an important source for assistance in their interpretation. The similarity between *Jubilees* and this literature is discernible on a linguistic level as well as in content, from their common ideas and beliefs to their comparable halakhic positions. Both promote a 364-day calendar, in contrast to the lunar-solar calendar of other Jewish groups in antiquity. The precise relationship between the sectarian literature and *Jubilees* has yet to be defined precisely, but the similarities between them inform us that they both emerged from the same spiritual and religious milieu. The study of each one therefore complements the other: the analysis of *Jubilees* allows for a broader and more developed perspective of the Dead Sea Scrolls, and in the other direction, the sectarian background of the scrolls contributes to our understanding of the book. In light of the conclusion of the publication of the Dead Sea Scrolls, it is necessary now, more than ever, to go back and reanalyze *Jubilees*, in addition to other compositions from the latter part of the Second Temple period.

In contrast to those works that are only found in the Dead Sea Scrolls, *Jubilees* is preserved in its entirety in a Geʿez translation. Although the reconstruction of the *Vorlage* of this translation presents its own methodological challenges, the completeness of the composition makes a particularly well-suited object of study, and moreover, provides a solid basis for a comprehensive analysis. Although we count today over 900 scrolls, a not insignificant number of them are primarily collections of fragments in which the reconstructed passages are greater than what is actually preserved. All Scrolls scholars have experienced the frustration of a break in the text right in the place that they are investigating. At times, there is no alternative other than to forego the analysis of a fragment (and often, it is better to forego this analysis rather than reconstructing what is not there). The study of a complete composition, which contains an entire world of biblical interpretation, early halakhah, and ideas and beliefs, allows for a broad and comprehensive understanding of one of the most important compositions known to us from the Jewish literature of the Second Temple period, and as a result, of fundamental notions of the scrolls as well.

The Book and its Contents

The book of *Jubilees* rewrites the Torah from Genesis through the middle of Exodus. However, in contrast to Gen 1, *Jubilees* does not open with the creation of the world, but rather, with a narrative framework dated to the 16th of the third month (1:1), the day after the Sinaitic covenant according to the *Jubilees* calendar. According to *Jub.* 1, the opening of which is parallel to Exod 24:12–18,[1] when Moses ascended Sinai for a second time, the Lord revealed to him "[the di]visions of [the ti]mes for the la[w and for the testimony]" (1:4; according to 4Q216 I, 11–12; DJD 13, pp. 5–6). At the end of the chapter, the Lord commanded

---

[1] The most prominent difference between *Jub.* 1:1–4 and the passage from Exodus is the disregard for all of the characters in the story (Joshua, the elders, Aaron, Hur) except for Moses; cf. van Ruiten 1995.

the angel of the presence "to dictate [to Moses from the beginning of creation unti]l my sanctuary is built [among them for all the ages of eternity]" (1:27; according to 4Q216 IV, 6–8; DJD 13, pp. 11–12). The angel of the presence took the tablets of the divisions of times (1:29), and immediately proceeded to fulfill God's command. The creation story (parallel to Gen 1) is therefore presented as the continuation of the narrative framework: "[The angel of the presence said to Moses by the word of the Lord: 'Write all the wor]ds of the creation...'" (2:1; 4Q216 V, 1). The influence of the narrative frame is discernible throughout the book, as the angel of the presence is presented as the speaker and narrator.[2]

One can divide the content of *Jubilees* into a number of units or cycles of stories:

(1) Chapter 1: Introduction, narrative framework
(2) Chapters 2–10: Stories about Adam and Noah (Primeval History)
(3) Chapters 11–23:8: Stories about Abraham
(4) Chapter 23:9–32: Appendix following Abraham's death
(5) Chapters 24–45: Stories about Jacob and his sons
(6) Chapters 46–49: Slavery in Egypt and the Exodus
(7) Chapter 50: Conclusion

Sections 2–3, 5–6 are based upon the stories in the Torah. However, alongside the material common to the rewriting and its sources, one also finds numerous changes and additions, including a number of lengthy, new passages. For example, many testaments and blessings from parents to their offspring were added.[3] The sequence of the stories within each unit generally follows the biblical order, but they were sometimes reordered due to chronological considerations. For example, the story of the sale of Joseph was moved earlier, to *Jub.* 34, prior to Isaac's death (36:18), in contrast to the order in which they are presented in the Pentateuch (Isaac dies in Gen 35:29; Joseph is sold in Gen 37).[4] Units 1, 4, and 7 are formally anomalous: both regarding their location and their content; they are not direct rewritings of the pentateuchal

---

[2] For the biblical roots of the angel of the presence and his functions in *Jubilees*, see Dimant 1994; VanderKam 2000b.
[3] Testament of Noah (7:20–39); Testament of Abraham (to all of his descendants in ch. 20; to Isaac in ch. 21); Abraham's blessing of Jacob (22:10–30); Rebecca's blessing of Isaac (25:11–23); Rebecca's testament to Jacob (35:1–8).
[4] For the exegetical and chronological considerations, see p. 121, n. 49.

stories, but rather serve as a literary framework, both surrounding and within the rewritten stories.

We do not know the original name of this book with certainty. The prologue opens with the words, "These are the words regarding the divisions of the times of the law and of the *te'udah*, of the events of the years, of the weeks of their jubilees…," and the expression "divisions of times" recurs a number of times in ch. 1 (vv. 4, 26, 29). One can also rely upon *Damascus Document* XVI, 2–4, in order to arrive at the conclusion that the original title of *Jubilees* was based upon its opening: "And the explication of their times, when Israel was blind to all these; behold it is specified in *the Book of the Divisions of the Times in their Jubilees and in their Weeks*."[5] The meaning of this sentence appears to be that the periods of Israel's "blindness" from the pentateuchal laws are listed in detail in the book entitled "Divisions of the Times in their Jubilees and in their Weeks." The term "blindness" refers to one of two subjects: either the periods of time prior to the giving of the various laws to Israel, or the forgetting of the laws by Israel. Both possibilities fit *Jubilees*, which maintains that the commandments were revealed gradually to Israel, and which attempts to precisely date the various events in Genesis and Exodus.

The Literary Genre

Jubilees is rightly considered one of the prominent examples of "Rewritten Bible".[6] The work generally follows the content and order of Genesis and Exodus, although sometimes certain changes in sequence have been introduced, often due to chronological considerations. In the rewriting of the Torah, a new work was created, which contains new ideas and biblical interpretation (in the broadest sense of the word), but one can almost always identify the biblical passage underlying the reworking. Entire passages from the Pentateuch were copied into the new literary work, often with only minor changes. As in any case of Rewritten Bible, the dependence upon the Torah reflects the author's desire to impart legitimacy and authority to his book, a desire that is fulfilled by connecting the new work to the holiest of compositions, the

---

[5] Translation according to Baumgarten and Schwartz 1995: 39.
[6] For the term Rewritten Bible, see the descriptions and discussions of Vermes 1973, esp. p. 95; Nickelsburg 1984; Harrington 1986; Alexander 1988; Segal 2005; Bernstein 2005. Werman (1995a: 368–372) discussed the categorization of *Jubilees* as Rewritten Bible in light of Alexander's definition of the term.

Pentateuch. The new worldview and the reading of the Bible in a different light are not presented as if created *ex nihilo*. Once the rewriter integrated his thoughts within the Torah itself, they became part of the accepted and authoritative collection of beliefs and ideas. Although the views expressed in *Jubilees* sometimes contradict those expressed in the Pentateuch, their presentation within the biblical framework granted them legitimacy in the eyes of the target audience.[7] One can explain some of the new elements in the book as the author's attempt to solve exegetical problems in the biblical text.[8] In contrast, there are new components in *Jubilees* that did not arise from a difficulty in the reading of the Bible (exegesis), but rather reflect the beliefs and ideas that have been imposed on the biblical stories (eisegesis).[9] It is not always a simple methodological task to distinguish between exegetical and ideological considerations.[10] First, the interpreter's worldview may cause him difficulty when coming to interpret a work based upon a different perspective. Second, an interpreter is liable to solve an actual exegetical problem by inserting a new idea into the composition. Both of these cases reflect interpretation, and in both, one must differentiate between the worldview of the rewriter and the exegetical difficulties that arise in every reading of a text.

Ideology and Theology in Jubilees

The unique outlook of *Jubilees* has been described in various studies. The four primary ideological and theological positions that *Jubilees* has introduced into the stories of the Torah, with the first two unique to this work, can be described as follows:[11]

---

[7] Therefore, a rewriting cannot replace the Bible itself, because without the biblical source, the rewriting will lose the authority that it needs. This is the paradox of the phenomenon of Rewritten Bible: the connection to the Bible is intended to bolster the claims of the rewriter, who essentially claims that what he is suggesting is not new, but is present in the Bible itself. However, at the same time, by including new ideas in the text of the Torah (at times contrary to the views expressed there), the rewriter undermines the same authority upon which he relies. The rewriter in effect asks the reader to rely upon the biblical source, but to understand it according to the rewriting.

[8] As emphasized by Endres 1987; compare also the numerous examples from *Jubilees* compiled by Kugel 1997; 1998.

[9] Cf. Testuz 1960, who emphasizes this aspect of *Jubilees*.

[10] As emphasized recently by Halpern-Amaru 1999: 133–146.

[11] The description here is based principally upon my own research, but also on the descriptions suggested by others; compare especially VanderKam (1997: 16–19), who also delineated four characteristics, but defined them differently.

(1) *The Giving of Laws to Israel prior to Sinai*: One of the most prominent features throughout the book is the combination of stories from the patriarchal period with the pentateuchal laws. In the Torah, almost all of the laws are first presented within legal collections that appear following the Sinaitic revelation, while in *Jubilees*, the laws are generally adduced within the framework of stories of the preceding period; there are very few collections of laws,[12] as most appear within the context of a narrative. Some of these stories are presented as precedents for the laws: the forefathers behaved in a certain way, and their actions are obligatory for later generations. For example, Adam entered the Garden of Eden forty days after he was created and his wife was brought there eighty days after her creation (*Jub.* 3:9). Basing itself upon these narrative details, *Jub.* 3:8–14 derives the periods of time in the law of the parturient mother (Lev 12) before which a new mother is prohibited from entering the temple or from coming into contact with sancta, forty days for the birth of a boy and eighty days in the case of a girl. In other cases, if a patriarch violated a law mentioned elsewhere in the Torah, *Jubilees* feels it necessary to explain the biblical account in light of this law (see the story of Reuben and Bilhah in *Jub.* 33), because the laws are written on the Heavenly Tablets, and are thus in existence from the beginning of time.[13]

The pentateuchal laws are the stipulations of the covenant between the Lord and Israel, which was established at Mount Sinai. In the Torah, the election of Israel as a special nation is understood as recompense for their acceptance of God's commandments: "Now then, if you will obey me faithfully and keep my covenant, you shall be my treasured possession among all the peoples, for the earth is all mine. And you shall be to me a kingdom of priests and a holy nation…" (Exod 19:5–6). But in the view of *Jubilees*, Israel was already awarded this special status from the time of creation:[14]

> (19) [He said to us: "I will now separate for myself] a people among my nations. And [they will keep Sabbath. I will sanctify them as my people, and I will bless them. They will be my people and I will be their God."]

---

[12] Except for the Passover laws in *Jub.* 49 (parallel to the Passover laws in Exod 12), and the Sabbath laws at the end of the book (50:6–13a).

[13] García Martínez 1997; Werman (1999) 2002; Kister 2001.

[14] The text here is according to 4QJub^a (4Q216) VII, 9–13 (eds. VanderKam and Milik; DJD 13, pp. 19–20).

(20) And he chose the descendants of Jacob among [all of those whom I have seen. I have recorded them as my first-born son and have sanctified them for myself] for all the age(s) of eternity. The [seventh] day [I will tell them so that they may keep Sabbath on it from everything, (21) as he blessed them and sanctified them for himself as a special people] out of all the nations and to be [keeping Sabbath] together [with us.] (2:19–21)

This notion has consequences for the other part of the covenant: if Israel is indeed the Lord's "[special people]" from the time of creation, then their requirement to observe the commandments was also in force from that time as well. The giving and observance of the commandments in the patriarchal period are thus the direct result of the special relationship between God and Israel during this early period. The stipulations of the covenant are recorded on the Heavenly Tablets, which come in the place of the earthly "Tablets of the covenant/ '*ēdut*," because these were only given later at Mount Sinai.

(2) *A Heptadic Chronological System (instead of the decimal system used throughout the Bible)*:[15] All events from creation until the entry into the promised land are dated according to a chronological system of jubilees (49 years), weeks (7 years), and years. The book extends over a period of fifty jubilees, or a "jubilee of jubilees" (2450 years). The foundational events in Israelite history, the Exodus, the giving of the Law, and the entry into the Land, all took place in the fiftieth jubilee (50:4). The release from slavery and the return to the ancestral land are the focus of the jubilee law of Lev 25. *Jubilees* thus transformed the biblical law, which relates to the individual, into a description of national redemption in a specific historical context, when Israel left Egypt, and returned to their inheritance, the land of Israel.[16]

Other works from the Second Temple period also describe periods of history using the terminology of "jubilees" and "weeks" (cf. Dan 9:24–27; the *Apocalypse of Weeks* [*1 Enoch* 93; 91]; *Testament of Levi* 17; *Assumption of Moses*; *Apocryphon of Joshua* [DJD 22]; *Apocryphon of Jeremiah* [DJD 30]; 11QMelchizedek [DJD 23]), but *Jubilees* is the only one to apply this chronological system in a systematic, detailed fashion throughout

---

[15] Elior 2004 traced the motif of the the number seven in priestly literature from the book of Ezekiel, through the Qumran Scrolls, until the Hekhalot literature, and demonstrated that its use in *Jubilees* is part of broader, priestly phenomenon, and not the invention of the redactor of *Jubilees*.
[16] VanderKam (1995) 2000: 540–544.

the composition.[17] The bounding of the period described in *Jubilees* by a "jubilee of jubilees," from creation until the entry into the Land, informs us of the editor's worldview: the world functions according to predetermined periods of time, at the end of which it returns to its original state. A complete period of history has passed and a new one begins with Israel's receiving of the Torah and its arrival in the Promised Land. This cyclical view of history is based upon the establishment of a fixed chronological system, and the events that occur within it, from the beginning of the world.

The solar calendar used in *Jubilees* is also based on a similar concept.[18] According to the description in *Jub.* 6:23–38, a year lasts for 364 days (see especially vv. 32, 38). The number 364 is divisible by 7, and the year therefore contains exactly 52 weeks: "All the days of the commandments will be 52 weeks of days; (they will make) the entire year complete" (v. 30). Since the number of days in the year is divisible by 7, every date in the calendar falls out on a set day during the week, which remains constant from year to year. Moreover, the calendar is divided into four quarters, each of which consists of three months of 30 days, with an extra day in the third month.[19] The calendar begins each year on Wednesday,[20] apparently because the celestial bodies were

---

[17] The vast quantity of chronological details sometimes also led to complications (apparently the editor was unaware of these), and one can point to certain inconsistencies within the chronological framework. Wiesenberg (1961) identified some internal chronological contradictions, and relied upon them to build a theory of a double redaction of *Jubilees*. VanderKam ([1995] 2000: 532–540) addressed the chronological problems in the Abraham story cycle, and instead of proposing a comprehensive solution, solved each of the problems individually, including correcting some of the dates that he deemed to be textually corrupt. It seems that most of the problems (except for those that arose from transmissional errors) are the result of the editor's attempt to impose the new chronological framework on all of the events in Genesis, without noticing all of the chronological inconsistencies that were created. Despite the editor's clear abilities in the area of chronology, he was unable to steer clear of all errors in the many dates that he added to his composition.

[18] Ben-Dov and Horowitz (2003) have suggested that the Mesopotamian roots of the 364-day calendar indicate that this was not in fact a solar calendar. But as they note, *Jub.* 2:8–9 (parallel to Gen 1:14–18), asserts the exclusive status of the sun for the determination of time and seasons. *Jubilees* differs in this respect from the calendrical texts that have been preserved from the Second Temple period (Ben-Dov and Horowitz 2003: 17, 23–24). Cf. also *Jub.* 6:36 ("There will be people who carefully observe the moon with lunar observations..."), which polemecizes against those who incorporate lunar observations in their calendars.

[19] For a summary of these calendrical issues, see VanderKam 1998.

[20] Jaubert (1953) arrived at the same conclusion based upon an analysis of the dating of events in *Jubilees* (see also VanderKam 1979). Jaubert's theory was confirmed with

created on that day (Gen 1:14–19). The calendar therefore suggests an internal cyclical pattern, within the broader chronological framework of the book.

(3) *Angelology*: In common with other works of the Second Temple period, *Jubilees* assigns an important role to heavenly beings in the administration of the world.[21] The angels are divided into two camps, good and evil. Among the good angels, the angels of the presence and the angels of holiness are the "two great kinds"[22] (2:18). They were created on the first day of creation, together with angels of lower status, who are responsible for the forces of nature (2:2).[23] The angels of presence and holiness assist God and his nation, Israel (18:9 [Abraham]; 48:11, 13, 15–16). They observed the Sabbath laws with the Lord from the time of creation (2:17–21), and were even created already circumcised (15:27).[24] The angels also have the responsibility of teaching: they taught Adam how to work in the Garden of Eden (3:15), and angels, known as the Watchers, "descended to earth to teach mankind and to do what is just and upright upon the earth" (4:15). They serve as intermediaries between God and human beings (cf. 3:1, 4–5, 12, 15; 4:6, 15; 5:6, 23; 8:10; 10:7, 10–13 et al.). In certain instances, an angel or angels in *Jubilees* come in the place of God in the Pentateuch.[25] The most conspicuous case of the replacement of God by an angel is the narrative frame of the entire book, in which the angel of the presence speaks to Moses at Sinai, and dictates to him from the Heavenly Tablets.

---

the publication of the Dead Sea Scrolls, which include calendrical texts that assume an identical calendar, which begins each year on a Wednesday; see Talmon (1958) 1989.

[21] Regarding the belief in angels in the Bible, see Rofé 1979; Dimant (1994) addressed the status and functions of angels in *Jubilees*.

[22] The adjective "great" appears in the Geʻez translation, but is absent in 4Q216 VII, 8–9 (DJD 13, pp. 19–20), and it is possible that it was introduced secondarily under the influence of "a great sign" in v. 17. However, it is clear that both of these classes had a special status amongst the angels.

[23] Kugel (1998a: 124–125) referred to these lower-class angels as "heavenly Sabbath gentiles," because in contrast to the other angels, they do not rest on the Sabbath (2:17–18). However, as will be suggested, the distinction between the angels of presence and holiness, and those divine beings of lesser status, is the result of a fundamental theological position regarding the creation of the world and all that it contains.

[24] These two commandments serve as signs of the covenant between God and his nation. One can also add the festival of Weeks (or: Oaths), the festival of the covenant, which was celebrated by presumably the same angels "from the time of creation until the lifetime of Noah—for 26 jubilees and five weeks of years" (6:18).

[25] See the list of sources adduced by VanderKam 2000b.

The general effect of the insertion of the angels into the stories is the distancing of God from the everyday events of the world, transforming him into a transcendental deity.

Parallel to the good heavenly forces, there are also evil beings that operate in the world. The head of the evil forces is named either Belial (1:20; 15:33) or Mastema (10:1–13; 11:5, 11; 17:16–18:19; 19:26; 48; 49:2). Mastema's role in the Akedah story (17:15–18:19) is identical to that of Satan in the narrative frame of Job, and *Jub.* 10:11 even refers to him as Satan. Evil spirits, the descendants of the Watchers (10:5), serve under Mastema's control in order to cause humanity to sin, and bring about their punishment, possibly even death (7:27; 10:1–13). They are also responsible for the illnesses in the world (10:12–13). According to the story in *Jub.* 10:1–13, God imprisoned the spirits in the place of judgment in response to Noah's prayer, but released one-tenth of them at the request of Mastema. The evil forces are appointed over the nations, while YHWH alone has responsibility for Israel (15:31–32).[26]

(4) *Priestly Outlook:*[27] In the rewritten stories in *Jubilees*, the patriarchs behaved like priests: Adam and Enoch offered incense (3:27; 4:25), and other forefathers brought sacrifices (Adam, Noah, Abraham).[28] When Jacob blessed his sons, Levi received the preferred blessing (31:12–17), and in general, he is elevated above his brothers in chapters 30–32. In addition, Levi is the only one of Jacob's sons to inherit his father's and ancestors' books, "so that he could preserve them and renew them" (45:16).[29] Based upon these considerations, it has been suggested that the author of this book was of priestly origins.

In addition to the elevated status of Levi, and the transformation of the forefathers into priests, one can add the following details or ten-

---

[26] Cf. also 12:20; 19:28.

[27] See Charles 1902: 73; Testuz 1960: 29–30; Berger 1981: 298; Schwarz 1982: 108–111, 127–129; Wintermute 1985: 45; Endres 1987: 238–249; VanderKam 1997: 19; Halpern-Amaru 1999: 149–159.

[28] As noted by Kugel (1993: 17–19), the forefathers also offered sacrifices in the Pentateuch; however, it is characteristic of early exegetes to assume that anyone who does so must be a priest. This view is not limited to *Jubilees*. Thus for example, Chronicles traces Samuel's lineage as a Levite (1 Chr 6:13, 18), since the book of Samuel describes how he served in the House of the Lord in Shiloh, and offered sacrifices on behalf of the people.

[29] Similarly, Noah transmitted his books to his preferred son, Shem (10:14).

dencies in the book that hint to a priestly provenance: (a) The laws of sacrifices and the cult are given special emphasis throughout the book (for example, 7:30–32; 21:5–8 et al.). (b) All Israelites are considered priests, apparently in light of the description of the covenant in Exod 19:5–6:[30] "... and you shall be my treasured possession among all the peoples... and you shall be to me a kingdom of priests and a holy nation...." This motif recurs a number of times in *Jubilees*, and has also influenced a number of halakhic positions expressed therein, specifically regarding purity, impurity, and fornication. For example, the prohibition against fornication directed at the daughter of a priest (Lev 21:9) has been expanded in Abraham's testament to apply to all Israelite women (*Jub.* 20:4),[31] and the prohibition against sexual impropriety attached to the story of Reuben and Bilhah is formulated as follows: "No sin is greater than the sexual impurity which they commit on the earth because Israel is a holy people for the Lord its God. It is the nation which he possesses; it is a priestly nation; it is a priestly kingdom; it is what he owns. No such impurity will be seen among the holy people" (33:20). (c) According to Halpern-Amaru, the emphasis on genealogy, and in particular the addition of women's names, stems from a priestly perspective that integrally connects lineage and holiness.[32]

The State of Scholarship

The predominant method for the study of *Jubilees* is the result of its literary genre. The book rewrites the Torah from the beginning until Exod 12, while adding (sometimes extensively), omitting, or changing the biblical text; however, beyond the new components, one can still usually identify the text of the Torah that was the source for this rewriting. The similarity between the biblical source and the rewriting allows for a comparison between the two layers, and then an analysis of the characteristics of the new material. Scholars generally compare the rewritten stories directly with the Pentateuch. Every difference, except for those that can be attributed to a textual witness of the Torah that

---

[30] Schwartz (1992b) traced the interpretive history in antiquity of the expression "kingdom of priests" (see especially his discussion of *Jubilees* on pp. 59–60); see also Halpern-Amaru 1999: 150–151.
[31] Finkelstein 1923: 56–57; Halpern-Amaru 1999: ibid.
[32] Halpern-Amaru 1999: 154–155, based upon Schwartz 1990a: 126–127; 1990b: 165.

Jubilees may have relied upon (including the [pre-]Samaritan Pentateuch, Hebrew manuscripts from Qumran, the Septuagint, the Peshitta, Aramaic Targumim, or the Geʿez translation of the Torah),[33] is considered the work of "the author of *Jubilees*." All of the many, various phenomena have been attributed to this one putative author.[34]

The study of the ideology and theology of *Jubilees* reflects this same general approach. The numerous studies that have been written on the worldview of the composition have examined the book from two directions:

(1) In their discussion of the passages that rewrite the biblical stories—whether it be through the addition of new material, omissions, or changing of details in the biblical stories—interpreters have analyzed the differences between the rewritten version and its source, and attempted to explain the motivations for these differences. If the difference does not seem to be the result of exegetical considerations, then it can be attributed to the worldview of the author.

(2) Scholars have addressed the long additions to the biblical text that appear throughout the composition, sometimes in the form of a testament of one of the patriarchs or matriarchs, and sometimes in other forms. For example, ch. 21 includes Abraham's testament to Isaac, ch. 22 conveys Abraham's blessing to Jacob right before Abraham's death, and in ch. 23, following the description of Abraham's death, an extensive eschatological passage was added. None of these additions can be classified as a rewriting of the biblical story, but rather are the original work of "the author of *Jubilees*," and they explicitly express his viewpoint.

---

[33] VanderKam (1977: 103–205) compared *Jubilees* to all available textual witnesses of the Pentateuch in order to determine upon which version of the Torah *Jubilees* is based.

[34] VanderKam (2001: 17–18), reflecting the prevailing perspective in *Jubilees* scholarship, notes:
> It has indeed been argued that *Jubilees* is a composite work, consisting of an original text and two subsequent revisions of it (Davenport). The evidence on which this thesis rests, however, has not proved very convincing to scholars...
> It has also been argued (Wiesenberg) that chronological inconsistencies in the book point to the activity of more than one writer... The overall chronology of the book appears to be unified, even if, quite understandably, occasional errors have crept into the author's numerous calculations.

I accept VanderKam's reservations regarding these two theories (which indeed are unconvincing), but not his final conclusion: "Assuming then that the book is a unity as we have it..." (ibid., p. 18). In this study, I will suggest that it is possible to distinguish between a crystallized editorial layer, and the sources included therein.

These two kinds of sources complement one another when examined together, and allow for a complete picture of the ideology and theology of the composition. The differences that are identified from the rewriting are combined with the set of ideas that appear in the large additions. At the same time, scholars sometimes interpret certain details in the rewritten sections, which differ from the biblical source, in light of the ideas expressed extensively in the long additions.

In the last century, a number of comprehensive studies of the beliefs and ideas of *Jubilees* have been written. Testuz (1960), the author of the last such comprehensive study, gathered a significant amount of material from *Jubilees*, but did not analyze it in depth.[35] In addition, since his work, great progress has been made in the field of Jewish literature of the Second Temple period, first and foremost due to the publication of the Dead Sea Scrolls, the vast majority of which were unavailable to Testuz when he composed his study. This progress necessitates a renewed, comparative study of all of the compositions from this period. Earlier studies of *Jubilees*, such as those of Charles (1902), Martin (1911), and Büchler (1930), were composed prior to the discovery of the Qumran Scrolls, and therefore necessarily present only a partial picture of the place of *Jubilees* within the context of Second Temple literature. The introductions to the translations of *Jubilees* provided by Berger (1981) and Wintermute (1985), although more recent, provide only brief sketches of the views of *Jubilees*.

In addition to the general overviews of the ideology and theology of *Jubilees*, specific topics within this area of study have been investigated:

(1) **Law:** Albeck (1930); Anderson (1994)
(2) **Chronology:** Wiesenberg (1961); VanderKam ([1995] 2000); Scott (2005); **Calendar:** Jaubert (1953); Talmon ([1958] 1989); Baumgarten ([1963] 1977); VanderKam (1979)
(3) **Eschatology:** Davenport (1971)
(4) **Determinism and the Heavenly Tablets:** Böttrich (1997); García Martínez (1997)
(5) **Belief in Angels:** Dimant (1974; 1994); Eshel (1999)
(6) **Uniqueness of Israel and the Relationship to the Nations:** Schwarz (1982); Werman (1995a)

---

[35] As VanderKam (1997: 12) wrote: "much of his book proves to be little more than a repetition of what *Jubilees* says on a variety of subjects, with less analysis than one might have expected...."

(7) **Status of Women:** Halpern-Amaru (1994, 1999)
(8) **Writing as an Authority Conferring Strategy:** Najman (1999)

Two additional comprehensive studies of *Jubilees* were written in the past twenty years, neither of which focus on ideology and theology, but both of which touch on these areas: Endres (1987) analyzed the biblical interpretation in *Jubilees*, and specifically in the narratives about Jacob. He studied the difficulties in the biblical text that caused "the author of *Jubilees*" to add or insert exegetical comments into his biblical source, and described the outlook expressed in the book in very general terms. Van Ruiten (2000) analyzed *Jub.* 2–10 parallel to Gen 1–11, including its ideological and theological aspects.

Almost all of the studies mentioned above share the assumption that *Jubilees* is a unified, homogenous composition. In general, scholars have been content with a comparison between *Jubilees* and the Torah, and have attributed any difference between them to "the author of *Jubilees*." The negation of the assumption that the composition is the product of one author (as I will attempt to demonstrate in detail), would therefore have far-reaching implications for the study of the ideology and theology of this book. If the book is composed from different sources or traditions,[36] one cannot describe its worldview without distinguishing between passages of different origins.

Among the studies of *Jubilees*, a few have suggested that it is composed of different layers, or that isolated passages are secondary additions to the original version of the book. Two scholars, Wiesenberg and Davenport, suggested comprehensive theories regarding the redaction of *Jubilees*.

Wiesenberg (1961) addressed inconsistencies and contradictions within the chronological framework of the composition, and concluded that *Jubilees* is composed of different strata, and that its current form

---

[36] Throughout this study, I use the term "source" to denote a written text, often a single passage, which the editor of *Jubilees* incorporated into his composition. It is not my intent to allude to the use of the term "sources" in pentateuchal criticism, which describes ancient, lengthy, continuous compositions that were combined with one another. I use the term "tradition" to indicate dependence upon earlier material, written or oral, which cannot be classified as direct literary dependence. Direct dependence upon another composition can be demonstrated through three common characteristics: content, sequence, and terminology. Common content alone is not sufficient to demonstrate direct dependence, and at most points to a "tradition" and not a "source".

is the result of redactional activity. However, his claims are generally not convincing. One of the main contradictions that he adduced is the result of an error in textual transmission: the Ethiopic text to *Jub.* 22:1 reads the "44th" jubilee, but Dillman already suggested to correct this to the "43rd". Dillman's suggestion has been confirmed by a Hebrew version of the verse preserved in one of the Qumran Scrolls (4Q219 II, 35; DJD 13, pp. 47, 50).[37] Most of the other chronological problems upon which Wiesenberg built his theory, more likely result from the difficulties created in attempting to apply a detailed chronological framework to the many events from Genesis and Exodus. Despite a few inconsistencies, it appears that the entire chronological framework throughout *Jubilees* is the product of a single author.[38]

Davenport investigated the eschatology of *Jubilees*. He suggested that the book can be separated into an original composition, and two subsequent recensions.[39] Davenport relied upon two considerations: (a) the analysis of eschatological passages and the views expressed therein; (b) inconsistencies in the composition, for example, regarding the roles of the angel of the presence and Moses in the recording of the revelation at Sinai. However, most of Davenport's distinctions are not convincing. His interpretive considerations, and especially the inconsistencies that he identified, do not stand up to critical analysis. For example, according to the Ethiopic translation, in some verses Moses records the contents of the revelation (1:5, 7, 26; 2:1; 23:32; 33:18), while in others the angel of the presence writes them down for Moses (1:27; 30:12, 21; 50:6). Davenport relied upon this distinction to distinguish between two redactions of the book (B: Second Edition of Jubilees;

---

[37] Dillman 1851: 71, n. 14. According to *Jub.* 11:15, Abraham was born in the 39th jubilee, 2nd week, 7th year (A.M. 1876). 22:1 dates Abraham's death, at the age of 175 (Gen 25:7; *Jub.* 22:7; 23:8) to the 44th jubilee, 1st week, 2nd year (A.M. 2109). According to these dates, 233 years passed from Abraham's birth until his death. If the original text of *Jub.* 22:1 is the 43rd jubilee, then Abraham died in the year 2060 to creation, leaving only 184 years from birth until death, a number much closer (but not identical) to the 175 years mentioned explicitly. Charles (1902: 137) wanted to fully adjust the dates in the chronological framework to the number 175, and therefore corrected *Jub.* 22:1 to the 42nd jubilee, 6th week, 7th year (A.M. 2051). However, as noted above, Dillman's suggestion has been confirmed by the text preserved in 4Q219. See the textual discussion in VanderKam 1989b: 127; VanderKam and Milik 1994 (DJD 13): 53.

[38] So too VanderKam (1995) 2000: 532–540; 2001: 18.

[39] Davenport 1971. Testuz (1960: 39–42) had previously suggested that three eschatological passages (1:7–25, 28; 23:11–32; 24:28b–30) were added to *Jubilees* between the years 63–38 B.C.E. However, he did not go as far as to suggest a comprehensive redaction.

C: Sanctuary-oriented Redaction).[40] However, VanderKam conjectured that in the original Hebrew reading of 1:27, God commanded the angel of the presence "to dictate (להכתיב)" the revelation to Moses, and not "to write (לכתוב)" as in the Ge'ez translation.[41] VanderKam's suggestion was subsequently confirmed in a Hebrew copy of *Jubilees* from Qumran (4Q216 IV, 6).[42] All told, Davenport's theory is difficult to accept.

In addition to these two theories, which suggested that *Jubilees* is a complex composition, the product of editorial activity and literary development, a few scholars have suggested the possibility that specific passages in *Jubilees* originate in other sources or traditions:

(A) Dimant (1983: 21, esp. n. 17) identified a verse that conflicts with the rest of the book. In all of *Jubilees*, the duration of a "jubilee" period is 49 years; see for example *Jub.* 23:8: "He had lived for three jubilees and four weeks of years—175 years" (3 * 49 = 147; 4 * 7 = 28; 147 + 28 = 175). But *Jub.* 4:21, which describes Enoch's sojourn with the angels following the birth of his son (when he was 65 years old according to MT, SP, and *Jubilees*; 165 according to LXX), is based upon a different understanding of this term. According to this verse, "he was, moreover, with God's angels for six jubilees of years…",[43] the period of six jubilees is parallel to the period described in Gen 5:22: "And Enoch walked with God after he begat Methusaleh 300 years.…" A simple calculation reveals that according to *Jub.* 4:21, a "jubilee" lasts for 50 years, in contrast to the rest of the book.[44] Dimant correctly

---

[40] Davenport 1971: 29 (and also 10–16).

[41] VanderKam 1981: 209–217; 1989b: 6. He suggested that the error occurred during the translation from Hebrew to Greek, and that it was the result of a *waw/yod* interchange, transforming the form לָכְתִיב (without the letter ה) into לכתוב. Kister (1995: 240, n. 9) described the linguistic background for the interchange of *qal* and *hiphil* forms in Hebrew of this period.

[42] VanderKam and Milik 1994: 11–12, and cf. their textual note on this word (p. 12).

[43] As noted by scholars (Milik 1976: 12; VanderKam [1978] 2000: 316, n. 51; Dimant 1983: 22; VanderKam and Milik 1994: 174), the description of Enoch's sojourn with the angels for six jubilees (parallel to *Jub.* 4:21) is also reflected in a composition entitled 4Qpseudo-Jubilees^c (4Q227; ed. VanderKam and Milik; DJD 13, pp. 171–175), frg. 2, 1–2 (ibid., pp. 173–174):

```
1  [                              E]noch after we taught him
2  [              ]°[              ] six jubilees of years
```

[44] VanderKam (1998: 121, n. 18; 2001: 33) interpreted this verse in accordance with the general meaning of "jubilee" in *Jubilees* (49 years), and arrived at the conclusion that Enoch spent 294 (6 * 49 = 294) years in heaven, and returned to the earth six years prior to his death. However, it is difficult to accept this harmonistic interpretation that overlooks the direct usage of Gen 5:22.

concluded that, "This shows that Jub. borrows from various sources, often without reconciling the contradictions."⁴⁵

(B) Kister analyzed two passages that exemplify the characteristic phenomenon of the juxtaposition of a legal passage to a rewritten story:⁴⁶

(1) Lev 19:23–25 defines the halakhic status of fruits during the first five years of a tree's life: during the first three years, it is prohibited to partake in these fruits (v. 23), while in the fifth year it is permitted to eat from them (v. 25). Regarding the fourth year, the pentateuchal law (v. 24) defines the fruit as "*qodeš hillûlîm* to the Lord" (according to MT) or "*qodeš ḥillûlîm* to the Lord" (according to SP). Rabbinic exegesis interpreted this expression as an obligation to eat the fourth-year fruits in Jerusalem, or to redeem the fruits with money and to buy food with this money in Jerusalem, as is done with the second tithe.⁴⁷ In contrast, Qumran sectarian compositions posit a different meaning for this

---

Scott (2005: 23–71) also interprets the "six jubilees of years" as 294 years, and suggests that this verse has fundamental significance for the chronological conception of *Jubilees*. In an extended treatment, he adduces this detail as "the most compelling evidence that *Jubilees* presupposes the '*otot*' cycle" (p. 37), in addition to the extensive system of jubilees and weeks, as part of an "implied cultic cycle" (p. 23) that is attested explicitly in the Qumran calendrical scrolls. Even if Scott's interpretation that this verse refers to a 294-year period were correct, his suggestion that this refers to an implied *'otot* cycle is difficult to accept, as it is highly unlikely that such a fundamental notion (as Scott claims) was left unstated. More significant to the discussion here, the notion that there is any reference here to a 294-year period is predicated upon the assumption that the chronological note in *Jub.* 4:21 refers to a 49-year period, in contradiction to Gen 5:22. Dimant's suggestion, that this verse demonstrates that *Jubilees* borrows from other sources, will be bolstered below (ch. 4) by other examples in which the chronological framework of the book contradicts the rewritten stories.

⁴⁵ VanderKam ([1978] 2000) investigated the Enoch traditions in *Jubilees*, and focused of course on the important passage in 4:16–25. Dimant (1983) tried to demonstrate that the Ethiopic Enochic corpus focuses on one theme, the biography of Enoch, and the passage from *Jub.* 4 serves as a central source for her argument. In contrast to her predecessors (Charles 1902: 36–37; and especially VanderKam [1978] 2000), Dimant suggested that the *Jubilees* passage is based upon a tradition that interprets Gen 5, and is not directly dependent upon *1 Enoch*. Despite the ideological and theological affinities between *Jubilees* and *1 Enoch*, they do not share common vocabulary or style, and they therefore each represent independent evidence to the same aggadic tradition.

⁴⁶ Kister 1992, and see the discussion below. Anderson 1994 (notes 43, 45) noted the disparity between the rewritten story and the admonition-legal passage in two additional places in *Jubilees*: the stories of the rape of Dinah (*Jub.* 30) and Judah and Tamar (*Jub.* 41). He even suggested that *Jub.* 30:12 was secondarily added to the text. However, he refrained from arriving at a more general conclusion regarding the literary development of *Jubilees*.

⁴⁷ M. *Ma'as. Š.* 5:1; *Sifre Numbers* 6; *y. Pe'ah* 7:6 (20b–c), and similarly Josephus, *Ant.* IV §227. See Albeck 1930: 32–33; Baumgarten 1987: 196; Kister 1992: 577–578.

enigmatic expression: the fourth-year fruits are considered one of the priestly prerogatives.[48] *Jub.* 7:35–37 agrees with the sectarian position: "...in the fourth year its fruit will be sanctified. It will be offered as firstfruits that are acceptable before the most high Lord...so that they may offer in abundance the first of the wine and oil as firstfruits on the altar of the Lord who accepts (it). What is left over those who serve in the Lord's house are to eat before the altar which receives (it)" (v. 36). However, according to the story at the beginning of the chapter, in the fourth year, Noah picked grapes from which he made wine, which he proceeded to put in a container. Noah did not offer the grapes on an altar, nor did he drink from the wine until the fifth year (vv. 1–6).[49] According to the sectarian halakhah, Noah and his sons should have offered the wine on the altar, and then been allowed to drink from it already in the fourth year, in light of their priestly status (compare the detailed description of his offering of sacrifices in vv. 3–6). Scholars have attempted to harmonize the laws in vv. 35–37 with the story in vv. 1–6;[50] Kister, however, concluded from this contradiction that *Jubilees* includes multiple traditions, not all of them sectarian. Therefore, when one encounters tensions or contradictions between these traditions, it is better to identify the source of their differences in their different provenance, instead of employing a harmonistic approach in order to create an artificial sense of homogeneity between them.

(2) Following the story of the elevation of Levi to priesthood in *Jub.* 32:1–8, there is a section that addresses the laws of tithes (vv. 9–15). According to the story, Jacob separated off one-tenth of his property: he offered the pure animals as a sacrifice, and gave the impure animals and his slaves to Levi (v. 8). However, according to the law in v. 15, "The entire tithe of cattle and sheep is holy to the Lord, *and is to belong to his priests* who will eat (it) before him year by year." Verse 9 describes a "second" tithe performed by Jacob, following which (vv. 10–15) the laws of the second tithe are adduced, including the obligation to eat it "before the Lord". But v. 9 itself does not describe the consumption of the tithe before the Lord, as mandated in the next verses, but

---

[48] 11QT LX, 3–4; 4QMMT B 62–64; in addition to *Tg ps.-Jon.* to Lev 19:24; cf. Baumgarten ibid.; Kister ibid.

[49] The story at the beginning of the chapter is very similar to that presented in 1QapGen XII, as Kister (1992: 583–585) noted. For the text of col. XII, see Greenfield and Qimron 1992.

[50] Albeck 1930: 33; Baumgarten 1987: 198, n. 20.

rather the giving of the tithe to Levi. Therefore, Kister suggested that in the original version of v. 9, the word "*dāgəma*, second, again" did not appear, and this verse functioned as the end of the story in *Jub.* 32:1–8. The redactor wished to include the laws of the second tithe in his composition,[51] and therefore added them after the story of the tithe in vv. 1–9; in order to adapt the story to the legal passage, he added the word "again" to v. 9.

(C) Ravid (2000) examined the Sabbath laws at the end of the book (50:6–13), and came to the conclusion that the passage was added as an appendix to *Jubilees* by a Qumran scribe, based upon the following considerations: (1) The legal passage is not an appropriate conclusion to the book. At the end of the composition, parallel to the opening, one expects words of admonition and encouragement. Indeed, such an ending is found in *Jub.* 50:5: "The jubilees will pass by until Israel is pure of every sexual evil, impurity, contamination, sin, and error. Then they will live confidently in the entire land. They will no longer have any satan or any evil person. The land will be pure from that time until eternity." (2) The laws in *Jubilees* are generally juxtaposed to stories, and there is no such connection in 50:6–13. (3) It is difficult to explain why one section of Sabbath laws appears in 2:24–33 and the other at the end of the book. (4) One can identify a fundamental theological difference underlying the Sabbath laws in ch. 2 as opposed to those in the list at the end of the book. In the first collection, the Sabbath is particular to Israel, while according to 50:7, the prohibition against work on the Sabbath applies also to "your male and female servants, all your cattle, or the foreigner who is with you."

In response to Ravid, Doering (2002) has claimed that the passage of Sabbath laws is actually appropriate to *Jubilees*: (1) Verse 13, the end of the passage of the Sabbath laws, is a fitting end to the book, both in its reference to the future, and in its terminology: "so that the Israelites may continue observing the sabbath in accord with the commandments for the sabbaths of the land as it was written in the tablets which he placed in my hands so that I could write for (or: dictate to)[52] you the laws of each specific time in every division of its

---

[51] The law of the first tithe already appeared in *Jub.* 13:25–27. That passage has suffered an omission in the text, and it is therefore difficult to know whether the law there matched the story or not.

[52] Regarding the interchange of "to write" (in the Geʿez translation) and the *hiphil* "to dictate," see above p. 16, and the textual witnesses to *Jub.* 1:27.

times."[53] (2) The Sabbath laws appear after the Passover laws (Exod 12; *Jub.* 49) and before the giving of the Law at Sinai (Exod 19–20; narrative frame of *Jubilees*). If one compares this order to Exodus, and specifically the Sabbath laws mentioned in the manna story (Exod 16:5, 20–22), then the Sabbath laws in *Jub.* 50 are in their proper place.[54] (3) The inclusion of foreigners, servants, and animals in the Sabbath laws does not contradict the focus on Israel in ch. 2. One can attribute their inclusion in ch. 50 to the quotation or paraphrase of the Sabbath law from the Decalogue (Exod 20 or Deut 5). (4) There is tension between *Jub.* 50:8, 12 and the Qumran Sabbath laws, and it is therefore difficult to ascribe Qumran origins to *Jub.* 50:6–13.[55]

Most of Doering's arguments are convincing, but Kister has offered another argument in favor of the assumption of the secondary nature of this passage, which at the same time improves Ravid's suggestion by explaining the process by which the section was inserted into the text.[56] One can identify two different meanings of the term "Sabbath" in v. 13: (a) "a man who does any of these things on the **sabbath day** is to die" = the day of Sabbath; (b) "so that the Israelites may continue observing the **sabbath** in accord with the commandments for the **sabbaths of the land**" = the Sabbatical Year. The combination of these two meanings has created a certain inconsistency and tension within this verse. Verse 13b ("so that the Israelites may continue observing the Sabbath…") is the natural continuation of vv. 1–5, which describe the future condition of Israel in its land: "(3) The land will observe its sabbaths when they live on it…(5)…then they will live confidently in the entire land; They will no longer have any satan or any evil person; the land will be pure from that time until eternity. (13b) so that the Israelites may continue observing the sabbath in accord with the commandments for the sabbaths of the land as it was written in the tablets.…" One can therefore conclude that vv. 6–13a, which include the Sabbath laws, were secondarily inserted into this passage.

---

[53] So too Kister (2001: 297, n. 47), who noted that the end of v. 13 forms an *inclusio* with *Jub.* 1:27–29. In his opinion, at least the final part of the verse belongs to *Jubilees* itself.

[54] Kister (ibid.) understands the laws in vv. 6–13 as an explanation of the vague description in *Jub.* 50:1 (parallel to the manna story in Exod 16), "after this law I informed you about the sabbath days in the wilderness of Sin which is between Elim and Sinai," but wonders why the author of these verses does not refer to the manna story explicitly, in contrast to the method he used throughout the book.

[55] See Doering 2002: 385–387.

[56] Prof. Kister suggested this to me in an oral communication, thus revising his suggestion found in Kister 2001: 297, n. 47.

These three suggestions, which have identified different and sundry traditions within *Jubilees*, are convincing, and the recognition of the different origins of each passage is significant for our discussion. One cannot view *Jubilees* as a completely homogenous composition if specific passages are interpolations, traditions, or sources that the redactor has included in his composition. Dimant and Ravid limited their discussions to the specific verse or passage in question, while at the end of his article, Kister called for a reassessment of the relationship between the rewritten stories and the juxtaposed legal passages, in light of the two examples that he analyzed.[57] Both Dimant and Kister suggested that *Jubilees* in general adopts material from different traditions, without adapting them to each other. They each, however, limited their discussions to one or two passages, and did not expand their discussions to the entire book. The question of the literary development of *Jubilees*, its traditions, its sources, and its redaction, thus still remains open.

A New Approach to the Study of the Book of Jubilees

The assumption that a comparison between *Jubilees* and textual witnesses of the Bible is sufficient, and that one can attribute every difference and alteration to one author, does not explain a number of phenomena in the book, and especially, it does not account for the internal contradictions, doublets, and tensions within the text. Of course, one can expect a few of these to occur, even in the work of one author, but the cumulative effect of many examples of internal tension raises serious questions about the unity of the book. I would therefore like to present here, in concentrated form, all of the instances of discrepancies or disparities between verses that I have been able to identify. The following is a list of these phenomena, starting with the most significant in terms of its implications for the question of the unity of the composition.

Contradictions: A number of explicit contradictions between verses can be identified, in reference to details in the narratives, biblical interpretation, and the halakhic positions reflected in the narratives. The examples can be divided into two groups: (I) contradictions between the legal passages and the rewritten stories; (II) contradictions between

---

[57] So too, Anderson (1994: 24, n. 43) asserted that the topic needs to be investigated comprehensively before the precise relationship between these two genres in *Jubilees* can be determined.

the chronological framework and the chronological data (or interpretation of biblical chronological data) embedded in the rewritten narratives.

Contradictions between the Legal Passages and the Rewritten Stories

(1) The Date of the Entry into the Garden of Eden:[58] According to *Jub.* 3:17, which is part of the rewritten narrative, Adam entered the Garden of Eden on the seventeenth of the second month. However, the legal passage within the rewritten story (3:8–14) connects the entries of Adam and his wife to the law of the postpartum mother from Lev 12; according to the legal passage, Adam entered the Garden forty days after he was created (v. 9). Based upon the 364-day calendar used throughout *Jubilees*, which begins each year on a Wednesday, the calculation of the dates reveals that forty days after the creation of Adam is the thirteenth of the second month, and not the seventeenth. It is impossible to ignore this discrepancy of four days between the dates, because this story is supposed to serve as the precedent for the law.

(2) Did Judah Sin?[59] According to the rewritten story of Judah and Tamar, Judah did not sin when he had intercourse with his daughter-in-law Tamar (cf. Lev 18:15; 20:12), because his sons had not consummated their marriage with her, and she was therefore not legally considered his daughter-in-law (*Jub.* 41:2, 5, 27). In contrast, according to the legal passage (vv. 23–26), Judah indeed sinned, but repented, and was forgiven.

(3) The Source for the Method of Tamar's Punishment:[60] After Judah heard that his daughter-in-law Tamar was pregnant, he decided that she should be put to death by burning (Gen 38:24). The punishment of fire in cases of sexual impropriety appears twice in the Pentateuch: "the daughter of a priest who profanes herself through harlotry" (Lev 21:9), and "a man who takes a wife and her mother" (Lev 20:14). In the rewritten story in *Jub.* 41, Judah wished to have Tamar killed based upon "the law which Abraham had commanded his children" (v. 28). This refers to Abraham's warning in his testament to his descendants: "If any woman or girl among you commits a sexual

---

[58] See the discussion in ch. 1.
[59] See the discussion on pp. 62–66.
[60] See the discussion on pp. 64, 67–69.

offence, burn her in fire" (*Jub.* 20:4), an expansion of the prohibition and punishment of Lev 21:9 to all Israelite women. In contrast, the legal passage in *Jub.* 41:23–26 preferred to derive this punishment through legal exegesis according to which the punishment of burning for intercourse with a daughter-in-law (expressly prohibited in Lev 18:15; 20:12, but without the method of punishment) is the same as that of a mother-in-law ("a wife and her mother"), mentioned explicitly in Lev 20:14.

(4) **Fourth-year Fruits:** See above, pp. 17–18.

(5) **The Source of the Festival of *Maṣṣot*:**[61] According to the rewritten story in *Jub.* 17:15–18:17 (parallel to the Akedah story in Gen 22:1–19), God appeared to Abraham on the night of the twelfth of the first month (17:15), and commanded him to offer his son Isaac as a sacrifice. Abraham woke up in the morning, departed on his journey, and on the third day (the 14th [= Passover] or perhaps the 15th of the first month) arrived at the location where the Akedah took place (*Jub.* 18:3). Following the trial, Abraham returned with his servants to Beer-sheba, a distance of no more than a three-day journey. All together, the roundtrip trip took no longer than six days (and perhaps only five). In contrast, the legal passage at the end of ch. 18 (vv. 18–19) transforms the story into a precedent for the seven-day festival of *Maṣṣot*, and assumes that the journey lasted seven days. Moreover, even if one assumes that the rewritten story posited a seven-day journey, the dates of this trip do not correspond to the festival of Unleavened Bread.

(6) **The Plague of the Firstborn:**[62] In the rewritten story regarding the plagues and the Exodus from Egypt, the Lord worked against the will of Mastema in the bringing of all the plagues, especially in the slaying of the firstborn, and in the salvation of Israel (*Jub.* 48). In contrast, according to the legal passage in *Jub.* 49, the Lord sent "the forces of Mastema" to kill the firstborn (49:2).

(7) **The Punishments for Reuben and Bilhah:**[63] In the brief story in Gen 35:22, which describes how Reuben slept with his father's concubine Bilhah, there is no reference to a punishment for Reuben or Bilhah. Other biblical passages criticize Reuben for his behavior (Gen 49:3–4), and describe how this led to his loss of the birthright

---

[61] See the discussion in ch. 9.
[62] See the discussion in ch. 10.
[63] See the discussion in ch. 3.

(1 Chr 5:1–2). But even in these two passages, there is no mention of a punishment for Reuben himself for his actions. This absence of a personal punishment appears to be at odds with biblical laws that prohibit intercourse with one's father's wife (Lev 18:8; 20:11; Deut 23:1; 27:20), and especially Lev 20:11, which calls for the death penalty for both the man and the father's wife. It would seem that both Reuben and Bilhah should therefore have been punishable by death, but none of the biblical stories mention this possibility. The rewritten story in *Jub.* 33:1–9a absolves Bilhah of any punishment by presenting her as the victim of rape, while the legal passage (vv. 9b–20) acquits both Reuben **and** Bilhah from any punishment for a different, technical reason: "for the statute, the punishment, and the law had not been completely revealed to all" (v. 16).

The following table presents a list of the legal passages in *Jubilees*:

2:24b–33; 50:6–13a: Sabbath	18:18–19: Festival of *Maṣṣot*
3:8–14: Impurity of Postpartum Mother	21:5–20: Sacrifices
3:30–31: Covering of Nakedness	28:6–7: Marrying the Older Sister
4:5–6: Murder	30: Marriage with a Foreigner
4:31–32: *Lex talionis*	32:9–15: Second Tithe
6:17–22: Festival of Weeks (or: Oaths)	32:27–29: Eighth Day of Festival of Booths
6:23–38: Calendar	33:9b–20: Intercourse with Father's Wife
7:1–6, 35–37: Fourth-year Fruits	34:18–19: Day of Atonement
13:25–27: First Tithe	41:23–26: Intercourse with Daughter-in-law
15:25–34: Circumcision	49: Passover
16:20–31: Festival of Booths	

Contradictions between the Chronological Framework and the Rewritten Stories

(8) The Length of a "Jubilee" Period:[64] See above, pp. 16–17.

(9) The Order of the Births of Jacob's Sons:[65] The births of Jacob's sons (except for Benjamin) are listed in Gen 29–30, and organized there according to their mothers: Leah (first group), Bilhah, Zilpah, Leah (second group), Rachel. According to a simple reading of Gen 31:41, all of the children were born during a seven-year period, and it is therefore reasonable to assume an overlap between the births.[66] According to the chronological framework of *Jub.* 28 (vv. 14–15, 18), there was such an overlap between the births of Leah's first children and the births of Bilhah's sons: Dan was born before Judah, and was conceived prior to the birth of Levi. In contrast, according to 28:17, all four of Leah's children were born before Bilhah was even given to Jacob.

(10) "Let the days allowed him be 120 years" (Gen 6:3):[67] Interpreters from antiquity until today are divided as to the meaning of the 120-year limitation that was instituted in response to the intercourse between the sons of god with the women, and the subsequent birth of the giants. Some posit that this limitation applies to human beings in general, including the giants, who were half divine and half human. The establishment of a maximum age for human life expectancy drew a boundary between the heavenly and earthly realms. Other interpreters have suggested that the sons of god story is related to the flood story that follows, and in fact provides a justification for this cataclysmic punishment. According to this position, 120 years is the length of time from the Watchers' descent until the flood. Within *Jubilees*, the limitation of 120 years in the rewritten story applies to the giants (5:7–9), the offspring of the Watchers, in accordance with the first interpretive approach to Gen 6:3. In contrast, according to the chronological framework, the Watchers sinned in the 25th jubilee, A.M. 1177–1225 (*Jub.* 5:1, referring to 4:33), and the flood occurred in the year 1308 (5:22–23). The difference between these two dates fits a period of 120 years, and reflects the second interpretive approach to Gen 6:3.

---

[64] Dimant 1983: 21, and especially n. 17.
[65] See the discussion in ch. 4.
[66] However, see *S, 'Olam Rab.* 2 (quoted on p. 85, n. 8), which posits that each pregnancy lasted for only seven months.
[67] See the discussion on pp. 119–125.

(11) The Placement of Noah's Testament:[68] Noah's testament appears in *Jub.* 7:20–39, following the story of the planting of the vineyard (vv. 1–19, parallel to Gen 9:18–27). In line with the testament genre, one would expect it to be given close to Noah's death, and this is actually hinted in the testament itself: "and now I fear regarding you that *after I have died* you will shed human blood on the earth" (7:27). However, according to the chronological framework, it was transmitted in the 28th jubilee (7:20), more than 300 years before Noah's death (10:15–17).

Tensions: In addition to the many contradictions throughout the book, one can also point to another phenomenon that might influence our understanding of the literary development of *Jubilees*: the compilation of varied ideological and theological traditions throughout the book. For example, the Heavenly Tablets have a number of different functions, such as a register of events, past and future, as well as a record of various halakhot. Some of these roles already appear in literature prior to *Jubilees*, but the function of the Tablets as a record of laws is unique to *Jubilees*.[69] In this case, there is no real tension between these traditions, because they do not contradict one another. As more and more traditions about the Tablets are accumulated, so their functions and status become more complex. A diachronic investigation into the Heavenly Tablets traditions reveals their different provenance, but their combination does not create an interpretive problem for the reader.

However, there are instances in which the accumulation of traditions does indeed lead to interpretive problems in *Jubilees*, and makes it difficult to precisely describe the worldview of the composition. For example, the redactor of *Jubilees* tried to combine a number of traditions on the origin of evil in the world, but their synthesis has produced theological tensions and hermeneutical difficulties. The book combines three different approaches to the origin of evil: evil as the result of the Watchers story; evil as the result of the sin in the Garden of Eden; evil as part of a dualistic system of good and evil created by God from the dawn of time.[70] Sometimes these traditions stand side-by-side, but at other times, there is an attempt to combine them, and this synthesis

---

[68] See the discussion on pp. 158–163.
[69] Cf. García Martínez 1997; Kister 2001: 291–292; and the analysis below, pp. 311–314.
[70] See the extensive discussion in Part II.

creates an inconsistent viewpoint. For example, in Noah's prayer (*Jub.* 10), the spirits, descendants of the Watchers, have been transformed into the servants of Mastema, the head of the forces of evil in the dualistic system, known from the Qumran sectarian literature.

One can suggest a number of possible approaches in order to resolve the problems detailed above, and one can divide the studies of *Jubilees* written until today according to their approaches to the resolution of these questions:[71]

(A) Individual Harmonistic Solutions: One can resolve a contradiction between two passages by reinterpreting one in order to agree with the other. Thus, for example, regarding the fourth-year fruits, Albeck and Baumgarten both attempted to harmonize the legal exegesis embedded in the rewritten story with the laws at the end of the chapter.[72] Regarding the question of whether Judah sinned or not, one can suggest that Judah supposed that he had sinned, but later learned that he was innocent because his sons had not consummated their marriages with Tamar.[73] In the case of the contradiction regarding the order of the births of Jacob's sons, Rönsch emended the dates in the chronological framework so that they would match the order presented in the rewritten story. In each and every example, one can consider whether the solution of the contradiction is reasonable, or whether the disparity between the two passages is too great to be resolved through exegetical means. At times the contradiction remains, and despite the reader's desire to view his text as an organic composition, the harmonistic solution suggested is less satisfying than the original contradiction that it came to solve.

As the number of contradictions and tensions identified grows, the likelihood of individual solutions shrinks. A reader can overcome an occasional interpretive problem, but when a text is filled with many such problems, each of which demands exegetical efforts, it is preferable to search for a single solution that will solve all of them at once. It is

---

[71] Scholars have discussed only a few of the contradictions listed here, but one can infer their general approaches from those discussions.

[72] Albeck (1930: 33) reinterpreted the story in order to make it match the laws (Noah was a priest, but his sons were not). Baumgarten (1987: 198, n. 10) reinterpreted the laws to make them match the story. Cf. Kister (1992: 585), who rejected a harmonistic approach.

[73] Zakovitch and Shinan (1992: 120–121) suggested a harmonistic approach, but also raised the possibility that this passage is the work of more than one author; cf. also Halpern-Amaru 1999: 116–117.

possible that some of the contradictions listed above can be resolved through the reinterpretation of one (or both) of the passages but it is hard to accept the possibility that each and every one is the result of a local exegetical issue.

(B) Local Interpolations: In every case of a contradiction between two passages, it is possible to conjecture that one of them has been added to the composition at a later stage, thus creating the disparity between them. The advantage of this approach over the previous one is that it avoids resolving the different contradictions by means of unconvincing solutions. When two sources cannot be reconciled, it is better to recognize the contradiction than to combine both sources through harmonistic explanations. This is true in particular of the contradictions regarding chronology; it is especially difficult to offer satisfactory explanations that combine all of the relevant details, because the numbers themselves cannot be reinterpreted. The suggestion of an interpolation is therefore preferable to the harmonistic solution, but as in the previous approach, its usefulness is limited to a small number of instances. Here too, the accumulation of numerous examples strengthens the suggestion that the differences reflect a literary process, and not a textual phenomenon that recurs in a number of places.

(C) Collection of Existing Exegetical Traditions: One can view the multiplicity of exegetical traditions as part of a broader phenomenon in Jewish literature of the Second Temple period: the accumulation of earlier exegetical traditions in later works, a phenomenon that Kugel labeled "overkill."[74] According to his description, when an exegete in antiquity encountered an interpretive difficulty in the biblical text, he did not limit himself to one solution, but rather collected a number of interpretations, and wove them together in his composition. The internal contradictions are therefore characteristic of literature of this period, and they are therefore not significant for the question of the literary development of *Jubilees*, but at most, for the history of biblical interpretation in this period.

---

[74] Kugel 1990: 256–257. In a later study (Kugel 1998: 24–29), he does not use the term "overkill," but still relates to the collection of multiple exegetical traditions: "The composite nature of such retellings or reflections on Scripture is the rule among ancient interpreters, not the exception—and such composites are sometimes found even in our earliest sources, like *Jubilees* or *1 Enoch*" (p. 26).

Kugel's approach to the body of interpretive literature of this period bypasses the problems generated by the contradictions as described above. Each contradiction or doublet, such as the two sources for Judah's verdict to kill Tamar by fire, can be explained as the result of different traditions, which have been adopted and combined by the author. However, this approach does not assist in explaining the cases in which there are contradictions between narrative details, and especially in those cases when there are discrepancies in the chronological data in the stories. One cannot reconcile the differences in birth-order of Jacob's children by claiming that an author wove together alternative traditions for understanding the story in Gen 29–30, because the final product is an illogical and impossible story. The same is true regarding the connection between the date of the entry to the Garden of Eden and the law of impurity of the parturient mother: the data do not match according to the *Jubilees* calendar. One author can adopt two traditions, but he will then combine them together to create a meaningful, sequentially logical narrative.

The "overkill" approach also overlooks the distinction in location within *Jubilees* of the different interpretive traditions. In the cases of contradictions between the narrative framework and the chronological details embedded in the rewritten stories, the different interpretive approaches are not only differentiated by their content, but also by their literary genre. Similarly, regarding the other contradictions, one can identify a sharp, generic distinction between the rewritten stories and the juxtaposed legal passages. There is no reason that the phenomenon of "overkill" should set the different traditions apart by dividing them between the different literary genres. Why not combine two traditions within one rewritten story or in a single legal passage? (It is more difficult to imagine two contradictory traditions within the chronological framework.) The consistent classification of the traditions according to the different genres informs us that the contradictions are not merely a byproduct of the history of traditions, but rather are of significance for the history of the literary development of *Jubilees*.

(D) A New Suggestion: A Literary-Critical Approach. This study suggests that these contradictions are the result of the literary development of *Jubilees*. Rewritten biblical stories and extant exegetical texts were adopted, and assimilated into the new composition. The tensions and contrasts within the book result therefore from the integration of this existing material into a new framework. Within the context of a literary-critical approach,

one can suggest a number of models in order to describe the process of literary growth of *Jubilees*. For example, it is possible that the redactor inherited all of the material from his sources and did not add anything new; it is possible that the different strata in the book reflect different recensions; it is also possible that certain passages were found in extant sources and others are the contribution of the redactor himself. Over the course of this study, the different passages will be analyzed in order to determine which model is most appropriate.

The literary-critical approach solves the questions raised by the other approaches:

(1) The Accumulation of Examples: As noted above, as the number of examples of contradictions and tensions increases, the likelihood that the book has undergone a process of literary development grows accordingly.[75] If the composition includes passages of different origins, it is easy to understand why the verses sometimes disagree with one another.

(2) The Division into Genres: The distinction between the redactional stratum and its sources suits the generic divisions throughout the book, between the rewritten stories, legal passages, and chronological framework. In all of the cases that I have identified, the divergent details always appear within two different genres, with one detail in the rewritten story, and the contradictory element either in a juxtaposed legal passage or in the chronological framework. This distinction suggests that the different genres are the works of different authors, each of which has contributed from their own unique viewpoint.[76]

(3) Contradictions that Create an Incoherent Narrative: In some of the examples adduced above (and especially those related to chronological details), the contradiction between the verses has created an illogical and incoherent story. For example, the description of the order of the births of Jacob's children in *Jub.* 28 includes chronological details in both the chronological framework and in the rewritten narrative, which for all intents and purposes cannot be reconciled, and should therefore not be attributed to one author. Assuming that these

---

[75] The theory of multiple traditions (or "overkill") also explains the accumulation of contradictions as the result of traditions of different provenance.

[76] It is important to stress that I was not able to identify contradictions between the chronological framework and the legal passages appended to the rewritten stories. The absence of any such tension allows for the claim (as I will suggest below) that the chronological framework and the legal passages are the work of the same author.

discrepancies are not the result of textual corruption,⁷⁷ the only way to understand the literary history of this passage is to assume that it is composed of materials of different origins, and at least one of its sources was extant in writing prior to this combination.⁷⁸

A number of additional considerations support this literary-critical approach, and simultaneously offer assistance in choosing the appropriate model for the literary development of *Jubilees*:

(4) The Unique Terminology: One can identify uniform terminology in two out of the three literary genres listed above: in the legal passages (appended to the rewritten stories) and in the chronological framework of the book. In the legal passages, Ravid has identified "the special terminology of the Heavenly Tablets," a vocabulary which functions as a literary device in order to mark those passages that belong to the Heavenly Tablets.⁷⁹ As I will try to demonstrate in this study, this unique, uniform terminology is not merely a literary device, but also an indication that the passages in which it is found belong to the redactional stratum; this terminology is a sign of the halakhic editor's contribution to this work. The same is true of the data in the chronological framework. The uniformity of terminology, formulation, and the system of jubilees and weeks in the different dates leads to the conclusion that the chronological framework belongs to one stratum, the product of one author. In contrast, there are no indications of uniformity, neither in formulations nor in vocabulary, between the many rewritten stories throughout the book.⁸⁰ Similarly, there is no ideological or theological uniformity between the different rewritten narratives, even though one can identify a number of recurring motifs throughout the book. The lack of homogeneity amongst the stories suggests that they cannot be

---

⁷⁷ See the discussion on pp. 85–91.
⁷⁸ The two possibilities are: (1) An extant, written source was adopted by an editor who added his own material; or (2) Two extant sources were combined together by an editor.
⁷⁹ Ravid 1999: 470–471; Werman (1999) 2002: 100–103. Both scholars collected the passages that mention the Heavenly Tablets, and that are marked by this unique vocabulary.
⁸⁰ Certain stories, such as the rewritten creation story in ch. 2, and the covenant between God and Noah in ch. 6, include vocabulary that is similar to the terminology of the legal passages. We can infer that the rewritten stories that are marked by this terminology belong to the same stratum as the legal passages; see pp. 238–239, nn. 24, 26. Similarly, the narrative frame of *Jubilees* (ch. 1; 50:1–5, 13b) and the eschatological passage in 23:9–32 use the same vocabulary, and can thus be attributed to the same legal layer.

combined into a consecutive, unified narrative layer. It is therefore reasonable to view the legal passages and the chronological framework as one stratum[81] which relied upon a variety of extant rewritten stories. The literary phenomenon of Rewritten Bible was very common in the Second Temple period,[82] and the redactor of *Jubilees* apparently adopted stories that were already reworked, and incorporated them into his book, while adding his own new material.

(5) The Literary Constitution of *Jubilees* 5:[83] One passage in the book, *Jub.* 5:1–18, allows us to determine the process of literary development of *Jubilees*. That passage addresses the story of the sons of god and the daughters of men (Gen 6:1–4), and vv. 1–12 describe the Watchers' actions and their drastic implications for the entire world. An analysis of vv. 1–12 reveals that this section is based upon *1 En.* 10–11, a passage that is itself based upon two traditions regarding the Watchers' sins and the results of their actions. The literary dependence finds expression in the order of events in *Jub.* 5, which matches the unique sequence created by the combination of traditions in the *Book of Watchers* (*1 En.* 1–36). One can therefore deduce that the following verses (*Jub.* 5:13–18), which describe the Lord as a righteous judge and transform the Watchers story into a paradigm of reward and punishment, were added to the rewritten story from *1 Enoch*. The use of the unique legal terminology described above is prominent in vv. 13–18, while it is completely absent in the rewritten story (vv. 1–12). As I will try to demonstrate, the passages marked by this special halakhic terminology belong to the halakhic redactional layer. *Jub.* 5:1–18 thus validates the theory suggested here: the halakhic redactor appropriated a rewritten story, in this case about the sons of god and the women, and added a passage with nomistic ramifications. There is no contradiction in *Jub.* 5 between the legal passage and the rewritten story, but its literary makeup allows us to reconstruct the compositional process of *Jubilees*.

The rewriting of the Watchers story in *Jub.* 5 is not only a proof for the halakhic redaction of *Jubilees*, but also an example of the chronological redaction described above. Included in the list of contradictions

---

[81] In support of the assumption that the person responsible for the legal redaction and the person responsible for the chronological redaction are one and the same, one can note the combination of the two motifs in the narrative frame (*Jub.* 1; 50:1–5, 13a); see p. 83.

[82] See the studies quoted above, n. 6.

[83] For a comprehensive discussion, see ch. 5.

above was the question of the interpretation of the 120-year period mentioned in Gen 6:3. According to the chronological framework (5:1), this period denoted the amount of time from the Watchers' sin until the flood, while according to the rewritten story it alludes to the maximum life expectancy of the giants (5:7–9). The analysis of *Jub.* 5 suggested here, according to which the rewritten story (vv. 1–12) is based upon *1 En.* 10–11, leads to the solution that the second interpretation (life expectancy of the giants) was inherited from the rewritten story in *1 En.* 10, while the first understanding (time until the flood) reflects the chronological editor's viewpoint.

(6) Beliefs and Ideas: When I began this study, I assumed that *Jubilees* was a homogeneous composition, and I attempted to describe the totality of beliefs and ideas that it contained. However, as my investigation progressed, it became clear to me that this book is composed of a variety of sources that have been combined together. The recognition of the complexity of this composition led me to change the focus of this study, and it now also addresses questions of redaction and literary development, and their implication for understanding the worldview of this editor. If the theory suggested here is correct, and the legal passages appended to the rewritten stories (and other passages that contain the special terminology of the legal passages) indeed represent one stratum composed by the halakhic redactor, then one can expect a crystallized set of ideas and beliefs within this layer. One person presumably possesses a unified worldview. For example, if one examines the functions of the Heavenly Tablets within the passages that are marked by the special terminology, it can be seen that this editor viewed them as tablets of covenant and commandments (stipulations of the covenant). This view is expressed in the use of the hendiadys "Torah and *teʿudah*" to describe the content of the Tablets, a word pair that can be exchanged by "law and covenant."[84] The importance of the terminology of the legal passages is not limited therefore to literary-critical questions, but is also of significance for understanding the worldview of the redactor.

The same is true regarding the question of the origin of evil in the world. An analysis of all the relevant passages in *Jubilees* leads to the conclusion that, according to this redactor, evil was created as part of a dualistic system of good and evil which God created from the beginning

---

[84] For a comprehensive discussion, see ch. 14.

of time. Other traditions that appear in the book (the Watchers story; the sin in the Garden of Eden) do not reflect the position of the redactor, but appeared in the extant sources that he adopted and included in his new composition. For example, if we return to the example of *Jub.* 5, the Watchers story, which was originally (in *1 Enoch*) intended to explain the origins of evil, was transformed into a paradigm of reward and punishment.[85] Chronological considerations demonstrate that the redactor of *Jubilees* did not compose Noah's testament (7:20–39), which describes the spirits, descendants of the giants (who are themselves descendants of the Watchers), as the cause of humanity's sins.[86] The date of the entry into the Garden of Eden in the rewritten story, and afterwards of the sin that was committed there, the seventeenth of the second month (3:17), matches the date of the beginning of the flood (Gen 6:11), and thus creates a connection between the first sin in history and the cataclysmic punishment by which all of humanity, except for Noah and his family, were destroyed. However, the legal passage in *Jub.* 3:8–14 connects this date of entry to the law of impurity of the parturient mother in Lev 12, and thus shifted the focus of this date from addressing the origin of evil to the legal realm.[87]

If it is possible to distinguish between the work of the redactor and his sources based upon literary-critical considerations, it is also possible to differentiate between the worldview of this author and those ideas contained in his sources. If *Jubilees* is composed of different materials, then the description of the viewpoint of the book needs to reflect this complexity. It is methodologically essential to differentiate between the final redaction and its sources, in order to isolate (with the help of the unique terminology) those passages that can be identified with confidence as the work of the redactor. Such an investigation will contribute to the understanding of the ideology and theology of this redactor, and simultaneously will serve as a control for the entire theory. Ideological and theological uniformity (in the legal passages) will not only confirm the existence of a redactional layer, but will also attest to the different provenance of the proposed sources of the book.

In light of these considerations, I would like to propose a new approach to the study of *Jubilees*. *Jubilees* is not a homogeneous book composed by one author. It is possible to identify in it internal contra-

---

[85] For a comprehensive discussion, see pp. 137–143.
[86] For a comprehensive discussion, see pp. 158–163.
[87] For a comprehensive discussion, see ch. 1; and pp. 264–265.

dictions, doublets, tensions, and discrepancies, both in details and in reference to the biblical stories in general. This situation attests to the variety of traditions that can be found side-by-side within the book. The redactor sometimes relied upon the Pentateuch itself, but often adopted other compositions as well, similar to the other examples of Rewritten Bible known to us from the Second Temple period.[88] The ideas embedded in these traditions do not always agree with the views of the redactor, thus creating the internal problems described here. The final product, as known to us today, is not the work of one individual, but a compound of different traditions and sources. The redactor's contribution can be found in the chronological framework throughout the book, in the legal passages juxtaposed to the rewritten stories, and in those passages that share the same unique terminology with the legal passages.

The thesis proposed here regarding the literary development of *Jubilees* is an outgrowth of close textual analysis of the contrasts and tensions between different passages in *Jubilees*. Some of these instances can certainly be interpreted differently, but I believe that it is difficult to ignore the cumulative effect of this claim. In any event, it is my hope that the analysis of these passages, the identification of the disparities, and the clarification of the connections between the different verses presented here, will be of value even for those readers who do not accept (in full or in part) the comprehensive theory regarding the literary development of *Jubilees* that I have proposed here.

THE DATE OF COMPOSITION

Scholars have debated the date of composition and the social-cultural context of *Jubilees*.[89] One can divide the studies that have addressed this topic according to the dates that they assigned to the book. Most scholars have located it within the 2nd century B.C.E., while others have dated it earlier or later than that.

---

[88] Charles (1902: xliv–xlvii) viewed *Jubilees* as the work of one author who relied upon earlier compositions and traditions. He even presents a list of those passages that he attributes to other sources, but neither justifies his remarks, nor does he suggest any methodological criteria in order to distinguish between the work of the author and his sources. Some of his suggestions can be substantiated (by means of explanations that Charles himself did not offer), while others are harder to defend.

[89] VanderKam (1997: 4–16) surveyed the different opinions, except for Kister's position (as well as those of Werman and Ravid that were published later).

The prevailing opinion today in *Jubilees* scholarship is that of VanderKam, who dates the composition of the book to 161–140 B.C.E., and especially prefers the period between 161–152 B.C.E.[90] VanderKam's view is based upon four main claims: (a) references in *Jubilees* to historical events; (b) the paleographic evidence of the Qumran copies of *Jubilees*; (c) the dependence of *Jubilees* upon earlier compositions; (d) the attitude towards the rest of the nation expressed in *Jubilees*.

Each of VanderKam's arguments can be contested: (a) VanderKam identified references to the Maccabean wars in the description of the battles between Jacob and his sons and the seven Amorite kings (*Jub.* 34), the battle with Esau and his sons (chs. 37–38), and in place-names in the two stories. However, it is difficult to accept the identification of place-names in *Jubilees* with locations from the Maccabean wars, both due to methodological problems raised by the evidence provided by the Ethiopic version and because of the gap between the retroverted names in *Jubilees* and the place-names from the Maccabean wars.[91] (b) Based upon paleographic considerations, the oldest copy of *Jubilees* from Qumran, 4Q216 (4Q Jubilees^a), is dated to the final quarter of the second century B.C.E.[92] The *terminus ad quem* for the composition is therefore between the years 125–100 B.C.E.[93] (c) According to VanderKam, *Jub.* 4:19 borrowed directly from the *Animal Apocalypse* (*1 Enoch* 83–90), which was composed soon after 164 B.C.E. However, this claim is difficult to defend, as *Jub.* 4:19 is too general to be connected to specific chapters from *1 Enoch*. (d) According to the prevailing opinion amongst scholars, "*Jubilees* gives no indication that its author has separated from the Jewish community of his day,"[94]

---

[90] For a comprehensive discussion of the topic, see VanderKam 1977: 214–285; for an updated, abridged version see VanderKam 1997: 19–20; 2001: 18–21.

[91] Goldstein 1983: 77–86; Nickelsburg 1984: 102. Cf. also Doran (1989), who cautions against arriving at historical conclusions based upon literary texts. In later studies, VanderKam refrains from the identification of references to the Maccabean wars. Doran's methodological argument can also be directed at Mendels (1987: 57–58), who dates *Jubilees* to ca. 125 B.C.E., based upon some of the same historical references that VanderKam analyzed.

[92] VanderKam and Milik 1994: 2. The editors note in a parenthetical statement that, "Milik prefers to date the script nearer to the mid-second century B.C.E." We can thus conclude that the date quoted above is that proposed by VanderKam.

[93] The Qumran evidence invalidates various suggestions proposed in the nineteenth century (for example, Dillman 1851: 88–94; Rönsch 1874: 496–523) to date *Jubilees* as late as the first century C.E., and to interpret it in light of Christianity.

[94] VanderKam 2001: 21.

in contrast with the Qumran sectarian literature. However, indications of inner-Jewish tensions do appear in *Jubilees*, both in the description of the civil war in *Jub.* 23:9–32, and in the halakhic polemic surrounding circumcision in *Jub.* 15:25–34, neither of which necessarily reflects a Mac-cabean backdrop.[95]

Two other suggestions for dating the book have been raised based upon the analysis of *Jub.* 23:9–32. This apocalyptic passage describes a revolt of the young people in the nation against the older establishment, as a reaction to the latter's sins:

> (14) All of this will happen to the evil generation which makes the earth commit sin through sexual impurity, contamination, and their detestable actions...(16) During that generation the children will find fault with their fathers and elders because of sin and injustice, because of what they say and the great evils that they commit, and because of their abandoning the covenant which the Lord had made between them and himself...(19)... regarding the law and the covenant. For they have forgotten commandment, covenant, festival, month, sabbath, jubilee, and every verdict.

According to Finkelstein, Goldstein, and Nickelsburg, this passage polemecizes against Hellenizers, and they posit that the book was composed a short time before Antiochus's decrees. They base their claim upon the (surprising—according to VanderKam's suggested date) absence of any reference in the passage to either Antiochus Epiphanes or to his decrees. In addition to this omission, they adduce the polemical demand, found elsewhere in the book, to separate completely from the nations. These scholars view this demand as a reaction to the Hellenistic reform that took place in 175 B.C.E. in Jerusalem.[96]

Based upon this same passage, Kister suggested that the absence of any reference to Antiochus's decrees is due to the fact that they had already passed. The sins mentioned in *Jub.* 23:9–32, forgetting "commandment, covenant, festival, month, sabbath, jubilee, and every verdict," which repeats an accusation already made in *Jub.* 1:14–15, does not constitute a willful violation of the laws, but rather forgetfulness or lack of knowledge. These sins are not related to foreign worship (as opposed to the sins mentioned in Deut 31, the biblical passage upon which the formulation in *Jub.* 1:14–15 is based), as one would have expected in the context of the Hellenizers, nor joining the nations,

---

[95] See Kister 1986: 5–9, and especially n. 26; and the discussion below, pp. 243–245.

[96] Finkelstein 1943: 21, 24; Goldstein 1983: 69–72; Nickelsburg 1984: 102–103.

but instead refer to the sectarian calendar used by *Jubilees* (cf. 6:34–36). The dispute between the "children" and the "fathers" in *Jub.* 23 focuses therefore on the halakhic realm, and is similar to the description of the founding of the sect in *Damascus Document* I, 8–11 both in terms of content and terminology.[97]

Other suggestions, earlier and later, have been put forth regarding the dating of *Jubilees*. Zeitlin posited the earliest date of composition for *Jubilees*, in the fourth century B.C.E. In his opinion, the author opposed the laws and traditions of the Torah, a position that would have been unacceptable in the Hellenistic period.[98] He also claimed that the angelology in the *Book of Watchers* is more developed than that of *Jubilees*, and therefore the latter must have been composed prior to the third century B.C.E. (the date of composition of the former).[99] However, it is difficult to accept his suggested dating, because: (1) *Jubilees* does not polemecize against the pentateuchal laws, but rather, interprets them; (2) the Watchers story in *Jubilees* is based upon the *Book of Watchers*.[100]

Ravid dated the composition to the end of the third century or the beginning of the second century B.C.E.[101] This date is based upon her conclusions regarding a number of central topics in the study of *Jubilees*: (1) In her opinion, *Jubilees* is not a sectarian composition, and its calendar is different from that preserved in Qumran (364 days). (2) *Jubilees* does not reflect the division into sects, but the opposition in *Jub.* 6 to the lunar-solar calendar does reveal signs of an internal rift. (3) There is no expectation in *Jubilees* of the end of the world, and the author therefore lived in a relatively peaceful era. (4) The author's "historical horizon" refers to Hellenistic culture. However, her conclusions are not convincing for the following reasons: (1) Ravid (and Kugel) suggested that the *Jubilees* calendar includes an extra day (364 + 1) that is not mentioned in the book, and it is therefore not a set calendar as is generally accepted in scholarship.[102] This suggestion, however, is contradicted

---

[97] Kister 1986: 5–9; Werman (1995a: 30–35; 2004) accepted Kister's position, and further strengthened the connection between *Jubilees* and the Qumran sect. In contrast to Werman's suggestion (2004: 39–53) that *Jub.* 23:9–32 is composed of two layers, a base text and a sectarian editorial stratum, I view the entire passage as the product of one author.
[98] Zeitlin 1939–40: 29–31.
[99] Zeitlin 1939–40: 8–16.
[100] See pp. 109–118.
[101] Ravid 2001: 181–184. Kugel (1998: 922) dates *Jubilees* to the beginning of the second century B.C.E., but does not offer any explanation.
[102] Kugel and Ravid 2001; Ravid 2003.

by explicit verses in *Jubilees*: "Now you command the Israelites to keep the years in this number—364 days. Then the year will be complete and it will not disturb its time from its days or from its festivals because everything will happen in harmony with their testimony. They will neither omit a day nor disturb a festival" (6:32); "because after your death your children will disturb (it) so that they do not make the year (consist of) 364 days only. Therefore, they will err regarding the first of the month, the season, the sabbath, and the festivals" (6:38). Ravid's conclusions regarding the *Jubilees* calendar, and the alleged difference between it and the Qumran version, compelled her to speculate why the Qumran sectarian literature does not polemecize against *Jubilees*, and instead reflects a level of admiration for the book. She solves this problem by dating *Jubilees* to a much earlier time than the foundation of the Qumran sect.[103] However, if the *Jubilees* calendar is identical to the Qumran version, there would be no reason to posit such an early date for *Jubilees*. The other differences that Ravid identified between *Jubilees* and the Qumran Scrolls (regarding purity and impurity, and the status of the Zadokite priests) were not so significant that the sect could not accept them. (2) As noted above, two passages (23:9–32; 15:25–34) actually point to inner-Jewish tension, and even the beginnings of a rift within the nation. (3) A number of passages refer to the eschatological era (1:26–29; 23:9–32; 50:5). (4) The relationship with Greek culture is appropriate for most of the suggestions for the dating of the book.

Charles attributed the book to a Pharisaic author who supported the Hasmoneans, and dated the book between the year John Hyrcanus ascended to the position of High priest (135 B.C.E.) and the time he broke away from the Pharisees (105 B.C.E.).[104] However, one can raise two arguments against this suggestion:[105] (1) Some of the allusions to the Hasmoneans adduced by Charles are unconvincing. For example, there is no support for the assumption that the epithet assigned to Levi, a "priest of the most high God" (32:1) is an allusion to the Hasmoneans,[106] and as noted above, it is difficult to confirm a connection between the Maccabean wars and the stories in *Jub.* 34–38. (2) If the composition

---

[103] Ravid 2001: 181–182.
[104] Charles 1902: xiii–xiv, lviii–lxvi; Testuz (1960: 25–42, 197) followed Charles, but limited the date to approximately 110 B.C.E. (except for a few interpolations from the years 63–38 B.C.E.).
[105] Nickelsburg 1984: 101–102.
[106] As claimed by Charles 1902: lix, 191; Testuz 1960: 35.

reflects a pro-Hasmonean approach, it is hard to understand why so many copies of *Jubilees* were preserved in the Qumran Scrolls, as well as the many links between the two.

The literary-critical analysis suggested in this study is also of significance for the dating of *Jubilees*. As VanderKam noted:[107]

> One issue that could complicate the search for the time when the author did his work should be noted first. It would be simpler to find that date if the book was a literary unity, but if it was written in stages the search would become much more difficult.

If the book is composed from sources and their redaction, one cannot speak of one date for all the material in the work, but rather the dates of each particular source or stratum, and especially the redactional layer.[108] The full discussion of the date (or dates) of composition of *Jubilees* will therefore only take place at the end of this study, after the redactional layer has been separated from its sources.

This book is composed of three parts: in the first, I analyze a number of passages that demonstrate the heterogeneous nature of *Jubilees*. Chapters 1–3 present instances of halakhic redaction, in which the legal passages either contradict or are at odds with the rewritten narratives, while ch. 4 focuses on cases of chronological redaction, in which inconsistencies between the chronological framework and the rewritten narratives demonstrate that the former was superimposed upon the latter.

Additional instances in which such redactional activity is discernible are discussed in Part II, but these also address the origin of evil in the world as presented in *Jubilees*. Chapter 5 plays a significant role both as a paradigm for the literary development of the book (halakhic and chronological redactions), and at the same time, as an important example of the reinterpretation of earlier traditions (from *1 Enoch*) regarding the question of evil. Similarly, ch. 6 presents an example of chronological redaction, thus leading to the conclusion that a passage from *Jub.* 7, which relates to the question of the origin of the evil, was

---

[107] VanderKam 2001: 17.

[108] As noted above, Davenport (1971) suggested a theory of literary development for the book. Even though his arguments are not convincing, it is worth noting that in his description of the stratification of the book, he also discussed the dating of the different layers.

not composed by the redactor of *Jubilees*. In chs. 7–8, I suggest that the redactor adopted an earlier tradition and incorporated it within a new ideological framework. Chapters 9–10 offer two more examples of legal redaction, each with implications for this theological question. Finally, chs. 11–13 address passages that can be attributed with reasonable certainty to the redactional layer of the book, and which have consequences for this discussion.

Part III addresses another topic regarding the ideas and beliefs of the redactional layer, the question of the origin of law. This analysis complements the earlier chapters by demonstrating that the law, similar to evil in the world (in addition to the chronological system according to which the world functions), was fashioned by God at the dawn of creation, thus leading to a comprehensive description of the redactor's worldview.

PART I

THE EDITORIAL LAYER:
REWRITTEN STORIES, LEGAL PASSAGES,
AND THE CHRONOLOGICAL FRAMEWORK

Introduction: The Halakhic Redaction

One of the most distinctive features of *Jubilees* is the juxtaposition of laws generally known from the legal corpora of the Pentateuch, with stories of the patriarchal period. In the Torah, almost all of the laws first appear in legal collections following the Sinaitic theophany, while in *Jubilees* most of them appear in the framework of stories that preceded this revelation. These laws are sometimes presented as deriving from the actions of the biblical characters, and in other cases as laws that already existed, preserved on the Heavenly Tablets, which were either observed or violated by the ancestor in question. The pentateuchal legends are thus transformed into etiological narratives, designed to impart legal lessons to the reader of the work. The patriarchs lend their authority to the antiquity of the laws, and the observance of the laws testifies to the religiosity of the patriarchs.

The collocation of specific laws with the patriarchal narratives reflects halakhic interpretation of the biblical stories. Although the laws are often presented as the result of the actions of the forefathers, and thus theoretically apply only following the story in question, *Jubilees*' presentation of the legislation is always the result of its interpretation of the story. First, the choice of which specific law to append to the narrative points to a particular understanding of the story and its details. Second, especially in cases in which the patriarchal narratives do not accord with any known biblical directives, the legal passages resort to exegesis that can be described by the later term, *midrash halakhah* (in method but not in form), in order to adapt the narrative to pentateuchal regulations. Finally, the laws in *Jubilees* make certain assumptions concerning the circumstances of each story; for example, that the focal character sinned or that impurity was created by his or her actions. Similarly, the derivation of a great number of rules concerning festivals and the calendar, based upon biblical events, assumes that those events took place on specific dates. In light of the above, an examination of the legal exegesis both explicit and implicit in the legislation appended to the stories is an essential component of the study of *Jubilees*.

The narrative portions of *Jubilees* also reveal halakhic interpretation, now already embedded in the stories. Here too one can discern the specific circumstances surrounding a given story that are the result of exegesis of biblical laws applied to the narratives. These include the dating of events, questions of purity and impurity, and whether the sin was the result of choice or compulsion. In those instances in which the law underlying the biblical story does not reflect any of the laws found in the biblical corpora, the rewritten narrative itself sometimes attempts to resolve the apparent contradiction between the two with its own *midrash halakhah*.

According to the general scholarly consensus, both processes, the rewriting of the stories and the addition of laws, are the work of the same author. According to this widespread view, one can attribute all differences between *Jubilees* and the extant textual witnesses of the Torah to one person, "the author of *Jubilees*." However, the analysis of the relationship between the laws and the narratives sometimes leads to the opposite conclusion: the laws derived from the narratives often do not correspond with the exegetical tendencies reflected in the rewritten stories themselves. Sometimes, the laws even contradict the stories. If one author were responsible for both processes, one would expect agreement between the legal passages and the rewritten narratives. Contradictions between them suggest that the person who incorporated the legal material is not the same individual who rewrote the story. Menahem Kister has already identified two instances of this phenomenon.[1] I will now present additional examples of the combination of law and narrative, and will attempt to demonstrate that the exegesis embedded in these rewritten narrative sections either contradicts or is at cross-purposes with the interpretation implicit or explicit in the legal passages. The weight of the cumulative evidence of all of these cases suggests some interesting possibilities regarding the relationship between the legal and narrative passages in *Jubilees*, and the literary development of the book as a whole.

---

[1] Kister 1992.

CHAPTER ONE

THE ENTRY INTO THE GARDEN OF EDEN (*JUBILEES* 3)

The Connection between the Entry into the Garden of Eden and the Law of Impurity due to Childbirth (3:8–14)

Jubilees 3 describes the period of time immediately following the week of creation (*Jub.* 2). In the second week of the world's existence, the animals were brought before Adam so that he could name them.[1] After they had all passed before him, God decided that Adam should not be alone, and he therefore fashioned a woman from one of his ribs (vv. 1–7, parallel to Gen 2:18–24). In the next section, in vv. 8–14, one finds a legal passage that has no parallel in Genesis. This passage links the dates of the first couple's births and entries into the Garden of Eden with the law of the impurity of the postpartum mother found in Lev 12:

> 3:8 In the first week Adam and his wife—the rib—were created, and in the second week he showed her to him. *Therefore, a commandment was given to keep (women) in their defilement seven days for a male (child) and for a female two (units) of seven days.*
> 3:9 After 40 days had come to an end for Adam in the land where he had been created, we brought him into the Garden of Eden to work and keep it. His wife was brought (there) on the eightieth day. After this she entered the Garden of Eden. *3:10 For this reason a commandment was written in the heavenly tablets for the one who gives birth to a child: if she gives birth to a male, she is to remain in her impurity for seven days like the first seven days; then for 33 days she is to remain in the blood of purification. She is not to touch any sacred thing nor to enter the sanctuary until she completes these days for a male. 3:11 As for a female she is to remain in her impurity for two weeks of days like the first two weeks and 66 days in the blood of her purification. Their total is 80 days.*
> 3:12 After she had completed these 80 days, we brought her into the Garden of Eden because it is the holiest in the entire earth, and every tree which is planted in it is holy. *3:13 For this reason the law of these days*

---

[1] This stands in contrast to the order presented in Gen 2:18–20—first the Lord's comment that "it is not good for man to be alone" (v. 18) and then the creation of the animals—which indicates that the purpose of bringing the animals to the man was to find him a mate.

> *has been ordained for the one who gives birth to a male or a female. She is not to touch any sacred thing nor to enter the sanctuary until the time when those days for a male or a female are completed.*
> 3:14 These are the law and *teʿudah* that were written for Israel to keep for all times.

The legal passages in *Jubilees* consist of narrative details that serve as legal precedents. In this instance, the legal passage consists of three parts, each with information from the Garden of Eden story (vv. 8a, 9, 12), followed by the law derived from that narrative detail (vv. 8b, 10–11, 13). The legal derivations, italicized above, are based directly upon the law of the parturient in Lev 12 mentioned above:

> (1) The Lord spoke to Moses, saying: (2) Speak to the Israelite people thus: when a woman at childbirth bears a male, she shall be impure for seven days; as during the days of her menstrual infirmity, she shall be impure...(4) She shall remain in [a state of] blood purification for thirty-three days; she shall not touch any consecrated thing, nor enter the sanctuary, until the days of her purification are completed. (5) If she bears a female, she shall be impure for two weeks as during her menstruation, and she shall remain in [a state of] blood purification for sixty-six days.

This pentateuchal law establishes that a woman who gives birth to a boy is impure for seven days, parallel to the period of impurity for a menstruant woman (cf. Lev 15:19–33). Following this week, the woman remains in an "in-between" status for 33 days, during which she is no longer impure, but is still prohibited from entering the temple or coming in contact with sancta (Lev 12:4). In the case of the birth of a girl, the numbers are doubled, fourteen days in which the woman is impure, and 66 additional days before entering the temple. This law presents two puzzling questions: first, what is the source for the different periods of 7, 14, 33, and 66 days? And second, why is there a difference between the births of boys and girls?[2] *Jub.* 3:8–14 is the earliest attempt to deal with these interpretive difficulties.

According to this legal passage, Adam and "his wife—the rib" were both created at the end of the first week, but she was only brought to him during the second. These two periods, one week for the creation of man and two weeks until the woman was brought before him, parallel the first two intervals in the postpartum law, one week of impurity for the birth of a boy, and two weeks for the birth of a girl (3:8). The

---

[2] See Milgrom 1991: 742–763.

dating of the creation to the first week, culminating in the creation of human beings on the sixth day, is set in Gen 1 (vv. 26–28). However, dating the introduction of the woman to Adam to the end of the second week is the result of a specific chronological-exegetical stance regarding the relationship of the stories in Gen 1 and 2. In the same way that the first week of creation culminated in the creation of man on the sixth day, on the sixth day of the second week, woman was created from the man's rib (*Jub.* 3:1, 5–6). Verse 9 adds two additional periods: Adam only entered the Garden forty days after his creation, and Eve was brought there on her eightieth day. These dates have no foundation whatsoever in the biblical story, and have been introduced as a source for the times found in the law of Lev 12, during which the woman was prohibited from entering the temple or from coming in contact with sancta (*Jub.* 3:10–13).

Jubilees 3:12 links the Garden of Eden to the temple, and thus creates the connection between the Eden story and the law of the parturient woman (which addresses entering the temple): "After she had completed these 80 days, we brought her into the Garden of Eden because it is the holiest in the entire earth, and every tree which is planted in it is holy." The identification of the temple with Eden is found elsewhere in *Jubilees*: "He knew that the Garden of Eden is the holy of holies and is the residence of the Lord" (8:19). The temple is associated with Garden of Eden in the Bible itself,[3] and this motif is developed further in postbiblical literature.[4] The author of this legal passage drew a parallel between the birth of a child, the beginning of life, and the creation of the first man and woman. Just as the birth of the baby causes impurity and prevents the mother from entering the temple, so too the creation of the first person caused impurity and prevented him from entering into the Garden.

Shlomo Naeh identified an additional exegetical motive for connecting the creation of man with the periods of time in the law of the parturient woman.[5] The Hippocratic treatise *Nature of the Child*, dated to the end of the fifth century B.C.E., expresses the medical opinion that the duration of a woman's postpartum bleeding is equal in length to the period of time from conception until the fetus is formed:[6]

---

[3] See Mazor 2002, and the detailed list of secondary literature adduced there.
[4] See Anderson 1989; Hayward 1992; Milgrom 1993; Baumgarten 1994; Ego 1997; Halpern-Amaru 1999: 11–12; van Ruiten 2000: 85–89.
[5] See the more detailed analysis in Naeh 1997: 170–174.
[6] The original Greek text was published in Littré 1851: 502–504. The translation here is according to Lloyd 1978: 330.

> The reason that I have introduced these details, is to show that the limbs are differentiated at the latest, in the case of girls, in forty-two days, and thirty days for boys; and I take as evidence for the assertion the fact that the lochial discharge (ἱστόριον ἡ κάθαραις τῶς λοχίων) lasts for forty-two days after a girl, and for thirty after a boy, these being the maximum periods.

Naeh noted that the same view is reflected in the position of R. Ishmael recorded in *m. Nid.* 3:7:

> A woman who miscarries on the fortieth day does not take account of the possibility that it is a human fetus. On the forty-first day, she shall sit [the days of impurity] for a male, for a female, and for menstruation. R. Ishmael says, "On the forty-first day, she shall sit [the days of impurity] for a male and for menstruation; on the eighty-first day, she shall sit for a male, for a female, and for menstruation, for the male is completed on the forty-first day and the female on the eighty-first." And the sages say: "Both the formation of the male and the formation of the female are [complete] on the forty-first day."

In the situation described in the Mishnah, a woman miscarried a fetus, and it is unknown whether the unborn child was male or female—it is consequently unknown whether she is required to wait forty or eighty days before she can enter the temple. According to all opinions, the fetus has no form during the first forty days following conception. The Rabbis opined that the gender of the baby is established at forty days, and therefore if the miscarriage occurred following the fortieth day, the mother must observe the regulations of impurity as if the baby could possibly have been either a boy or girl. If so, she must wait the longer periods of time required following the birth of a girl, fourteen days of impurity and eighty days before she can enter the temple. According to R. Ishmael, the gender of a male fetus is established at forty days after conception, and at eighty days for a female fetus. Therefore, if a woman miscarried between forty and eighty days, she needs to observe the laws of impurity for a male child, but not those for a female child, because the fetus could not yet be established as a female. The principle underlying R. Ishmael's position is expressed explicitly in the *baraita* in *b. Nid.* 30b:

> It was taught, R. Ishmael said: "(The Torah prescribes periods of) impurity and (blood) purity in the case of the male, and impurity and (blood) purity in the case of the female. Just as the (periods of time of) impurity and purity in the case of a male correspond to (the time of) his formation, similarly the (periods of time of) impurity and purity in the

case of a female correspond to (the time of) her formation. They said to him: The (duration of the time of) formation cannot be derived from (the periods of) impurity.

According to R. Ishmael, the two periods of time—the impurity following childbirth (טימא) and the time during which she is prohibited from entering the temple or from coming into contact with sancta (וטיהר)—are together equal in duration to the period of time necessary for the formation of the fetus, and the establishment of its gender, both for male and female babies. In contrast, the Rabbis claimed that the duration of the time of "formation cannot be derived from (the periods of) impurity"—there is no connection between the periods of impurity for the postpartum mother and the creation of the fetus at the beginning of the pregnancy.

Philo also posited that the gender of a male fetus is set at forty days and for a female at eighty days, but offers a different reason for this discrepancy: the longer period necessary for the female fetus is the result of her being imperfect relative to the male, and therefore a double period is required for her creation.[7] Although he does not explicitly connect the numbers forty and eighty to law from Lev 12, we can assume that his position represents the same tradition expressed later by R. Ishmael, and Philo used it in his discussion of Genesis.

The position of R. Ishmael and Philo is fundamentally similar to the one expressed in the Hippocratic composition quoted above, with one important difference: in the medical work, the periods of postpartum bleeding were ascertained through empirical, physiological evidence. Philo and R. Ishmael derived the same periods from the contents of the law in Lev 12.

It appears that the author of the legal passage in *Jub.* 3 adopted the same principle of "deriving creation from impurity," but his approach differs from that of R. Ishmael in three ways:

(1) The objects of creation are not each and every fetus, but rather only Adam and Eve: "(10) For this reason a commandment was written in the heavenly tablets for the one who gives birth to a child: if she gives birth to a male, she is to remain in her impurity for seven days *like the first seven days*...(11) As for a female she is to remain in her impurity for two weeks of days *like the first two weeks*...." Corresponding to the first week of the world, during which Adam was

---

[7] Philo, *Questions and Answers on Genesis* 1:25 (according to Marcus 1953: 14–15).

created, the mother of a newborn boy remains impure for seven days; in parallel to the first two weeks, at the end of which Eve was brought to Adam, the mother of a newborn girl remains impure for fourteen days.

(2) The derivation of the periods of impurity from the periods of creation in the legal passage in *Jubilees* applies only to the shorter periods of impurity, seven and fourteen days. In contrast, R. Ishmael derived the periods of creation of the fetus from the longer periods of time in the law in Lev 12, forty and eighty days.

(3) The story of the entry into the Garden of Eden is presented as a precedent for the law, and therefore, the exegetical principle found in other sources, "deriving creation from impurity," functions here in the reverse direction, "deriving impurity from creation."

THE RELATIONSHIP BETWEEN THE LEGAL PASSAGE AND THE SURROUNDING STORY

The legal passage is appropriately placed within the narrative context of *Jub.* 3. However, one can identify a significant contradiction between the two sections. As noted, the legal passage assumes a certain chronological sequence: Adam was created at the end of the first week of creation, and forty days later he entered the Garden of Eden. Do these numbers correspond to the dates in the narrative section? According to *Jub.* 3:17, the snake came to tempt the woman to eat from the forbidden fruit on the 17th of the second month: "When the conclusion of the seven years which he had completed there arrived—seven years exactly[8]—in the second month, on the seventeenth, the serpent came and approached the woman." The description of the time in the Garden as "seven years exactly (*tenquqa*)" emphasizes that the entrance to the Garden and the exile due to their sin, both occurred on the same date, the 17th of the second month. This is the meaning of the phrase "a complete year"[9] in 6:30—"All the days of the commandments will be 52 weeks

---

[8] The Ge'ez reading here, *sab'āta 'āmata **tənquqa***, "seven years exactly," emphasizes the complete years. In *Jub.* 6:30, 32, the Ge'ez translation uses a different formula to express complete years, *'āmata **fəṣṣuma*** (perhaps equivalent to the Hebrew שנה תמימה). However, despite the difference between them, it is difficult to find an alternate Hebrew *Vorlage* for *Jub.* 3:17, and therefore the Hebrew translations of Goldmann and Hartom (שבע שנים תמימות) in 3:17 seem likely. The emphasis on exactly seven weeks justifies such a translation.

[9] The adjective "complete" modifies a period of time in three instances in the

of days; (they will make) the entire year complete"; and 6:32—"*Now you command the Israelites to keep the years in this number—364 days. Then the year will be complete....*" This is also the meaning of the phrase in 4Q252, an exegetical scroll found at Qumran, in its description of the end of the flood (II, 1–3; DJD 22):[10]

> 1 in the six hundred and first year of Noah's life and on the seventeenth day of the second month,
> 2 the earth dried up, on the first day of the week, on that day Noah went forth from the ark **at the end of a**
> 3 **complete year** (לקץ שנה תמימה) of three hundred and sixty-four days...

Does the date of entry into the Garden according to *Jub.* 3:17, the 17th of the second month, match the chronological data from the legal passage (vv. 8–14)? As is commonly accepted, *Jubilees* assumes a 364-day calendar (6:32, 38), based upon solar calculations (as opposed to the lunar or lunar-solar calendars used by other Jewish groups; cf. 6:36). The year is divided into four quarters, each one consisting of 91 days, or 13 weeks (6:29), all together 52 weeks exactly (6:30). As has been noted by many scholars, since the number of days in a year according to this calendar, 364, is divisible by 7 (364/7 = 52), every date on the calendar falls out on a set day of the week every year. Moreover, each quarter of 91 days, a period of exactly 13 weeks, also has this same cyclical property, by which the dates in the calendar fall out on specific days of the week. Each quarter is divided into 3 months of 30 days, with an extra day at the end of the third month.[11] Jaubert studied the calendar used by *Jubilees* before the publication of the vast majority of the Qumran Scrolls, and came to the conclusion that the year in

---

Bible: (1) In Lev 25:30, the identical phrase, "a complete year," occurs with a similar meaning, but without the emphasis on the exact date found in *Jubilees*. (2) From Lev 23:15–16, "and you shall count off seven complete weeks. You must count until the day after the seventh week—fifty days," one can deduce that the Hebrew adjective תמימות refers to a complete period. (3) Josh 10:13: "Then the sun halted in midheaven, and did not press on to set for a whole (תמים) day." According to the interpretation in Sir 46:4: "Was it not by his hand that the sun stood still and one day [became two]?" (the reconstructed words are according to the Greek translation ἐγενήθη πρὸς δύο), i.e., the sun stood still for a complete day. B. *'Abod. Zar.* 25a cites other opinions regarding the duration of the sun's delay.

[10] Brooke 1996: 198. This source focuses on the same date that appears in *Jubilees* regarding the sin in the Garden of Eden.
[11] For a summary of the calendar in *Jubilees* and the Dead Sea Scrolls, see VanderKam 1998.

Jubilees began on Wednesday,[12] a position now confirmed in light of the calendrical evidence from Qumran.[13] The following table presents the order of events in *Jub.* 3, according to the 364-day calendar used by *Jubilees*:

Month 1

Sunday	Monday	Tuesday	Wednesday	Thursday	Friday	Sabbath
			1	2	3 Man Created	4 End of the first week
5	6	7	8	9	10 Seven days after the creation of man	11 Seven days after the first week
12	13	14	15	16	17	18
19	20	21	22	23	24	25
26	27	28	29	30		

Month 2

Sunday	Monday	Tuesday	Wednesday	Thursday	Friday	Sabbath
					1	2
3	4	5	6	7	8	9
10	11	12	13 Forty days after the creation of man	14 Forty days after the first week	15	16
17 Adam entered the Garden (*Jub.* 3:17)	18	19	20	21	22	23
24	25	26	27	28	29	30

Adam, who was created on the sixth day, came into being according to this calendar on the third day of the first month, which was followed immediately by the first Sabbath in history, on the fourth of the month. According to the legal passage, Adam entered the Garden forty days

---

[12] Jaubert 1953; VanderKam 1979. The calendar apparently begins on Wednesday because that is the day on which the celestial bodies were created as described in Gen 1:14–19.

[13] Talmon (1958) 1989; VanderKam 1998.

after the first week, or forty days after the fourth of the first month. Calculating the entry into the Garden according to the *Jubilees* calendar[14] leads to the conclusion that it occurred on the fourteenth of the second month, and not on the seventeenth as stated explicitly in *Jub.* 3:17.[15] The discrepancy is especially glaring in this case because the author of the legal passage has based the entire law of the parturient mother upon these dates, and it is in this most basic detail that the contradiction has been identified. This analysis leads to the conclusion that the legal passage, which draws a parallel between the entry to the Garden of Eden and the law of impurity of the postpartum mother, was not composed by the rewriter of the surrounding narrative, because its presence in the composition creates a blatant contradiction.

Moreover, one can identify an exegetical motive for dating the entry into the Garden to the seventeenth of the second month, independent of the chronological data in the legal passage. An investigation into the dates throughout *Jubilees* as compared to Genesis reveals some that are adopted from the biblical source, and others that are the creation of *Jubilees*. One date common to both texts is the beginning of the flood: according to both MT and SP to Gen 7:11, and *Jub.* 5:23, the flood began on the 17th of the second month.[16] As noted above, according

---

[14] Kugel and Ravid (2001; and more recently Ravid 2003) suggested, contrary to the prevailing scholarly consensus, that the calendar in *Jubilees* is not identical to the Qumran system. In their opinion, the length of the *Jubilees* calendar is 364 days, but with the important addition of an extra day which is not part of this count. This kind of calendar begins each year on a different day. It is worth noting that the story of the entrance to the Garden of Eden could provide them with a proof that the calendar in the first year of history began on Sunday. If that was the case, forty additional days after the first week, which would have ended on the seventh of the first month, would indeed end on the seventeenth of the second month (cf. the chronology presented by Syncellus discussed by Kister 2003), the date set by *Jub.* 3:17. However, Kugel and Ravid's suggestion does not accord with unambiguous verses in *Jubilees* (especially 6:32, 38), which state explicitly that a "complete year" is 364 days long, and do not mention an additional day. It seems to me therefore that the contradiction between the legal passage and the date contained in the story remains unresolved.

[15] Baumgarten (1982: 489, n. 8) noted that the *Jubilees* calendar begins on Wednesday, and therefore according to this scheme, Friday of the first week falls on the third of the first month. In his opinion, the author ignored this discrepancy of three days and calculated the Friday as the sixth of the first month instead. Considering the central role of the calendar throughout *Jubilees*, it is difficult to accept that this author ignored the basic fact that it began each year on a Wednesday.

[16] This stands in contrast to LXX, which reads "the 27th." For a discussion of the relationship between the various textual witnesses regarding the dates recorded in the flood story, see the recent studies that were written in light of the publication of 4Q252: Lim 1992, 1993; Hendel 1995; Zipor 1997; Kister 1999a: 360–363.

to *Jub.* 3:17, the sin in the Garden of Eden took place on the same date, the 17th of the second month, a detail that is not found in any textual witness of Genesis. By dating the entry into Eden to the same date as the beginning of the flood, *Jub.* 3:17 appears to link the first sin in history with the most severe punishment in history.[17] This connection expresses the important idea of reward and punishment: the paradigmatic sin leads to the paradigmatic punishment.[18]

According to the chronological approach of *Jubilees*, complete periods consisted of complete "weeks of years."[19] Similarly, in the case of the Garden of Eden story, the sin occurred "when the conclusion of the seven years which he had completed there arrived—seven years exactly" (3:17). In other words, the period of time from the entrance into the Garden until the sin was a complete period, the first seven years of history. If the sin occurred on the 17th of the second month, in the first year of the second week, then the entrance to the Garden happened on the same date, the 17th of the second month, in the first year of the first week. The entry to the Garden on this date is the result of the sin and exile on the same date seven years later. The choice of this date for the entry into Eden can thus be justified on theological and exegetical considerations, without any connection to the dates of the law of the parturient mother.

---

[17] See Baumagarten 1982: 488. It is possible that another date also hints at a connection between the Eden and flood stories. *Jub.* 5:29 and 6:26 recount that "on the first of the fourth month the openings of the depths of the abyss below were closed." The downpour thus ended 45 days after it began (although it is unclear how this date can be reconciled with the fact that Gen 7:12 and *Jub.* 5:25 both state that the water continued for 40 days). On that same date, the first of the fourth month, "Adam and his wife departed from the Garden of Eden" (*Jub.* 3:32), and thus concludes the story of the sin in Eden. However, this date was of special significance in the *Jubilees* calendar (see 6:23), and it is therefore questionable whether there is indeed any connection between the two events. It is possible that both stories reflect attempts to connect stories from Genesis with the solar calendar.

[18] In contrast to Stone's (1999: 141–149) claim that in Enochic and Qumranic literature, specifically the Watchers' sin led to the flood, and not the sin in the Garden. The correlation between these dates shows that both traditions existed in parallel, perhaps already in the Pentateuch, and certainly afterwards in Second Temple literature, and they were each emphasized in different degrees in the various compositions.

[19] 12:15—two weeks; 19:1—two weeks, 12—two weeks; 24:12—three weeks; 47:9—three weeks, 10—three weeks.

Summary and Conclusions

The legal passage in *Jub.* 3:8–14 stands in tension with the surrounding story with regard to the dating of events. If so, this passage appears to have been composed by a different author than the surrounding, rewritten narrative.[20] This demonstrates that one cannot assume *a priori* that *Jubilees* is the work of one author.[21] As mentioned above, the juxtaposition of legal passages to rewritten narratives is one of the most prominent characteristics of the entire book. This conclusion is therefore highly significant for understanding the literary development of the entire book. One can suggest a number of models for the literary development of this chapter, and especially regarding the combination of law and narrative. However, at this early stage of the discussion, we cannot yet substantiate one theory over another. It will only be possible to arrive at a preferred model following the analysis of additional cases of the juxtaposition of legal passages to rewritten narratives throughout the book.[22]

Jub. 3:8–14 is characterized by specific terminology, which is similar to the language used in other legal passages throughout the book:

8: Therefore, a commandment was given...
10: For this reason a commandment was written in the heavenly tablets...
13: For this reason the law of these days has been ordained...
14: These are the law and *te'udah* that were written for Israel to keep for all times.

---

[20] In Segal (2003; 2004), I attempted to show that the legal passage in *Jub.* 3 is based upon a parallel passage partially preserved in 4Q265, frg. 7. However, I now tend to accept the contrasting position, that the Qumran text adopted and incorporated the *Jubilees* legal passage (as suggested by Baumgarten 1994: 60–61, 72; 1999 [the official publication of the scroll]). The most important argument for this suggested order of literary development is the heterogeneous nature of the Qumran scroll (hence the title 4QMiscellaneous Rules in the final publication), which includes seemingly unrelated excerpts parallel (or similar) to various sectarian compositions from Qumran, including 1QS, CD, and the pesharim.

[21] In response to my analysis of *Jub.* 3, Kister (2003) suggested an alternate solution to the chronological anomaly identified between the legal and narrative sections, according to the *Jubilees* calendar. Kister's explanation also assumes that *Jub.* 3 underwent a process of literary development. Furthermore, he suggests that the written sources used by the person who reworked this chapter can be identified, and are attested in the writings of Syncellus, a Byzantine chronographer from the eighth century C.E.

[22] See especially the analysis of the Watchers story (*Jubilees* 5) presented in ch. 5.

It is reasonable to assume that all of the legal passages in *Jubilees*, which are marked by the same special terminology, were written by the same person responsible for *Jub.* 3:8–14. In contrast, the rewritten story in *Jub.* 3 contains no hints or allusions to it origins, and therefore, its relationship to other passages in the book cannot be determined. This difference between the literary genres, and the presence or absence of special terminology, will play a significant role further on in this investigation.

CHAPTER TWO

JUDAH AND TAMAR (*JUBILEES* 41)

Another example of the tension between a rewritten narrative section and an appended legal passage is found in *Jubilees*' story of Judah and Tamar (Gen 38). A comparison between the biblical story and its retelling in *Jubilees* reveals the exegetical motives behind the reworking. *Jub.* 41:1–21 parallels Gen 38, with changes by the reviser,[1] whereas *Jub.* 41:23–28 has no parallel in Gen 38, and the material contained therein adds both legal and moral considerations to the story. The relationship between the end of *Jub.* 41 and 41:1–21 deserves attention. Are the exegetical tendencies and aims present in the rewritten section identical to those found at the end of the chapter? If so, one can safely assume that the same individual composed both the earlier section and the concluding passage. Alternatively, if one can identify differences between the rewritten passage and the legal-moral exhortation regarding their exegesis of the biblical story, and perhaps even contradictions, then it is likely that the rewriting of the biblical story and the addition of legal material were performed by different individuals.

Moreover, the unity of the legal passage itself may be called into question. The Judah and Tamar story presented the ancient reader

---

[1] Verse 22 offers a chronological note intended to locate the Judah and Tamar story at the appropriate time, a common feature of *Jubilees*. Genesis 38 is sandwiched between the sale of Joseph (Gen 37) and the story of Joseph and Potiphar's wife (Gen 39). It is unclear from the biblical narrative when Gen 38 occurred, because the chapter details the birth of Judah's sons, their marriages to Tamar, their deaths, Tamar's pregnancy, and the birth of Perez and Zerah. All these events certainly took place over many years. The only chronological reference in Gen 38 is found in v. 1: "And about that time...." The interruption in the narrative between Gen 37 and 39, and the use of resumptive repetition in Gen 39:1 indicate the simultaneity of the stories of Joseph and Judah; cf. Talmon, 1978: 18–19. In contrast, *Jubilees* employs a chronological principle, by which the narratives are arranged sequentially according to the order in which they occurred. The Judah and Tamar story is located in *Jub.* 41, after Joseph had already risen to power in Egypt; *Jubilees* 41:1 dates Er's marriage to Tamar in the year 2165. The story continues until 2170 (*Jub.* 41:21), the year in which Perez and Zerah were born. These five years occurred during the years of plenty in Egypt, which according to *Jub.* 41:21 lasted from 2164 to 2170. *Jubilees* 42 then begins the story of the years of famine. By moving the Judah and Tamar story to a different location, *Jubilees* removes any doubt concerning its chronological details.

with many difficult legal questions, such as the possibility of intercourse between a man and his daughter-in-law, an act which is explicitly prohibited in Lev 18 and 20; or Judah's decision to punish Tamar for harlotry with death by means of fire, a punishment not found elsewhere in the Pentateuch.² Interpreters throughout the ages have offered various solutions to these and other problems raised by the story. The presence of legal or moral additions at the end of the chapter does not therefore indicate the internal unity of this section. Different approaches, from different hands, could have stood side by side, both attempting to explain the same difficulties in the text. Each addition must therefore be investigated independently, and only then be evaluated to determine whether or not they present corresponding solutions to the issues found in the biblical narrative. While keeping in mind the distinction between the rewritten narrative and the additional material, it is important to note the possibility that some of the material in the passage appended to the chapter may agree with the exegetical positions presented in the rewritten narrative, while other material may not. In such a case, I will suggest that the supplementary material that agrees with the rewritten narrative is indeed the work of the reviser of the story, while any data which do not match the rewritten narrative are the product of another hand.

The Rewritten Narrative (41:1–21, 27–28)

A careful comparison of *Jub.* 41:1–21 with Genesis 38 reveals the larger exegetical goals of the reworking. Most of the differences, including alterations, additions, and omissions, are intended specifically to mitigate Judah's guilt throughout the narrative:

(1) The cause of the unfavorable outcome of the story is Bat-Shua, Judah's Canaanite wife:

(A) Judah erred by marrying a Canaanite woman,³ but from that point on, she became the prime cause behind the death of their sons.

---

² For a discussion of the many exegetical problems raised by the Judah and Tamar story in its canonical context, see Menn 1997: 48–73.

³ This aspect is emphasized in *T. Jud.* 11, 13–14. Judah's marriage to a Canaanite woman is noted explicitly in Gen 38:2. *Jub.* 34:20 had already mentioned her in a list of Jacob's sons' wives, and presumably avoids repeating this information here (cf. Anderson 1994: 25). Alternatively, in light of the other details in the story that attempt to mitigate Judah's actions, it is possible that this detail was omitted to moderate his condemnation.

Judah, attempting to rectify his mistake in the selection of a wife, chose an Aramean woman for his son.[4] Thus, in this latter respect, he followed in the footsteps of his ancestors (Abraham: Gen 24:10; 25:20; Isaac: Gen 28:2, 5, 6).

(B) The reason for Er's death is not mentioned in Gen 38. According to *Jub.* 41:2, Er refused to sleep with Tamar because she was not of Canaanite origin, as was his mother. Immediately after this, in v. 3, *Jubilees* cites the biblical description of Er's wickedness and death at the hands of God. Although it is not explicitly stated that the sin for which Er died was his refusal to sleep with Tamar,[5] the juxtaposition of the two statements strongly suggests this.[6] A similar position is found later in rabbinic literature, without the nationalistic component. In *b. Yeb.* 34b, Er's refusal to sleep with Tamar is derived from the use of the adverb גם in Gen 38:10, to stress that both Er and Onan were killed as a result of their actions. If their punishments are identical, then presumably their crimes were too. The provision of missing details based upon the immediate context is a known midrashic technique; thus, perhaps the tradition of Er's refusal to sleep with Tamar was not the creation of *Jubilees*. Rather, the rewriter adopted an earlier tradition, and adapted it for his own purposes.

(C) According to Gen 38:11, Judah sent Tamar to her parents' house with the promise that she would marry Shelah when he matured. In fact, Judah apparently never intended to fulfill this promise, for he feared that Shelah might die as the result of this union, just as his older brothers had before him. According to *Jub.* 41:6–7, Judah sent Tamar to her parents' house with the full intention of marrying her off to Shelah. Once again, Bat-Shua the Canaanite is at fault, because she prevented Shelah from marrying Tamar when he was old enough. This change improves Judah's image in two respects: first, Judah is not responsible for preventing the marriage of Shelah and Tamar. Second, Judah did not lie to or mislead Tamar when he sent her to her parents' home. He intended to fulfill his promise. If so, Judah's only mistake was marrying a Canaanite woman. From that point on, he acted fairly and righteously.

---

[4] Tamar's origins are left unstated in the biblical story, thus allowing for her description as an Aramean in *Jub.* 41; cf. *T. Jud.* 10:1.
[5] As noted by Zakovitch and Shinan 1992: 49.
[6] Zakovitch and Shinan 1992: 49; Halpern-Amaru 1999: 114.

(2) According to *Jubilees*, neither of Judah's sons slept with Tamar. In the biblical story, there is no reason to assume that Er, the elder son, did not sleep with her. The story is less clear regarding Onan: "But Onan, knowing that the seed would not count as his, let it go to waste whenever he came in to his brother's wife..." (Gen 38:9). This verse is ambiguous about the nature of Onan's intercourse with Tamar. *Jubilees* appears to reinterpret Onan's actions: in place of "came in to his brother's wife," בא אל אשת אחיו, *Jubilees* provides "entered the house of his brother's wife" (v. 5). The verbal stem ב-ו-א is thus interpreted not in a sexual sense,[7] but as a description of their marriage.[8] *Jubilees* reiterates and emphasizes at the end of the chapter that Er and Onan never had intercourse with Tamar: "We told Judah that his two sons had not lain with her" (v. 27a), a fact of which he was unaware at the time of the event. If neither son had slept with Tamar, then she was still a virgin when Judah encountered her in Timna.

Verse 27b continues, "For this reason his descendants were established for another *family*,[9] and would not be uprooted." Why is this the result of Tamar's virginity? One can suggest two possible interpretations of this verse:

(i) The first statement, "his descendants were established for another family," is constructed from the subject *zarʿu*, 'his descendants/offspring', the verb *qoma*, and an object introduced by the preposition *la-*. The same construction is found in v. 4 (as well as Gen 38:8), Judah's request to Onan that he marry Tamar following Er's death: "and establish descendants for your brother." Based upon the parallel to v. 4, v. 27 informs the reader that Judah has performed the duties of levirate marriage instead of his sons, and this offspring is thus for a different family, that of Er.[10] The same use of the verbal stem ק-ו-ם is found in

---

[7] Found with this meaning in Gen 6:4, 16:2, 19:31, 30:3; Deut 22:13, 25:5; 2 Sam 16:21, 20:3; Ezek 23:44; Prov 6:29; cf. BDB, בוא §1e.

[8] Halpern-Amaru 1999: 114.

[9] The meaning of *nagad* in Ethiopic is "tribe, clan, kin, stock, kindred, progeny, lineage, family" (see Leslau 1997: 391). Goldmann 1956: 300, and Rabin 1984: 121, both translated "family," while Charles 1902: 231 and VanderKam 1989b: 276 offer "generation." However, in three places within the Hebrew fragments of *Jubilees* preserved at Qumran, one finds the word דור in Hebrew translated by a different Geʿez word, *tawlədd* (1:5 [4Q216 I, 13]; 21:24 [4Q219 II, 30]; 21:25 [4Q219 II, 33]). It is likely that *tawlədd* was used with the meaning "generation," and *nagad* with the meaning "family."

[10] *Contra* Menn 1997: 60, n. 84: "I have not come across an explicit interpretation of Tamar and Judah's union as levirate marriage in Second Temple or rabbinic literature."

the law of levirate marriage in Deut 25:5–6, where it is specified that the brothers of the deceased must fulfill the obligation. Apparently, according to *Jubilees*, the father of the deceased may also perform this duty, an idea already implicit in Gen 38.[11] However, this assumption contradicts laws from other biblical corpora, specifically the prohibition of sleeping with one's daughter-in-law (Lev 18:15; 20:12), which is punishable according to Lev 18:29 by being cut off (*karet*) from one's people. If so, *Jubilees* must address the tension between the story in Gen 38 and the explicit prohibitions in Leviticus—how can the father perform the levirate duties without being punished by *karet*?[12] *Jubilees* suggests that the laws of Leviticus do not apply in a case where the marriage of the son and daughter-in-law has not been consummated. The daughter-in-law is still considered the son's widow however, i.e. subject to the requirement of levirate marriage; thence Judah first tried to give Tamar to Onan to "establish descendants for his brother." When Onan failed to do this, Judah was able to fill this role without being subject to *karet*.

(ii) Alternatively,[13] v. 27 does not refer to levirate marriage, and instead, the sentence "his descendants were established for another

---

Menn does not address *Jubilees*' reading of the Judah and Tamar story, even though it is chronologically earlier than those she chose to discuss.

[11] The law of levirate marriage in Deut 25 differs from the Judah and Tamar story in Gen 38 from a number of perspectives: (1) Deuteronomy 25 limits the marriage to brothers alone, while in the narrative, Judah performs this duty. However, even in Gen 38, Judah first turned to his other sons to perform this obligation, thus indicating that it is preferable for brothers to do so (cf. Nahmanides to Gen 38:10); (2) according to Deut 25:5, the brother actually marries the widow, while Gen 38:26 relates that Judah did not approach her again; (3) Deuteronomy 25:7–10 allows the brother to refuse to fulfill his obligation. Although the Bible views this decision negatively (vv. 9–10), an escape mechanism does exist. In Gen 38, this option seems to have been unavailable to Judah's sons; the somewhat unpleasant ceremony described in Deut 25:7–10 would certainly have been a preferable option for Shelah, instead of Judah misleadingly sending Tamar to her father's home.

[12] In reality, the contradiction between the laws of levirate marriage (Deuteronomy 25) and forbidden sexual practices (Leviticus 18, 20) is found in the Bible itself: the former prescribes the marriage to one's brother's wife, a relationship expressly forbidden in the latter (Lev 18:16, 20:21), and punishable by *karet* (Lev 18:29); cf. *y. Ned.* 3:2 (37d): "'Do not uncover the nakedness of your brother's wife' (Lev 18:16), 'her husband's brother shall unite with her' (Deut 25:5)—both of them were stated in a single act of speech," as part of a list of biblical laws which contradict one another. Rabbinic law viewed the specific case described in the law of Deut 25, a levirate marriage where there is no offspring from the original relationship, as an exception built into the original law of prohibited relationships.

[13] The following suggestion was raised by the students in my course Introduction to Early Biblical Exegesis, Hebrew University, 2005–2006.

family," relates to *Judah*'s other families. Since his sons did not have intercourse with Tamar, she was not legally his daughter-in-law.[14] Their intercourse was consequently not prohibited according to the *'arayot* prohibitions in Lev 18:15; 20:12, and was therefore not considered a sin for Judah. The expression, "another family," perhaps then refers to the list of Judah's progeny in Num 26:19–22: "(19) The sons of Judah: Er and Onan; Er and Onan died in the land of Canaan. (20) And the descendants of Judah according to their *families*: of Shelah, the family of the Shelanites; of Perez, the *family* (משפחת) of the Perezites; of Zerah, the *family* (משפחת) of the Zerahites...." Perez and Zerah had the legal status of Judah's children, and not his grandchildren, and were therefore another one of Judah's families.

(3) Judah's verdict and its nullification point away from any guilt or negligence:

(A) In Gen 38:24, Judah decreed that Tamar be put to death by burning. *Jubilees* 41:28 explains that the source for Judah's ruling was the law which Abraham commanded his sons. This presumably refers to Abraham's statement in *Jub.* 20:4 that any Israelite woman or girl who commits a sexual offence must be burned with fire. As has been noted by many scholars, this law is a general expansion of Lev 21:9, which applies only to the daughter of priests.[15] Judah's verdict against Tamar was thus based upon sound legal principles.

(B) As Tamar was being taken out for burning, she sent Judah his pledge to show him that he was the father. In the biblical story, when he sees these signs, Judah states: "She is more righteous than I, *inasmuch* (כי על כן) as I did not give her to my son Shelah" (38:26). This statement presents a certain criticism of Judah, since his refusal to give Shelah to Tamar in marriage had led to her masquerading as a harlot. As mentioned previously, according to *Jubilees*, Judah intended to allow Tamar to marry Shelah, but his wife Bat-Shua had prevented this from happening. For this reason, the nullification of the verdict cannot

---

[14] See Rothstein 2004, who suggested that in this section, and in other passages in *Jubilees*, sexual intercourse between a man and woman creates the legal bond of marriage between them.

[15] Halpern-Amaru (1999: 150–151) correctly connects this extension to the general tendency in *Jubilees* to view all of Israel as priests. *Jubilees* thus continues the process of democratization typical of the Holiness Code in the Pentateuch; cf. Knohl 1995.

Some rabbinic sources describe Tamar as the daughter of a priest, thus justifying the means of punishment; see *Gen. Rab.* 85:10; *Tg. Ps-Jon.* to Gen 38:24: הלא בת כהין היא הנפקוהא ותיתוקד.

include Judah's words of self-condemnation. Instead, *Jub.* 41:19–20 reads: "'Tamar has been more just than I; therefore, do not burn her.' *For this reason* (על כן) she was not given to Shelah, and he did not approach her again." By this interpretation, the failure to give her to Shelah was not the reason for her superior righteousness, indicated by כי על כן, but rather the result of the circumstances of the story, reading על כן. Once Judah had impregnated her, the levirate marriage had been accomplished;[16] therefore, Shelah was prohibited from sleeping with his brother Er's wife as in Lev 18:16; 20:21, and with his father's wife according to Lev 18:8; 20:11. Since the purpose of the union of Judah and Tamar was to produce descendants for Er, once this had been accomplished, there was no justification for them to be intimate again, and this was in fact prohibited by the law against sleeping with one's daughter-in-law found in Lev 18:15; 20:12.

(C) The biblical expression צדקה ממני was expanded in *Jub.* 41:19 by the addition of the clause "therefore, do not burn her." In v. 28, the narrative relates that Judah intended to apply Abraham's prohibition in *Jub.* 20:4 to Tamar. He originally thought that she was guilty of fornication, and was thus deserving of death by fire. However, when Tamar sent him his pledge, he understood that she had not acted as a harlot, and should therefore not be put to death. The interpretation of v. 19 is illuminated by v. 28: צדקה ממני, "she is more just/correct than me," with reference to the legal question, and "therefore do not burn her," annulling his verdict.

In sum, *Jub.* 41:1–21, 27–28, presents a story in which Judah erred in the choice of a Canaanite wife, but from that point on, he neither made any mistakes nor did he sin.

The Legal Passage (41:23–26)

In Jub. 41:23–26, one finds a completely different evaluation of Judah's actions:

---

[16] Zakovitch and Shinan 1992: 172. Anderson (1994: 27–28) suggests that the narrator's statement, "for this reason she was not given to Shelah," refers to the period *before* Tamar's pregnancy—Tamar was not given to Shelah so that her offspring would be free of any Canaanite blood. However, that interpretation places the statement about Shelah at a different stage of the story than the phrase which immediately follows, "and he [Judah] did not approach her again," which clearly describes a consequence of the pregnancy.

(23) Judah knew that what he had done was evil because he had lain with his daughter-in-law. In his own view he considered it evil, and he knew that he had done wrong and erred, for he had uncovered his son's covering. He began to lament and plead before the Lord because of his sin. (24) We told him in a dream that it would be forgiven for him because he had pleaded very much and because he had lamented and did not do (it) again. (25) He had forgiveness because he turned away from his sin and from his ignorance, for the sin was a great one before our God. Anyone who acts this way—anyone who lies with his mother-in-law[17]—is to be burned in fire so that he burns in it because impurity and contamination have come on them. They are to be burned. (26) Now you order the Israelites that there is to be no impurity among them, for anyone who lies with his daughter-in-law or mother-in-law has done something that is impure. They are to burn the man who lay with her and the woman. Then he will make anger and punishment desist from Israel.

This passage can be shown to differ from the narrative discussed above in three essential points:

(1) Instead of attempting to mitigate Judah's guilt, this passage relates Judah's recognition that he is guilty of "revealing his son's covering" (גלה כסות בנו). This formulation, based upon the prohibition of sleeping with one's father's wife in Deut 23:1; 27:20, implies that Judah has violated the prohibition of sleeping with his daughter-in-law. In this passage, the fact that Tamar did not have intercourse with Er or Onan does not function as a mitigating factor, and therefore does not help to justify Judah's actions. After he pleads with God, the angels inform Judah that he has been forgiven. This forgiveness proves that the intercourse with Tamar was in fact a sin. According to the narrative passage, on the other hand, *karet* was not to be enforced because Tamar had not previously had intercourse with Judah's sons. That logic implies that Judah was *not* in violation of the prohibitions of Lev 18:16; 20:12, against intercourse with a daughter-in-law. These two perspectives on the union of Judah and Tamar are diametrically opposed: was there a sin or not?[18]

---

[17] All Geʿez manuscripts read here "mother-in-law." Littman 1900: 108; Goldmann 1956: 300; and Hartom 1969: 121 all suggest correcting the text to "daughter-in-law." As will be shown below, the reading as preserved in the Ethiopic texts is both correct and crucial to the understanding of this passage.

[18] Attempts have been made to harmonize the rewritten narrative (vv. 1–21, 27–28) and the legal passage (vv. 23–26), by suggesting that Judah only thought that he had sinned until the angels revealed to him in v. 27 that in fact he had not. The forgiveness in v. 25 renders this possibility untenable. Zakovitch and Shinan (1992: 120–21) suggest the harmonistic approach, but also posit the possibility of two separate hands as the cause of this tension.

(2) According to 41:28, Judah's ruling that Tamar be burned was based upon the law commanded by Abraham, presumably in *Jub.* 20:4. As noted earlier, according to that verse, any Israelite woman who is guilty of fornication should be burned; this is an expansion of the law in Lev 21:9 which mandates this punishment for the daughter of a priest. It is possible that this law has been expanded specifically to justify the verdict of burning in the story of Judah and Tamar.[19] Placed in the mouth of Abraham, this law has achieved authoritative status, and can thus be applied by Judah in this specific case.

In the Torah itself, burning is meted out as a punishment in only three cases of prohibited sexual activity: the story in Gen 38, the law of the daughter of the priest in Lev 21:9, and the prohibition of intercourse with a woman and her mother in Lev 20:14. This was recognized in *m. Sanh.* 9:1—"These are the ones to be burned: he that lies with a woman and her daughter, and the daughter of a priest that has committed fornication." *Jubilees* addresses the death penalty by burning in vv. 25–26. Verse 25 first deals with the case of one who has intercourse with his mother-in-law: "Anyone who acts this way—anyone who lies with his mother-in-law—is to be burned in fire." Both Goldmann and Hartom emend this text to read "daughter-in-law" instead of "mother-in-law," as the context of this passage is intercourse between a man and his daughter-in-law. However, this correction, unattested in any textual witness, corrupts the *midrash halakhah* employed by these verses. The prohibition against intercourse with a daughter-in-law in Lev 20:12 mandates the death penalty for both the man and his son's wife. However, the method of capital punishment is left unspecified. In contrast, Lev 20:14, the prohibition of intercourse with a woman and her mother (i.e., one's mother-in-law), does include a punishment, death by fire. *Jub.* 41:26 draws an analogy between the cases of intercourse with a daughter-in-law and with a mother-in-law, applying the method of punishment explicitly described in the latter case to the former.[20] *Jub.* 41:25–26 thus presents an alternative halakhic explanation for Tamar's punishment than that offered in the rewritten narrative. Although Judah was unaware that Tamar was guilty of intercourse with her father-in-law when he sentenced her to death by fire, the legal passage justifies the appropriateness of the punishment to the offense.[21]

---

[19] Finkelstein 1923: 56–57.
[20] In contrast to this approach, rabbinic law determined the method of punishment for intercourse with a daughter-in-law to be stoning; see *m. Sanh.* 7:4.
[21] According to Lev 20:14, intercourse with one's mother-in-law results in death by

What is the internal logic of this comparison?[22] Lev 20:14 describes the case in which a man has intercourse with both a woman and her mother, for which they are all punished by fire. The law of sleeping with one's daughter-in-law, which appears in its immediate context (Lev 20:12), describes a symmetrical situation: a woman (the daughter-in-law) has intercourse with both a man (her husband) and his father (her father-in-law). These two prohibitions, intercourse with one's mother-in-law and intercourse with one's daughter-in-law, are thus mirror images of each other, in which the men and women have switched roles.

The claim that the ʿarayot prohibitions apply equally, or symmetrically, to both men and women, is found in the often quoted ruling of CD V, 7–11:[23]

7	ולוקחים
8	איש את בת אחיה׳ם ואת בת אחותו ומשה אמר אל
9	אחות אמך לא תקרב שאר אמך היא ומשפט העריות לזכרים
10	הוא כתוב וכהם הנשים ואם תגלה בת האח את ערות אחי
11	אביה והיא שאר

7) ... and they marry
8) each one his brother's daughter or sister's daughter. But Moses said, "To
9) your mother's sister you may not draw near, for she is your mother's near relation." Now the precept of incest is written
10) from the point of view of males, but the same (law) applies to women, so if a brother's daughter uncovers the nakedness of a brother of
11) her father, she is a (forbidden) close relationship.

Leviticus 18:13 prohibits intercourse between a man and his aunt. The biblical law leaves the symmetric case, a woman and her uncle, unstated. The author of CD here polemicizes against those who marry their nieces, a position not explicitly prohibited in the Bible. While accord-

---

fire of all those involved: the man, the woman, and her mother. By analogy, in the case of intercourse with a daughter-in-law, all parties involved should be sentenced to death by fire as well. This is in fact stated explicitly in *Jub.* 41:25b–26: "because impurity and contamination have come on them. They are to be burned... for anyone who lies with his daughter-in-law or mother-in-law has done something that is impure. They are to burn the man who lay with her and the woman." Verses 24b–25a describe Judah's atonement through repentance, but do not mention a similar process for Tamar. Presumably, the author of the legal passage derived her innocence *a fortiori* from Judah's.

[22] Rosenthal 1993: 454, n. 19; Shemesh 2002: 514; and Rothstein 2004: 379–382 have independently suggested the same argument.

[23] Text and translation from Baumgarten and Schwartz 1995: 20–21.

ing to CD, the laws of incest are formulated from the perspective of men, but apply equally to men and women, the author's opponents appear to have read the incest prohibitions from a strict literal approach, holding that only those cases expressly prohibited by the Torah are in fact forbidden.[24]

The internal logic of *Jub.* 41:25–26, which draws an analogy between intercourse with a mother-in-law and that with a daughter-in-law, is formulated succinctly in CD: ומשפט העריות לזכרים הוא כתוב וכהם הנשים, "the precept of incest is written from the point of view of males, but the same (law) applies to women." As in the case of intercourse with one's niece, one finds a similar opposing view in rabbinic literature that interprets the laws of incest in a strict, literal fashion, limiting their jurisdiction to cases mentioned explicitly in the Torah. *M. Sanh.* 7:4 includes intercourse with one's daughter-in-law among a list of incestuous relationships for which one is put to death by stoning, while *m. Sanh.* 9:1 limits the punishment of fire to intercourse with a mother-in-law.

(3) According to vv. 23–24, Judah sinned, and therefore needed atonement to be free of punishment. He received this atonement for two reasons: (1) "because he turned away from his sin" and (2) "from his ignorance." Judah's ignorance differs from that in the case of Reuben and Bilhah, for in the latter, according to *Jub.* 33:16, they were ignorant of the existence of the prohibition itself. In *Jub.* 41, immediately upon realizing the nature of his sin, Judah regrets his actions and begs for forgiveness. He was aware when he committed his act that intercourse with one's daughter-in-law was prohibited. His lack of knowledge resided in the fact that he was unaware that the woman whom he had slept with was Tamar. The notion of the coexistence of two types of ignorance, of the law and of the circumstances, is found explicitly only later in rabbinic literature.[25] Ignorance of the law was enough for the author of the legal material in the story of Reuben

---

[24] This opposing position is adopted in a later period by the rabbis; note the positive appraisal of marriage between an uncle and niece expressed in *b. Yeb.* 62b–63a. Cf. Schwartz 1992a, who identified two different legal conceptions, nominalism and realism, to explain the many differences between Qumran and rabbinic law; and see Rubenstein's (1999) response, which attempts to show that in most of Schwartz's examples, the disagreements can be shown to result from different methods of biblical interpretation.

[25] See for example *t. Šabb.* 8:5.

and Bilhah to absolve them of any punishment, while ignorance of the circumstances was not sufficient to absolve Judah—he was also required to "turn away from his sin."

The process of Judah's "turning away from his sin" takes place in three stages: (1) he "knew that what he had done was evil"; (2) "he began to lament and plead before the Lord because of his sin"; and (3) he "did not do (it) again." These three elements reflect an understanding of Gen 38:26 that differs from the way in which it was understood in the narrative section:

Gen 38:26	Jub. 41:23–24
(1) Judah recognized [them] (ויכר יהודה)	(1) Judah knew that what he had done was evil because he had lain with his daughter-in-law. In his own view he considered it evil, and he knew that he had done wrong and erred, for he had uncovered his son's covering.
(2) and said, "She is more right than I inasmuch as I did not give her to my son Shelah."	(2) He began to lament and plead before the Lord because of his sin...because he had pleaded very much and because he had lamented
(3) And he did not know her again.	(3) and did not do (it) again.

Genesis 38:26 leaves the object of Judah's recognition unstated. From the similar language in v. 25, it is clear that on the *peshat* level, this recognition refers to the signs he left with Tamar. *Jubilees* 41:23 reinterprets this verb to indicate Judah's self-recognition of his sins: "Judah knew (or recognized)[26] that what he had done was evil." The second statement in Gen 38:26, in which Judah declares that Tamar was

---

[26] The Geʿez verb *'a'mara* can be translated as either "know" or "recognize," and thus translates the Hebrew י-ד-ע or נ-כ-ר (*hiphil*). Both Hebrew verbs are translated in many instances (including Gen 38:26) by the LXX using the same verb, ἐπιγινώσκω. It is therefore likely that the Hebrew text of *Jubilees* was ויכר יהודה, identical to that of Gen 38.

more right than he, has been interpreted by early exegetes as a public act of confession and repentance, which assisted in his attainment of atonement.[27] This passage in *Jubilees* also appears to understand Judah's words as a confession, but a private, rather than public one. In the narrative portion of *Jubilees*, v. 19, these words were understood as the annulment of Judah's earlier verdict: "Tamar has been more just than I; therefore do not burn her." The use and interpretation of Gen 38:26 is clear in the third element found in *Jubilees*: "and (Judah) did not do (it) again." In *Jub.* 41:24, Judah is never again intimate with Tamar because this would be considered the repetition of a sin, intercourse with one's daughter-in-law. Thus the interpretation of Gen 38:26 in the legal passage differs considerably from the exegesis of this verse in the narrative section.

Summary and Conclusions

The cumulative weight of the discrepancies between the rewritten narrative and the legal passage, regarding: (1) the nature of Judah's actions; (2) the source for the penalty of death by burning; and (3) the interpretation of Gen 38:26, suggests that the narrative (vv. 1–21, 27–28) and legal (vv. 23–26) passages of *Jub.* 41 originate from two different hands. Each passage interprets the biblical story independently, and each one solves the exegetical problems in its own way. The legal passage is unaware of both the punishment of death by fire for any Israelite woman guilty of harlotry (20:4; 41:28), and the special circumstances surrounding this story, namely that Judah's sons had not had intercourse with Tamar. This section therefore suggests alternative solutions to these same questions: the comparison of the mother-in-law and the daughter-in-law, and Judah's process of repentance.

Kugel noted the phenomenon of the collection and combination of interpretive traditions found in many postbiblical compositions. These later authors, who were aware of various approaches to solving these difficulties, assembled them in their works, even though these traditions were sometimes at odds with one another.[28] It is possible that one of

---

[27] Cf. *Tg. Neof.* to Gen 38:26; *Mek. R. Ishmael Beshallaḥ* 5; *Sifre Deut.* 348; *y. Soṭah* 1:4 (5b); *Gen. Rab.* 97; *b. Soṭah* 10b, and elsewhere.
[28] Kugel 1997: 28–34. Kugel (1990: 256–257) used the term "overkill" to describe cases in which an author quoted multiple interpretive solutions to address one problem. See the discussion above in the Introduction, pp. 28–29.

the differences identified above, specifically the two interpretations of Gen 38:26, is a product of this process. However, it is difficult to use this same model to explain the other two differences, the source for the punishment by fire and the question of whether Judah sinned or not. It is hard to imagine that one rewriter combined two such contradictory readings of the same story. Moreover, the difference in their location within the chapter is significant: the distinction between the two approaches corresponds to the distinction between the literary genres. If one author was combining multiple traditions, they could appear anywhere throughout the entire section, without the generic differentiation.[29] It is preferable therefore to view the combination of these two traditions as part of the process of literary development of *Jubilees*.[30]

---

[29] The same generic differentiation can be found in all the examples discussed in this study: the entry into the Garden of Eden (*Jub.* 3; see ch. 1); the Watchers story (*Jub.* 5; see ch. 5); the Akedah (*Jub.* 17–18; see ch. 9); Reuben and Bilhah (*Jub.* 33; see ch. 3); the Exodus (*Jub.* 48–49; see ch. 10).

[30] Verse 28 seemingly hints to understanding this process: Judah set the punishment for Tamar "on the basis of the law which Abraham had commanded his children." As explained above, this verse is related to another passage in *Jubilees*, Abraham's testament to his sons and grandsons: "If any woman or girl among you commits a sexual offence, burn her in fire" (20:4). The use of an internal reference from the story in ch. 41 to the testament in ch. 20 suggests that the rewritten narrative in *Jub.* 41 was composed as part of a broader work, which also included this earlier passage (and probably much more). However, it is also possible that Abraham's warning against harlotry was known to the rewriter of *Jub.* 41 from another source, viz., from the same tradition which also found expression in *Jub.* 20.

CHAPTER THREE

REUBEN AND BILHAH (*JUBILEES* 33)

The story of Reuben and Bilhah, which appears in an abbreviated fashion in Gen 35:22, was expanded to an entire chapter in *Jubilees*. While Jacob is away, Reuben, his first-born son, sleeps with Jacob's concubine Bilhah. The Bible records no consequences of this act, but simply notes, וישמע ישראל, "and Jacob heard." However, one finds negative evaluations of Reuben's action elsewhere, particularly at Gen 49:4, in Jacob's blessings for his sons: "פחז כמים אל תותר כי עלית משכבי אביך אז חללת יצועי עלה, Unstable as water, you shall excel no longer; for when you mounted your father's bed, you brought disgrace—my couch he mounted." According to 1 Chr 5:1, Reuben's act resulted in the revocation of his birthright and its transfer to Joseph. Despite the negative assessment found in these two passages, neither of them prescribes a punishment against Reuben himself; rather, they describe the penalty incurred by the tribe of Reuben as a whole for the actions of their forefather.

This punishment differs from that generally meted out in the Pentateuch for this type of behavior, and from that prescribed by the specific law prohibiting intercourse with a father's wife.[1] According to Lev 20:11, in the case where a man sleeps with his father's wife, both of the participants, the son and the wife, are to be put to death. One finds a similar prohibition, but without stipulation of the punishment, at Lev 18:8; Deut 23:1; 27:20.

The Rewritten Narrative (33:1–9a)

The short description in Genesis does not express any appraisal of Bilhah's role in this story. She is not a developed character there, and possibly plays the part of a prop in Reuben's premature attempt to

---

[1] In the immediate story of Reuben and Bilhah, Gen 35:22 describes Bilhah as the פילגש, "concubine," of Jacob. However, in Gen 30:4, Rachel gives Bilhah to Jacob "as a wife," and Gen 37:2 describes Bilhah and Zilpah as נשי אביו, "the wives of his father."

inherit Jacob's position.² Sleeping with one's father's wife is proposed as this kind of political tactic in 2 Sam 16:21–22 and 2 Sam 3:7, as well as in ancient Near Eastern sources. In the narrative section of its retelling (vv. 1–9a), *Jubilees* attempts to defend Bilhah by presenting her as the victim of rape, adding or changing the following details:³

(1) Reuben saw Bilhah bathing, and thus desired her. This theme appears to be taken from the story of David and Bathsheba in 2 Sam 11.⁴ But, in contrast to the biblical story, in which Bathsheba washed herself on the roof, a semi-public area, *Jub.* 33:2 emphasizes that Bilhah bathed in "a private place" (*ba-ḥəbu'*). Bilhah cannot be accused of attempting to seduce Reuben.⁵

(2) Bilhah was asleep during the act of intercourse. *Jub.* 33:4 says she only awoke *after* Reuben had lain with her, a sure sign of her lack of participation.⁶

(3) As soon as she realized that she had been raped, Bilhah grabbed Reuben and screamed out. In the laws concerning the rape of the betrothed virgin in Deut 22:23–27, the shouts of the woman are evidence of the fact that she protests the actions of the man, and thus she is not culpable.⁷ After she released him, Reuben immediately ran

---

² See for example Sarna 1989: 244–245.
³ Halpern-Amaru 1999: 110–111.
⁴ Heinemann 1954: 24; Anderson 1994: 21. Kugel (1995: 528–531; 1997: 272–273) has suggested that the motif of seeing Bilhah bathing derived from exegesis of Jacob's blessing to Reuben in Gen 49:4, "פחז כמים." It seems more economical, however, to assume a direct borrowing from a detailed story about sexual impropriety (David and Bathsheba) in the expansion of the briefer story about Reuben and Bilhah, a common midrashic technique, than to assume that it is the result of creative exegesis of the enigmatic phrase in Jacob's blessing.
⁵ Halpern-Amaru 1999: 110, n. 20. Kugel (1997: 272) suggests that the element of privacy was added to mitigate Reuben's guilt—the circumstances caused him to sin. However, in light of the tendency found elsewhere in this rewritten narrative, it is preferable to view this detail as an attempt to portray Bilhah more favorably, and exonerate her from any guilt.
⁶ Kugel (1995: 533–535; 1997: 273–274) suggests that the motif of Bilhah sleeping is also the result of the interpretation of Gen 49:4: "יצועי...אביך משכבי עלית כי"—"עלה"—"you (sing.) went up to your father's bed...he went up to my couch." If Reuben alone went up to Jacob's bed, then Bilhah must have been there already, and was thus presumably asleep when Reuben entered the bed. This motif, however, should be viewed in light of the general tendency of the rewritten narrative, present in almost all of its new elements, to absolve Bilhah of any guilt in the story. As a general methodological principle, Kugel has suggested that, "Ancient biblical interpretation is an interpretation of verses, not stories" (1997: 28), a statement which he has amply demonstrated in his many studies. At the same time, his focus on individual exegetical motifs can obscure the general interpretive tendencies present in complete narratives.
⁷ Halpern-Amaru 1999: 111.

away (33:4–5). These three elements, grabbing, shouting, and escape, appear together in the biblical account of Joseph and Potiphar's wife (Gen 39), but with the opposite intent. *Jubilees* recasts Bilhah, who grabs Reuben and shouts her objection, as a mirror image of Potiphar's wife, whose intentions are diametrically opposed to hers.[8] Both Reuben and Joseph run away—the latter from sin and the former as the consequence of it.[9]

(4) The words of Bilhah herself, in *Jub.* 33:7, emphasize the fact that she had been sleeping while Reuben lay with her, and was unaware until after the fact.

Bilhah is not punished in *Jubilees*' retelling. She is described as both defiled and impure as a consequence of the intercourse, an outlook whose origin can be traced to Lev 18:24–30, and this prevents Jacob from approaching her again. This is not a penalty aimed at her, but rather, impurity that is automatically created by the act itself. The existence of impurity prohibits any further sexual contact between Jacob and Bilhah.[10]

Why does the author of this version of the story emphasize that Bilhah was an unwilling victim? It is useful to compare this exegetical motif of Bilhah's unwillingness in *Jubilees* to two other compositions in which it appears:[11]

(1) In *T. Reu.* 3:9–15, Reuben warns his offspring against the dangers inherent in involvement with women. As an example, the *Testament* refers to the story of Reuben and Bilhah, and describes it in a similar fashion to the portrayal in *Jubilees*, albeit with some crucial differences. Some of these differences may originate in the *Testament*'s concern to impart to readers a more pronounced moral message; other differences may derive from the use of different traditions, while still others may result from different interpretations of the biblical text. Reuben describes how he observed Bilhah bathing in a private place, and desperately desired to sleep with her. One night, she became drunk, and fell asleep naked in her bed. Seizing the opportunity, Reuben raped her while she was

---

[8] Thus, Kugel's suggested correction (1997: 273, n. 5), that in the original version of the story Reuben grabbed Bilhah and not the reverse, is less convincing than the text preserved.
[9] Halpern-Amaru 1999: 110–111.
[10] Milgrom 1993: 281.
[11] Interestingly, throughout the rewritten narrative section, there is nothing characteristically unique to *Jubilees*, except for the addition of a date, the first of the tenth month (33:1), one of the ימי התקופה in the *Jubilees* calendar; cf. 5:17, 6:27–28.

asleep, and she was therefore unaware of his deed (vv. 12–14). Among the differences between *Jubilees* and the *Testament*: (a) *Jubilees* does not record that Bilhah was exposed, a point emphasized in *T. Reu.* 3:13–14. This detail perhaps provides an immediate catalyst that caused Reuben to sin, although it does not excuse his behavior; (b) Bilhah's drunkenness in the *Testament* transfers some of the blame from Reuben to herself.[12] These first two differences serve to mitigate Reuben's guilt in the story, even though this version of the story at the same time describes how Bilhah slept through the entire incident. Further differences include: (c) According to *Jub.* 33:4, Bilhah awoke while Reuben was in her bed, while in *T. Reu.* 3:14, Bilhah slept through the entire incident; and (d) Gen 35:22 does not name the source who disclosed to Jacob that Reuben slept with Bilhah. In *Jub.* 33:7, Bilhah herself reported this to him, while in *T. Reu.* 3:15, an angel informed him.[13]

The most prominent difference between the account in *Jubilees* and that in the *Testament of Reuben* relates to Reuben's punishment. According to the latter, Reuben *was* punished: "he struck me with a severe wound in my loins for seven months" (1:7), a measure for measure penalty. This personal punishment meted out to Reuben was added to the one he received on a national level, loss of the birthright to the tribe of Joseph, recorded in 1 Chr 5:1. The *Testament* does not record any punishment for Bilhah, and notes, as in *Jubilees*, that Jacob never touched her again. Her passivity, or nonparticipation, appears to have absolved her of any culpability, while Reuben himself is responsible for his own actions.

The literary relationship between *Jubilees* and the *Testament of Reuben* is not completely clear. The similarity of the rewritten story in *Jubilees* to the version in the *Testament* appears to indicate the dependence of the latter on the former, with the differences between them resulting from the exegetical tendencies of *Testament of Reuben*,[14] and from additional exegetical traditions known to its author.[15] At the same time, it should be emphasized that the similarity between *Jubilees* and the *Testament*

---

[12] For the strongly negative view of drunkenness in the *Testaments of the Twelve Patriarchs*, see, e.g., *T. Jud.* 14.

[13] For a fuller discussion of the story in the *Testament of Reuben*, see Kugel 1995.

[14] In particular, the attempt to partially justify Reuben's actions by passing some of the blame to Bilhah based upon her behavior; see above regarding the motifs of Bilhah's nakedness and drunkenness.

[15] Kugel 1995: 550–554.

of Reuben applies only to the rewritten narrative section of the former (vv. 1–9a), and not to the legal passage appended to the chapter (vv. 9b–20).

(2) A similar suggestion is found explicitly in Ephrem's *Commentary on Gen 49:4*: "'*You went up to your father's bed*' also indicates that he went into Bilhah when she was sleeping, and therefore, **she** was not cursed with him [Reuben]."[16] Ephrem states explicitly what was implied in *Jubilees* and the *Testament of Reuben*, that emphasis on Bilhah's nonparticipation, and specifically the motif that she was sleeping, are only significant if they come to exonerate her from punishment, placing the onus on Reuben alone.[17] Despite the chronological distance between Ephrem's commentary and these other compositions, the interpretation that he suggested explains the motif of Bilhah's slumber in the earlier works—Bilhah was absolved of any punishment, because she was not an active participant.

The Legal Passage (33:9b–20)

Following the rewritten story, a legal passage (vv. 9b–20) discusses the halakhic aspects of this episode. This passage is inundated with the terminology characteristic of the other legal passages in *Jubilees*:

10: "For this reason it is written and ordained on the heavenly tablets"
12: "Again, it is written a second time"
13: "Now you, Moses, order the Israelites to observe this command"
18: "Now you, Moses, write for Israel"; "because the Lord our God, who shows no partiality and accepts no bribes, is the judge"[18]

According to Ravid, this vocabulary is a literary stratagem, intended to mark those passages that belong to the Heavenly Tablets. In light

---

[16] Translation according to Matthews and Amar 1994: 201; emphasis mine.

[17] According to Ephrem, Reuben's punishment was not personal, but rather affected his future offspring: "'*You wander about like water, you shall not remain*' (Gen 49:4), that is, in the reckoning of the tribes. This is the reason why when Moses blessed him he said, '*Let Reuben live and not die and let him be in the reckoning of his brothers*'" (Deut 33:6) (tr. Matthews and Amar 1994: 201). Unlike *T. Reu.* 1:7, this punishment appears to be related to the national punishment recorded in 1 Chr 5:1.

[18] The motif of God as a righteous judge is emphasized in the legal passage in *Jub.* 5:13–18, and is also expressed in *Jub.* 1:6, which describes the circumstances surrounding the composition of *Jubilees* itself. It is also possibly the basis for the technical exemption given to Reuben and Bilhah in *Jub.* 33:15–16: YHWH, as a righteous judge, does not penalize those who have not fulfilled all of the legal conditions for punishment.

78 CHAPTER THREE

of the forthcoming analysis, I will suggest that the special vocabulary in the legal passage is not the result of a literary technique, but rather, the product of the unique process of literary development of *Jubilees*.

A different picture regarding Bilhah's legal status emerges in the legal passage appended to this story (vv. 9b–20). The laws quoted here refer to the prohibition of intercourse with one's father's wife, found in four places in the Pentateuch (Lev 18:8; 20:11; Deut 23:1; 27:20). Each of these prohibitions is formulated from the perspective of the man: "Do not uncover the nakedness of your father's wife..." (Lev 18:8); "And a man who lies with his father's wife..." (Lev 20:11); "A man shall not take his father's wife..." (Deut 23:1); "Cursed is one who lies with his father's wife..." (Deut 27:20). Only one of these four laws, Lev 20:11, records a punishment, and it applies to both the man and the woman involved in the case: "they shall both surely die, their blood is upon them." *Jubilees* relies primarily upon this verse, with some differences, when it quotes the prohibition against intercourse with one's father's spouse inscribed on the Heavenly Tablets (33:10):

> For this reason it is written and ordained on the heavenly tablets that a man is not to lie with his father's wife and that he is not to uncover the covering of his father *because it is impure*. They are certainly to die together—*the man who lies with his father's wife and the woman, too—because they have done something impure on the earth*.

The biblical prohibitions against intercourse with one's mother-in-law do not distinguish between cases of rape and consent,[19] and the same is true of the legal passage in *Jubilees*. The phrase "because they have done something impure on the earth" in *Jub.* 33:10, added to the biblical law, provides the reason as to why they are both punishable by death. The idea that their action led the creation of impurity amongst humanity on earth presumably originates in the conclusion of the list of *'arayot* prohibitions in Lev 18:24–30, which also includes the prohibition of intercourse with a mother-in-law (v. 18).

Verses 15–16 address the non-punishment of those involved in this incident:

> (15) They are not to say: 'Reuben was allowed to live and (have) forgiveness after he had lain with the concubine-wife of his father, *and she also*,[20]

---

[19] *Contra* Milgrom 2000: 1749, who states, "Her culpability presumes her consent," without providing any proof for this assertion.

[20] For reasons of Ethiopic syntax, I follow a translation of v. 15 similar to those proposed by Charles and Rabin, as opposed to that of VanderKam and others. The

while she had a husband, and while her husband—his father Jacob—was alive.²¹ (16) For the statute, the punishment, and the law had not been completely revealed to all but (only) in your time as a law of its particular time and as an eternal law for the history of eternity.

This passage also requires the death penalty as the general rule for both the man and the woman. This rule is stressed for a third time at the end of v. 17, "On the day on which they have done this they are to kill *them*." The reason for the non-punishment of Reuben and Bilhah according to v. 16 is that "the law had not been completely revealed to all." According to this legal passage, their ignorance of the law exempted them from punishment. Had they been aware of the law, they would both have been liable for their actions and deserving of death.

Rabin added a number of words in his translation of v. 16: "and the law in its completeness, *to cover every case*, had not been revealed."²²

---

²¹ Geʿez version at this point reads: *wa-yəʾəti-ni ʾənza bāti məta*. Charles (1902: 199) translated "and to her also though she had a husband." In the body of his revision of the Charles translation, Rabin offers a similar, yet slightly freer translation: "and so also was Bilhah, although she had a husband" (Rabin 1984: 103). Most other translators connect the Ethiopic *wa-yəʾəti-ni* ('and/now she [also]') to the beginning of the next clause: VanderKam 1989b: 222: "while she had a husband"; Berger 1981: 489: "derweil sie ihren Mann hatte"; Goldmann 1956: 287: "והיא לה בעל." VanderKam rejects Charles' translation because *wa-yəʾəti-ni* is not 'to her' but 'and/now she.' The disagreement between the two suggested translations revolves around the Ethiopic construction *wa- -ni*. Goldmann, Berger, and VanderKam understand it in accordance with Dillman 1907: §168, par. 4, which compares the Ethiopic suffix *-ni* to the Greek construction (μέν...) δέ..., in which the particle δέ indicates a new syntactical subject. Against this interpretation of the *-ni* in *Jub.* 33:15 is the fact that it is followed only by subordinate clauses (governed by *ʾənza*, 'while'). This leaves the second half of the verse without a main verb, making it difficult to assume the existence of a new subject. It is thus preferable to understand *-ni* here as 'even, also,' and translate "and she also" as did Charles and Rabin.

Support for this interpretation can be found in the Geʿez translation of v. 10:... *mota yəmut ḥəbura bəʾəsi za-yəsakkəb məsla bəʾəsita ʾabuhu **wa**-bəʾəsit-**ni**, ʾəsma*..., "They are certainly to die together (*ḥəbura*,)—the man who lies with his father's wife **and the woman too** because...." This verse paraphrases the law in Lev 20:11, according to which both the man and woman are to be put to death as the result of their sexual impropriety. The verse is translated using the same syntactical structure, *wa- -ni*, as *Jub.* 33:15. The syntactical construction indicates a compound subject, and not the beginning of a new sentence. (I would like to thank M. Mulgatta for her verification of the details of this argument.)

²¹ The formulation of this law suggests that the prohibition of intercourse with a father's wife applies only to one whose father is still alive; after his death, the woman is no longer legally his wife. As C. Albeck noted, (Albeck 1930: 29 and n. 197), this view stands in opposition to the rabbinic position expressed explicitly in *m. Sanh.* 4:7 and further discussed in *b. Sanh.* 54a.

²² Rabin 1984: 103. The body of his translation reads "to cover every case." In his notes, however, he remarked that the literal sense is "for all." VanderKam 1989b: 222, translated "to all."

This translation was adopted and interpreted by Anderson,[23] who explained that the justification for the pardon was that only certain laws regarding fornication were known during Reuben's lifetime; only those already known were punishable. The penalty against a woman who committed a sexual offense had already been commanded by Abraham (*Jub.* 20:4),[24] and thus was known in Reuben's time. Therefore, according to Anderson, *Jubilees* could not absolve Bilhah for the same reason as it did Reuben. Anderson suggested that the author therefore stressed Bilhah's non-participation; without this mitigating factor, there was no justification for her to go unpunished.

But it is difficult to accept Rabin's translation and Anderson's explanation that *Jub.* 33:16 refers to the revelation of only a partial list of sexual prohibitions for the simple reason that, as these scholars themselves admit, the translation that they suggest is not a literal translation of the Geʿez. In addition, Anderson assumed that if Judah knew Tamar's punishment in the story of Judah and Tamar in *Jub.* 41 (discussed above), then Bilhah's punishment also had to be known at the time of Bilhah's rape. Therefore, Anderson suggested a significant innovation: the case of a woman guilty of fornication is different from that of a man guilty of the same crime, and they are governed by different laws. Even if one were to assume this distinction, it would still be difficult to accept the claim that no such law existed for men, in light of *Jubilees*' retelling of the story of Joseph and Potiphar's wife. In that narrative, at the moment when Potiphar's wife attempted to seduce Joseph:[25]

> He remembered the Lord and what his father Jacob would read to him from the words of Abraham—that no one is to commit adultery with a woman who has a husband; that there is a death penalty which has been ordained for him before the most high Lord. The sin will be entered regarding him in the eternal books forever before the Lord. (39:6)

Just as Abraham had commanded a law to cover women guilty of fornication, he also had legislated, and apparently written, a law applicable to men. Although the words of Abraham that Jacob read to Joseph

---

[23] Anderson 1994: 21.

[24] Anderson 1994: 23–24 suggested that there were two considerations for ascribing this prohibition to Abraham: (1) the fact that Judah knew what Tamar's punishment should be, according to *Jub.* 41:28 (see above); (2) Reuben's awareness of a punishment for women who are guilty of fornication (Bilhah).

[25] The text is partially preserved in 4QJubilees[f] (4Q221), frg. 7, 4–9 (ed. VanderKam and Milik; DJD 13, pp. 79–80). Cf. also *T. Jos.* 3:3, in which Joseph refers to the words of Jacob (without explicit mention of Abraham) in the same context.

applied specifically to adultery with a married woman, it is certain that this more general case included the more specific case of intercourse with one's father's wife, including the demand for the death penalty.[26] If so, it is difficult to accept the explanation that v. 16 applies only to legislation concerning men. It is preferable, I think, to understand the lack of punishment for both Reuben and Bilhah as the result of the publication of the laws to only select individuals: "For the statute, the punishment, and the law had not been completely revealed *to all*." Joseph and Judah knew the law, while Reuben and Bilhah did not.[27] Thus, Reuben and Bilhah were exempt from punishment, even though at the same time Judah knew Tamar's penalty, and Joseph prevented himself from sinning with Potiphar's wife under threat of a known penalty. Only in the time of Moses, at the Sinaitic revelation, were all the laws revealed to all of Israel; thus, from then on, all Israel was liable for punishment.

Summary and Conclusions

The narrative rewriting of the story pardons Bilhah for her lack of participation, and is silent regarding Reuben's fate. She is rendered impure by this action, however, and thus prohibited to Jacob. The legal categories implicit in the narrative passage are those of אונס and רצון, compulsion and free will. According to the legal passage, both people in a case of intercourse with a father's wife are to be put to death

---

[26] Anderson 1994: 21–22, n. 38, notes the incongruity between the story of Reuben and Bilhah and that of Joseph and Potiphar's wife, in that the law was known by Joseph, but seemingly not by Reuben. Following Rabin's suggested reading, Anderson posits that the difference in knowledge resulted from the difference between the cases. He proposes that Reuben *was* aware that his behavior was inappropriate, but since it was not the exact same case as referred to in his father's teaching, he chose to be lenient with himself.

[27] Anderson (1994) rightly emphasizes the relationship between the perspective suggested in the Reuben and Bilhah story in *Jubilees* (the laws were revealed gradually) and the position found in certain sectarian compositions, such as the *Damascus Document*; see also Kister (1988: 323, n. 38) regarding *Jub.* 36:20. In light of the understanding of *Jub.* 33:16 suggested here, one can further the comparison, by noting that according to both *Jubilees* and the sectarian corpus, knowledge of the laws was limited to specific people or groups at different stages of history. In *Jubilees*, Judah and Joseph know the law, while Reuben does not. According to the Qumran writings, only the sect is aware of the mysteries of God and of the correct interpretation of the law (1QS V, 10–11; VIII, 13–15; IX, 17–18; 1QH IV, 9; XIII, 9; XIX, 9; 1QpHab II, 8–9; VII, 4–5; CD II, 14ff. and elsewhere); see Licht 1965: 48–49.

because of the impurity created by their actions. Both Bilhah and Reuben should have been punished, but were instead pardoned because the law had not yet been revealed to them. The narrative emphasis on Bilhah's non-participation is meaningless for the legal passage, which applies different legal categories, i.e., knowledge or lack of knowledge of the law. These different perspectives to the biblical story of Reuben and Bilhah are separated clearly by their location in *Jub.* 33; one is found exclusively in the narrative passage and the other only in the legal material. This clear literary division between the two perspectives suggests that the joining of these two passages is not merely a case of "overkill," in which one author quotes multiple traditions in order to solve one interpretive question, but results from the exegetical activity of **two different interpreters**. This argument is strengthened by the observation made above, that a version of the events parallel to that described in the narrative passage of *Jub.* 33, can be found in the *T. Reu.* 3, without the additional material presented in the legal section.

CHAPTER FOUR

THE CHRONOLOGICAL REDACTION OF THE BOOK OF *JUBILEES*

In addition to the legal redaction of the stories in *Jubilees*, which is expressed in the juxtaposition of legal passages to the rewritten stories, it is possible to identify a chronological redaction. Throughout this work, various events in Genesis and Exodus are dated in years from creation, using a triplet of numbers consisting of jubilee, week, and year.[1] The legal editing and the chronological editing appear to be the handiwork of one and the same person. The legal and chronological are intertwined together already in the narrative framework (*Jub.* 1), in the expression "the divisions of the times of the law and of the *teʿudah* (of the weeks and of the jubilees),"[2] which occurs four times in the Prologue and ch. 1 (vv. 4, 26, 29) and again in the last verse of the book: "which he placed in my hands so that I could write for you *the laws of each specific time in every division of its times*" (50:13).[3]

---

[1] *Jubilees* also dates some events to the month and day of the month, and in a number of instances, there is significance to these dates. For example, the 15th day of the 3rd month (14:10; 15:1; 16:14; 28:15; 29:7); the 1st day of the 1st month (5:20; 6:25; 7:2; 13:8; 24:22; 27:19; 28:14); the 1st of the 4th month (3:32; 5:29; 6:26; 16:1; 28:24); the 17th day of the 2nd month (3:17; 5:23,31).

[2] Compare CD XVI, 1–4: "to return to the Torah of Moses, for in it everything is specified. And the explication of the times of Israel's blindness from all these, it is specified in the *Book of the Divisions of the Times according to their Jubilees and Weeks*." This passage apparently refers to *Jubilees*, which is also called "The Book of the Division of the Times according to their Jubilees and their Weeks." In the heading of the book quoted in the *Damascus Document*, the legal component "law and *teʿudah*" is absent. But the content of the passage—the proper understanding of the Law of Moses and its observance, and the periods wherein the Israelites were blind to the laws—implies the integration of law and chronology in the "Book of the Divisions of Times." Even so, it is still unclear whether the book referred to in the *Damascus Document* is actually *Jubilees* (as we have it), because *Jubilees* does not refer to any period after the revelation at Sinai; see Kister 2001: 297, n. 44.

[3] Ravid (2000) suggested that *Jub.* 50:6–13 is not a suitable ending of the book, and should be viewed as an appendix which was added secondarily. Doering (2002) dissented and argued that v. 13b is especially appropriate as a conclusion. Kister (oral communication) improved on Ravid's suggestion and showed that the addition ended with v. 13a, and that v. 13b is indeed the original conclusion of the book. See the Introduction, pages 19–20.

The chronological framework of jubilees and weeks is common to other works of the Second Temple period that divide world history into eras of predetermined length. Underlying all of them is the idea of periodization: at the end of a pre-defined length of time, the world returns to its primordial state. *Jubilees* extends over a jubilee of jubilees, and this period ends with the fiftieth jubilee, during which the Exodus from enslavement in Egypt and the entry into the Promised Land takes place (50:4).[4] VanderKam noted the direct connection between the events at the end of this period in history with the laws of Lev 25 that deal with the jubilee and the Sabbatical Year. The release from servitude in Egypt and the return to the ancestral, promised land implement in the national plane the law of the jubilee from Lev 25 (vv. 10, 13), which is incumbent on the individual.[5]

Beyond the conceptual significance of the chronological framework for *Jubilees*, one can also identify its influence on the literary form of the work. The biblical stories are often reordered to maintain chronological continuity from creation to the revelation at Sinai.[6] In the previous chapters, I have tried to demonstrate that legal passages were joined by an editor to pre-existing, rewritten stories, and in this chapter I would like to suggest that the chronological framework was also superimposed upon extant rewritten stories. The editor who inserted the chronological data into *Jubilees* did not base his work directly on Genesis and Exodus, but on stories that had already been rewritten.

It is possible to demonstrate that the chronological framework was superimposed upon the already existing stories from instances in which the chronological framework contradicts chronological data that are embedded in the rewritten story itself, either in the details of the narrative or in the exegesis that underlies the rewriting. Dimant has

---

[4] The term "jubilee" in *Jubilees* connotes in general 49 years (with the exception of 4:21, where six jubilees equal 300 years; see Dimant 1983: 21, n. 17; and above, pp. 16–17). In contrast, *As. Mos.* 1:2 dates the entry into the Promised Land to the year A.M. 2500, and this equates to 50 jubilees of *50* years each.

[5] For the chronological conception of *Jubilees*, see VanderKam (1995) 2000.

[6] Glatt (1992: 132–138) deals with two instances of chronological displacement in *Jub.* 34–41: the story of the sale of Joseph (*Jub.* 34) is transposed to a point in time before the death of Isaac (36:18), and the story of Judah and Tamar is transposed to the period of the seven plentiful years in Egypt (*Jub.* 41). As Glatt notes, the chronological displacement of the sale of Joseph arises from chronological considerations of the biblical data (see below, p. 121, n. 49). However it is more difficult to explain the Judah-Tamar displacement based upon chronological considerations. Cf. Bernstein (1996) regarding the phenomenon of rearrangement in the *Genesis Apocryphon*.

already identified one such example, regarding the length of the jubilee period. Throughout the chronological framework, this period of time lasts 49 years, while in 4:21 it extends over 50 years.[7] The following three additional examples lend further support to the presence of a chronological redaction in *Jubilees*.

THE BIRTHS OF JACOB'S SONS (JUBILEES 28)

The story of the births of Jacob's sons provides an example *par excellence* of the imposition of the chronological framework on an independently rewritten story. The biblical account of the births raises chronological difficulties that have engaged the attention of biblical commentators throughout history. Genesis 29–31 describes the period of Jacob's sojourn with Laban and the birth of his children (except for Benjamin). According to Gen 29:18, 20, Jacob worked for Laban for seven years in order to marry Rachel, but at the end of this period Laban gave Jacob his daughter Leah instead. Laban then proposed that Jacob marry Rachel and work another seven years in return (Gen 29:27, 30). After completing the fourteen years of work to which he committed, Jacob remained in Laban's house for another six years, shepherding his father-in-law's flocks: "These twenty years I have spent in your service... of the twenty years that I spent in your household, I served you fourteen years for your two daughters, and six years for your flocks" (Gen 31:38, 41). The period of six years accords well with the story of how Jacob acquired Laban's flock, which took place after the birth of Joseph, the last son in the list given in Gen 29–30. During the first seven years of his stay with Laban, Jacob had no children, since he was not yet married. This leaves seven years in all for the all the births mentioned in Genesis. This schedule of births is possible, although very crowded.[8]

---

[7] Dimant 1983: 21, esp. n. 17; see above, pp. 16–17.

[8] Compare *S. 'Olam Rab.* 2: "Twenty years he spent in the house of Laban: seven years until he married the matriarchs, seven years from when he married the matriarchs, and six more years after the birth of the eleven tribes and Dinah. Thus all the tribes were born in seven years, each one every seven months." Based upon the chronological data in the Pentateuch, the Midrash determined that eleven sons and one daughter were born in the second period of seven years. But its conclusion that the gestation period of each child was seven months is based upon the assumption that there was no overlapping between the pregnancies, and therefore each pregnancy lasted only seven months (7 years [84 months]/12 children = 7 months per pregnancy). For a different approach, compare the comments of Ibn Ezra to Gen 30:23; Exod 2:2 (long commentary).

According to the dating of the events in *Jubilees*, all the births took place in the thirteen year period, which includes the seven year period that Jacob worked for Rachel and the ensuing six year period which is mentioned in Gen 31:41.[9] The following table gives the dates of the birth of Jacob's children:

	Event	Jubilee	Week	Year	Year from Creation
27:19	Jacob arrives in Bethel	44	2	1	2115
28:2	Jacob marries Leah	44	3	1	2122
28:11	Birth of Reuben	44	3	1	2122
28:13	Birth of Simeon	44	3	3	2124
28:14	Birth of Levi	44	3	6	2127
28:15	Birth of Judah	44	4	1	2129
28:18	Birth of Dan	44	3	6	2127
28:19	Birth of Naphtali	44	4	2	2130
28:20	Birth of Gad	44	4	3	2131
28:21	Birth of Asher	44	4	5	2133
28:22	Birth of Issachar	44	4	4	2132
28:23	Birth of Zebulun and Dinah	44	4	6	2134
28:24	Birth of Joseph[10]	44	4	4	2132
29:5	Jacob leaves the House of Laban and goes to Gilead	44	4	7	2135

The order of the pregnancies and births given in Gen 29–30 does not necessarily reflect the actual order of events. Some biblical commentators have already noted that given the multitude of Jacob's wives

---

[9] It is not clear why the chronological framework in *Jubilees* extends the period of births from 7 years to 13 years. It is possible that the redactor thought that the average period between pregnancies for any given woman was two years. Such a duration of two years is consistent with the chronological data regarding the births of Noah's children (*Jub.* 4:33).

[10] The only attested reading of *Jub.* 28:24 (as preserved in the Ethiopic translation) fixes Joseph's birth to the 44th jubilee, the 4th week, the 6th year (A.M. 2134). However, this date leads to an internal problem in the chronology of *Jubilees*. *Jub.* 34:10 states that Jacob sent Joseph to inquire about the welfare of his brothers in the 44th jubilee, the 6th week, the 7th year (A.M. 2149), when Joseph was seventeen (cf. *Jub.* 39:2; 46:3; Gen 37:2); thus Joseph was born in A.M. **2132**. Charles (1902: 173) suggested emending *Jub.* 28:24 to read "in the 4th year," to accord with the birth of Joseph in 2132. The erroneous "6th year" reflects the influence of v. 23, which dates the birth of Zebulun and Dinah to the 6th year of the 4th week.

(Rachel, Leah, Bilhah, and Zilpah), it is quite possible that two wives were pregnant at the same time.[11] At the same time, whoever takes the description of the pregnancies and births in Genesis as being an uninterrupted story, which is presented in sequential order without any overlap, is likely to encounter the difficulty of having them all take place in the seven year period.[12]

In *Jubilees* there is an internal contradiction between the two exegetical approaches, at least with regard to the first five births. In the biblical narrative, after the description of the birth of Leah's first four sons (Gen 29:32–35), it is related that Rachel was jealous (because she had not borne any children), and gave Bilhah her maidservant to Jacob, so that Bilhah might have children with Jacob in her stead (30:1–4). Bilhah became pregnant, and bore a son, Dan (vv. 5–6). A sequential reading of the events leads to the conclusion that Dan was born after Leah's fourth child, Judah. But this is not the only possible interpretation of the events, for Rachel could have been frustrated with her predicament long before her sister Leah had given birth to her fourth child. An examination of the chronological data added to the rewritten story in *Jub.* 28 indeed points to the second interpretive approach:

	Event	*Jubilee*	*Week*	*Year*	*Year from Creation*
28:11	Birth of Reuben	44	3	1	2122
28:13	Birth of Simeon	44	3	3	2124
28:14	Birth of Levi	44	3	6	2127
28:15	Birth of Judah	44	4	1	2129
28:18	Birth of Dan	44	3	6	2127

In contrast to a sequential reading of the biblical narrative, in *Jubilees*, Bilhah's son Dan was born in the same year as Levi, the son of Leah, and two years before the birth of Judah. In addition, the chronological framework made due with adding the dates to the text, but left the order as found in the biblical text, where the births of the sons are grouped according to their respective mothers.

A similar tension between the *Jubilees* chronological framework and the biblical order of the births as preserved in the rewritten story in

---
[11] Cf. the commentary of Ibn Ezra (see n. 8 above).
[12] Cf. *S. 'Olam Rab.* 2 (n. 8 above).

Jubilees occurs at the border between the births of the sons of Zilpah (Gad and Asher) and the second cycle of the births of Leah's children (Issachar, Zebulun and Dinah).

28:20	Birth of Gad	44	4	3	2131
28:21	Birth of Asher	44	4	5	2133
28:22	Birth of Issachar	44	4	4	2132

Here too, the birth of Asher the son of Zilpah is mentioned before the birth of Issachar the son of Leah, even though the chronological data in *Jubilees* imply that Issachar was born before Asher. This is another instance of where the rewritten text preserves the thematic order of the biblical story (according to the matriarchs), even if this contradicts the chronological ordering principle of *Jubilees*, which is systematically applied throughout the book.

Another verse in this context points to the fact that this chapter indeed developed in a complex, gradual process. As mentioned above, according to the birth dates, Dan the son of Bilhah was born in the same year as Levi, Leah's third son. One can infer therefore that when Rachel gave Bilhah to Jacob so that she might have children in Rachel's place, Leah had given birth to only her first two children (Reuben and Simeon).[13] This conclusion, which is inferable from the chronological data that have been added to the composition, contradicts *Jub.* 28:17, which provides an explicit statement of the order of the events:

> When Rachel saw that Leah had given birth to **four sons for Jacob—Reuben, Simeon, Levi, and Judah**—she said to him: "Go in to my servant girl Bilhah."

The rewritten story therefore clearly contradicts the dates in the chronological framework, as the addition to the biblical narrative in v. 17 explicitly establishes that Jacob's first four sons were born before Bilhah was given to Jacob.

Rönsch attempted to resolve this contradiction between the dates in ch. 28 and v. 17 by emending the data contained in the chronological framework, with the assistance of chronological information drawn

---

[13] Levi was born on the 1st day of the 1st month (28:14), prior to Dan who was born on the 9th day of the 6th month (28:18). However, one can deduce from these dates that Bilhah became pregnant before the birth of Levi.

from other works, and in particular from the *Testaments of the Twelve Patriarchs*.[14] He suggested that the dates of Judah's and Dan's births were interchanged, and what was formerly Judah's date (and is now Dan's) should be emended to the "seventh" year of the third week, instead of the "sixth."[15] Rönsch's reconstructed reading is as follows:[16]

28:11	Birth of Reuben	44	3	1	2122
28:13	Birth of Simeon	44	3	3	2124
28:14	Birth of Levi	44	3	6	2127
28:15	Birth of Judah	*44*	*3*	*7 (6)*	*2128*
28:18	Birth of Dan	*44*	*4*	*1*	*2129*

Rönsch suggested a similar emendation to resolve the second chronological anomaly relating to Zilpah's sons (Gad and Asher) and Leah's second set of children (Issachar, Zebulun, and Dinah). In order to restore the chronological continuity, Rönsch suggested interchanging the birth dates of Issachar and Asher as follows:

28:20	Birth of Gad	44	4	3	2131
28:21	Birth of Asher	44	4	*4*	*2132*
28:22	Birth of Issachar	44	4	*5*	*2133*

But Rönsch's suggested emendations are based upon certain assumptions regarding the composition of *Jubilees*. These conjectures are not supported by any textual witness, but emanate from the preconceived notion that the chronological data and the rewritten stories are indeed completely consistent. Moreover, Rönsch's emendations necessitate further emendations in the formulation of the dates in ch. 28. In the formulaic method found in the chronological framework in *Jubilees*, every year is denominated by a triple of numbers: jubilee, week, and

---

[14] Rönsch 1874: 327–331.
[15] After Rönsch interchanged the dates of Judah's and Dan's births, he was forced to correct the number 6 to 7, for otherwise Levi and Judah would have necessarily been born in the same year.
[16] Charles (1902: 170–172) adopted Rönsch's suggestions in light of the contradiction between the chronology and v. 17: "From the context (cf. verses 15 and 18) *it is obvious that the dates in the text are corrupt* (italics—mine). Judah was born before Rachel gave Bilhah to Jacob. Yet the text sets the birth of Bilhah's son two years before that of Judah."

year in the week. In this system, a successive date does not repeat any information that is already contained in its predecessor. For example, in *Jub.* 4:28–33 the chronological data is formulated as follows:

> (28) In the fifteenth jubilee, in the third week...during this week...
> (29) And at the end of the nineteenth jubilee, during the seventh week, in its sixth year...(31) At the conclusion of this jubilee...one year after him...(33) In the twenty-fifth jubilee...during the first year in the fifth week. In its third year...and in its fifth year...and in the first year during the sixth week...

The number of the jubilee, week, or year is mentioned only when it differs from that of the preceding date. *Jub.* 4:33 opens with the designation of the twenty-fifth jubilee, because it is different from the previous date which refers the nineteenth jubilee (v. 29). Verse 33 describes the events of the fifth week of the twenty-fifth jubilee, and mentions the week again only when moving to the next one, namely the sixth.

The dates in ch. 28 are formulated according to this same principle:[17]

> (11)...during the first year of the third week [Reuben]....(13)...during the third year of this week [Simeon]. (14)...during the sixth year of this week [Levi]. (15)...during the first year of the fourth week [Judah].... (18)...during the sixth year of the third week [Dan]. (19)...during the second year of the fourth week [Naphtali].

Between the birth dates of Levi and Judah, the week changed from the third to the fourth, and therefore explicit mention is made of the fourth week. Verse 18 then returns to the third week, and therefore, the number of that week is mentioned explicitly. Naphtali was born in the following week (the fourth), so the chronological framework mentions its number explicitly. Rönsch's suggested emendations, which arose from his computations, needed to have taken into account the characteristic formulation of the chronological framework, resulting in a text such as the following:

> (11)...during the first year of the third week [Reuben]....(13)...during the third year of this week [Simeon]. (14)...during the sixth year of

---

[17] I do not deal here with the question of the dates within the year (i.e. month and day of the month), which were provided for the births of each of the sons. It is difficult to know if there is any significance to these dates, except for the dates of the births of Levi (the 1st of the 1st month), of Judah (the 15th of the 3rd month) and of Joseph (the 1st of the 4th month), which are important dates in the *Jubilees* calendar (Levi and Joseph—dates marking the beginning of the seasons; Judah—the day of the covenant).

this week [Levi]. (15)...*during the seventh year of this week* [Judah]....
(18)...during the *first year of the fourth week* [Dan]. (19)...during the second
year of *this* week [Naphtali].

But this kind of reconstruction cannot merely assume a mechanical interchange of the birth-dates of Judah and Dan (as claimed by Rönsch): the "original" date formula of the birth of Judah did not include an explicit mention of the third week, whereas the existing dating of the birth of Dan mentions it explicitly. According to Rönsch's conjecture, the "original" date of Naphtali's birth (v. 19) would not have included an explicit mention of the fourth week, but this would have been inferred from the information contained in v. 18. Rönsch's claim necessitates the assumption that in the wake of the mechanical interchange of the two dates, the date formulae were systematically corrected to make them accord with the usual "conservation" principle of dating in *Jubilees*.

In my opinion, the necessary conclusion from the contradiction between the chronological details and the rewritten story is not that the text is corrupt (as suggested by Rönsch), but that ch. 28 developed through a complex literary process. The chronological editor of *Jubilees* copied a rewritten story, which reflected a specific approach to understanding the order of the births (v. 17), and superimposed a chronological framework upon this base that reflected a different approach to the interpretation of the biblical story (vv. 15, 18). Any attempt to resolve the tension between the two will necessarily fail, because these two approaches reflect two exegetical traditions arising from two different sources.

The existence of a chronological redaction in *Jubilees* can be demonstrated from two additional examples: the different interpretations offered for the period of 120 years mentioned in Gen 6:3, as well as the location of Noah's testament.[18]

"Let the Days Allowed Him be One Hundred and Twenty Years" (Genesis 6:3)[19]

Genesis 6:1–4 describes the descent of the sons of god (known as Watchers in later literature), their intercourse with the earthly women,

---

[18] These two examples are analyzed here only briefly, because they are discussed at great length in Part II (The Origin of Evil).
[19] For a comprehensive discussion of this example, see pp. 119–125.

and the birth of their progeny. In the midst of this short narrative, God renders the following judgment: "My breath shall not abide in man forever, since he too is flesh; let his days be one hundred and twenty years" (v. 3). Commentators have disagreed as to the meaning of this period of 120 years:

(1) 120 years is the period from when the Watchers sinned until the punishment of the flood. This explanation assumes a direct, causal connection between the two stories.
(2) 120 years is the upper bound for the life expectancy of all earthly creatures; the progeny of the sons of the divine beings and the daughters of men, who are half human and half divine, cannot exceed this limitation on their life expectancy. This explanation does not assume a direct causal connection between the sons of god story (Gen 6:1–4) and the flood narrative (Gen 6:5ff.).

In line with the first interpretation, *Jub.* 5 (and according to the Asael tradition in the *Book of Watchers* in *1 Enoch*) describes that the descent of the Watchers caused the sins of earthly beings, and these led eventually to the punishment of the flood on the earth. The dating of the events in the chronological framework reflects this first interpretation: the descent of the sons of god and their interactions with the women is dated to an unspecified year in the 25th jubilee (5:1; according to 4:33), A.M. 1177–1225.[20] The flood waters reached the earth in the 27th jubilee,[21] the 5th week, the 6th year (5:22–23), A.M. 1308. The difference in time between these two events, 83–131 years, matches the 120-year period described in Gen 6:3.

In contrast, the rewritten story itself in *Jub.* 5 reflects the second interpretation as to the significance of the 120-year period:

> 5:7 Regarding their children (of the Watchers) there went out from his presence an order to strike them with the sword and to remove them from beneath the sky. 5:8 He said: "My spirit will not remain on people forever for they are flesh. Their lifespan is to be 120 years." 5:9 He sent his sword among them so that they would kill one another. They began to kill each other until all of them fell by the sword and were obliterated from the earth.

---

[20] Instead of designating the precise year as usual, the story is dated to "a certain (year) of this jubilee." See pages 121–122 for possible reasons for the lack of precision in this date.

[21] For the reasons for choosing the reading "27" in v. 22, see VanderKam 1989b: 35, and similarly, below p. 123, n. 52.

Genesis 6:3, which was interpreted in the chronological framework as the time remaining until the flood, was understood within the rewritten story to have a different meaning, the life-expectancy of the giants, the sons of the Watchers. As I will show below in greater detail, the Watchers story in *Jub.* 5 is dependent upon *1 En.* 10–11, which itself is derived from two basic traditions which rewrite and broaden the biblical story of the sons of god.[22] According to *1 En.* 10:9–10 (part of the Shemihazah tradition which does not see a causal connection between the Watchers story and the flood), Gen 6:3 addresses the life expectancy of the giants. When *Jub.* 5 made use of *1 En.* 10–11, this interpretation of Gen 6:3 remained as it was in *1 Enoch*. However, the chronological redactor received the *Book of Watchers* in its complex literary state, according to which there is already a causal connection between the stories of the Watchers and the flood. For this reason, this redactor's interpretation of Gen 6:3, as it is reflected in the chronological framework, differs from the approach that is assumed in *1 En.* 10–11, the source used in *Jub.* 5.

THE TESTAMENT OF NOAH (7:20–39)[23]

Following a description of the flood, *Jubilees* presents two consecutive literary units, the story of the planting of the vineyard and Noah's testament to his children. Testaments in Jewish literature of the Second Temple period are generally transmitted close to the death of the deliverer of the testament.[24] And indeed, from the concern expressed by Noah in his testament about the future behavior of his children, it would seem that his death was near: "For I myself see that the demons have begun to lead you and your children astray; and now I fear regarding you that *after I have died* you will shed human blood on the earth" (v. 27). In contrast, according to the dating of the chronological framework, the testament was delivered in the 28th jubilee (7:20; A.M. 1324–1372), the jubilee immediately after the flood (5:23; A.M. 1308). Noah died 350 years after the flood (10:16–17), in accord with Gen 9:28. It is therefore difficult to understand the placement of Noah's testament immediately after the vineyard story. According to the general chronological ordering principle in *Jubilees*, all of the stories from Genesis and Exodus are

---

[22] See pp. 109–118.
[23] For a broader discussion of this example, see pages 158–163.
[24] See Collins 1984: 325–326.

presented in the order that they occurred (compare the Joseph stories in *Jub.* 34–41), and Noah's testament should therefore have been presented just before Noah's death in *Jub.* 10.

The current placement of Noah's testament can be explained by the biblical order of events surrounding the vineyard story (Gen 9:18–29). Noah's death is mentioned immediately after the story (vv. 28–29), even though Noah lived for an additional 350 years. In contrast to the chronological ordering principle generally followed throughout *Jubilees*, the order of events in the Bible is usually determined according to theme—the cycle of Noah stories is completed before moving on to the next subject. The testament in *Jub.* 7:20–39 appears in the same place where the death of Noah is mentioned in Gen 9, immediately after the vineyard story. The juxtaposition of the testament to the story in *Jub.* 7 results therefore from the dependence upon a source whose arrangement accorded with the principle of biblical, thematic ordering. The editor of *Jubilees* copied the rewritten story of the vineyard planting in its entirety, including the attached testament, and did not separate the story from the testament. However, when he added the date to the testament, he did so in accordance with the chronological ordering principle (according to which all the events in *Jubilees* are presented in the order that they occurred). The testament was therefore given immediately after the vineyard planting, and not near the death of Noah. The tension that was created between the chronological framework and the content of the rewritten story informs us about the literary development of this passage.

Summary and Conclusions

The many dates that were added throughout *Jubilees* to the chronological framework often derive from a source that is different from the rewritten stories. The "chronological editor" (who can be identified with the "halakhic editor") adopted extant rewritten stories, which he adapted and integrated into a new work. In general, there are few traces left of the process that we have just reconstructed. But the three examples discussed here (the birth of Jacob's children, the 120-year limitation, and the placement of Noah's testament), in addition to the one identified by Dimant concerning the length of the jubilee period, attest to the fact that *Jubilees* developed through a process of chronological redaction, not only of the biblical stories of Genesis and Exodus, but of already existing rewritten stories.

PART II

THE ORIGIN OF EVIL IN THE WORLD

Introduction

Evil in this world takes many forms: sickness, pain, death, suffering, and more. No one can deny its existence because its presence in the world affects each and every person. The existence of evil in the world poses a serious theological problem for anyone who believes in a single, omnipotent and omniscient god who is completely good. According to the formulation of modern philosophers, the following three sentences cannot all be simultaneously true in a monotheistic belief system:[1]

(1) Evil exists in the world.
(2) God is omniscient and omnipotent.
(3) God is completely good.

As noted above, everyone agrees that evil does exist (sentence 1). If sentences (1) and (2) are correct, such that God has the power to prevent evil, and he knows that it exists, then by refraining from doing so, he reveals his acceptance of the existence of evil in the world. A god who allows for evil to continue cannot be completely good, thereby negating sentence (3). If sentences (1) and (3) are correct, assuming that God is completely good, then he must be limited either in his power or in his knowledge: if he could prevent the evil, he would do so, and if he knew that it existed, he would act. Sentences (2) and (3) can therefore both only be correct if there is no evil in the world. From the day-to-day reality, it is clear that evil does in fact exist, and therefore any monotheistic religion has to assume that its god is limited either in his power, his knowledge, or his goodness.

The solution to the problem of the existence of evil can therefore be found in one of two approaches: either God is not completely good, and is therefore responsible for both good and evil, or he is either not omnipotent or not omniscient. The limitation of God's power according to this second approach is based upon the assumption that other forces exist in the world, which can act with a certain degree of independence from God's intervention, and sometimes even against his will.

---

[1] See the collection of articles in Adams and Adams 1990, and especially Mackie (1955) 1990.

Both approaches can be found in the Bible, and one can trace these approaches into postbiblical literature (as will be done below).[2]

Another question arises, particularly in sources from the Second Temple period, regarding the point in time at which evil began to exist in the world. If God created evil, it is reasonable to assume that it was created with the rest of the universe. If however, evil was created against God's will, from when does it exist? Two possibilities can be suggested: either evil existed before the creation of the world, or it came into existence at some point in history. If it existed before creation, then there are powers in the world that were not created by God, an idea that is difficult to accept in a monotheistic religion. If so, the possibility remains that evil came into existence at some point in time, as the result of a specific event. The event that led to the existence of evil could either be in the earthly realm (such as the sin in the Garden of Eden) or in the heavenly sphere (such as the sin of the sons of god). However, if evil was brought into existence at a specific point in history by a power created by God, then the creation of evil limits God's power, since an outside force (created by God) is able to cause damage to the world, and God is unable to protect his creation or fix the world. God is therefore limited by the world that he himself created, and if so, his creation is imperfect. Therefore, there is also a tension between God's goodness and his omnipotence regarding the question of when evil came into existence.

The Origin of Evil in the World

Methodologically, the study of the view of evil in *Jubilees* should not be limited to *Jubilees* alone. It needs to also take into account the sources used by *Jubilees*, in order to ascertain when it follows these earlier sources, and when it expresses a new theological idea. The identification of the sources or traditions used by the author or editor can be accomplished by one of two processes: (1) if it is possible to identify passages in *Jubilees* that are identical to passages from earlier compositions, then

---

[2] For example, the idea that YHWH created evil is explicitly expressed in Isa 45:7: "I form light and create darkness, I make weal and create woe—I the Lord do all these things." Knohl (2003: 11–14, 16–19) identified the second approach in the Creation account (Gen 1:1–2:4a) and the scapegoat ritual (Lev 16), and claimed that the Priestly source (P) attributed evil to an independent evil force, which already existed from before the creation of the world.

it is reasonable to assume that the redactor of *Jubilees* adopted and incorporated them when he came to compose his new composition.[3] (2) In those instances when there is no independent textual evidence of sources or traditions that this editor found before him, then literary-critical analysis of the relevant passages can assist in the process of differentiating the "building blocks" used by the redactor from his own new material.

Regarding the question of the origin of evil, *Jubilees* is seemingly characterized by the tendency to attribute evil to an outside force or being, thus defending God's goodness. This character is known as Prince Mastema (or Belial), the leader of a group of spirits or demons who serve before him.[4] Mastema acts according to his own will, but is limited in his powers by other forces: God and the angels of the presence. By transferring evil actions from God to Mastema, the rewriter succeeds in vindicating the former of responsibility for evil in the world, thus offering one possible solution to the question of evil.[5]

According to *1 Enoch*, which preceded and influenced *Jubilees*, the existence of evil began at a specific point in history, at the time of the descent of the sons of god, named "Watchers," from heaven to earth in order to mate with women (based upon the story in Gen 6:1–4). Subsequent to this cataclysmic sin of the combination of the heavenly and earthly spheres, evil increased on earth, which eventually led to the flood.[6] According to this outlook, evil did not exist from the time of creation, but only entered the world at a later point. A similar approach is expressed in an alternate tradition, which ascribes the origin of evil to the sin in the Garden of Eden.[7] These two traditions differ

---

[3] See for example the discussion in ch. 5 regarding the literary development of the Watchers story in *Jub.* 5.

[4] As I will attempt to demonstrate, in the original tradition about Prince Mastema embedded in chs. 17–18, 48, he acted alone against God and his council, similar to Satan in the book of Job. However, in the other passages in which Mastema is mentioned, the tradition has been expanded to include assistants, the spirits or demons.

[5] The solution is not perfect, since there is a contradiction between the assumption that God has the power and authority to limit Mastema's actions (as with Satan in the narrative frame of Job), and the claim that if God is completely good, he would prevent Mastema from behaving in this manner. The rewriter apparently supposed that there is a fundamental and qualitative difference between the performance of an evil act by God himself, and his lack of prevention of such behavior by another.

[6] In *1 Enoch* itself, different traditions have been combined regarding the nature of the Watchers' sin. For a detailed discussion of the traditions surrounding the Watchers story, see Dimant's comprehensive study (Dimant 1974).

[7] Stone (1999) viewed these two traditions as two different "axes" concerning the

fundamentally regarding the question of whether evil is the result of supernatural, heavenly processes, or of earthly, human behavior; both, however, share the assumption that the world was created without any human suffering, and that the nature of the world was changed as a consequence of a specific sin.

One can suggest another possible approach: evil was not created at some point in history, but already existed at the time of the creation of the universe. According to this approach, either the external evil force existed before creation,[8] or alternatively, God created everything in the world, including evil. According to the final option, evil is part of the divine plan, and God created the world at the outset with evil forces that exert influence over people. This approach is found in the sectarian scrolls from Qumran.[9]

What is the position of *Jubilees* regarding this question? Scholars tend to identify the worldview of *Jubilees* in this area with that of *1 Enoch*, that evil came into existence as a consequence of the Watchers' sin.[10] However, a more complex picture emerges from the different passages in *Jubilees* that relate to the question of the origin of evil. On the one hand, continuing the many traditions about the sons of god story that appear in *1 Enoch*, *Jubilees* also contains a number of references to this myth.[11] The book also hints at the sin in the Garden of Eden as the origin of human sin that eventually brought about the flood.[12] In addition to the references to these two traditions that appeared in earlier sources, one also finds in *Jubilees* the approach characteristic of the Qumran sect, according to which God created evil from the beginning of time, together with good, in heaven and on earth.[13] Both the heavenly

---

problem of evil in Jewish sources in antiquity. As we will see below, one can add another approach, according to which evil was in existence from the beginning of time as part of the divine plan, and was created by God himself. Contrast Stone's (1999: 147) attempt to harmonize this dualistic approach with the approach that attributes evil to the Watchers story.

[8] See Knohl 2003: 11–19.

[9] For example, the famous Treatise on the Two Spirits in 1QS III, 13–IV, 26; see Licht 1965: 88–105 for the interpretation of this passage.

[10] Thus Eshel (1999: 48–57) recently addressed the origins of the evil spirits in *Jubilees* immediately after her discussion of *1 Enoch*, both under the category of compositions that attribute the origins of the evil spirits to the story of the Watchers and the women.

[11] 4:15; 5:1–18; 7:20–39; 8:1–4; 10:1–14; 20:5.

[12] 3:17, and see the discussion on pp. 55–56.

[13] In the earthly realm, the "good" beings are the Israelites, who were already chosen during the first week of creation according to *Jub.* 2:19–24, while the evil

forces and the earthly nations are divided according to a dualistic system from the beginning of the world:[14] the evil divine powers rule over the wicked people, while the good forces govern the righteous.[15] This approach is expressed in the references to Mastema, who is in charge of the evil spirits.[16] Mastema has the status of an angel,[17] and the angels were created on the first day of the world according to *Jub.* 2:2.[18] These three approaches stand side by side in *Jubilees*, and it is imperative for us to clarify their status in the eyes of the redactor. As I will attempt to demonstrate, the study of the ideas and beliefs of *Jubilees* in general (and the subject of the origin of evil in particular) is significant for the study of Jewish thought in the late Second Temple period, as well as for the analysis of the literary development of the book in its entirety.

---

ones are the other nations. One can identify a development within this approach in the Qumran literature, in which the righteous "sons of light," refers to a select group within Israel, the members of the sect (a development that perhaps already began in *Jub.* 15:25–34; see ch. 11).

[14] This view is not completely dualistic, since God is in charge of all other forces in the world. In a monotheistic religion, there is no room for pure dualism.

[15] According to *Jub.* 15:31–32, YHWH himself is responsible for Israel, without any other heavenly intermediaries (cf. Deut 32:8–9 according to the LXX and 4QDeut^j), and protects them from all of the evil spirits that lead the nations astray.

[16] Cf. 10:8; 19:28.

[17] Cf. *Jub.* 17–18 and 48, which describe struggles between Mastema and the angel(s) of the presence.

[18] One could claim that Mastema is not included within the category of "all the spirits *who serve before him*," if he acts in defiance of God's will. However, Mastema remains subordinate to God throughout *Jubilees*, even though his behavior is often at odds with God's bidding. The biblical Satan, parallel to Mastema, is also considered a member of the heavenly retinue (Job 1–2; Zech 3:1–2).

CHAPTER FIVE

THE WATCHERS STORY (*JUBILEES* 5)

The Biblical Background

Genesis 6:1–4 tells a short, enigmatic story (attributed to the J source)[1] about the sons of god and the daughters of men. The sons of god saw the women, and took them as wives. The sons that were born from this union were "the Nephilim...they were the heroes of old, the men of renown" (Gen 6:4). In reaction to these deeds, God decided: "My breath shall not abide in man forever, since he too is flesh; let the days allowed him be one hundred and twenty years" (v. 3). In the immediate context of the story, God's decision expresses his opposition to the union of earthly women with the heavenly beings. The offspring of such unions inherited their divine dimension from their fathers and their physical, human dimension from their mothers. Therefore, God established that such offspring could not live beyond 120 years. This limitation confines the Nephilim to be among mankind, and separates them from the divine realm. The determination that eternal life is a characteristic of the gods appears in Gen 3:22 (also attributed to J): "And the Lord God said, 'Now that man has become like one of us, knowing good and bad, what if he should stretch out his hand and take also from the tree of life and eat, and live forever.'" In other words, the last thing that separates mankind from the divine (aside from the knowledge of good and evil) is eternal life.[2]

This short story does not take note of any negative influence on the earthly population that can be attributed to the descent of the sons of god. God's concern, expressed in v. 3, focuses on the reverse influence, and reflects his desire to prevent earthly beings from mixing in the divine domain. Essentially, the story of the sons of god and the daughters of men is a myth about the boundary between heaven and earth, and

---

[1] Cf. Skinner 1930: 139–147; Speiser 1964: 44–46.
[2] This motif is very prominent in ancient Near Eastern literature. Cf. for example the legend of Adapa the ancient wise man, and the Gilgamesh Epic that tells of the protagonist's search for eternal life (as noted by Speiser 1964: 27–28).

it establishes in an unambiguous manner that these are two separate worlds, and that crossing this boundary is strictly forbidden.[3]

This explanation of this story assumes that it exists (or existed) independently of the neighboring stories.[4] But reading Gen 6 in its entirety raises the possibility of an alternative understanding of the meaning and purpose of this story. The juxtaposition of the sons of god story (vv. 1–4) with the story of the flood (vv. 5ff.) solves an exegetical problem that perplexed readers in antiquity. In the biblical narrative, there is a general description of the sins that led God to destroy the world with the flood: increase of evil in the world (ibid. 5), the corruption of the earth, and lawlessness (ibid. 11–12), and it is difficult to understand from the story which sin could have provoked the punishment of total destruction of the world. It is hard to justify this cataclysmic punishment for ordinary sins. One solution for this conundrum appears to be the proximity of the flood story to the mythic, enigmatic story about the sons of god. If one views the cohabitation of the sons of god with the women as a sin, or even (more seriously) as an assault upon the natural order of the world, then the proximity of the stories supplies the justification for the flood.

---

[3] Cf. also Gen 11:1–9 (the story of the Tower of Babel). Some scholars have interpreted the sons of god story as an etiology for the presence of the Nephilim on earth (they are mentioned in the spies story as giants who lived in Canaan—Num 13:33); see for example Cassuto (1943) 1973; von Rad (1953) 1972: 113–116.

[4] An "independent" reading of the story of the sons of god and daughters of men apparently serves as the basis for LXX Ezek 32:27 (probably reflecting the original text of the verse): καὶ ἐκοιμήθησαν μετὰ τῶν γιγάντων τῶν πεπτωκότων ἀπ' αἰῶνος οἳ κατέβησαν εἰς ᾅδου ἐν ὅπλοις πολεμικοῖς καὶ ἔθηκαν τὰς μαχαίρας αὐτῶν ὑπὸ τὰς κεφαλὰς αὐτῶν ("And they lay down with the giants who fell from old, who descended to Hades with weapons of war, and they placed their swords under their heads..."). According to this reading, "the giants who fell from old," the same beings present in Gen 6:4, died in battle. The prophet accuses them, in addition to other groups, of terrorizing mankind. There is no hint of the giants being punished by the flood, but rather, they perished through warfare. The brief description in Ezek 32:27 is almost identical to the basic outline of the Shemihazah tradition in *1 Enoch*, which will be discussed below. The verse in Ezekiel consists of elements that recur throughout the prophetic unit in which it is found, including: the descent to Sheol, death by sword, and the terror of the inhabitants of the land. These motifs, which play a central role in the Shemihazah tradition, and afterwards in *Jub.* 5, appear therefore to originate in this verse.

A Comparison between Jubilees 5 and Genesis 6

The juxtaposition of stories in Gen 6 only hints at a possible relationship between the two, but in *Jub.* 5 the causal relationship between them is expressed explicitly. After summarizing Gen 6:1-2, 4 in *Jub.* 5:1, *Jub.* 5:2-5 then integrates the two descriptions of sins that appear in Gen 6:5-8 (attributed to J) and in vv. 9-12 (attributed to P), that eventually brought about the flood:

Jubilees 5	Genesis 6
(2) Wickedness[5] increased on the earth.	V. 5a: The Lord saw how great was man's wickedness on earth, or v. 11b: the earth was filled with lawlessness
All animate beings corrupted their way	V. 12b: for all flesh has corrupted its ways on earth
From people to cattle, animals, birds, and everything that moves about on the ground.	V. 7aβ: from men to cattle, creeping things and birds of the sky
All of them corrupted their way *and their prescribed course.*	V. 12b: for all flesh had corrupted its ways on the earth
They began to devour one another, And wickedness increased on the earth.	V. 5a: The Lord saw how great was man's wickedness on earth, or v. 11b: the earth was filled with lawlessness
Every thought of all mankind's knowledge was evil like this all the time.	V. 5b: And every plan devised by his mind was nothing but evil all the time
(3) The Lord saw that the earth was corrupt, (that) all animate beings had corrupted *their prescribed course,* and (that) all of them—everyone that was on the earth—had acted wickedly before his eyes.	V. 12: God saw the earth, and it was corrupt, for all flesh had corrupted its ways on earth V. 5a: The Lord saw how great was man's wickedness on earth

---

[5] The Geʿez translation *'amaḍā* (injustice, wickedness) is the equivalent of the Hebrew חמס; thus in *Jub.* 35:13 the word ח[מ]ס is translated *'amaḍā* (according to 4Q223-224, Unit 2, II, 6 [DJD 13, p. 106]; see the editors' note [ibid., p. 107]). Therefore, from among the two parallel verses, Gen 6:5 and 6:11, the latter is preferable (in contrast to the opinion of van Ruiten 2000: 186).

(*cont.*)

Jubilees 5	Genesis 6
(4) He said that he would obliterate people and all animate beings that were on the surface of the earth which he had created.	V. 7aα: The Lord said, "I will blot out from the earth the men that I created…"
(5) He was pleased with Noah alone.	V. 8: But Noah found favor with the Lord

The Pentateuch provides two descriptions of God's decision to bring about a flood to destroy the world. The first, Gen 6:5–8, focuses on descriptions of the sins of man: "The Lord saw how great was man's wickedness on earth, and how every plan devised by his mind was nothing but evil all the time" (Gen 6:5). On account of this wickedness, the Lord decided to wipe all living things off the face of the earth: "The Lord said, 'I will blot out from the earth the men whom I created—men together with beasts, creeping things, and birds of the sky; for I regret that I made them" (ibid. 7). The second description (vv. 9–12) focuses on the earth itself: "The earth became corrupt before God; the earth was filled with lawlessness" (v. 11). The earth is destroyed because "all flesh had corrupted its ways on earth" (v. 12). In reaction to the corruption of all flesh, God himself decides to destroy the world: "I am about to destroy them with the earth" (v. 13). The two descriptions, which both relate to the unseemly behavior that brought about the flood, are integrated in *Jub.* 5, as the editor-rewriter has combined both of these passages.[6]

---

[6] While combining both descriptions, *Jubilees* includes the full content while assiduously avoiding a particular idea: the Lord's regret that he created man (Gen 6:6, 7b). Van Ruiten (2000: 191) attributes this omission to the editor's desire to avoid imputing a deficiency to God—if the Lord regrets creating humankind, then his knowledge of the future is limited. This same tendency is present in the Septuagint, which uses the verb ἐνθυμέομαι (lay to heart, ponder) in order to translate the verb נ-ח-ם in Gen 6:6 and the verb διανοέω (have in mind) as a translation for "and his heart was saddened." (The Septuagint uses the very same verb, διανοέω, to translate "plan devised [by his mind]" in the previous verse); cf. Salvesen 1991: 34–36.

At first glance, there is no explicit connection in *Jub.* 5:1–6 between the story of the sons of god and God's decision to bring the flood. Verse 1 summarizes the mythic story and v. 2 transitions to the next account ("Wickedness increased on the earth...") without indicating that there is a causal relationship between them. The wickedness for which all "animate beings" are responsible—"from people to cattle, animals, birds, and everything that moves about on the ground,"[7]—is described in v. 2: "All of them corrupted their way, and their prescribed course. They began to devour one another." The rewritten version in *Jub.* 5:2 expands the expression "(all flesh has corrupted) its ways (on earth)" in Gen 6:12 to "their way *and their prescribed course*" (*fənotomu* **wa-šərʿātomu**). The term *šərʿat* ("prescribed pattern") occurs in the context of the flood in *Jub.* 6:4 (in the rewriting of Gen 8:21–22): "...that there would be no flood waters which would destroy the earth...seedtime and harvest would not cease; cold and heat, summer and winter, day and night *would not change their prescribed pattern* and would never cease." Gen 8:21–22 relates that after the flood, during which the laws of nature were suspended temporarily, God promised that such a suspension would never recur. The flood was a one-time, extraordinary event in the history of the world. *Jub.* 6:4 emphasizes the cyclical nature of the seasons—after the flood, the laws of nature return to their original and now eternal state.[8] Based upon the usage of the same term (*šərʿat*) to denote both mankind's sins before the flood and the punishment by the flood, one may suggest that it was precisely mankind's violation of the natural order that

---

[7] The rewriter here identifies "all flesh" in Gen 6:12 with the list of man and animate beings in Gen 6:7 as a way of harmonizing and summarizing the two descriptions of the world's sins in Gen 6.

[8] VanderKam (2000a: 95) suggested that the promise of the cyclical nature of the seasons in Gen 8:22 is the reason that the editor of *Jubilees* decided to incorporate the long passage about the calendar at the end of ch. 6 (as he noted, the term *šərʿat* appears both in *Jub.* 6:4 and also in the passage about the calendar in *Jub.* 6:34). Another motivation for the discussion of the calendar may have been the multitude of dates in the biblical story of the flood. The question of reconciling the dates to different calendrical systems engaged the attention of ancient commentators (Cf. 4Q252 I–II; DJD 22, 193–200; *S. 'Olam Rab.* 4), and it is reasonable to explain the juxtaposition of the passage about the calendar with the flood story in light of these exegetical exercises. As Werman discerned (1995b: 188), the goal of the rewriting in 4Q252 was to reconcile the dates of the biblical flood story with a certain calendar, whereas the goal of the rewriting of the biblical story in *Jubilees* is to endow that calendar with authority.

caused suspension of the laws of nature by the flood. The assault on the natural order of the world did not begin with human behavior, but with the fornication of the sons of god with the daughters of men, as described in *Jub.* 5:1. The cohabitation of the divine beings with the women, which produced the giants, represented a callous violation of the clear boundaries between heaven and earth, and led to destructive results. This behavior then led to the people's violation of the laws, and in the end brought about the flood.[9]

The connection between the acts of the sons of god, otherwise known as "Watchers" or "angels," and the flood story is made explicit in *Jub.* 5:6ff. After the Lord decided to destroy the world, he directed his anger towards the Watchers and their offspring. Below we bring in summary form *Jub.* 5:6ff., until God's decision to bring the flood in v. 20:

- 6: The command to the angels of the presence to incarcerate underground the angels who descended to the earth
- 7–9: The killing by sword of the offspring of these rebellious angels in a civil war; the limitation on their life expectancy to 120 years (cf. Gen 6:3)
- 10: The rebellious angels observe their offspring being killed; the rebellious angels are incarcerated underground until the "day of great judgment"
- 11–12: The creation of the world anew, without sin
- 13–18: YHWH as a righteous judge
- 19: The wickedness of the entire world in the time of Noah, except for Noah himself
- 20: God's decision to destroy the world

The additional element of a punishment for the angels after God's decision to bring the flood gives expression to the causal connection between the story of the sons of god and the implementation of the punishment of the flood. In the biblical story there is no punishment prescribed for the sons of god for their deeds.[10] In *Jub.* 5, despite the different punishments that each group receives, the sons of god and

---

[9] The second part of this addition, "they began to devour one another," is also connected to the story of the sons of god, and will be discussed below.

[10] As was posited above, the limitation on the length of life in Gen 6:3 was indeed a result of the deeds of the sons of god, though not to punish them, but rather to draw the boundary between the earthly and heavenly worlds.

their offspring on the one hand, and humanity and all animate beings on the other, all receive their punishment *en masse*.

The connection of the sons of god story to the flood narrative supplies a fitting answer to the exegetical-theological problem of the justification for the flood, and helps us understand the overall intent of *Jub.* 5. But alongside the novel exegesis in its understanding of Gen 6, one should take note of quite a few difficulties that emerge from a reading of the rewritten story in *Jub.* 5. For example, there are duplications in *Jub.* 5, such as the repeated mention of the incarceration of the angels in the depths of the earth, both before the angels' offspring are killed (v. 6) and also thereafter (v. 10). There are motifs that have no clear connection to the biblical narrative, such as the notion that mankind was guilty of cannibalism: "They began to devour one another" (*Jub.* 5:2). There are even internal contradictions, such as the two answers given to the question of the significance of the period of 120 years: is it the limitation on the length of life of the giants (v. 8) or the number of years remaining until the flood (as can be deduced by calculation of the chronological data)?[11]

These and other difficulties can be solved by a detailed analysis of the development of the story of the Watchers in *1 Enoch*, which was the source used by the editor-author of *Jub.* 5.[12] The understanding of the literary development of the diverse traditions that have been integrated in *1 Enoch* will enable us to discuss in detail the different difficulties, and to suggest a comprehensive explanation for the development of the story in *Jub.* 5. Furthermore, the literary analysis that will be offered for this passage will allow for a description of the literary development of *Jubilees* as a whole.

THE WATCHERS STORY IN 1 ENOCH 6–11

In order to resolve the issues just raised, it is necessary to trace the development of the traditions about the Watchers in Second Temple Jewish literature. The issues will be resolved only by understanding the literary complexity of the different sources that deal with the Watchers,

---

[11] This question was discussed briefly on pp. 91–93 in connection with the chronological redaction of *Jubilees*.
[12] The evidence for this claim will be presented below.

especially those traditions that were woven together in *1 Enoch*, for *Jub.* 5 depended on this book while composing its version of the Watchers story.

1 Enoch, and in particular the *Book of Watchers* (chs. 1–36), constitutes the oldest and most important source for the interpretation of the story of the sons of god and the daughters of men.[13] In contrast to the interpretation of the biblical story suggested above, where it was posited that these liaisons did not have a negative effect on humanity, the Enochic story of the Watchers involves a negative outcome for humanity. Special importance can be attached to chs. 6–11, which are dedicated to the sins of the sons of god.[14] However, one can identify within this unit a variety of descriptions of their sins; there are even internal contradictions and literary tensions that one can utilize to identify the seams between different sources.[15] Dimant identified three different traditions in chs. 6–11 surrounding these sins:[16]

(1) A legend about angels under the leadership of Shemihazah, who consorted with the daughters of men, and gave birth to giants (or the Nephilim). According to this tradition, the angels themselves are the sinners. This story interprets Gen 6:1–4 without any dependence on the flood story, and there is no connection between their punishment and the flood.[17]

---

[13] Cassuto ([1943] 1973) posited that Gen 6:1–4 is an implicit polemic against mythological traditions known from the ancient Near East. In his view, the traditions in *1 Enoch* are a later development of Gen 6:1–4. Alternatively, Milik (1976: 30–32), Black (1985: 124–125), and Barker (1987: 18–19) claimed that the story in Gen 6:1–4 is a summary of the more ancient sources found in *1 Enoch*. Precisely because of the cryptic nature of Gen 6:1–4, it is better to view this narrative as older than the traditions in *1 Enoch* (cf. the ancient Near Eastern parallels cited by Speiser 1964: 45–46). This ancient story was then elaborated in *1 Enoch*, sometimes for exegetical reasons, and sometimes under the influence of other cultures. For a broader discussion, see Nickelsburg 2001:166–168.

[14] These sins are mentioned elsewhere in *1 Enoch*, such as chs. 12–16, 86–89, but the most ancient traditions appear in chs. 6–11; cf. Dimant 1974: 21–22. Regarding the status of *1 En.* 6–11 as an example of "Rewritten Bible," see Dimant 2002.

[15] Dimant 1974: 23–72; Nickelsburg 2001: 165. Bhayro 2005 conveniently assembled all of the textual evidence for these chapters, and offered an interesting interpretation of the traditions in this passage.

[16] Dimant 1974: 65. A detailed division of the sources appears ibid., pp. 25–29. In the table there, Dimant sometimes distinguishes between the first two traditions, while at other times she does not make this differentiation.

[17] As noted above (n. 4), LXX Ezek 32:27 presents a concise version of the Watchers story that is very similar to the Shemihazah tradition, which appears to have been influenced by this verse, and thus supports its separation into an independent tradition.

(2) A legend about angels who taught the daughters of men sorcery and mysteries, and thus caused the women to sin. This legend is intended to explain Gen 6:1–4, but it also supplies the cause for the punishment of mankind by the flood.
(3) A legend about the angel Asael who taught the women objectionable handiworks, and thus caused them to sin. According to Dimant, this legend is intended to explain Gen 6:11–12, verses which describe the corruption of the earth, as well as to justify the flood.

According to Dimant, the first two traditions were merged together in the first stage, inasmuch as they explain the same biblical verses. Afterwards, the third tradition, about Asael who taught the women about the mysteries of the world and thus caused them to sin, was blended with the first two. According to Dimant, one can infer from the difficulty of distinguishing between the first two traditions in the current version of *1 Enoch* that they were merged at the earliest stage of the development of the book. In contrast, one can easily differentiate the Asael tradition from the surrounding text.[18] According to other scholars, there are only two traditions that are merged in *1 En.* 6–11, one about Shemihazah and the other about Asael (similar to Dimant's first and third traditions), and these offer an identical distinction between angels that sinned and angels that caused humanity to sin.[19]

According to Dimant, the integration of the first two sources at the earliest stages led to the difficulty of differentiating between them. However, one can resolve this difficulty in another way: it is possible that the verses that are assigned to the second tradition do not represent an independent tradition, but were added by the redactor of

---

[18] Dimant 1974: 65. Nickelsburg (2001: 171) asserts that the original tradition described Shemihazah and his band, into which a string of different interpolations was introduced: first 7:1b; 9:8b, then 8:3, and finally the material about Asael. The difference between Dimant and Nickelsburg cannot be reduced or confined to different ways of partitioning the story into the different sources (in particular, see below the discussion with regard to *1 En.* 10). In contradistinction to Dimant, Nickelsburg does not view the verses describing the instruction of sorcery provided by the Watchers as being a separate tradition that was combined with the central tradition about Shemihazah, but as discrete insertions with an anti-magical tendency. Despite this disagreement, these two scholars agree as to the order of the steps in the process of redaction.

[19] Beer (1900: 225) identified two main traditions in chs. 6–11: (1) the revelation of hidden knowledge to mankind, and the flood as a punishment for the sins that are a direct result of these secrets (7:1b; 8:1–3; 9:6–8; 10:1–3); and (2) the descent of the angels, the evil of the Nephilim, and their punishments (6:2b–8; 7:3–6; 8:4; 9:1–5, 9–11; 10:4–11:2).

1 Enoch in order to integrate the Asael tradition ("the third tradition"), which refers to the teaching of forbidden handiworks, into the central tradition about Shemihazah ("the first tradition"). These verses transfer the instruction of the mysteries of the world by Asael to Shemihazah and the Watchers in general, and in so doing, the redactor attempts to present a unified story about a group of angels led by Shemihazeh.[20]

1 Enoch 6–8 surveys the sins of the rebellious angels, and ch. 9 describes the disastrous results of their actions: much blood being spilled on the earth and lawlessness (9:1, 9–10). On account of the dismal state on earth, God (or to be more precise, the Supreme One) sent four angels for different assignments:

(1) Sariel[21] was sent to Noah in order to inform him about the plan to bring the flood upon the earth (*1 En.* 10:1–3).
(2) Raphael was sent to bind the angel Asael underground until the day of great judgment on which Asael will be punished by fire. Afterward, Raphael will heal the earth that had been corrupted by the Watchers, and will save mankind whose lives had been endangered by the secrets revealed to them by the angels (vv. 4–8).
(3) Gabriel was sent to destroy the giants, the offspring of the Watchers, by involving them in internecine warfare. God decided that the giants will not live eternally, and they will not even reach the age of 500 years (vv. 9–10).[22]
(4) Michael was sent to bind Shemihazah and his colleagues who defiled the daughters of men. After the fathers will watch the killing of their sons, Michael will bind Shemihazah and his band underground for a period of seventy generations until the day of great judgment, at which time they will be punished with fire and eternal incarceration. Then wickedness shall be vanquished from the earth, the righteous will attain fruitfulness, peace, abundance, and earthly blessing, and the earth will be cleansed from all evil and defilement. (*1 En.* 10:11–11:2).

The redundancies discernible in chs. 10–11 lead to the conclusion that the different traditions about the angels' sins that were detected already in chs. 6–8 continue through to chs. 9–11. Scholars of *1 Enoch* all agree with this conclusion, but there is no unanimity among them as to the division of material among the different traditions. It is possible to point to the following contradictions and/or doublets:

---

[20] *Contra* Nickelsburg (above, n. 18), who asserts that these few verses were inserted with an anti-magical intent, and *before* the integration of the Asael tradition.
[21] *1 Enoch* 9:1, according to 4QEn^b 1 III, 7 (Milik 1976: 170). Cf. Nickelsburg 2001: 202, 216.
[22] Relying on Gen 6:3; cf. *Jub.* 5:8 and the discussion below.

(1) Both Raphael and Michael were sent to deal with problems of the earth, the first to heal and the second to remove all evil (10:7, 16, 20).[23]
(2) Both Gabriel and Michael were commanded to kill the offspring of the angels (10:9, 15).[24]
(3) Both Asael and Shemihazah and his band receive identical or at least similar punishments (10:4–6, 11–14).

The third point is the clearest testimony that *1 En.* 10 continues the traditions reflected in the earlier chapters. Scholars have argued over how to partition this chapter into different sources. Based on the first two arguments, Nickelsburg determined that the earlier legend about the group of sinning angels under the leadership of Shemihazah continues in 10:1–3 (Sariel's mission) and 10:11–11:2 (Michael's mission). The tradition about Asael includes *1 En.* 10:4–10, the punishment of Asael followed by the punishment of the Watchers.[25] Nickelsburg himself admits that including Sariel's mission in the Shemihazah tradition is not without difficulties—until this point, there has been no mention of mankind's sins for which it deserved to be punished by the flood.[26] In general, the Shemihazah tradition did not draw a connection between the sons of god story and the punishment of the flood. Therefore, Sariel's mission to inform Noah about the imminent flood is more appropriate to the Asael tradition, which tells about the teaching of the secrets of the world to the daughters of men, the knowledge of which caused the people to sin for which they were punished by the flood.

Dimant differentiates between the missions in a different way: Sariel's mission, in which he warns Noah about the impending flood, and Raphael's mission, which describes the punishment of Asael (10:4–6, 8),[27] both belong to the tradition about Asael and the angels who misled mankind into sinning. In contrast, Gabriel's mission to kill the giants, Michael's mission against Shemihazah and his henchmen, and the

---

[23] Dimant 1974: 60–61; Nickelsburg 2001: 165.
[24] Nickelsburg 2001: 165.
[25] Nickelsburg 1977: 383–386; 2001: 165.
[26] Nickelsburg 2001: 167.
[27] *1 Enoch* 10:7 describes how all the Watchers taught the secrets of the world to mankind. The inclusion of v. 7 specifically within the tradition about Asael in 10:4–8 supports my suggestion above that v. 7 is one of the verses inserted by the redactor in order to transfer the mission of instruction to Shemihazah and his group. Dimant (1974: 63) views this verse as a continuation of the tradition about the Watchers who instructed the daughters of men.

verse within Raphael's mission regarding the Watchers (*1 En.* 10:7), all have their origins in the merged tradition (that is, the combination of Dimant's first and second traditions) about the angels that sinned.[28] There is no contradiction between 10:15 (Michael's mission to kill the offspring of the angels) and v. 9 (Gabriel's mission to kill the giants), because v. 15 is a later addition, as can be argued from the following:

(1) From a literary perspective, Michael's mission ends with the punishment of the angels on the day of judgment "for all eternity" (v. 14).[29]
(2) The offspring of the angels are called "evil spirits" in v. 15. Prior to this, there is no occurrence of this phrase "evil spirits" in *1 Enoch* (but it is widespread afterwards in chs. 12–16). It also does not fit the preceding story (from the Shemihazah tradition), according to which the offspring of the angels oppressed mankind and spilled much blood on the earth.[30]

If so, there is no justification to separate the missions of Michael and Gabriel. Both together constitute the conclusion of the tradition about Shemihazah and his fellow angels (and their offspring the giants) who sinned, inasmuch as each one received his due punishment.

In light of the survey presented here, it is possible to describe the literary development of *1 En.* 6–11 as the merger of two main traditions, together with some additions. The following is the division of *1 En.* 6–11 according to its various sources:

(1) The Shemihazah source ("angels that sinned"): 6; 7:1a, 2–6; 8:4; 9:1–5, 7–8a, 9–11; 10:9–14
(2) The Asael source ("angel who caused others to sin"): 8:1–2; 9:6; 10:1–6, 8
(3) Verses added by the redactor: 7:1b; 8:3; 9:8b; 10:7
(4) Concluding addition: 10:15–11:2

1 Enoch 10–11, which is part of this literary unit, therefore presents a version that is composed of several sources or traditions, additions,

---

[28] Dimant 1974: 60–64; but cf. the previous footnote.
[29] The Byzantine chronographer Georgius Syncellus preserved passages from the *Book of Watchers*, 6:1–10:14, but not the rest of chs. 10–11 (cf. Mosshammer 1984: 11–13, 24). Dimant (1974: 61) correctly viewed this fact as an additional proof for its original literary state.
[30] Dimant 1974: 61–62.

and adaptations. In its current literary form, it includes five essential components:

(1) 10:1–3: The announcement of the flood—from the Asael tradition
(2) 10:4–8: Punishment of Asael and the Watchers—continuation of the Asael tradition (v. 7 is an insertion of the redactor)
(3) 10:9–10: Punishment of the giants, the offspring of the sons of god—from the Shemihazah tradition
(4) 10:11–14: Punishment of Shemihazah and his band after they observed the destruction of their children—continuation of the Shemihazah tradition
(5) 10:15–11:2: Destruction of the spirits, a new creation—later addition

The Relationship between Jubilees 5 and 1 Enoch 10–11

As Charles noted,[31] the description of the angels' sins and punishments in *Jub.* 5 is parallel to the story in *1 En.* 10–11. Moreover, as several scholars have pointed out, the parallel between the two texts is extremely close, and is not confined to similar expressions, but also extends to the literary structure: the sequence of events in *Jub.* 5 and *1 En.* 10 is identical.[32] Below is a synoptic table of the two descriptions:

Jubilees 5	1 Enoch 10–11
1–3: The sins of the sons of god with the women and their consequences	Chs. 6–9: The sins of the sons of god with the women and their consequences
4–5: The Lord's decision to destroy the world and to save Noah	10:1–3: The Lord's decision to destroy the world and to save Noah
6: First judgment against the angels—they are bound underground	4–8: The judgment against Asael—he is bound underground (7: the Watchers)
7–9: The judgment against the offspring of the angels: "My breath shall not abide"; the offspring shall kill each other	9–10: The judgment against the offspring of the angels: the children shall kill each other; they request to live forever

---

[31] Charles 1912: lxxii–lxxiii, in an extensive table that summarizes the influence of *1 Enoch* on Jewish literature.
[32] Van Ruiten 1997: 72–73; 2000: 196–197; Nickelsburg 2001: 73; García Martínez (1997: 248) also noted the general similarity of the Watchers story in *Jub.* 5 to the version in *1 En.* 10.

(cont.)

Jubilees 5	1 Enoch 10–11
10: Second judgment against the angels—the fathers will see the sons kill each other; they are bound underground until the day of the great judgment 11: The day of judgment 12: A new creation.	11–12: The judgment against Shemihazah—the angels will see their children kill each other; the angels are bound underground until the day of the great judgment 13–15: The day of judgment 10:16—11:2: A new creation.

A comparison of these two works reveals the strong similarity between them with regard to the sequence of events, in their descriptions and in their formulations. In particular, it is worth emphasizing that *Jub.* 5 even presents a double version of the judgment against the angels precisely in those places where it appears in *1 En.* 10.[33]

As mentioned above, it is still possible to trace the traditions that have been merged together in *1 Enoch*, because they are distinguishable from each other by means of the usage of the names of the different angels and the nature of their sins on the earth. Aside from this, two passages in *1 En.* 10–11 (10:7; 10:15–11:2) are later additions to the text. *1 Enoch* 10–11 is the product of a literary development unique to the *Book of Watchers*, and it is possible to trace this development throughout *1 En.* 6–11. Therefore, one can conclude that the specific combination of the traditions and their sequence, as they are preserved in *1 En.* 10–11, cannot be based on any other source, but originates in the *Book of Watchers*.[34] In light of this consideration, the similarity between *1 En.* 10–11 and *Jub.* 5, with regard to content, sequence of events, and terminology, can lead to only one conclusion: *Jub.* 5 used *1 En.* 10–11 (or another composition which used *1 En.* 10–11) as a source when it rewrote the Watchers story.

With all these points of similarity between these two texts, it is still possible to identify certain differences:

---

[33] Van Ruiten 2000: 197.
[34] In contrast with van Ruiten (2000: 197) who suggested, based upon the differences between *1 En.* 10–11 and *Jub.* 5, that they both drew material from the same tradition, perhaps the well-known and problematic "Book of Noah," and each of these two editors rewrote this source according to his needs.

(1) The formulation of the story. The two stories use similar terminology,[35] but in general the formulations are different. Most prominently, the story in *Jub.* 5 is shorter than that in *1 En.* 10–11, and certain parts of *Jub.* 5 are a paraphrase of the story in *1 En.* 10–11.

(2) Differences in content.[36] There are certain differences in content between the two works, but most of them are not significant. The difference that led scholars to deny the direct dependence of *Jub.* 5 upon *1 En.* 10–11 relates to the purpose of the angels' descent[37]—according to *1 Enoch*, such a descent was itself a sin, whereas according to *Jub.* 5:6 (and more explicitly in *Jub.* 4:15), the descent was at the behest of God and for a positive purpose, and only afterwards did the angels sin.[38]

An additional difference with regard to content pertains to the nature of the sin of the angels: in *Jub.* 5 there is no mention of the angels teaching the women crafts of a questionable nature (as is articulated in the Asael tradition in the *Book of Watchers*).[39] On the other hand, one finds in *Jubilees* a description that reflects the tradition of the band of angels under Shemihazah who sinned with earthly women. Yet whereas in the Shemihazah tradition in *1 Enoch* there was no causal connection between the defiled angels and the flood, in *Jubilees* this sin is presented explicitly as its prime cause.[40] The transformation of the myth of the defiled angels from an event unrelated to the flood story to one that is the central factor in the flood, already took place in the editorial stages of the *Book of Watchers*, when the various traditions about the descending angels were integrated. In other words, when the redactor of *Jub.* 5 made use of the text of *1 En.* 10 (in its present form), the connection between the flood (*1 En.* 10:1–3, Sariel's mission) and the punishment of the defiled angels (*1 En.* 10:9–14, the missions of Gabriel and Michael) already existed.

(3) Names of the angels. The names of Shemihazah and Asael in *1 En.* 10 assist in identifying the different, original traditions. In contrast, *Jub.* 5 does not make explicit mention of the different angels who

---

[35] Cf. Charles (above, n. 31).
[36] In principle, a difference in content does not negate the possibility of direct literary dependence, since such a difference can emanate from a reworking of the original.
[37] Cf. for example van Ruiten 2000: ibid.
[38] Cf. below pp. 125–132 for an explanation of the origins of this tradition in *Jubilees*.
[39] Despite the fact that there is no hint of the angels instructing women in the mysteries of the world, the punishment in *Jub.* 5:6 parallels that of Asael.
[40] Cf. also *Jub.* 7:22–25; 20:5. See Dimant 1974: 94–95.

sinned and were punished. This difference between *Jubilees* and *1 Enoch* is the result of a general tendency in *Jubilees*, which does not mention the names of angels throughout the entire book.

Exegetical Issues in Jubilees 5

The author of *Jub.* 5 did not perceive the source from which he worked as being composed of different traditions, but saw it as a unified, organic whole. The integration in *1 En.* 6–11 of the sources about Shemihazah and his band of sinning angels and the punishment by the flood (which originated in the Asael tradition) led to the difficulties in the Watchers story in *Jub.* 5 which were alluded to above. We can now return to these difficulties and discuss them in greater detail.

Cannibalism: At first glance, it is not clear what the source is for the addition in *Jub.* 5:2, "they began to devour one another," for in the biblical story there is no hint of cannibalism. However, it is possible to explain the introduction of this motif against the backdrop of the development of the flood story in *1 Enoch*.

According to the Shemihazah tradition as preserved in *1 En.* 7:3–6, the giants ate all the produce grown by mankind. When there was no more food left for them, the giants began to devour the people (v. 4). Afterwards, the giants turned to eating animals and they then turned on each other. Eating animals necessarily entailed the consumption of their blood. This is specifically prohibited in Gen 9:4 and eventually led to their punishment. According to the Shemihazah tradition in the *Book of Watchers*, mankind was therefore the victim of the giants' hunger. But as previously noted, consequent to the literary complexity of *1 En.* 10–11, *Jub.* 5 posited a connection between the sons of god story and the flood, in which all of mankind was killed (except for Noah and family). In order to justify the bringing of the flood upon the entire world for sins that were originally attributed only to the Watchers and their offspring, the sins of the giants were transferred to mankind: "They began to devour one another" (5:2).[41] The victims thus became the aggressors, and a justification was provided for the flood.

---

[41] Dimant 1974: 95.

Repetition of the Imprisonment of the Angels: *Jubilees* mentions the binding of the angels underground twice, both before and after the killing of their offspring (*Jub.* 5:6, 10). The explanation for this redundancy can be found in the process of literary development of *1 En.* 6–11, in which there are descriptions of separate punishments for Asael and Shemihazah. When the author of *Jub.* 5 rewrote the Watchers story, basing himself on *1 En.* 10–11, he deleted the names of angels in accord with the general tendency throughout *Jubilees*. Following the disappearance of the primary criterion by which the two punishments were distinguished in *1 En.* 10, all that remained in *Jub.* 5 were traces of the two versions of the anonymous angels' punishment.

The transition from the punishment of a single angel (Asael, *1 En.* 10:4–8) to the punishment of many angels (*Jub.* 5:6) was made possible by virtue of *1 En.* 10:7, which is the verse identified above as being added by the redactor of the *Book of Watchers*, with the goal of unifying the tradition of (many) angels led by Shemihazah who sinned, together with the punishment of Asael. If the intent of this addition (*1 En.* 10:7) was to transfer the punishment of Asael to all of the Watchers, then *Jub.* 5 is testimony to the success of this editorial intervention.

The Interpretation of Genesis 6:3 as Referring to the Giants in the Light of the Chronology of Jubilees: Genesis 6:3 can be interpreted in two different ways. If the sons of god story (Gen 6:1–4) is unrelated to the flood narrative, then the limitation to 120 years presumably refers to the life expectancy of non-divine creatures, established to demarcate the boundary between the heavenly and earthly realms. The term האדם in the clause "My breath shall not abide in *man* forever," which denotes the being whose life expectancy is being limited, can refer either to both human beings and the semi-human offspring of the sons of god,[42] or only to the offspring of the sons of god and the daughters of men.[43] Another possible interpretation arose in light of the broader biblical context: according to the continuation of Genesis, various biblical characters did indeed live longer than 120 years (see for example, the genealogical list in Gen 11 and the stories

---

[42] Cf. *L.A.B.* (pseudo-Philo) 3:2; Josephus, *Ant.* I, 75; the opinion of R. Joshua b. Nehemiah in *Gen. Rab.* 26:6 (Theodor-Albeck edition, pp. 251–252).

[43] According to the plain sense of Gen 6:3; cf. also *1 En.* 10:9–10 and the discussion below.

of the patriarchs and matriarchs). Therefore, various exegetes suggested that the 120 years referred to the duration of time until the flood. This limitation of 120 years therefore only applied to the flood generation.[44] Some of these interpreters viewed the period of 120 years until the flood as a flexible limitation that could be overcome with repentance. This approach supplied an answer to the theological problem that emerges from the biblical story—did God deprive the flood generation of the opportunity to repent?[45]

According to *Jub.* 5:7–9, Gen 6:3 is intended only for the giants:

> (7) Regarding their children (of the Watchers) there went out from his presence an order to strike them with the sword and to remove them from beneath the sky. (8) He said: "My spirit will not remain on people forever for they are flesh. Their lifespan is to be 120 years." (9) He sent his sword among them so that they would kill one another. They began to kill each other until all of them fell by the sword and were obliterated from the earth.

The limitation specifically upon the lives of the giants, even though the giants and mankind sinned in tandem, seemingly points in the first exegetical direction, that the sons of god story is independent of the flood narrative, and is concerned with demarcating the boundary between the heavenly and earthly realms.

However, there is a discernible contradiction between the body of the story and the chronological framework within which *Jub.* 4–5 is set. In contrast to 5:7–9, which follows the first exegetical approach outlined here, the chronological framework reflects the second exegetical approach, according to which the 120-year period in question refers to the time until the flood. *Jub.* 5:1 dates the sighting of the daughters

---

[44] Cf. 4Q252 I, 1–3; *S. 'Olam Rab.* 28; *Tg. Onq.* to Gen 6:3; *Tg. Neof.; Frg. Tg.; Tg. ps.-Jon.; Mek. R. Ishmael Shirta* 5; *Gen. Rab.* 30:7; *b. Sanh.* 108a; *'Abot R. Nat.* A 32; Rashi, Ibn Ezra, and Radaq to Gen 6:3. Jerome, *Questions on Genesis* on Gen. 6:3 (Hayward 1995: 37, 131–132) and Augustine, *City of God* XV, 24:24 (Dods 1977: 305) both cite the opinion that Gen 6:3 relates to the limitation on life expectancy for all humankind, but reject this opinion in favor of the interpretation that 120 years refers to the duration of time until the flood. See Bernstein 1994: 5–7; Kugel 1997: 112–114.

[45] In light of the general exegetical goal in certain sources to connect the sons of god story with the flood narrative, it is preferable to assume that the motif of repentance reflects a later stage of the tradition that interpreted the 120 years of Gen 6:3 as the time remaining until the flood. Bernstein (1994: 6) noted that in 4Q252, only the first stage of exegetical tradition appears, viz., that 120 years is the length of the period until the flood, without the addition of the possibility of repentance.

of men by the sons of god "in a certain (year) of this jubilee."[46] "This jubilee" refers to the last specified jubilee, which appears in *Jub.* 4:33, namely the 25th jubilee (A.M. 1177–1225), without specifying the year within the jubilee.[47]

The reason for the absence of the precise year is not clear, and one can posit two possibilities to explain this anomaly:

(1) *Jubilees* is arranged entirely according to continuous chronological order, from the creation of the world to the revelation at Sinai. This principle of maintaining the sequential order of events sometimes led *Jubilees* to reorder the stories of the Torah.[48] For example, according to the computation of *Jubilees* (and also according to a simple computation of the biblical data),[49] the sale of Joseph (Gen 37) occurred before the death of Isaac at 180 (Gen 35:29). The organization of stories in the Pentateuch is based upon their theme or content—the stories of Isaac are finished before the stories of Joseph are begun. In contrast, *Jubilees* prefers a chronological principle: first the story of the sale of Joseph in the 44th jubilee, the 6th week, the 7th year (A.M. 2149; *Jub.* 34:10), and only afterwards the death of Isaac appears in the 45th jubilee, the 1st week, the 6th year (A.M. 2162; *Jub.* 36:18). The obscure date presented in *Jub.* 5:1, "in a certain (year) of this

---

[46] The text in the Ge'ez reads: *ba-'aḥatti* ('āmat 42ᶜ 47 58) *za-'iyyobelwu zəntu*. Most of the translations (Littman, Charles, Goldmann, VanderKam, and Wintermute) translate here "in one (of the years) of this jubilee." Berger (1981: 349) translates: "am Anfang dieses Jubiläums," or "at the beginning of this jubilee." VanderKam (1999: 161) adopted Berger's translation for exegetical needs (see the discussion below) even though this does not agree with the translation in his own edition of *Jubilees*. But Berger's translation does not seem correct. First, this is not the literal meaning of the Ge'ez translation in *Jub.* 5:1. Second, in the story of Cain and Abel (*Jub.* 4:2) the notation for the beginning of the jubilee is formulated differently: *wa-**ba-qadāmi**-hu la-'iyyobelwu*. Syncellus dates the death of Abel to the year 99, which is the first year of the third jubilee, i.e. the actual beginning of the jubilee (see Mosshammer 1984: 8). It is not clear why VanderKam translates 4:2 as "during the first (week) of the...jubilee" instead of "at the beginning of jubilee," which is the plain meaning. Berger (1981: 339) also translated *Jub.* 4:2 as "Und am Anfang des...Jubiläums," despite the difference between the Ethiopic texts of *Jub.* 4:2 and *Jub.* 5:1.

[47] *Contra* Berger 1981: 349; VanderKam 1999: 161 (see the previous footnote).

[48] However, there are a few instances in which it is possible to identify the original order, which is not chronological; see ch. 4 regarding the chronological redaction in general, and the significance of these exceptions for the literary development of the entire work.

[49] Isaac was 60 years old when Jacob was born (Gen 25:26); he died 120 years later at the age of 180 (ibid. 35:28); Jacob went down to Egypt at the age of 130 (ibid. 47:9), 10 years after the death of Isaac, following the seven years of plenty and the first two years of the famine (ibid. 45:6); Joseph was 30 years old when he stood before Pharaoh (ibid. 41:46). Therefore, Joseph was 39 years old when Jacob was 130, and thus Jacob was 91 (and Isaac was 151) at the time of Joseph's birth. Joseph was 17 when he was sold (Gen 37:2), 12 years prior to the death of Isaac, who was then 168 years old.

jubilee", refers, as noted, to the date at the end of ch. 4 pertaining to the birth of Japheth in the 25th jubilee, the 6th week, the 1st year (A.M. 1212; *Jub.* 4:33). On the assumption that the chronological comment in *Jub.* 5:1 refers to a date before the birth of Japheth,[50] this raises a problem with regard to the principle of the preservation of chronological sequence: on the one hand, it is impossible to transplant the whole story of *Jub.* 5 to before 4:33 (or even earlier) because of the need to connect the flood and the sins of the angels, the giants, mankind, and all animate beings; on the other hand, the two stories no longer appear in chronological order. Since the tension between these possibilities is irreconcilable, it is possible that the problem was solved by some creative ambiguity: if the sin occurred "in a certain (year) of this jubilee," there is no conspicuous chronological deviation between these two stories. *Jubilees* 4 ends in the 6th week of the 25th jubilee, and ch. 5 opens in this same jubilee, without explicitly mentioning that the narrative is doubling back on itself chronologically.

(2) The chronology of the entire book ends with the entrance into the land of Canaan during the 50th jubilee (*Jub.* 50:4). As noted by VanderKam, the arrival into the land of Canaan is an implementation on the national plane of the law of jubilee from Lev 25, which establishes "and you shall hallow the fiftieth year. You shall proclaim release throughout the land for all its inhabitants. It shall be a jubilee for you: each of you shall return to his holding and each of you shall return to his family" (ibid. 10). The Israelites fulfilled the law (originally a social law directed to individuals) on the national plane when they departed Egypt (= "You shall proclaim release"), and returned to the land of Canaan, the land of their inheritance (= "each of you shall return to his holding") during the fiftieth jubilee.[51] In this chronological system of ancient history, the 25th jubilee is the midpoint, and one can think of it as the "half-jubilee." The first half of the narrative time ends therefore with destruction that is the result of the mixing of the earthly and heavenly spheres. According to *Jub.* 5:11–12, this event brought about a new creation and therefore constitutes an important historical juncture. But the likelihood of this possibility is slight for two reasons: (a) the concept of "half-jubilee" appears nowhere in *Jubilees*, and in truth it does not accord with a method of enumeration based upon the number seven; (b) the new creation mentioned in *Jub.* 5:11–12 did not occur in the 25th jubilee but in the 27th.

---

[50] See the discussion below regarding the reasons to assume that the angels' sins occurred approximately 120 years before the flood, which took place when Japheth was only 97 years old.

[51] VanderKam (1995) 2000; 1997: 16–17.

According to *Jub.* 5:23, Noah entered the ark with his family in the 27th jubilee,[52] the 5th week, the 6th year (A.M. 1308). The flood, therefore, occurred between 83–131 years after the sin of the angels mentioned in *Jub.* 5:1, and these numbers accord with the 120 years that are mentioned in Gen 6:3. According to the dating of the sin in *Jub.* 5:1 to "a certain (year) of this jubilee" (i.e. the 25th jubilee, between 1177–1225), the punishment of the giants, death in civil war, was realized 120 years after this: thus the giants perished sometime between A.M. 1297–1345. It is possible to even more precisely bound the span of time in which the punishment of the giants was realized, if we assume (in accordance with the sequence of events in *Jub.* 5) that this civil war did not take place after the flood itself, which took place in 1308 (*Jub.* 5:23). The punishment of the giants thus took place between the years 1297–1308, and the sins of the sons of god took place 120 years earlier, between the years 1177–1188.

VanderKam suggested that if the angels sinned during the first year of the (25th) jubilee (A.M. 1177),[53] and the punishment was imposed

---

[52] All the Ethiopic manuscripts read in *Jub.* 5:22: *ba-kālə'etu 'iyyobelwu 'āmatāt*, "in the second jubilee of years." Dillman (1850) translated here "twenty-seven." Charles (1902: 47) commented that the Ge'ez text is a corruption of the reading "27." Littman and Goldmann both translate here "26"; Wintermute translated "22" (seemingly under Charles' influence, who claimed that this is the reading of all the Ethiopic manuscripts). VanderKam (1989b: 35) discussed this textual crux and offered two proofs that the original reading was "27": (1) According to *Jub.* 4:33, Noah's sons were born near the end of the 25th jubilee (between A.M. 1205–1209). According to Gen 5:32, Noah was 500 years old when he begat Shem, Ham, and Japheth, and according to Gen 7:6, Noah was 600 years old when the flood began. The flood thus took place between A.M. 1305–1309, and this date agrees precisely with the reading of the 27th. (However, we should note that there exists a chronological problem in *Jubilees* with regard to the date of Shem's birth, which arises from the biblical data themselves. According to *Jub.* 4:33, Shem was born in the 25th jubilee, in the 5th week, the 5th year [A.M. 1207]. According to Gen 11:10, Shem's son Arpachshad was born when Shem was 100 years old, i.e. in the year 1307. But both Gen 11:10 and *Jub.* 7:18 assert that Arpachshad was born two years after the flood, i.e. in the year 1310 [recall *Jub.* 5:23 which dates the flood to 1308]. *Jub.* 4:33, which states that Shem was Noah's first-born, does not address this issue.) (2) According to *Jub.* 6:18, the festival of Weeks/Oaths was given to Noah following the flood, 26 jubilees and 5 weeks after creation, in the year 1309.

One can add a third proof to the reading "27": According to Gen 7:6, Noah was 600 years old at the beginning of the flood. *Jub.* 4:28 dates Noah's birth to the 15th jubilee, the 3rd week (A.M. 701–707). Therefore, the flood (or at least the admonition about the flood) took place between 1301–1307, and this date agrees with *Jub.* 5:22, if the correct reading is "27." All of the evidence cited here proves without any doubt that the original text of *Jub.* 5:22 referred to the 27th jubilee, and thus also *Jub.* 5:23, 31. It is difficult to know what caused this textual mishap.

[53] Thus Berger (1981: 349) translated the chronological note in *Jub.* 5:1 (in contrast

on their offspring in 1177+120 = 1297, then there was sufficient time for the giants to be annihilated before the flood (1308–1297 = 11 years), and there is therefore no need to assume that the giants died in the flood: "they would still have died comfortably before the flood."[54] Yet his suggestion raises several problems: (1) the assumption that the sons of god saw the women precisely in the first year of jubilee (1177) does not accord with version of this verse in the Ge'ez.[55] (2) Even if we accept this suggestion for understanding this chronological datum, several events or processes occurred between the sighting of the women and the Lord's decision to punish the giants: the giants were born, the lawlessness (both of men and animals) increased, and mankind began to devour one another (5:2). Only then did God decide to destroy all that was on earth because of the corruption (5:4). These events did not take place in the blink of an eye, but were spread over a period of many years, and without exerting much effort one could distribute them over a period of 11 years. God's decision to kill the giants occurred therefore about the year 1188, 120 years before the flood (1308). A contradiction thus emerges, for while the rewritten story assumes that the limitation of 120 years from Gen 6:3 refers to the lifespan of giants (in accord with *Jub.* 5:7–9), according to the chronological framework the 120 years refers to the duration of time until the flood, which affected both the giants and all of humanity in that generation.

It is not clear from *Jubilees* itself why *Jub.* 5:8 emphasizes that the limitation on the length of life was imposed only on the giants, and not on humanity. This emphasis of *Jub.* 5:8 has its source in *1 En.* 10:9–10, which emphasized the limitation on the life expectancy of the giants:[56]

> ...[and destroy the chil]dren of the Watchers [...and send them into] a war of destruction; [and] len[gth of days they will not have. And] no req[uest from their fathers on their behalf shall be granted that they should expect] to li[ve an eternal] life [or that each of them should live for five hundred years]

---

with VanderKam's own translation of *Jubilees*). For this expression, see the discussion above in footnote 46.

[54] VanderKam 1999: 160–161.
[55] See above, footnote 46.
[56] The text and the reconstruction of the lacunae (based upon the versions of *1 Enoch*) are quoted from 4QEn[b] 1 iv, 6–8 (see Milik 1976: 175; *DSSR* 3:467). There is no explicit mention here of 120 years, but this is the sole reference in *1 En.* 6–11 to the limitation of life expectancy, and for this reason it is reasonable to assume that it is based on Gen 6:3. Cf. Nickelsburg 2001: 224.

This passage belongs to the Shemihazah tradition that does not draw a connection between the angels' sins and the flood itself. According to this tradition, the sons of god and their offspring (the giants) are the sinners, and not mankind; thus only within this framework is it understandable why Gen 6:3 is interpreted as relating to the giants alone. The period of 120 years in the Shemihazah tradition refers only to the giants born from the problematic cohabitation of the divine and human beings, and bears no chronological connection to the flood. When *Jub.* 5 adopted the description of the giants' punishment from the *Book of Watchers*, it also inherited the explicit reference to the limitation on human life expectancy. The emphasis in *Jub.* 5:8 that this limitation was applied only to the giants, while according to the chronological framework this limitation fell upon all of mankind in the generation, is the result of its literary dependence on the angel story from the *Book of Watchers*, and of the connection that was created in the redaction of *1 Enoch* between the sinning angels tradition and the description of the sins of mankind that led to the flood.

The Descent of the Angels for a Positive Purpose: According to all the traditions in *1 Enoch*, the angels' descent was an act of rebellion against God, and their intentions were nefarious—to defile the daughters of man or to teach humanity the mysteries of the world. In contrast, *Jub.* 5:6 states that the angels arrived on a mission from God: "*Against his angels whom he had sent to the earth* he was angry...." The same perspective is found in a note that was added to the genealogical list in *Jub.* 4:15 (which is parallel in part to Gen 5:15): "He named him Jared because during his lifetime the angels of the Lord who were called Watchers descended to earth to teach mankind and to do what is just and upright upon the earth." The biblical narrative itself is silent as to when the angels descended. Most scholars agree that the tradition about the sinful descent in *1 Enoch* precedes the one found in *Jubilees*. Dimant explained the modification of the Watchers' motive for descending, from negative to positive, as an expression of a later tendency that attempted to soften the motif of the sinning angels.[57] But one has to question whether changing the initial motivation from a negative to a positive one mitigates the ultimate outcome, which is that the Watchers sinned. According to VanderKam, the change in the nature of the Watchers' descent is intended to distance this evil act from the heavenly realm—if

---

[57] Dimant 1974: 100.

the angels sinned *after* they arrived on earth, then one cannot draw a connection between God and the responsibility for evil in this world.[58] This change is therefore derived from the theological outlook of the rewriter of *Jubilees*, namely that sin has its origins on earth and not in heaven. But it is difficult to accept this explanation, because *Jubilees* itself introduces an evil, heavenly angel, Mastema, into other stories, including the Akedah (chs. 17–18), the bridegroom of blood and the plagues in Egypt (ch. 48).[59] In those stories, Mastema struggles against the angel of presence and in opposition to God's will, even though there is no allusion to Mastema in the biblical narrative.[60] If the addition of Mastema to these stories is intended to mitigate God's share in the introduction of evil and negative deeds on earth, it is reasonable to posit that the assumption of an evil angel in heaven did not trouble the rewriter theologically.

In contrast, one can point to an exegetical motivation that would explain the transformation in the nature of the Watchers' descent, a motivation unrelated to the theological outlook of the "rewriter." I would like to suggest that the merging of the two traditions about the angels, those who sinned and those who caused others to sin, also influenced the purpose of the Watchers' descent in *Jub.* 4:15: "He named him Jared because during his lifetime the angels of the Lord who were called Watchers descended to earth to teach mankind and to do what is just and upright upon the earth." The play upon words in this verse supplies an etymology for the name Jared, which is absent in Gen 5:15. The etymology was not the invention of *Jubilees*, but was already present in its sources, and in particular *1 En.* 6:6, "[and they were all of these two hundred who descended] in the days of Jared" (according to 4QEn^a 1 iii, 4–5),[61] a verse that belongs to the Shemihazah tradition about angels who descended and sinned.[62] This etymology appears also

---

[58] VanderKam (1978) 2000: 328–331; 1999: 154–155.

[59] On the other hand, one could argue that two different authors were responsible for the distancing of evil from heaven and the introduction of Mastema into the other stories, and this contradiction can therefore be explained as emerging from their different origins. As will be suggested in chs. 9–10, the rewritten stories in which Mastema appears, in fact, do not belong to the redactional layer.

[60] However, it is possible that the rewriter of the bridegroom of blood story had before him a version of the text similar to LXX Exod 4:24: "an angel of the Lord encountered him"; see pp. 207–210.

[61] Milik 1976: 150–151.

[62] Scholars point out that the play on words is meaningful only in Hebrew, and not in Aramaic (י-ר-ד and not נ-ח-ת), and therefore this tradition antedates the *Book of*

in *1 En.* 106:13[63] and in 1QapGen III, 3[64] and apparently reflects a well-known ancient *aggadah*. In the context of the sinning angels tradition from the *Book of Watchers*, these angels descended during Jared's lifetime with the intention of sinning (*1 En.* 6:6). Their offspring, the giants, caused an increase in the acts of lawlessness on the earth, and as a result, these giants were finally punished by a civil war, and by a limitation on their life expectancy (ibid. 10:9–10). It is noteworthy that the descent of the angels in the days of Jared is not related to the flood, neither causally nor chronologically.

The situation in *Jubilees* is different because the tradition about the sinning angels (led by Shemihazah) was already linked with the flood in the source used by the redactor of *Jubilees*. This linkage apparently occurred in one of the redactional stages of the *Book of Watchers*. According to the chronology of *Jubilees* (*Jub.* 4:15, based upon Gen 5), Jared was born in the 10th jubilee, the 3rd week, the 6th year (A.M. 461),[65] and the angels descended "during his lifetime." VanderKam argues that from this chronological datum, it turns out that Mahalalel, Jared's father, gave Jared his name through prophecy, as the angels had not yet descended at the time of Jared's birth.[66] But an investigation into the formulation of this etymology leads to a different conclusion—Mahalalel did not give him his name through prophecy, but on account of circumstances in the world at the time of his birth.

The derivation of the name in *Jub.* 4:15 is based on the descent of the angels: "He named him Jared *because during his days* the

---

Watchers; cf. Charles 1912: 15; Dimant 1974: 41; Milik 1976: 152; Nickelsburg 2001: 177.

[63] Cf. 4QEnᶜ 5 ii, line 17 (according to Milik 1976: 209).

[64] The text there is fragmentary, and only part of the sentence is preserved: "for in the days of Jared, my father," but it is reasonable to assume that it refers to the same tradition (the translation is according to Fitzmyer 2004: 70–71).

[65] According to all textual witnesses of Gen 5, Jared was born when his father Mahalalel was 65 years old. According to *Jub.* 4:14 (and consistent with all textual witnesses to Gen 5, which agree up to this point), Mahalalel was born in A.M. 395. According to this, Jared should therefore have been born in the year 460, and not 461 as stated in *Jub.* 4:15. Perhaps there is an error here, and the original text read "in the 5th year." This emendation is supported by the very next verse (4:16), which dates the birth of Enoch to the 11th jubilee, the 5th week, the 4th year (A.M. 522). If the original reading in *Jub.* 4:15 was actually 460, then Jared was 62 years old when he begat Enoch. This accords with the Samaritan Pentateuch to Gen 5:18 (in contrast to 162 years in MT and LXX). This small emendation does not affect the general argument presented here.

[66] VanderKam 1999: 155.

angels of the Lord who were called Watchers descended to earth." This collocation, "because during his days (כי בימיו)," occurs in the Bible only in Gen 10:25 (and in its parallel in 1 Chr 1:19): "Two sons were born to Eber: the name of the first was Peleg, for *in his days* the earth was divided; and the name of his brother was Joktan." Early exegetes disagreed as to the meaning of "his days" of Peleg. *Jub.* 8:8 interprets the time of the event, described as "in his days," as a reference to the time of Peleg's birth: "He named him Peleg because *at the time when he was born* Noah's children began to divide the earth for themselves." According to the interpretation in *Jubilees*, this name was not based on prophecy, but rather was based on events that were transpiring at the time of his (Peleg's) birth.[67] In contrast, rabbinic exegesis dates the "division of the earth" to the end of Peleg's days.[68] According to this approach, "Eber was a great prophet, for he called his son Peleg through the holy spirit."[69] The source of the disagreement can be traced to an exegetical dispute regarding the meaning of the phrase "the earth was divided." *Jubilees* 8:8 takes this division of the earth to refer to a division by lots performed by Noah's sons (as described in 8:9–9:15). This division began in the year of Peleg's birth (32nd jubilee, 7th week, 6th year, A.M. 1567) and continued until the official, authoritative division in *Jub.* 8:10, two years thereafter. In contrast, the prevalent explanation in rabbinic literature is that "the division of the earth" refers to the story of the Tower of Babel (Gen 11:9), at the end of which the nations were dispersed all over the earth, and God mixed their languages.[70] This is the meaning of the common rabbinic expression, "the generation of division (דור הפלגה)," namely the generation of the Tower of Babel.[71] *Jub.* 8:8 was not compelled to assume that the

---

[67] Compare Radaq to Gen 10:25.
[68] *S. 'Olam Rab.* (ed. Milikowski) 1; *Gen. Rab.* 37:25; Rashi to Gen 10:25.
[69] This statement is attributed to R. Jose in *Sed. 'Olam Rab.* 1; and to R. Jose b. Halaftha in *Gen. Rab.* 37:25.
[70] Kahana (1969: 36) and Sarna (1989: 79) noted that Ps 55:10 also hints to this interpretation. One can also add the evidence of *L.A.B.* (pseudo-Philo) 6, which presents Joktan, Peleg's borther, as the rebel leader in its rewritten Tower of Babel story.
[71] The identification of the division of the land with the Tower of Babel story according to the second approach created a chronological incongruity regarding the birth of Peleg in Gen 10:25–32. In v. 25, it is related that Eber gave birth to two sons, Peleg and Joktan. In general, rabbinic exegesis assumes that Joktan was the younger of the two (cf. *S. 'Olam Rab.* 1) for three reasons: (1) in the list of names in Gen 10:25, Peleg comes before Joktan (the order of the names does not necessitate this understanding; see the order of the births of Noah's children in Gen 5:32 and the different opinions of commentators to Gen 10:21: אחי יפת הגדול). (2) The etymology of the

name Peleg was given through prophecy, and therefore explained the naming of Peleg more simply: Peleg was named so on account of an event that his father had seen with his very own eyes.

If we assume that *Jubilees* is consistent in its usage of the phrase "in the days of" a person,[72] then the expression "in the days of" Jared

---

name Joktan was taken to be ק-ט-ן (small, young). (3) Peleg appears in the genealogical list in Gen 11, from which Joktan is absent (cf. R. Huna's statement in *Gen. Rab.* 37 [ed. Theodor-Albeck], pp. 349–350). According to Gen 10:26–32, Joktan's many descendants were part of Noah's family from which "the nations branched out on the earth after the flood" (v. 32). Reading the Table of Nations in Gen 10 in sequence with the Tower of Babel story at the beginning of Gen 11 leads to the conclusion that the nations listed in Gen 10 are the same ones dispersed throughout the land at the end of the Babel story. If Joktan's sons were amongst the nations dispersed, and if Joktan was the younger brother of Peleg, who "in his days the earth was divided" (Gen 10:25), then "in his days" cannot refer to his birth. This interpretation therefore needs to assume that Eber, Peleg's father, was a prophet. In contrast to this somewhat convoluted interpretive path found in rabbinic literature, *Jub.* 8:8 assumes that the "division of the land" refers to a different event in world history, the allocation of inheritances by lot to Noah's children. This explanation does not create any tension between the dating of the division of the land at the time of Peleg's birth and the genealogical information regarding Joktan's children in Gen 10.

[72] This formula also appears in *Jub.* 10:18–19: Peleg named his son Reu (רעו) "for he said: 'Mankind has now become evil through the perverse plan to build themselves a city and tower in the land of Shinar'...*because in his days* they built the city and the tower, saying: 'Let us ascend through it to heaven.'" According to the Ethiopic translation of v. 18, Reu was born in the 33rd jubilee, the 2nd week, the 4th year (A.M. 1579). However, according to vv. 20–21, the building of the tower commenced in the fourth week (1590–1596) and continued for 43 years (until 1633–1639), leading to the conclusion that Reu's name was given "prophetically." I would like to suggest, however, that according to the original text of v. 18, Peleg's marriage and the birth of Reu took place in the **34**th jubilee (and not the 33rd), and Reu was therefore born in A.M. 1628, during the building of the tower. The primary argument for this emendation is Peleg's young age at the time of his marriage, and subsequently at the time of Reu's birth (cf. the similar reasoning proposed by VanderKam 1989b: 51 [in the textual note] in reference to the correction of Shelah's birth date in *Jub.* 8:6). The following table presents the relevant chronological data:

	Event	Jubilee	Week	Year	Year to Creation	Age of Peleg
8:8	Birth of Peleg	32	7	6	1567	
10:18	Marriage of Peleg	33	2	1	1576	9 years old
10:18	Birth of Reu	33	2	4	1579	12 years old

The dates of these events are implausible in and of themselves. Moreover, they are also difficult to substantiate in comparison with other characters mentioned in *Jub.* 8–11 (parallel to Gen 11:10–32). Not including Peleg and Reu (who was much older), all of these people married and had children between the ages of 50–70. These problems are solved by correcting the date in *Jub.* 10:18 to the 34th jubilee:

(*Jub.* 4:15), which dates the angels' descent, simply refers to the time of Jared's birth. Against VanderKam's claim that Mahalalel gave Jared his name through prophecy, the wording of the text indicates that the angels descended precisely at the time of Jared's birth. According to the dating in *Jub.* 4:15, this descent occurred in A.M. 461.[73]

And when did the angels sin? According to the Shemihazah and sinning angels tradition in *1 En.* 6–11, the angels descended in the days of Jared, begat children, and these children died by the sword after 120 years (as already mentioned, in this tradition there is no connection between the angels' sin and the flood). It is therefore possible to estimate that in the Shemihazah tradition, the offspring of the angels died around the year 580 (461+120 = 581) or shortly thereafter. Gen 6:6 dates the flood to the 600th year of Noah's life. According to SP and *Jubilees*, Noah was born in A.M. 707 (Gen 5:28; *Jub.* 4:28); according to the Masoretic text, he was born in A.M. 1056.[74] According to

	Event	Jubilee	Week	Year	Year to Creation	Age of Character
8:8	Birth of Peleg	32	7	6	1567	
10:18	Marriage of Peleg	**34**	2	1	1625	Peleg 58 years old
10:18	Birth of Reu	**34**	2	4	1628	Peleg 61 years old
11:1	Marriage of Reu	35	3	1	1681	Reu 53 years old
11:1	Birth of Serug	35	3	7	1687	Reu 59 years old

Another argument for the correction of the date in *Jub.* 10:18 is based upon the chronological ordering principle used in *Jubilees*. Noah's prayer at the beginning of *Jub.* 10 is dated to the 33rd jubilee, the 3rd week (1583–1589), **after** Peleg's marriage and Reu's birth according to the date found in the Ethiopic translation to *Jub.* 10:18. However, in light of the suggested correction, the order of events of Noah's prayer, Peleg's marriage, and Reu's birth proceeds sequentially from earliest to latest.

At the same time, it is important to note that the suggested emendation gives rise to tension between 10:18 and 10:20, which dates the beginning of the building of the tower to the 4th week, without explicitly noting the jubilee. According to the standard method of date formulation in *Jubilees*, one could conclude that the number of the jubilee is the same as in the previous date (v. 18), the 34th jubilee (according to the correction). However, according to *Jub.* 10:27, which dates the end of the tower-building to the 34th jubilee, 4th week, 1st year (A.M. 1639), at the end of 43 years (cf. v. 21), the building started in the 33rd jubilee. It is possible that the formulation of the date in *Jub.* 10:20, without the explicit mention of the 33rd jubilee, is an outgrowth of the textual corruption to the 33rd jubilee in v. 18.

[73] According to MT and SP, Jared was born in the year 460 to creation. As suggested above, perhaps the date in *Jubilees* should also be corrected to reflect 460 years to creation (see above, n. 65). According to LXX, Jared was born in the year 960.

[74] According to LXX, he was born in the year A.M. 1642, and the flood therefore took place in 2242.

SP and *Jubilees*, the flood took place in the year 1307–1308 (or in the year 1656 according to MT). In the framework of the Shemihazah tradition, the great distance between the two events does not raise any problems, because there is no causal connection between them. But as we saw above, the editor of *Jubilees* used a text of the *Book of Watchers* in which both traditions, about Shemihazah and Asael, were integrated, and this combination caused the tradition about Shemihazah and the sinning angels to be connected with the punishment of the flood (as a result of the juxtaposition of the stories in Gen 6). In *Jubilees*, the sin of the angels is connected to the flood, not only in a causal fashion, but also chronologically. As we saw in the previous section, the limitation of 120 years in the chronological framework, in fact, corresponds to the number of years of the period from when the angels began to sin until the flood occurred.

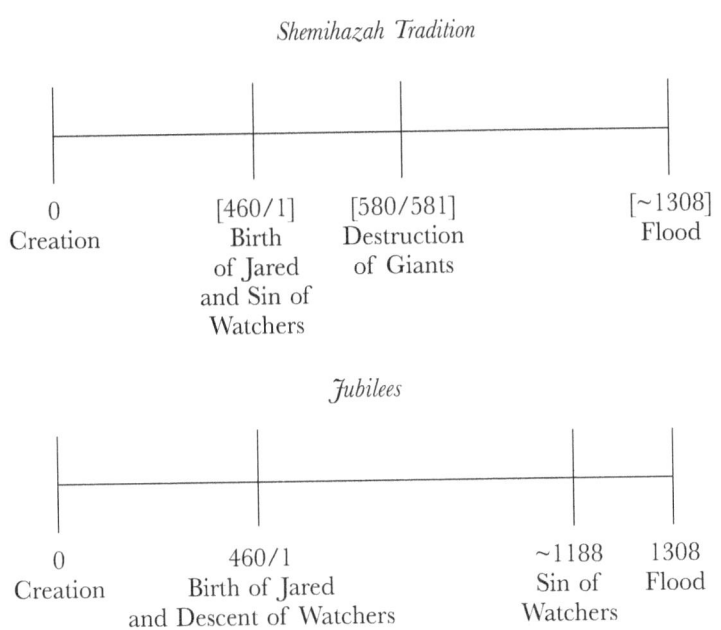

However, this dating in *Jubilees* generates a new problem, because it creates a chronological gap of more than 700 years between the angels' descent and their sin. The exegetical problem which arises in *Jubilees* is the result of the combination of: (1) the two traditions about the sinning angels and the angel who led them astray that were merged in the *Book of Watchers*, leading *Jubilees* to date the angels' sin chronologically close to the flood (approximately 120 years), between the years A.M. 1177–1188; and (2) the tradition about the descent of the angels in the days of Jared (A.M. 460–461, according to *Jub.* 4:15). The interpretive solution to this difficulty in *Jubilees* is to maintain the descent of the angels during the days of Jared, but to push off the angels' sin to a time closer to the flood. For this reason, their descent to earth cannot be construed as a rebellion, but must have been the result of other objectives. Thus, the mission of teaching mankind justice and righteousness was invented in order to provide an alternate purpose for this descent.[75] The commitment of *Jubilees* to the traditions that preceded it, even ones that contradicted one another, led to the invention of a solution to reconcile them.

The New Creation: After the sinning angels were bound underground for a second time "until the great day of judgment when there will be condemnation on all who have corrupted their ways" (*Jub.* 5:10), God obliterated the entire earth (ibid. 11), and formed "a new creation," *fəṭrata ḥaddās*. This creation is characterized by the fact that nobody will sin and each inhabitant of the earth will be righteous forever "according to his kind"[76] (ibid. 12). This world, in which nobody sins and all its inhabitants are righteous, stands in contrast to the state of affairs that preceded the flood. The flood came as a punishment upon all those who had "corrupted their way" (*Jub.* 5:2), whereas after the new creation, "everyone will be righteous—each according to his kind—for all time." The motif of the flood as leading to a new creation, after which humanity will no longer sin, is found in Josephus (*Ant.* I, 75). He relates that following the flood, God decided to create a new race, free from perversion: γένος ἕτερον πονηρίας καθαρόν.[77]

---

[75] Eshel (1999: 51–52) suggested viewing the angels' descent for didactic purposes as part of their regular responsibilities in *Jubilees* to maintain contact with human beings. For example, *Jub.* 3:15 tells how the angels taught Adam how to work the land. In my opinion, the correlation with other descriptions of the angels is not a sufficient reason to have changed the tradition regarding the purpose of their descent, but it might explain the specific task assigned to them in light of the exegetical-chronological problem raised here.

[76] The translation "in his generation" in Goldmann's edition, which seemingly refers to Gen 6:9, is the result of a random omission by the printers of the letter ב, and the subsequent, incorrect revocalization of the text.

[77] Charles 1902: 44; Berger 1981: 351. The other sources that Berger quotes relate to a second creation, and to Noah as a "second Adam," but not necessarily to a sin-free world. Philo, *Moses* II, 65, describes a new creation following the flood, in which humanity is created in the image of God, but is not pure from sin.

But the understanding of this new creation as referring to the period immediately following the flood is confounded by a number of problems:[78]

(1) This tradition of a halcyon period after the flood seemingly stands in contradiction with Gen 8:21. This verse relates that after God smelled Noah's sacrifice, he promised that he would not bring another flood, "since the devisings of man's mind are evil from his youth"—that is to say, God's expectations of human conduct were lowered after the flood, because he concluded that humanity could not meet the standard that had been set. The state of affairs after the flood was not that different from before: "great was man's wickedness on earth, and (how) every plan devised by his mind was nothing but evil all the time" (Gen 6:5).[79] A straightforward reading of the end of the flood story in Gen 8 ostensibly precludes the possibility of understanding that there was a new creation without sinning after the flood.

(2) The reality of the world, both in the time of Noah, and during the rewriting of this story, and also in the time of any potential reader, testifies that in every period of world history, mankind sins and apparently will continue to do so.

(3) *Jubilees* 5:10 dates the judgment of the whole world to the "great day of judgment," after which will come the new creation. When will the "day of judgment" take place? In the context of *Jub.* 5, "the great day of judgment" is identified with the flood. The identification is reflected in the personae of those who stand in judgment: "all who have corrupted their ways and their actions before the Lord" (ibid.). The expression "corruption of ways" is taken from the description of humanity's sins before the flood in Gen 6:12. However, the meaning of the term "the great day of judgment" is fundamentally different throughout the entire book, where it refers to the day on which evildoers will be punished, at the time of the transition from this world to the eschatological era (cf. 4:19; 9:15; 10:17, 22; 22:21; 23:11; 24:30, 33). This general meaning produces a problem regarding the usage of the

---

[78] The following questions (1–2) apply to Josephus as well.
[79] As noted by Sarna (1989: 59), Gen 6:5 judges humanity from God's perspective, while Gen 8:21 describes people's penchant for sinning as part of human nature.

term "the great day of judgment" in 5:10, which *prime facie* describes the flood from the earliest period of history, and not the judgment of the world in the end of days.

Because the sons of Noah did indeed sin after the flood, Charles argued that "the new creation" refers to an eschatological era, and not to the period of time close to the flood. Thus, in contrast to the Ge'ez translation (the only extant witness of this passage), Charles posited that in the original text of *Jub.* 5:11–12, all the verbs appeared in the conversive (or consecutive) perfect and not the simple perfect, and therefore described a future event. The translator from Hebrew to Greek did not understand the sense of this conjugation, and therefore translated all of the verbs as simple perfect, as they appear in the current text.[80] On the other hand, Davenport saw no problem with the Ethiopic version as is. In his opinion, v. 10b, which mentions "the great day of judgment," is to be taken as a parenthetical statement, and therefore it has no connection to the description of the new creation described in *Jub.* 5:11–12. He suggests that the motif of the new creation is already present in the biblical flood story, which describes primitive chaos, and transforms Noah into the first tiller of the earth.[81] However, from a syntactical viewpoint, it is difficult to construe v. 10b as parenthetical— for what relation does the first half of the verse have with "**until** the great day of judgment"? Aside from this objection, even though the story of the flood includes the idea of a new creation, it does not relate to a world in which there are no sinners. Like Davenport, Berger also understands vv. 11–12 as relating to a period after the flood, and not to an eschatological era; he even cites parallels from other works that have a second creation after the flood.[82] But the only one of these sources that describes a new race of men devoid of sin is the one cited above from *Antiquities*. Feldman refers to two Hellenistic works that present parallels to this sentence in Josephus,[83] and it appears that Josephus

---

[80] Charles 1902: 44–45; and subsequently Martin 1911: 508, n. 13; Rabin 1984: 26. These scholars do not address the other problems raised by the interpretation of these verses.

[81] Davenport 1971: 48, especially n. 3.

[82] See Berger 1981: 351; VanderKam 1999: 161–162; van Ruiten 2000: 197.

[83] Feldman (1998: 26) notes two parallels from classical literature in which Zeus intended or promised to destroy all of evil mankind, and to create a new race of people (Aeschylus, *Prometheus Bound*, lines 232–233 [Smyth 1922: 236–237]; Ovid, *Metamorphoses*, Book I, lines 250–252 [Miller 1977: 18–21]). Feldman explains Josephus' assertion as an attempt to attribute a positive purpose to God's obliteration of the world, and not just his desire to destroy everyone; this attempt was intended for the Greek reader familiar with Hellenistic literature.

was influenced by these Greek writings, which had no real connection or link to the works that influenced *Jubilees*.

Here too, it appears that the incongruity between the new creation of *Jub.* 5:11–12 and the biblical description of the flood (and in particular with the regard to the meaning of the expression "great day of judgment"), is a result of the literary development of *Jub.* 5. The description of "the day of judgment" in *1 En.* 10–11 belongs to the Shemihazah tradition about sinning angels, and is not connected to the flood: the giants (offspring of the angels) who caused the corruption of the earth, were punished by the sword, while the angels who sired them were bound in the earth "until the great day"[84] "of their judgment and of their consummation, until the judgment which is for all eternity is accomplished"[85] (*1 En.* 10:12). Their punishment will continue "for all eternity...until the end of all generations" (ibid. 13–14). In the original tradition, there is no connection whatsoever between "the day of judgment" and the flood—the former connotes a future punishment at the end of history, and the latter constitutes a punishment at a fixed point in the past. In the redaction of the *Book of Watchers*, when the two traditions, that of Shemihazah and the sinning angels and that of Asael who caused mankind to sin, were conflated, the stories of the sinning angels and the flood were artificially joined. *Jubilees* 5 therefore had no choice but to reinterpret the "day of judgment" in *1 En.* 10, which originally reflected an eschatological event, as being related to the flood. The new creation at the end of days, which is characterized by righteous people who do not sin, was transformed into a description of the world after the flood.

Other Doublets in the Story: In addition to the repetition of the punishment of angels (*Jub.* 5:6–7 and v. 10), there are other doublets in the story in *Jub.* 5:

(1) According to *Jub.* 5:2–3, 5 (following Gen 6:8, 11–12), God saw that men had corrupted their ways on the earth, and "he was pleased with *Noah alone*." Later on, v. 19 repeats this: "To all who corrupted their ways and their plan(s) before the flood no favor was shown except to *Noah alone*."

---

[84] According to 4QEn^b 1 iv, 11 (Milik 1976: 175).
[85] The Greek version reads: μέχρι ἡμέρας κρίσεως αὐτῶν καὶ συντελεσμοῦ ἕως τελεσθῇ τὸ κρῖμα τοῦ αἰῶνος τῶν αἰώνων (according to Flemming and Radermacher 1901: 32; Black 1970: 25); for the translation, see Knibb 1984: 196 (similarly for the translation of vv. 13–14 in the following sentence).

(2) According to *Jub.* 5:4 (following Gen 6:7), the Lord decided to liquidate humanity and all living creatures: "He said that he would obliterate people and all animate beings that were on the surface of the earth." Further on, in v. 20, the text repeats this decision: "The Lord said that he would obliterate everything on the land—from the people to cattle, animals, birds, and whatever moves about on the ground."

(3) In the current form of the story, by v. 11 God had already "obliterated all from their places; there remained no one of them whom he did not judge for all their wickedness." In the context of *Jub.* 5, this description seemingly relates to the punishment of the flood. The flood itself is described again in vv. 24–27.

These doublets can also be explained as the result of literary dependence of *Jub.* 5 upon *1 En.* 6–11, alongside the rewritten flood story at the end of *Jub.* 5. The first instance of each of these repetitions finds its source in *1 En.* 10: (1) God's decision to destroy the world and save Noah is mentioned in Sariel's mission (*1 En.* 10:1–3); (2) In Michael's mission (10:11–14), at the end of the Shemihazah tradition, there is a description of the obliteration of the Watchers. *Jubilees* 5 drew the Watchers story material from *1 En.* 10–11, but not the description of the flood itself. The rewritten flood story begins in *Jub.* 5:19, and continues until the end of the chapter. In that section, the author describes the destruction of the land and its inhabitants, except for Noah and his family, and God's decision to destroy the world, topics that were already mentioned in the passage borrowed from *1 Enoch*.

The development of the doublet describing the destruction of the world is slightly more complex, but is the result of the same process. The first reference to the destruction of the world (*Jub.* 5:11) is taken from Michael's assignment in *1 En.* 10, which details the punishment for Shemihazah and his band of angels on "the great day of judgment," i.e. in the eschatological age. This punishment was reinterpreted in *Jub.* 5 in reference to the flood. Similar to the previous examples, this detail, which originally referred to the Watchers in *1 En.* 10, was repeated in the description of the flood at the end of *Jub.* 5.

The Boundaries of the Story and the New Material

A crucial stage in the analysis of any story is the definition of its boundaries. The comparison with *1 En.* 10–11 not only solves the interpretive problems raised above, but also aids in determining the limits of the story in *Jub.* 5. This question is of special importance due to the literary genre of *Jubilees*, "Rewritten Bible." Methodologically, the present example demonstrates that one cannot attribute every difference between *Jubilees* and the Pentateuch to "the author" of *Jubilees*. At times, the rewritten story in *Jubilees* is itself based upon another, already extant rewritten story, which was part of a different composition. Thus *Jub.* 5 is based upon *1 En.* 10–11, which itself is based upon the pentateuchal story.[86] In the present case, one can ask: until what point in the text the rewriting of earlier materials continues, and where the new material, the work of the redactor, begins?

When the stories in *Jub.* 5 and *1 En.* 10–11 are compared synoptically, it can be concluded that the borrowed material in the former ends at *Jub.* 5:12. Both *Jub.* 5:12 and *1 En.* 10–11 end with a new creation: in *1 En.* 10–11, this creation refers to the eschatological era, while in *Jub.* 5 it refers to the flood. However, from a literary perspective, the two stories are in agreement regarding the conclusion of the passage. In addition, the sinning angels, so prominent in *Jub.* 5:1–12, are completely absent starting with v. 13. If so, v. 13 begins a new topic, even though it is related to the Watchers story to which it is juxtaposed. If the borrowed material in *Jub.* 5 continues until v. 12, what has been added in vv. 13ff.?

YHWH as a Righteous Judge and the Judgment of the World (5:13–18)

Following the Watchers story (vv. 1–12), *Jub.* 5 continues with a passage that describes the judgment of the entire world. This passage is replete with terminology and expressions found elsewhere in the book (these expressions are italicized):

> (13) The judgment of them all *has been ordained and written on the heavenly tablets; there is no injustice*.[87] (As for) all who transgress from their way *in which it was ordained for them* to go—if they do not go in it, *judgment has*

---

[86] As mentioned above, *Jub.* 5 did not merely copy its source, but changed some of the content (for example, the purpose of the Watchers' descent) and reformulated parts of the passage. However, despite the attempts to create a new, unified composition, the interpretive difficulties discussed above demonstrate that the author was not completely successful in his task.

[87] The meaning of the term *'amaḍā*, "injustice, wickedness," presumably reflects the Hebrew חמס (see above, n. 5) which appears in a number of biblical verses as the opposite of justice. Cf. the epithet "unjust witness (עד חמס)" (Exod 23:1; Deut 19:16; Ps 35:11), as well as the fuller expression, "false witnesses and unjust accusers" (Ps 27:12).

been written down for each creature and for each kind. (14) There is nothing which is in heaven or on the earth, in the light, the darkness, Sheol, the deep, or in the dark place—*all their judgments have been ordained, written, and inscribed.* (15) He will exercise judgment regarding each person—the great one in accord with his greatness and the small one in accord with his smallness[88]—each one in accord with his way. (16) He is not one who shows favoritism nor one who takes a bribe,[89] if he says he will execute judgment against each person. If a person gave everything on earth[90] he would not show favoritism nor would he accept (it) from him because he is the righteous judge. (17) *Regarding the Israelites it has been written and ordained*: 'If they turn to him in the right way, he will forgive all their wickedness and will pardon all their sins'. (18) *It has been written and ordained* that he will have mercy on all who turn from all their errors *once each year.*

From this addition to the story, it is apparent that the main message derived from the Watchers story is not related to the origin of evil in the world, even though this was the original objective of the Watchers traditions of the Second Temple period. Instead, this passage takes the Watchers story as a paradigm for the idea of reward and punishment,[91] and for the obligation of each and every creature to follow the path that God set for them. Each of the groups in this story (angels, giants, and people) received a punishment appropriate to them. These penalties were preordained on the Heavenly Tablets,[92] and it is therefore justified when they are imposed on the guilty parties. Alongside the punishments for those who sinned in antiquity, the Heavenly Tablets also record the punishments for every creature that will deviate in the future from their assigned path. This approach should not be viewed as deterministic: human behavior was not set in advance, but rather

---

[88] Apparently under the influence of Deut 1:17: "Hear out low and high alike." That verse continues, "for judgment is God's." It seems that *Jub.* 5 reflects exegesis of this verse from Deuteronomy that takes God as the judge.

[89] The Geʿez translation reflects the Hebrew נ-ש-א פנים, in its negative connotation (showing preference to an undeserving party in a legal context), as it appears in Lev 19:15; Deut 10:17; 16:19; Ps 82:2; Prov 6:35; 18:5; 2 Chr 19:7. Negative descriptions of accepting bribes appear in Exod 23:8; Deut 10:17; 16:19; 27:25; 1 Sam 8:3; Isa 1:23; 5:23; 33:15; Ezek 22:12; Mic 3:11; Ps 15:5; 26:10; Prov 6:35; 17:23; 21:14; 2 Chr 19:7. The combination of the two thus appears in Deut 10:17; 16:19; 2 Chr 19:7 (as well as Prov 6:35, but not in a legal context).

[90] The formula "If a person gave/will give..." followed by a negative result appears in Num 22:18; 24:13; Song 8:7.

[91] A similar perspective appears in Noah's testament in *Jub.* 7:20–39 and Abraham's testament in 20:5 ("the punishment of the giants"); cf. also CD II, 14—III.

[92] For a broader discussion of the Heavenly Tablets, see García Martínez 1997; Werman (1999) 2002; Ravid 1999; and below, pp. 313–316.

the way in which each person *should* behave, and the sanctions that will be used against them if they fail to act accordingly.[93]

The key to understanding the connection between the Watchers story and the motif of YHWH as a righteous judge is founded first and foremost upon the combination of the Watchers and flood stories. The flood was viewed as a paradigm for the punishment of sinners, and served as the subject for admonitions against sin.[94] However, in addition to the general motif of the flood as a symbol for reward and punishment, there is an additional literary motivation for this addition, based upon the terms and expressions that appear at the end of *1 En.* 10. *1 En.* 10:12 describes the final punishment of Shemihazah and his band: "... [and bind them for] seventy ge[nerations in the hills] of the earth *until the great day*"[95] "*of their judgment* and of their consummation, until the judgment which is for all eternity is accomplished." This verse, in its original context, does not describe the flood, but the "day of judgment" at the beginning of the eschatological age. In *Jub.* 5:10, this description was applied to the flood: "... afterwards they were tied up in the depths of the earth until the great day of judgment when there will be condemnation on all who have corrupted their ways and their actions before the Lord." The enumeration of those punished in *Jub.* 5, which is based upon the description of the flood generation in Gen 6:12 (and the rewriting in *Jub.* 5:2–3), reinterpreted this expression as a reference to the flood. On the basis of the expressions "day of judgment" and "punishment," and their implementation by God, the author

---

[93] García Martínez (1997: 248) viewed vv. 13–14 as equivocal: the idea that the punishment or judgment is already inscribed on the Heavenly Tablets might correspond to a biblical notion of predestination, or it might be closer to pure determinism. However, setting the judgment or punishment in advance is not the same as determining the actions themselves.

[94] See 4Q370 (C. Newsom [ed.], "4QAdmonition Based on the Flood," DJD 19, pp. 85–97); see also 4Q422 (T. Elgvin and E. Tov [eds.], "4QParaphrase of Genesis and Exodus," DJD 13, pp. 417–434), which presents three examples of sin and punishment; see Chazon 1997: 16–18. (As an additional note on this scroll, the word חו/יט in col. II, line 8, which the editors were unsure of its translation, can be taken as an alternative orthographic form of the word חטא ("sin"), a term that is appropriate to the general topic of the scroll; cf. col. III, line 7 on p. 429.) See further above, pp. 55–56, regarding the identical date in *Jubilees* for the sin in the Garden of Eden and the beginning of the flood, which points to a perspective that takes the flood as a paradigmatic punishment, although that tradition attributes the sin to a different event (Eden and not the Watchers).

[95] The first part of the verse is according to 4QEn^b 1 iv, 10–11 (Milik 1976: 175), while the rest follows Knibb 1984 (cf. n. 85), based here upon the Greek text.

of *Jub.* 5:13–18 projected the motif of judgment for the entire world on each and every individual in his generation. Since YHWH serves as a judge, it is incumbent upon all people to behave in accordance with the regulations that are in force for them. The Watchers story in *Jub.* 5 does not address the problem of the origin of evil in the world (in contrast with the Watchers story in *1 Enoch*), but rather calls on all people to behave according to "their way in which it was ordained for them to go," and thus to obey God's command.[96] The Watchers story has been transformed into a paradigm of reward and punishment, and the presentation of God as a just, righteous judge.

The special terminology that appears in this passage is bound up with the well-known phenomenon in *Jubilees*, according to which stories from the patriarchal period are connected with pentateuchal laws. In the vast majority of these cases, the connection refers to a specific law. Sometimes, in light of the forefather's behavior, a new law was established in the Heavenly Tablets, which was later given to all of Israel at Sinai. In other cases, the laws were already contained in the Heavenly Tablets, and the forefathers behaved accordingly. In every case where one finds new legislation of halakhot, or behavior according to existing laws, *Jubilees* notes this by the use of special terminology. Ravid labeled this vocabulary, which recurs throughout the entire book, "the special terminology of the Heavenly Tablets."[97] In her opinion, "the author of *Jubilees*" used this terminology when he wanted to present the information which appears on these tablets. According to her approach, this vocabulary is essentially a literary device that distinguishes between the laws that were inscribed on the tablets, in contrast to the Torah or to *Jubilees* itself. In the current passage, one can identify a number of expressions that Ravid included as part of this special vocabulary:[98]

> 13: "has been ordained and written on the heavenly tablets," "in which it was ordained for them," "judgment has been written down"
> 14: "all their judgments have been ordained, written, and inscribed"
> 17: "Regarding the Israelites it has been written and ordained"
> 18: "It has been written and ordained," "once each year"

---

[96] As suggested by Davenport 1971: 47–48, n. 2.
[97] Ravid 1999.
[98] Ravid (1999: 470–471) mentioned *Jub.* 5:13 as an example of "complete tablets" and 5:17 as an example of "incomplete tablets." Werman ([1999] 2002: 100–103) also differentiated between the two verses, but in a different way: v. 13 was categorized under the title "events", and v. 17 under "halakhot". However, it is preferable to take them both together as part of one legal passage, vv. 13–18.

Although there is no legislation of a specific law as a result of the Watchers story, both the terminology of the passage and its general topic (YHWH as a righteous judge) point to a connection between *Jub.* 5:13–18 and the legal passages interspersed throughout the entire book.[99]

In light of the literary analysis proposed here, one can understand the special terminology of the legal passages not as a literary device, as suggested by Ravid, but as the result of the literary development of *Jub.* 5. As demonstrated above, *Jub.* 5:1–12 is a reworking of *1 En.* 10–11, while vv. 13–18 is a passage that was added in order to emphasize the legal lesson of this story. The expressions characteristic of the Heavenly Tablets are concentrated in vv. 13–18, the new passage, which was added by the redactor to the source that he adopted. If so, the distinction in terminology is not the result of the author's attempt to create special terminology surrounding the Heavenly Tablets; instead, this terminology actually designates and characterizes the work of the redactor. After the editor of *Jub.* 5 paraphrased *1 En.* 10–11, he added an additional passage of his own composition, and the content of this passage informs us as to the aim of this redaction. The characteristic style of this passage, including the expressions mentioned above (in contrast with the rewritten story that is based upon *1 En.* 10–11) also attests to their different provenance.

---

[99] The idea of God as a righteous judge appears in other verses throughout the book, and especially in legal passages: 33:18: "Now you, Moses, write for Israel so that they keep it and do not act like this and do not stray into a capital offence; because the Lord our God, who shows no partiality and accepts no bribes, is the judge." As Anderson (1994) emphasized, according to the legal passage in *Jub.* 33:15–16 (as well as in sectarian scrolls, including the *Community Rule* and the *Damascus Document*), God does not punish sinners unless they received a warning about the specific law that they violated. The requirement of intentional sin is understandable in light of the description of God as a righteous judge, who does not mete out punishments unless it is clear that the law was known in advance. Similarly, in the narrative frame of the book (ch. 1), which describes the circumstances surrounding the writing of *Jubilees*, and which contains similar terminology to the legal passages (especially "Torah and *teu'dah*" which occurs four [or five times according to the reconstruction proposed by Werman (1999) 2002: 94–95; 2001a: 242–243]), the idea of God as a righteous judge appears as a reason for the composition of the entire book: "[So it will be that when] all of [these] things [bef]all th[em they will recognize that I have been more faithful than they in all] their [judgments]..." (1:6; according to 4Q216 I, 15–16; DJD 13, pp. 5–6). This motif also appears in Abraham's testament to Isaac, which reflects the halakhic emphases of *Jubilees*: "For he is the living God. He is more holy, faithful, and just than anyone. With him there is no favoritism nor does he accept bribes because he is a just God and one who exercises judgment against all who transgress his commands and despise his covenant" (21:4).

As noted, the vocabulary in *Jub.* 5:13–18 is similar to the terminology in the other passages throughout the book that have a legal emphasis. The juxtaposition of the rewritten stories and the legal passages is one of the most prominent characteristics of *Jubilees*. In the current example, the legal passage was added to an extant rewritten story. However, the editor of *Jub.* 5 was not responsible for both the rewriting of the story and the addition of the legal passage. The main argument to distinguish between the rewritten story and the legal passage in this example is the literary evidence, since the source for the rewriting can be identified in an existing composition. However, this model of literary development, an extant, rewritten story to which a legal passage was added, can also be used to explain the juxtaposition of narrative and law in the rest of the book. Instead of assuming that one author composed the entire book, both rewriting all of the stories and adding the legal passages, it is preferable to see here the work of a redactor of extant texts (mostly stories), whose primary efforts were dedicated to the emphasis of the observance of the proper, righteous halakhah.

The general theory proposed here in light of the analysis of *Jub.* 5 corresponds to the analysis presented in this study regarding other stories: the entrance into the Garden of Eden (*Jub.* 3), the Akedah (*Jub.* 17–18), Reuben and Bilhah (*Jub.* 33), Judah and Tamar (*Jub.* 41), the plague of the firstborn and the Exodus (*Jub.* 48–49). In these examples, I differentiated between the origins of the rewritten stories and the juxtaposed legal passages based upon contradictions between the two genres, such as in their exegetical tendencies regarding the biblical text, or in narrative details, such as the dates in the story. However, in these examples there was no textual evidence for the independent existence of the rewritten stories.[100] The current example thus complements those instances: *Jubilees* 5 does not present contradictions between the two passages, but textual support can be adduced to demonstrate their different provenance. In the other examples, there are contradictions, but no textual evidence of their different origins. By combining these two types of evidence, we can posit that in all of these examples, the redactor adopted extant, rewritten stories, and then refocused these narratives nomistically through the addition of legal passages from the "Heavenly Tablets."

---

[100] In the analysis of the story of Reuben and Bilhah, it was noted that *T. Reu.* 3:9–15 is similar to the rewritten story in *Jub.* 33:1–9a. However, it is not possible to demonstrate direct literary dependence between these two compositions.

SUMMARY

The purpose of the Watchers story in *Jubilees* 5 is not to explain the existence of evil in the world. Instead, the story functions as a paradigm for the observance of the commandments, and emphasizes the punishment awaiting anyone who fails to follow the proper path set for them by God. The story has thus undergone a transformation from a myth that explains the wretched state of this world to a story that suggests a juridical view of how this world is managed—YHWH functions as a righteous judge who acts according to predetermined rules.

CHAPTER SIX

THE TESTAMENT OF NOAH (7:20–39)

Analysis of the Testament

The Testament of Noah appears in *Jub.* 7:20–39 following the story of Noah's planting of the vineyard.[1] Two characteristics demonstrate that this passage does indeed belong to the testamentary genre: the terminology, such as the verb "prescribe, command" (*ya'azzəz*) at the beginning of the section, and the content, as Noah beseeches his sons to behave appropriately after his death.[2] An additional internal sign that this passage can be classified as a testament is found in v. 27: "and now I fear regarding you that *after I have died* you will shed human blood on the earth…"—Noah gives the orders to his sons with an eye toward the future, when he will no longer be around, and this perspective is appropriate for a testament.

In order to describe the structure of the passage, one can divide it into five sections according to their content:

(1) 20–26a: Noah commands his offspring to observe the commandments that he has learned in the past, and emphasizes the lesson learned from the Watchers and flood stories.
(2) 26b–33: Noah notes that his offspring are not acting righteously. He fears that their behavior will eventually deteriorate to the point of murder, and warns them both not to kill others and not to consume blood.

---

[1] The story of the planting of the vineyard in *Jubilees* rewrites the biblical story in Gen 9:20–29. On the halakhic interpretation of Gen 9 reflected in *Jub.* 7, see Albeck 1930: 32–33; Baumgarten 1987; Kister 1992; Werman 1995a: 92–98.

[2] For a description of the literary genre of testaments, see Collins 1984: 325–326. In his opinion, the most important characteristic of this genre is that it is a speech from a father to his children (or from a leader to his nation or successor), which is presented close to his impending death. The testament is generally introduced with a third-person description of the occasion on which it was imparted, but the testament itself is formulated in the first person. The testament is followed by the death of the speaker. This final element is absent in *Jub.* 7, and Noah's death is not mentioned until *Jub.* 10:15; for a discussion of the anomalous placement of the testament in *Jub.* 7, see the discussion below, pp. 158–163.

(3) 34: First conclusion of the testament: "Now listen, my children. Do what is just and right..."
(4) 35–37: The laws of the vineyard and firstfruits
(5) 38–39: Second conclusion of the testament

As noted already by scholars, the approach of the testament itself vis-à-vis the identity of the cause of evil in the world is similar to that reflected in the various traditions in *1 Enoch*—it attributes it to demons, offspring of the giants (children of the Watchers). However, literary-critical considerations will lead to the conclusion that the testament was not composed by the redactor of *Jubilees*, and therefore does not reflect his worldview.

Section (1): Similar to other compositions of the Second Temple period, Noah's testament emphasizes the Watchers story and the resulting flood punishment, since they function as paradigms of sin and punishment.[3] The content of this section is limited to those stories which Noah himself could have known, and those sins which he saw with his very own eyes. This limitation matches the summary of the content found in the introduction to the testament: "the ordinances and the commandments—every statute which he knew" (v. 20).[4] The description of the Watchers' sins in *Jub.* 7 is similar to that presented in the rewritten story in *Jub.* 5, but not identical with it, both in terms of some details of the content, and with respect to its literary genre (testament versus story). However, both passages share the same goal in their reading of the Watchers story. The purpose of the rewritten story in *Jub.* 5 (with the additional legal passage) is to advocate for the observance of the commandments, and to call attention to the calamitous repercussions resulting from noncompliance. The myth of the sons of god and the women plays a similar role in Noah's testament in *Jub.* 7,[5] as the Watchers episode is adduced following a list of laws that Noah implored his sons to observe.

---

[3] See pp. 139–140.

[4] It is possible that the emphasis on "every statute which he knew" is significant for understanding the view of the author regarding the status of the law: Noah's sons were only obligated in those laws which were already known (cf. Anderson 1994, and the systematic theological approach which he describes). However, it is also possible that according to the literary assumptions of the narrative, Noah was limited in his testament to those commandments that he could have known.

[5] So too *Jub.* 20:5; CD II, 14–III.

The sources for the different commandments that Noah mentions in the list are taken from either the Bible or from *Jubilees* itself:[6]

Commandment (Jub. 7:20–21)	Source
they should do what is right,	Gen 18:19[7] (Gen 6:9; 7:1)
cover the shame of their bodies,	Gen 9:21–23; *Jub.* 3:30–31; 7:7–9[8]
bless the one who had created them,	*Jub.* 2:3, 21[9]
honor father and mother,	Gen 9:22–23; *Jub.* 7:7–13
love one another,	*Jub.* 7:15
And keep themselves from fornication, uncleanness, and from all injustice. For it was on account of these three things that the flood was on the earth, since (it was) due to fornication that the Watchers had illicit intercourse—apart from the mandate of their authority—with women. When they married of them whomever they chose they committed the first (acts) of uncleanness.	Gen 6:1–4; *Jub.* 5

---

[6] For a similar analysis, see Lambert 2004: 99–100.

[7] As suggested by Kister (1995: 245–249), Gen 18:18–19 ("and all the nations of the land will be blessed through him. For I knew that he will command his children and household after him and they will keep the way of the Lord by doing what is just and right...) is the basis for the testaments attributed to Abraham and Isaac in *Jub.* 20:2–10 and 36:3–4. These testaments in turn influenced the "earlier" testament attributed to Noah here. The only instance of the root צ-ד-ק prior to the flood is the adjective used to describe Noah (Gen 6:9; 7:1), but it is questionable whether there is any connection between those biblical verses and Noah's testament in *Jubilees*.

[8] The story of the covering of Noah's nakedness in *Jub.* 7 is related directly to Noah. However, *Jub.* 7 contains no specific legislation related to this topic, in contrast to *Jub.* 3:30–31, which notes that nudity was explicitly prohibited in the Heavenly Tablets.

[9] The story of creation and the giving of the Sabbath law in *Jub.* 2 contains a double description of a blessing to the creator: the angels bless God at the end of the first day (v. 3), and then again in the description of the Sabbath (v. 21)—"they, too, would keep sabbath with us [the angels] on the seventh day to eat, drink, *and bless the creator of all* as he had blessed them and sanctified them for himself as a noteworthy people out of all the nations." According to this verse, blessing the creator is an integral part of Sabbath observance. Verse 21a appears in the Ethiopic translation of *Jubilees*, but there is not enough space to reconstruct it in 4Q216 VII, 12–13 (DJD 13, p. 19). VanderKam and Milik (1994: 22) noted this issue, and raised two possible explanations as to the cause of the difference between the two textual witnesses: an expansion in the Ethiopic translation or haplography (presumably they intended homoioteleuton) in the Hebrew text. They preferred the latter option, and the reconstruction of the scroll at this point is based upon the assumption that a Hebrew copyist deleted the text due to parablepsis. One can add that the parallel formulation in *Jub.* 7:20 perhaps strengthens the argument for the originality of the Ethiopic version of *Jub.* 2:21.

The Watchers story is emphasized more than any other story or commandment in the list, both in its conspicuous length (five verses of the testament address the story), and also in the anchoring of the specific commandments (refraining from fornication, impurity, and injustice) in the story itself. The purpose of the Watchers story, and of the commandments derived from it in *Jub.* 7, is identical in its goals to the other instructions in the list—to encourage Noah's offspring (and of course the reader) to observe the commandments.

Similar to the description in *Jub.* 5, the Watchers story in *Jub.* 7 is constructed from various materials: the story in Gen 6:1–4, elements taken from the *Book of Watchers* (*1 En.* 1–36), and new details added by the author of the testament. According to the version of the story in *Jub.* 7, the intercourse of the Watchers (sons of god) with the women led to the birth of the Nephilim. The Nephilim are made of flesh and blood, and could therefore kill each other. *Jubilees* 7:22 partially adopted what is conveyed in *1 Enoch* 7:4–5 (belonging to the Shemihazah tradition), and described how the giants ate one another: "They were all dissimilar (from one another) and would devour one another: the giant killed the Naphil...,"[10] and eventually the giants killed human beings. Similar to what is told in *Jub.* 5, the people themselves began to sin in response to the violence directed at them: they also killed one another, and consumed other animals.[11] When God became aware of the violence and the bloodshed on earth, he decided to destroy the entire world, including humanity and all living creatures.

---

[10] *Jubilees* 7:22 mentions three classes of giants: giant, Naphil, and Elyo. In the text of *1 En.* 7:2 preserved by Syncellus, one also finds three groups, with the additional idea that the three represent successive generations: the giants begat the Nephilim, and the Nephilim gave birth to Ἐλιούδ (= "Elyo" in *Jub.* 7:22). The origin of the first two classes can be traced easily to Gen 6:4 ("heroes" and Nephilim), and the third group is probably related to the third epithet found in that verse, "men of reknown" (so Kahana 1956: 32; Dimant 1974: 46–47; Nickelsburg 2001: 184–185). Charles (1902: 62) noticed that the *Animal Apocalypse* (*1 Enoch* 86:4; 88:2) describes three kinds of offspring of the stars (which represent the Watchers in the vison): elephants, camels, and donkeys.

[11] According to *1 En.* 7:4–5 (a passage that belongs to the Shemihazah tradition), the giants killed the people and animals, and ate them both. As I suggested in my analysis of *Jub.* 5 (p. 118), the combination of the two traditions in *1 Enoch* 6–11, one about angels that sinned (under the leadership of Shemihazah) and the other about an angel (Asael) that caused the people to sin, resulted in the transfer of the giants' sins to humanity. However, in contrast to *Jub.* 5:2, Noah's testament does not accuse the people of cannibalism. This difference perhaps strengthens the claim put forth later in this chapter, that Noah's testament in *Jub.* 7 reflects an independent reworking of the Watchers story from *1 Enoch*, and is not dependent on the rewritten story in ch. 5.

The description in *Jub.* 7:26a ends the first section of the testament with the comment that Noah and his sons were the only ones spared in the flood, just as *Jub.* 5:19 ends the Watchers story on a similar note. But the reference to the survival of Noah and his sons also functions as a transition to the next section, which criticizes Noah's offspring for their problematic behavior. The flood was brought in response to bloodshed (7:21, 23–24), and presumably Noah and his family were the only people who were not guilty of this sin (according to Gen 6:8–10); they themselves were not killed by the deluge, but if they behave in the future like those killed by the flood, then they too will be wiped off the face of the earth (*Jub.* 7:27–28). Verse 26a therefore has a dual function: as the conclusion of the description of the events that led to the flood, and as the introduction to Noah's words of warning to his descendants.

Section (2): The beginning of the second section is marked by the word *wa-nāhu*, "and/but now," which moves the time of the testament from commands for the future, based upon events from the past, to Noah's present. Although Noah advises his sons to "do what is right" (7:20), he sees that they are actually conducting themselves "in the way of destruction" (7:26b). Noah was also aware that in contrast to his request that they should "love one another" (v. 20), his sons were jealous of each other, and moved apart (see *Jub.* 7:14–19, and especially v. 15). While Noah reprimanded his sons for their problematic behavior, he also offered a possible motivation for their actions, blaming the demons (*'agānənt*) for leading them astray. The claim that an outside force, in this case "demons," caused the people to sin, points to a specific view regarding the source of evil in the world. This problematic behavior is not the result of God's intervention, and also not the result of man's free choice to defy him, but rather, this conduct is the result of an external power, demons, who wish to incite man to disobey him. At the same time, although these beings are the cause of the sins committed by Noah's sons, they do not absolve Noah's offspring of responsibility for their actions. Noah fears the potential punishment for his progeny in light of their activities, and therefore warns them of the dangerous influences of these demonic beings. His words of warning do not offer any solution for the existence of these demons. He is aware of their influence over his sons, but refrains from any action against them. He does not turn to God in prayer and request his protection for his sons, or even to release his sons from the control of these demons. Rather, he limits himself to warning his sons directly, imploring them not to sin.[12]

Who are the "demons" mentioned in *Jub.* 7:27? In order to answer this question, we must first analyze the structure of the testament. As noted above, section (2) presents Noah's present perceptions—he sees that his children and grandchildren are not observing certain commandments. These commandments match some of the instructions in section (1). For example, in v. 26, Noah sees that his sons have separated from one another and no longer live together, in contrast to his instruction that they should "love one another" (7:20). Noah's observation in v. 27, that the demons have begun to lead his sons astray, is adjacent to his concern that they will be guilty of bloodshed in the future. In light of the parallel between v. 26b and v. 20, it is reasonable to draw a parallel between v. 27, the description of the demons who cause bloodshed, and vv. 20b–25, which describe how the giants caused bloodshed in the antediluvian period. One can therefore conclude that there is some degree of continuity between the giants and the demons.[13]

Scholars of *Jubilees* generally understand *Jub.* 7:27 in light of 10:5 (from Noah's prayer):[14]

> You know how your Watchers, *the fathers of these spirits*, have acted during my lifetime. As for these spirits who have remained alive, imprison them and hold them captive in the place of judgment. May they not cause destruction among your servant's sons, my God, for they are savage and were created for the purpose of destroying.

Jubilees 10:5 describes the spirits as the actual children of the Watchers,[15] a position that stands in contrast with the description in *Jub.* 7 (and in ch. 5),[16] that the intercourse between the sons of god and the women

---

[12] Noah's abstention from requesting God's help against the demons is conspicuous in light of his request in ch. 10 (compare Moses' similar request in *Jub.* 1:20, and Abraham's appeal in 12:20). See the discussion below regarding the relationship between *Jub.* 7:20–39 and 10:1–15.

[13] Dimant 1974: 101, n. 288; Eshel 1999: 52.

[14] Charles 1902: 63; Berger 1981: 365; Eshel 1999: 52–54; van Ruiten 2000: 297.

[15] It is possible that Watchers are, broadly speaking, the "fathers" of the spirits, but it is important to note that *Jub.* 10 contains no allusion to the existence of giants. Furthermore, Noah compares the Watchers to the spirits, while according to the description in the testament, it would have been more fitting to compare the spirits to the giants.

[16] *Jubilees* 5 does not mention spirits or demons at all. Their absence is apparently the result of the rewriter's dependence upon *1 En.* 6–11, one the earliest parts of the Enochic corpus, which mentions these spirits in only one verse, 10:15. Dimant (1974: 61–62) determined that this verse is a secondary addition to chs. 6–11 (see the following note). Its absence from *Jub.* 5 possibly supports this conclusion.

produced giants. Both sources are in agreement that non-physical beings were eventually created by the Watchers' behavior, but they disagree regarding the process by which the spirits or demons were created, whether as the direct product of the problematic sexual relationship, or as offspring of the giants who themselves were the immediate descendants of the Watchers. These two traditions regarding the origins of the spirits are found side by side in *1 Enoch*:

(i) "And destroy all the spirits of the reprobate and the sons of the Watchers for they have wronged men" (*1 En.* 10:15).[17]

(ii) "(8) And now the giants who were born from the spirits and flesh will be called evil spirits upon the earth, and on the earth will be their dwelling. (9) And evil spirits came out from their bodies because from above they were created; and from the holy Watchers was the beginning of their creation and the beginning of their foundation...and evil spirits they will be called...(11) And the spirits of the giants lay waste, do wrong, and cause corruption and attack and fight and break on the earth, and cause sorrow; and they do not eat, but fast and thirst, and cause offence" (*1 En.* 15:8–11).[18]

(iii) "From the days of the slaughter and destruction and the death of the giants, the spirits, having gone out from the souls of their flesh, will destroy without judgment; thus will they destroy until the day of consummation, the great judgment in which the great age will be brought to an end, upon the Watchers and the impious ones" (*1 En.* 16:1).[19]

The first two sources (*1 En.* 10:15; 15:8–11 [except for v. 9a]) describe the spirits as the immediate offspring of the Watchers themselves, as suggested also in Noah's prayer in *Jub.* 10.[20] In contrast, the third source

---

[17] The translation is based upon Knibb 1984: 196 (body of translation combined with textual notes, especially from the Greek version); cf. also Eshel's (1999: 35–37) textual analysis. Dimant (1974: 61–62) identified the verse as a later addition based upon its use of the epithet "spirits" for the Watchers' offspring, in contrast with the rest of *1 En.* 6–11, which speaks of "giants." This verse was apparently added in light of *1 En.* 15:8–9; 16:1; 19:1, all of which use the term "spirits" to describe these beings.

[18] The translation is based upon Knibb 1984: 204–205 (body of translation combined with textual notes, especially from the Greek version; cf. the previous footnote); cf. the textual analysis of Eshel 1999: 38–42. Eshel noticed that v. 9a, which describes how the spirits emerged from the giants' bodies, is at odds with vv. 8, 9b, which equate the two.

[19] Knibb 1984: 205 (cf. above, notes 17, 18); cf. also Eshel 1999: 42–44.

[20] The tradition in the *Book of Watchers* in *1 Enoch* that takes the spirits as the direct

(*1 Enoch* 16:1 [as well as 15:9a]) describes the spirits as departing from the giants' bodies after they were punished, as reflected in Noah's Testament in *Jub.* 7.

1 Enoch 16:1 and *Jub.* 7 both preserve a complex tradition: Watchers → Giants → Spirits.[21] This development is possibly the result of a secondary combination of two earlier traditions: the first described only the birth of giants (attested in Gen 6:1–4; *1 En.* 6–11), and the second the creation of the spirits (*1 En.* 10:15; 15:8–11). In order to preserve both versions, they were arranged in sequence, as if they occurred chronologically: first the giants and then the spirits. Alternatively, it is possible that this is not a complex tradition, but rather the result of exegesis of Gen 6:3: "My spirit shall not abide in man forever, for he too is flesh." This verse can be understood as a verdict by God that the divine spirit cannot remain forever inside the giants, who are made from flesh and blood. However, the spirits can continue to survive on earth, just outside the giants' bodies. The evil spirits mentioned in *1 En.* 16:1 are therefore the heavenly-divine aspect of the giants, which can still survive even after the giants have perished.

Due to the basic similarity between *Jub.* 7:27 and 10:1–13 regarding the behavior of Noah's sons (both tell of evil spirits that began to lead Noah's sons astray), Charles suggested that both passages belong to a single, lost composition, which he called the *Book of Noah*.[22] If one combines both sources, and identifies the demons from one with the spirits (the offspring of the Watchers) in the other, then one can then theoretically complete the missing details in each description based upon the other passage. Thus for example, *Jub.* 10 does not mention giants at all, and only describes spirits, while *Jub.* 7 mentions both in its version of the Watchers story. In addition, in *Jub.* 10, Mastema appears for the first time in *Jubilees* as the figure in charge of the spirits, even though there is no hint of his existence in *Jub.* 7.[23]

---

offspring of the Watchers justifies the suggested interpretation of *Jub.* 10:5, "your Watchers, the fathers of these spirits," as actual fathers.

[21] This development should not be attributed to the author of the testament in *Jub.* 7. It is reasonable that this author inherited it from an earlier source, such as *1 En.* 16:1.

[22] Charles 1902: 62, 78. See also Stone 1972; García Martínez 1992: 1–44; Steiner 1995. For a more skeptical approach to the existence of this composition attributed to Noah, see Werman 1999.

[23] Mastema appears in *Jub.* 11:5 as the leader of the spirits that attempt to lead people astray, and to cause them to commit murder. This description is similar to the

If the two passages are combined, one can arrive at one of two possible conclusions:

(1) The giants, the offspring of the Watchers, are called "spirits," similar to the view expressed in *1 En.* 15:8.[24]
(2) The spirits (*Jub.* 7; 10) are the offspring of the giants (*Jub.* 5; 7). A similar perspective appears in *1 En.* 15:9a; 16:1, and it appears to be the result of the combination of the two traditions as to the offspring of the Watchers. The description of the Watchers as the "fathers" of the spirits in *Jub.* 10:5 must be taken in the broader sense of forefather.

Both of these conclusions raise difficulties. Regarding the first possibility, one should note that it is difficult to identify the giants of chs. 5 and 7 with the spirits, because of the difference in how they are treated: according to *Jub.* 7:22–25 (and also 5:9), the giants died by the sword, and they are therefore certainly mortal. In contrast, in *Jub.* 5:6, 10, the Watchers were imprisoned underground; since they are immortal, they cannot be killed, yet they cannot remain on earth (because of the damage that they will cause), nor can they return to heaven (because of their sins). The spirits in *Jub.* 10 suffer a similar fate: Noah asked God to imprison them in the "place of judgment" (v. 5), and that is what he did, except for one-tenth of the spirits whom he left under the control of Mastema (v. 9). If so, according to the story in *Jub.* 10, the spirits are not mortal, but rather, divine beings that cannot be killed. This position does not correspond to the death-by-sword of the giants, the offspring of the Watchers, in *Jub.* 5 and 7.

The second possibility, according to which the spirits are the offspring of the giants, is also difficult:

(1) *Jubilees* 10 does not mention the giants, but rather, only the Watchers and spirits. The tradition in *Jub.* 10 is more consistent with the viewpoint expressed in *1 En.* 10:15; 15:8–11.
(2) The Watchers are described as the fathers of the spirits in *Jub.* 10:5. Although it is possible to understand the epithet "fathers" in a

---

description of the spirits in *Jub.* 7:27, who have a similar goal. See pp. 181–185 for a discussion of the relationship between these two passages and *Jub.* 10:1–13.

[24] Eshel 1999: 55. It is possible that even the tradition that equates the giants and the spirits is the result of the combination of two traditions, one about the spirits and the other concerning the giants.

broad sense, it is more appropriate for the description of the giants according to the genealogy suggested in *Jub.* 7: Watchers → Giants → Demons.

In sum, despite the strong similarity between the two stories, the disparities between them regarding the Watchers story, and especially the reliance of each one upon different traditions, leads to the conclusion that they each reflect a different viewpoint regarding the origin of the spirits or demons.[25]

The inclusion of the Watchers story within the testament led to the transformation of this myth into another paradigmatic example of reward and punishment. A similar process of demythologization of the Watchers story occurred in Abraham's testament (20:5–6):

> He told them about the *punishment of the giants* and the punishment of Sodom—how they were condemned because of their wickedness; because of the sexual impurity, uncleanness, and corruption among themselves they died in (their) sexual impurity. "Now you keep yourselves from all sexual impurity and uncleanness and from all the contamination of sin..."

There too, the "punishment of the giants," similar to the "punishment of Sodom," is not intended to explain the origin of evil in the world, but rather functions as the basis for the admonition against sin found in that testament. The use of the story for a didactic-moral purpose necessitated the softening of its mythological character, and as a result, also limited the importance of this mythic event for the explanation of the origin of evil in the world. In contrast to the traditions in *1 Enoch*, which perceived the mixing of the heavenly and earthly realms as the catalyst for the entry of evil into the world, the interpretation of Gen 6:1–4 in Noah's (*Jub.* 7) and Abraham's (*Jub.* 20) testaments does not focus solely on the repercussions of this event on the world order. Instead, it transforms it into an archetype for YHWH as a righteous judge who punishes the wicked.

Section (3): The use of the term "and now" (*wa-yəʾəze-hi*) marks the transition from the second to the third section of the testament. Verse 34 repeats elements from the beginning of the testament, and it can

---

[25] Dimant (1974: 101–102) attributed the two chapters to two different traditions. I will adduce additional evidence below (pp. 158–163), based upon redactional considerations, for the different origins of the passages.

therefore be classified as a conclusion (at least an interim conclusion) of the admonition section of the testament (vv. 20–34). The recurring motifs in v. 34 are:

> "Do what is just and right" || "He testified to his sons that they should do what is right" (v. 20)
> "who saved me from the flood waters" || "We—I and you, my children, and everything that entered the ark with us—were left" (v. 26)

One additional component is found in v. 34: "so that you may be rightly planted on the surface of the entire earth." The image of Israel in general, and the righteous in particular, as planted in the land already appears in the Bible,[26] and afterwards in postbiblical, Jewish literature (*1 Enoch* 10:16; 93:5, 10).[27] The depiction of Israel as a plant appears in two other passages in *Jubilees*:

(1) 1:16: "I will transform them into a *righteous plant* with all my mind and with all my soul. They will become a blessing, not a curse; they will become the head, not the tail." The Lord promises Moses that the Israelites will receive an abundance of blessings, including their being "planted" in the land, when they repent from their sins "with all their minds and with all their souls" (v. 15). *Jubilees* 1 does not belong to the testament genre, but it does contain a similar description of reward and punishment for the righteous and the sinners from within Israel.

(2) 21:24: "He will bless you in all your actions. He will raise from you a *righteous plant* in all the earth throughout all the history of the earth." This verse appears at the end of Abraham's testament to Isaac. In the previous verses in ch. 21, Abraham warned his son not to sin. Similar to Noah's promise to his descendants at the end of his testament, in *Jub.* 21:24, Abraham addresses the potential benefit his offspring will receive if they follow God's commandments. *Jub.* 21:24 and 7:34 both use the same image to express these rewards, and these two passages are therefore similar in their location, their function, and their purpose within the testament.

---

[26] Charles (1902: 64) refers to Jer 11:17 and Amos 9:15, both of which refer to Israel planted in the earth, but without the additional element of righteousness. It is possible that this motif is connected to Isa 60:21: "And your people, all of them *righteous*, shall possess the land for all time; they are the shoot that I *planted*...," which describes all of Israel in these terms.

[27] Charles 1902: 64; Licht 1961. The more common expression in sectarian literature is "eternal planting (מטעת עולם)"; see the sources adduced by Licht.

Section (4): The beginning of this section (vv. 35–37) is marked by the word "And behold" (*wa-nāhu*), similar to the opening of section 2. The passage includes laws related to the fourth-year fruits, whose halakhic status was the subject of debate between Jewish sects in the late Second Temple period.[28] The legal passage appears here for two reasons: (1) the story of the planting of the vineyard at the beginning of the chapter, which includes details regarding the edibility of these fruits, necessitated a detailed halakhic discussion on the topic; (2) the image of Israel planted in the ground explains the location of the passage at this specific point in Noah's testament.[29] Kister identified a number of contradictions between the rewritten story at the beginning of the chapter and the laws presented in section (4),[30] especially vis-à-vis the status of the fourth-year fruits,[31] and raised the possibility that different traditions (not all of them sectarian) have been combined in this chapter. As Kister noted, the attempts to harmonize the laws with the rewritten story, as proposed by some scholars,[32] are unjustified. In addition to the discrepancies in content, the division of the conclusion into two parts (the first in v. 34 and the second in vv. 38–39) also points to the secondary nature of vv. 35–37. Another argument that supports the suggestion that vv. 35–37 were added at some stage in the literary development of *Jub.* 7:20–39 is the use of the technique of resumptive repetition at the end of the section: "...so that you may leave it in the *right and proper way*. Then you will be doing *the right thing*, and all *your planting* will be successful" (v. 37).[33] These verses return the reader to

---

[28] See Albeck 1930: 32–33; Baumgarten 1987; Kister 1992; Werman 1995a: 92–98.

[29] Van Ruiten 2000: 302; VanderKam 2001: 40.

[30] Kister 1992.

[31] They were viewed either as priestly prerogatives, as reflected in vv. 35–37 and in sectarian compositions (11QT LX, 3–4; MMT B 62–64), or alternatively as having the same status as the second tithe, as reflected in vv. 1–6 and in rabbinic literature (m. *Ma'aś. Š.* 5:1–4; *Sifre Numbers* 6).

[32] Albeck ibid.; Baumgarten ibid.

[33] I intentionally skipped the first words in the verse, "In the fifth year." The fifth year continues the list of laws regarding the fruits of the first four years (cf. Lev 19:23–25), and it is difficult to understand its connection to the law of release at the end of the verse. Charles (1902: 65) suggested that some of the text was omitted unintentionally. Baumgarten (1987: 197) interpreted the release here as a reference to the removal of limitations on the fruit that were in force during the first four years. Similarly, Kister (1992: 582) suggested that the idea of release was introduced here as the result of interpretation of the term *hillulim* (Lev 19:24), according to the meaning of the cognate Arabic verb *ḥll*. But the choice of the verb "release" is still anomalous

the end of section 3: "Now listen, my children. Do what is *just and right* so that you may be *rightly planted* on the surface of the entire earth" (v. 34). An author will often use resumptive repetition for stylistic reasons, but it was sometimes employed by scribes as a technique to introduce secondary material into their source.[34] In our case, the accumulation of arguments for the secondary nature of vv. 35–37 strengthens the possibility that this technique provides additional evidence that this section was added to the testament at a later stage.

A final argument for the secondary nature of the legal passage here will become apparent from the analysis of the final section, which closes the testament.

Section (5): Verses 38–39 describe the chain of transmission which Noah passes along to his sons:

> (38) For this is how Enoch, your father's father, commanded his son Methuselah; then Methuselah his son Lamech; and Lamech commanded me everything that his fathers had commanded him. (39) Now I am commanding you, my children, as Enoch commanded his son in the first jubilees. While he was living in its seventh generation, he commanded and testified to his children and grandchildren until the day of his death.

The transmission of knowledge from father to son plays a central role in *Jubilees*, and it imparts authority and validity to the commandments in the pre-Sinaitic period (see also 10:14; 12:27; 21:10; 39:6–7; 41:28; 45:16).[35] At the end of Noah's testament, he clarifies that what he just said was not the figment of his own imagination, but part of a tradition that he received from his forefathers. From the continuity between vv. 35–37 and v. 38, it seems that the words, "For this is how Enoch, your father's father, commanded his son," refers to what immediately precedes it, the laws of *'orlah* and fourth-year produce. *Jub.* 21:10 (Abraham's testament to Isaac) also describes things that "I (Abraham) found written in the book of my ancestors, in the words of Enoch and the words of Noah" This refers to the halakhot in the

---

in this context, and it seems preferable to take vv. 35–37 as a list of agricultural laws, which was the victim of textual corruption (perhaps homoioteleuton from "in the fifth year" to "in the seventh year").

[34] For a discussion and examples of this phenomenon, see Seeligmann 1992: 53–60.

[35] Najman 1999 discusses different "authority conferring strategies" within *Jubilees*, among them a chain of transmission from the earliest generations.

prior verses, which address foreign worship and sacrifices (21:5–10), and emphasize the prohibition against consuming blood (v. 6) and the requirement to pour it onto the altar (v. 7). If the suggestion above, that 7:35–37 was added to Noah's testament at a later stage, is correct, then in the original form of the text v. 38 immediately followed v. 34, creating a single, unified conclusion for the testament. Moreover, the complete conclusion, vv. 34, 38–39, follows the prohibitions against murder and the consumption of blood, similar to the topics covered in Abraham's testament in *Jub.* 21. It is therefore possible that both of these testaments (chs. 7, 21) are based upon a common tradition, which attributes the laws against violence and consumption of blood to Enoch and Noah.

The Arrangement of the Passages Concerning the End of Noah's Life[36]

The analysis of the differences between *Jub.* 7 and *Jub.* 10 regarding the Watchers story revealed the editorial process of these traditions. It is also possible to arrive at a similar conclusion, based upon the analysis of the chronological framework surrounding the stories that address the end of Noah's life. Noah was born in the 15th jubilee, in the 3rd week, A.M. 701–707, and died 950 years later (*Jub.* 10:15–16, according to Gen 9:29). A simple calculation reveals that according to the chronology of *Jubilees* (which is based upon chronological details attested in SP), Noah died between A.M. 1651–1657. As noted above, Noah's testament is dated to the 28th jubilee, A.M. 1324–1372.

		Jubilee	*Week*	*Year to Creation*
4:28	Marriage of Lamech and Birth of Noah	15	3	701–707
7:20	Testament of Noah	28		1324–1372
10:1	The demons begin to lead Noah's children astray	33	3	1583–1589
10:16	Noah dies at the age of 950			1651–1657

---

[36] This discussion has implications for the discussion of the chronological redaction of the book; see ch. 4.

From the dates in the chronological framework, Noah presented his testament to his children approximately 300 years before his death. The dating of Noah's testament so far in advance of his death is clearly atypical when compared to other testaments preserved in Second Temple literature in general,[37] and more significantly, from the other testaments in *Jubilees*. There are four other testaments in *Jubilees*:

(1–2) According to *Jub.* 20:1, Abraham's testament to all of his sons and grandsons was given in the 42nd jubilee, in the 7th week, in the 1st year (A.M. 2052); his testament to Isaac took place in the 42nd jubilee, in the 7th week, in the 6th year (A.M. 2057; *Jub.* 21:1). Abraham died three years later, in the 43rd jubilee, in the 1st week, in the 2nd year (A.M. 2060; *Jub.* 22:1). The Ethiopic version of *Jub.* 22:1 actually reads the 44th jubilee, but Dillman suggested emending this to the 43rd, a suggestion that was confirmed by 4QJub^d II, 35.[38]

(3) Rebecca's testament to Jacob is dated to the 45th jubilee, the 1st week, the 1st year (A.M. 2157; *Jub.* 35:1), when she was sure that she would die in that very same year (ibid. 6). After speaking with Esau, she once again commanded Jacob, and died that night (ibid. 27).

(4) Isaac's testament to his children is dated to the 45th jubilee, the 1st week, the 6th year (A.M. 2162; *Jub.* 36:1), and he died that same day.

The dating of Noah's testament according to the chronological framework, some 300 years prior to his death, deviates from the general pattern of the testaments, and demands explanation.

A comparison with the biblical story, which forms the basis of *Jub.* 7, explains the placement of Noah's testament, and solves the chronological anomaly.[39] The following synoptic table presents the contents of Gen 9:20–29 and *Jub.* 7:

---

[37] According to Collins (1984: 325), one of the primary characteristics of the testamentary literary genre is that they were transmitted close to the death of the speaker; see 7:27: "after I have died."

[38] Dillman 1851: 71, n. 14. The Qumran text is found in DJD 13, pp. 47, 50. For a detailed discussion of Dillman's arguments, see p. 15, n. 37.

[39] In contrast to van Ruiten (2000: 305) who writes: "There is no problem in the biblical text that justifies the insertion of this text."

Genesis 9	Jubilees 7
20: Planting of the vineyard	1: Planting of the vineyard
21: Noah's drunkenness and nudity	2–7: Preparation of the wine; festival; Noah's drunkenness and nudity
22–23: Ham sees Noah's nakedness; Shem and Japheth cover Noah	8–9: Ham sees Noah's nakedness; Shem and Japheth cover Noah
24–27: Noah curses Canaan, son of Ham, and blesses Shem and Japheth	10–19: Noah curses Canaan, son of Ham, and blesses Shem and Japheth; Ham moves away from Noah; the building of cities
28–29: Death of Noah	**20–39: Testament of Noah**

From this comparison, one can see that the testament is indeed in its appropriate place, parallel to the death of Noah, according to the order of events in the biblical story. The present place of the testament in *Jub.* 7, immediately after the story of the planting of the vineyard, therefore reflects the biblical order of the stories.

This observation has important implications for understanding the literary development of *Jubilees*. If the testament appears in its natural place according to the order of events in Genesis (the vineyard story followed by the notice of Noah's demise), it seems likely that Noah's testament originally appeared adjacent to the death notice, and not three chapters (Noah's death is described in *Jub.* 10:15–16) and some 300 years beforehand. A number of stories appear in between Noah's testament (7:20–39) and his death (10:15–16): Kainan's discovery of the Watchers' teachings and the births of additional generations (8:1–7), the division of the earth (8:8–ch. 9), and Noah's prayer against the spirits who were leading his children astray (10:1–13). These stories break the expected sequence of Noah's testament followed by his death. This current literary form can be attributed to two possible scenarios:

Jub. 8:1–10:13 was originally not part of *Jubilees*, and the addition of this section led to the separation of the testament from the death notice. However, these chapters contain details whose absence in an earlier form of the book is difficult to imagine. For example, the references to the births of Kainan, Shelah, Eber, and Peleg (8:1, 5–8) are based upon the genealogical lists in Gen 11, and correspond to the many references in *Jubilees* to the births (and marriages) of other characters that appear in the lists in Gen 5 and 11.[40] Similarly, the story of the

---

[40] Compare the many chronological references in *Jub.* 4.

division of the earth in chs. 8–9 is parallel to the Table of Nations in Genesis 10.[41] It is therefore difficult to imagine that these passages were secondarily added to an existing composition.

More likely, it is possible that the story of the planting of the vineyard, the attached testament, and the notice of Noah's death, together represent a rewriting of Gen 9:20–29. They existed independently (prior to being included in *Jubilees*) in their appropriate place, according to the order of Gen 9. The redactor of *Jubilees* refrained from separating the testament from the rewritten story when he included them in his composition, perhaps because they were juxtaposed in the text that he used as his source. Additional events, which occurred chronologically between the flood and Noah's death (the births of Kainan, Shelah, Eber, and Peleg; the division of the earth in the time of Peleg; and Noah's prayer),[42] were inserted by the redactor in their chronologically appropriate place, prior to the reference to Noah's death in *Jub.* 10:15–16, but the juxtaposition of the story of the vineyard and the testament attests to the original combination of these passages. When this unit was introduced into *Jubilees*, and woven into the chronological framework, the testament was dated in proximity to the story of the vineyard.[43]

The global principle in *Jubilees* for the ordering of stories is chronological—starting from the first week of creation until the Exodus from Egypt, the stories from Genesis and Exodus are presented in the order in which they occurred. Biblical stories were sometimes reordered so that they fit this chronological ordering principle.[44] This approach stands in contrast to the topical ordering principle found in the Pentateuch, according to which one subject was finished before moving on to the

---

[41] Charles 1902: 66 (title); van Ruiten 2000: 327–330; VanderKam 2001: 40–42.

[42] Noah's prayer against the evil spirits must appear after the testament because at the end of the story in *Jub.* 10:1–13, the spirits can no longer attack Noah's sons. In *Jub.* 7:27, Noah notes, "I myself see that the demons have begun to lead you and your children astray..."; if the prayer preceded the testament, then the spirits would not have been able to harm Noah's offspring.

[43] The dates in the story of the planting of the vineyard all fall within the 27th jubilee, during the 7th week (7:1–2), between the years A.M. 1317–1321. The testament is dated to the 28th jubilee (7:20), A.M. 1324–1372. The first event following the testament, the birth of Arpachshad, is dated to the first year of the 29th jubilee (8:1), A.M. 1373. It seems that the dating of the testament to the jubilee as a whole, without specifying which year, is an attempt to create the impression of complete chronological contiguity, without any gaps in time between the events.

[44] There are some exceptions to this rule (including Noah's testament), but I suggest that they all result from the inclusion of extant rewritten texts into the chronological framework of *Jubilees*; see ch. 4.

next. The biblical system is especially apparent when describing the lives and events of specific characters: the biblical authors first completed describing the life of one person (and his death) before moving on to the next person.[45] In the case of the stories about Noah, following the flood and the ensuing covenant between the Lord and Noah (Gen 6:1–9:17), the Pentateuch proceeds to tell the story of the planting of the vineyard, followed by Noah's death. According to Gen 9:28, Noah lived for 350 years following the flood, and some of the incidents mentioned in Gen 10–11 took place during this period of time: the births of Noah's grandchildren and great-grandchildren (Gen 10), and the first generations in the genealogical list in Gen 11.[46] However, in keeping with the topical ordering principle, the Pentateuch first tells of Noah's death, and finishes the cycle of stories that relates to him, and only then continues with the events of his descendants. In contrast, in *Jubilees*, the stories about Noah's descendants (8:1–8) were transferred to before his death, as was the description of the division of the land between his offspring (8:8–9:15, parallel to Gen 10). However, as noted above, the juxtaposition of the testament to the vineyard story in *Jubilees* is the result of the juxtaposition of the reference to Noah's death to the same vineyard story in Gen 9, i.e., according to the topical ordering principle. If so, the juxtaposition in *Jubilees* is not the result of the redactor's interference, since he normally worked according to a different (chronological) ordering principle. The redactor's contribution to this passage can be found in the date attached to the beginning of the testament, in an attempt to create chronological continuity between the testament and the surrounding texts.[47] Nevertheless, the order of the

---

[45] Compare for example the death of Isaac and the sale of Joseph (see p. 121), as well as the notice of Terah's death at the age of 205 in Gen 11:32 (according to MT and LXX), before the story of Abram's departure for Canaan at the beginning of Gen 12 (according to 12:4, Abram was 75 years old when left Haran; according to 11:26, Terah was 70 years old when Abram was born; Terah was therefore 145 years old when Abram departed for Haran, sixty years before his death). The SP to Gen 11:32 reads that Terah died at the age of 145, but this is a correction which is intended to create chronological continuity.

[46] There are many differences between the pentateuchal textual witnesses regarding the numbers in this list, and therefore the overlap between the lives of Noah and his descendants varies according to the specific text. The Tower of Babel story in Gen 11:1–9 is not dated, and there are no signs in the story regarding its chronologically appropriate place in Genesis.

[47] As we will see below, the reworking by the redactor includes the opening (vv. 20–21a) and conclusion (v. 39b) of the testament.

passages in *Jub.* 7 reveals the original ordering principle behind the juxtaposition of the story and the testament.

According to the possibility raised here, the redactor of *Jubilees*, who was responsible for the chronological framework of the book, was responsible neither for the rewriting of the vineyard story, nor for the juxtaposed testament. Rather, he copied a pre-existing text, and included it in his new composition. It is therefore difficult to accept that *Jub.* 7 and 10 both come from the same source, because: (1) they differ regarding the interpretation of the Watchers story;[48] (2) *Jubilees* 7 is supposed to appear at the end of Noah's life, and it is therefore difficult to posit that Noah's prayer (from ch. 10) originally appeared between the testament and his death. The duplication in the two passages regarding the spirits that were leading his sons astray also supports the conclusion that the two passages originated in different traditions.[49] The suggestion raised here based upon exegetical-redactional considerations corresponds to Kister's suggestion regarding the composition of *Jub.* 7 based upon halakhic-exegetical arguments. As he demonstrated, the halakhic stance regarding fourth-year produce reflected in the rewritten story at the beginning of ch. 7 contradicts the laws in vv. 35–37. Kister suggested that *Jubilees* preserves two different traditions which cannot be reconciled: according to the tradition embedded in the rewritten story, the fourth-year products of the vineyard have the same status as the second tithe which needed to be consumed in Jerusalem (as posited by the Pharisees), while according to the tradition in vv. 35–37, these fruits have the status of priestly gifts (as posited by the Qumran sect).[50] Verses 35–37 were apparently added secondarily to the rewritten story, and this addition led to the contradictions between the passages. It is possible that the chronological editor, who was responsible for the ordering of the chapters and addition of the dates, was the same person who added the legal passage in vv. 35–37, the redactor of *Jubilees* himself.[51]

---

[48] See above, pp. 146–154.

[49] It is possible that one story influenced the formulation of the other (it seems plausible that ch. 7 influenced ch. 10). This claim can help explain the disparity between the beginning of *Jub.* 10, which emphasizes how the spirits led Noah's sons astray, and the continuation of the story, which stresses the illnesses and suffering that the spirits caused them.

[50] See Kister 1992: 581–586. Werman (1999: 173–177) noted the common formulation of the story in *Jub.* 6–7 and in the *Genesis Apocryphon*.

[51] My slight hesitation to identify the author of this legal passage with the redactor (both halakhic and chronological) of *Jubilees* is the absence of the unique terminology found in the other legal passages throughout the book. In other legal passages, this

Did Enoch Die?

The identification of the exegetical problem regarding the dating of the testament allows us to understand a difficult verse in *Jub.* 7.[52]

The description of Enoch in the genealogical list of Gen 5 differs from all of the other people mentioned in a number of respects: (1) The length of his life, 365 years, is much shorter than any of the other people in that list; (2) the meaning of the statement, "Enoch walked with God" (5:22), is unclear; and (3) perhaps most perplexing is the absence of any explicit reference to his death with the formula generally used throughout Gen 5 ("and he died"), and in its place one finds an enigmatic description: "And Enoch walked with God; and then he was no more, for God took him" (Gen 5:24). Many early exegetes took this last verse to mean that Enoch did not die, but rather ascended to heaven and remained there with God.[53] This is the view expressed throughout *1 Enoch*, which describes Enoch's experiences and visions in heaven. *Jubilees* relates to the issue of the end of Enoch's time on earth in two passages:

> (4:23) He was taken from human society, and we led him into the Garden of Eden for greatness and honor. Now he is there writing down the judgment and condemnation of the world and all the wickedness of mankind. (24)...he was placed there as a sign and to testify against all people in order to tell all the deeds of history until the day of judgment.
>
> (10:17) He (Noah) who lived longer on the earth than (other) people except Enoch because of his righteousness in which he was perfect; because Enoch's work was something created as a testimony for the generations of eternity so that he should report all deeds throughout generation after generation on the day of judgment.

---

vocabulary bolstered the hypothesis of a halakhic redaction. If vv. 35–37 belong to the editorial stratum, and were not added at an even later stage, then one can suggest that the special terminology was not included by the redactor because it was not appropriate to the context of a testament. According to this explanation, the presence of the terminology is a sufficient, but not a necessary, condition to identify the work of the redactor.

[52] Prof. M. Kister suggested most of this solution based upon the analysis up to this point.

[53] Kugel (1997: 101) assembled many sources that express this view: LXX to Gen 5:24; *1 Enoch* 14:8; Sir 49:14; *2 En.* (recension J) 22:8; Philo, *Names* 38; Jospehus, *Antiquities* I, 85; IX, 28; Heb 11:5. As Kugel noted, there are some sources that explicitly establish that Enoch died—see *Tg. Onq.* to Gen 5:24.

Both sources reflect the same tradition about Enoch and his role in the world, and both are formulated in almost identical terms. Enoch will live separately from the rest of humanity, recording their actions until the "day of judgment," the point in time between this world and the eschatological era. Both express the idea that Enoch did not die, but rather lives apart from humanity.

In light of these two verses, scholars have noted the apparent contradiction with *Jub.* 7:39: "Now I (Noah) am commanding you, my children, as Enoch commanded his sons in the first jubilees, while he was living in its seventh generation, and he commanded and testified to his children and grandchildren **until the day of his death**." This verse seemingly refers to Enoch's death, which reflects a contradiction with the two other passages cited above.[54] One can explain this contradiction in one of two ways:

(1) Perhaps the various passages in *Jubilees* reflect two different traditions that were prevalent in antiquity regarding the question of whether Enoch died or not. This approach has implications for understanding the literary development of *Jubilees*. If one can identify an explicit contradiction between two verses, which cannot be reconciled, then that contradiction can be used to bolster the argument that the author or editor incorporated various traditions and sources into his new composition. Yet it seems that those exegetes who interpreted Gen 5:24 to mean that Enoch actually died (such as *Targum Onqelos*) are polemicizing against the more common opinion in the Second Temple period (which appears to be the simple meaning of the text), whether it be due to the difficulty in believing that a human being could ascend to heaven and live forever, or as part of the avoidance (attested in a later period) of traditions that venerate Enoch. There is no doubt that *Jub.* 7:38–39 respects Enoch, as he stands at the head of the chain of transmission that imparts authority to Noah's testament. Moreover, Enoch is a greater authority than any of the other characters specifically because he spent time in heaven and learned from the angels.[55] It is therefore difficult to interpret *Jub.* 7:38–39 as part of the tradition which minimized these aspects of Enoch's character.

---

[54] VanderKam 1989b: 50. Van Ruiten (2000: 343, n. 63) described the contradiction somewhat mildly: "It is somewhat curious that *Jub.* 7:39 states that Enoch testified to his children and grandchildren 'until the day of his *death*.'"

[55] Compare *Jub.* 4:16–24; and see Najman 1999: 384–385.

(2) *Jub.* 7:39b does not refer to Enoch, but to another character.[56] Syntactically, there is another option for the punctuation of v. 39, reading 39b as a new sentence, and not as the direct continuation of 39a:

> (a) Now I (Noah) am commanding you, my children, as Enoch commanded his sons in the first jubilees, while he was living in its seventh generation. (b) He commanded and testified to his children and grandchildren until the day of his death.

If v. 39b is read as the conclusion of the entire testament, then according to this division of the text, the subject of v. 39b should not be taken as Enoch, but rather, Noah.

The advantage of this interpretation is threefold: (1) It solves the contradiction with the other verses in *Jubilees* that claim that Enoch did not die. All of the relevant passages in *Jubilees* now reflect the tradition that Enoch ascended to heaven and lived forever. (2) This interpretation fits the literary structure of the testament, and creates a parallelism between its beginning and end:

> 20: During the twenty-eighth jubilee Noah began to <u>command to his grandchildren</u>... He <u>testified to his children</u>...
> 39b: And he <u>commanded</u> and <u>testified to his children and grandchildren</u> until the day of his death.

(3) Verse 39b can be seen as the redactor's attempt to solve the chronological-exegetical problem discussed earlier, of the testament being so far removed from Noah's death. In response to the question of why Noah offered his testament some 300 years before his death, v. 39b suggests an appropriate answer: this testament was not a one-time event, but rather, Noah continued to do so until the day of his death.

This interpretation of the opening and conclusion of the testament (vv. 20, 39) also allow us to more precisely understand the formulation "Noah *began* (*'aḫaza*) to command" (v. 20). The use of this verb is unusual in *Jubilees* for the introduction of testaments, as can be demonstrated by a comparison with the introductions to the other testaments in the book:

> 20:1–2:...Abraham summoned Ishmael and...He commanded them
> 21:1:...Abraham summoned his son Isaac and commanded him...
> 35:1:...Rebecca summoned her son Jacob and commandeded him...
> 36:1–3: Isaac summoned his two sons Esau and Jacob...This is what I am commanding you...

---

[56] As noted by VanderKam (1989b: 50), one Ethiopian manuscript (MS 58) added the word *la-matusālā*, reading "until the day of Methuselah's death." According to this manuscript, Enoch did not die—instead his son did, thus resolving the contradiction.

In each of these instances, the testament was a one-time event near the death of the speaker. However, Noah's testament, which was given approximately 300 years before his death, is described as the beginning of his testaments to his sons: Noah began to offer testaments to his descendants in the 28th jubilee, and continued to do so "until the day of his death." If in its original context the testament was given near the end of Noah's life (as evidenced by 7:27), it was transformed in the chronological framework into the opening round of a series of testaments that continued for 300 years until his death. In light of the theory proposed above regarding the literary development of *Jub.* 7, which assumes that the vineyard story and the testament were attached in the literary source used by the chronological editor of *Jubilees*, we can also add that the insertion of the story and the testament into the current location led to the adjustment of the introduction and the conclusion of the latter to the comprehensive chronological framework.[57]

---

[57] This change appears to have been implemented by this same redactor, but could theoretically have been created by a later scribe.

CHAPTER SEVEN

NOAH'S PRAYER (10:1–13)

Until now we have noted attempts to deemphasize the importance of the Watchers story for the question of the existence of evil in the world.[1] In contrast with the earlier traditions in *1 Enoch*, which viewed the sins of the sons of god and the women as the cause of a fundamental change in the nature of the world, *Jub.* 5 presents the story as a paradigm of reward for the righteous and punishment for the wicked, and emphasizes God's central role as a righteous judge. The story no longer revolves around the origin of evil in the world, but focuses instead on the appropriate behavior expected of every individual, thus blurring its original, mythological meaning.[2] Through the technique of adoption and adaptation of an earlier tradition, the reworked version succeeded in altering its emphases. Noah's prayer in 10:1–13 reflects a different kind of attempt to limit the importance of the Watchers story. Instead of the technique used in the earlier passages (moderation of a well-known tradition by transforming its message), *Jub.* 10:1–13 attempts to incorporate the Watchers traditions into a new theological construct.

Near the end of Noah's life, impure demons began to lead his children astray: "During the third week of this jubilee [33rd = A.M. 1583–1589] impure demons began to mislead Noah's grandchildren, to make them act foolishly, and to destroy them."[3] Noah's sons approached

---

[1] See the discussions in chs. 5–6 regarding *Jub.* 5 and 7.

[2] The traditions that attribute the origin of evil to the Watchers incident were well-known and authoritative in the late Second Temple period, and therefore could not be ignored. Cassuto ([1943] 1973) raised a similar claim regarding the biblical version of the sons of god story, describing it as a polemic directed against Canaanite mythology.

[3] The narrative background is almost identical to that of Noah's testament in *Jub.* 7:27: "For I myself see that the demons have begun to lead you and your children astray...," dated more than 200 years earlier, in the 28th jubilee (A.M. 1324–1372, according to *Jub.* 7:20). The repetition in these passages is problematic, particularly the use of the verb "began (*'aḥazu*)" in 10:1. If they began to lead Noah's children astray, how did they do so again in chapter 10? One can suggest a harmonistic solution, that the spirits first began to lead Noah's children astray immediately after the flood, stopped (perhaps due to Noah's testament?), and then began again close to Noah's death. However, there is no hint of such a development between the passages, and the

him and informed him of the demons' malicious behavior (10:2). As a result, Noah turned to God in prayer and implored him to protect his sons from these demons, and to imprison them in the place of judgment (10:3–7), a place where they will be unable either to harm his children and grandchildren or to cause them to sin. Their imprisonment in "the place of judgment" introduces an eschatological element into the story—the demons must presumably remain in this location until the great day of judgment. God answers in the affirmative, and commands his angels to bind the demons in the place of judgment. Noah's prayer was thus answered and succeeded in influencing the Lord's behavior.

The Relationship between Jubilees 10 and the Introduction to the Book of Asaph

Charles suggested that *Jub.* 10:1–15, together with 7:20–39, were part of a lost composition, entitled either the *Book of Noah* or the *Apocalypse of Noah*.[4] A parallel story to *Jub.* 10 appears in the introduction to a medieval medical text entitled *The Book of Asaph the Physician*.[5] The relevant passage in *The Book of Asaph* reads as follows:[6]

---

repetition remains. Regarding the literary development of *Jub.* 7, see pp. 158–163; in footnote 49, I suggested that the similarity between them is perhaps the result of the influence of 7:27 on ch. 10.

The issue of doublets is intensified when one compares Noah's prayer in ch. 10 to his testament in *Jub.* 7: if Noah was able to pray on behalf of his children, and therefore should have been able to help them when the spirits led them astray after the flood, why did he wait until the end of his life to pray for them? We have already noted that the order of chs. 7 and 10 is puzzling—not only does one expect Noah to have prayed when the problem first arose, but also that the testament should appear close to Noah's death, and not 300 years before then.

[4] For a survey of Noah traditions in Jewish literature of the Second Temple period, and the possible reconstruction of the *Book of Noah*, see Charles 1902: xliv, 62, 78; Flusser 1972; Stone 1972; García Martínez 1992: 1–44. However, Werman (1999) has expressed reservations regarding the idea that there ever was a *Book of Noah*.

[5] The text was published by A. Jellenik as part of a composition that he titled *The Book of Noah* (Jellenik 1938: 155–156). Regarding the date of the redaction of the *Book of Asaph* and the time in which Asaph actually lived, see Muntner 1957: 47–50. Muntner suggested that the original chapters, composed by Asaph himself, contain no Arabic medical terms, while in the later material, the Arabic influence is perceptible. He concluded that Asaph lived and wrote "before the Arab conquest of the Middle East" (Muntner 1972).

[6] This English translation is according to Himmelfarb 1994: 129–130, with minor variations. The translation is based upon the Hebrew text in Jellenik 1938: 155.

This is the book of remedies that the ancient sages copied from the book of Shem, the son of Noah. It was handed down to Noah on Mt. Lubar, one of the mountains of Ararat, after the flood. For in those days the spirits of the bastards began to attack Noah's children, to lead them astray and to cause them to err, to injure them and to strike them with illness and pains and with all kinds of diseases that kill and destroy human beings. Then all of Noah's children came, together with their children, and related their afflictions to Noah their father and told him about their children's pains. Noah was troubled, for he realized that it was because of human transgression and their sinful ways that they were afflicted with all kinds of sickness and disease. So Noah sanctified his children together with the members of his household and his house. He approached the altar and offered sacrifices, praying to God and beseeching him. He (God) sent one of the angels of the presence from among the holy ones, whose name was Raphael, to imprison the spirits of the bastards from under the heavens so they would do no more harm to mankind. The angel did so, imprisoning them in the place of judgment. But he left one in ten to go about on earth before the prince of enmity (משטמה) to oppress evil-doers, to afflict and torture them with all kinds of disease and illness and to afflict them with pain. The angel told him the remedies for the afflictions of mankind and all kinds of remedies for healing with trees of the earth and plants of the soil and their roots. And he sent the princes of the remaining spirits to show Noah the medicinal trees with all their shoots, greenery, grasses, roots and seed, to explain to him why they were created, and to teach him all their medicinal properties for healing and for life. Noah wrote all these things in a book and gave it to Shem, his oldest son, and the ancient wise men copied from this book and wrote many books, each one in his own language.

Charles supposed that the passage in the *Book of Asaph* is quoting the *Book of Noah*, and is not based upon *Jub.* 10:1–14.[7] However, I suggest that analysis of the version preserved in the *Book of Asaph* leads to the conclusion that it does indeed depend on *Jub.* 10:1–14.[8] After *Jub.* 10

---

[7] Charles 1902: xliv; Himmelfarb 1994: 128; Werman 1999: 172–174, especially n. 4.

[8] So also Stone 1999: 140. Dimant (1974: 128–130) suggested that this passage from *Asaph HaRofe* is "an excerpt of the text of *Jubilees* different from that known to us, and perhaps even a remnant of the Hebrew original of *Jubilees*" (translation mine—MS). Dimant explained the differences between *Jubilees* and *Asaph* as the result of the different aims of the two compositions. In particular, *Asaph* emphasizes medical illnesses and remedies, while *Jubilees* stresses moral or ethical ills. Himmelfarb (1994: 128–132) also addressed these differences and, following Charles, claimed that both *Jubilees* and *Asaph* are dependent upon a third work, the *Book of Noah*, and each one adapted details from the original in line with the new context (Himmelfarb identified an anti-magical tendency in *Jubilees*).

quotes Noah's prayer and tells how the angels informed him of the remedies, it is recorded that Noah "wrote down *in a book* everything (just) as we had taught him regarding all the kinds of medicine" (v. 13). This book of remedies is intended presumably for all of Noah's children, for according to *Jub.* 10:1–2, the demons attacked all of them. However, following this, it is described how Noah "gave *all the books* that he had written to his oldest son Shem because he loved him much more than all his sons" (v. 14). It is difficult to interpret that the books (in the plural) in v. 14 are the same as the book of remedies (in the singular) that was mentioned in v. 13, for the following reasons:

Werman (1999: 174, n. 4) claimed that the reference to remedies in *Jub.* 10:10, 12–13, in contrast to the beginning of the story that emphasizes ethical aspects, suggests that the author of *Jub.* 10 knew of the source of the introduction to *Asaph*, and made use of it in his own composition. According to her interpretation, *Jub.* 10:13b (which she quotes from VanderKam 1989b: "and the evil spirits were precluded from pursuing Noah's children") is the solution to the spirits leading Noah's descendants astray, and not the remedies mentioned in v. 12 (which in her opinion are a vestige of the joint source of *Jubilees* and *Asaph*). However, VanderKam's translation of this sentence is not literal (as he himself notes on p. 60). A more precise translation of this verse is: "And the evil spirits were *locked up from behind* (*ʾm-daḥra*) Noah's sons." The verse does not indicate that the spirits refrained from pursuing Noah's children, but rather, that they were unable to hurt them, once the angels had taught them both the remedies and the spirits' deceptions (v. 12a). As a result of the angels' teaching, the spirits no longer had any power over Noah's sons—they could not hurt them by means of illness, and could also no longer lead them astray. In any event, according to a number of biblical sources, illnesses are caused by sin, especially the violation of the covenant between the Lord and his nation (Lev 26:16; Num 12:10–11; Deut 28:22, 27, 35; so van Ruiten 2000: 340), and therefore the differences between physical illnesses and moral deceptions are not that far apart from each other.

Werman (ibid.) claimed that the version of the story in the *Book of Asaph* is more coherent than the one in *Jubilees*. However, there is a problem in the internal logic of the *Asaph* account, which does not exist in *Jub.* 10. According to the *Book of Asaph*, one tenth of the spirits were left under Mastema's control "to oppress evil-doers, to afflict and torture them...." In other words, the spirits punish the wicked, those who presumably deserve to be punished. However, if the wicked are the only ones being punished by the spirits, then why do Noah and his sons need to know the remedies? If Noah and his sons are righteous, then the spirits will not attack them, nor will they become sick; if they are evil, then their punishment is justified. The problem of the "spirits of the bastards," which caused Noah to pray to God, arose when they attacked those who were not deserving of punishment, such as Noah and his children. In contrast, in *Jub.* 10, the reason why the angels revealed the remedies to Noah and his sons is clear: "because he knew that they would neither conduct themselves properly nor fight fairly" (v. 10). If the Lord will allow one-tenth of the spirits to move around the world freely, they will harm both the evil and the righteous; therefore, the angels revealed to Noah all of the remedies and the spirits' deceptions so that they could defend themselves accordingly.

(1) The reason given in v. 14, "because he loved him much more than all his sons," does not fit the book of remedies, which was intended for all of Noah's offspring.
(2) The transition from the singular form "book" in v. 13, to the plural "all the books" seems to point to two different corpora.
(3) The nature of the books that Noah transmitted to his son Shem in v. 14 should be understood in light of the common idea in *Jubilees* of a (perhaps priestly) chain of transmission of knowledge from generation to generation.[9] Noah's death is reported (v. 15) immediately following the description of the giving of the books to Shem. The pattern of a father giving his books to one, special son close to his death recurs in *Jub.* 45:15–16: "He (Jacob) slept with his fathers...He gave all his books and the books of his fathers to his son Levi so that he could preserve them and renew them for his sons until today."[10] In light of the clear parallel between these two passages, *Jub.* 10:14 should be taken as part of the description of the chain of transmission, which began with Enoch and continued until Levi, the patriarch of the priests.[11] Therefore, v. 14 does not (only) describe the book of remedies mentioned in v. 13, but rather, all the knowledge passed on to the next generation.[12] The literary unit that contains Noah's prayer and the book of remedies therefore ends with v. 13; verse 14 opens the next unit, which describes the conclusion of Noah's life.

The nature of the "book(s)" in *Jubilees* is therefore not identical to its character in *Asaph*. It is clear from the introduction to *Asaph* that the book "which the ancient wise men copied...and wrote many books, each one in his own language," which Noah had given to Shem, is the book of remedies that Noah recorded from the angel. However, upon careful examination, the giving of the book first to Shem, which fits the general pattern in *Jubilees*, is extraneous in *Aspah*, as the wise men could have copied directly from Noah's (original) copy. Moreover, *Asaph* does

---

[9] Compare 7:38–39 (oral transmission); 12:27; 21:10; 39:6; 45:16, and see VanderKam 1997: 19; 2001: 43–44, 118–120.
[10] Charles (1902: 81, 244) noted the connection between the two verses.
[11] Adam is presented as a priest who covers his nakedness and offers incense in *Jub.* 3:27, but there is no reference to him writing books and then passing them on to his son.
[12] In contrast with scholars who interpret the two sentences as referring to the same thing; see Stone 1999: 139; van Ruiten 2000: 339; VanderKam 2001: 119.

not mention that Shem shared the contents of this book of remedies with his relatives, Noah's sons and grandsons, who were the demons' primary victims. The version found in *Asaph* appears therefore to be secondary, since it combined the two distinct kinds of books that Noah wrote, the book of remedies that he wrote for all of his children, and his books that he gave to Shem. In the combined version, the composition and transmission of the different books was transformed into the composition and transmission of one book, the book of remedies, which Noah gave to his son Shem. The version of the story in *Asaph* is thus dependent on the tradition in *Jubilees*.[13]

THE ORIGIN OF THE DEMONS AND THE ROOT OF EVIL IN THE WORLD

In the discussion above, I attempted to demonstrate that Noah's testament in *Jub.* 7 and Noah's prayer in *Jub.* 10 present two different versions of the story of the Watchers and their offspring.[14] According to the former, the intercourse between the sons of god and the women resulted in the birth of giants (נְפִילִים), while according to the latter it produced spirits (perhaps נְפָלִים).[15] It is therefore difficult to attribute both of them to the same (reconstructed) composition about Noah, unless the two disparate passages were already combined secondarily in the *Book of Noah*.[16]

The claim that these passages present different traditions, which were combined together in *Jubilees*, was bolstered by the analysis of the editorial considerations in *Jub.* 7.[17] In addition, the two traditions

---

[13] According to the description in the *Book of Asaph*, the spirits were imprisoned in בית המשפט. Grintz (1969: 127, n. 51) and Dimant (1974: 129, n. 352) demonstrated that this expression, meaning "place of judgment" (cf. 1QpHab VIII, 2), is an early expression (possibly reflecting the Hebrew *Vorlage* of the Ethiopic translation of *Jubilees*) that was no longer used in the Middle Ages, and therefore demonstrates that the Hebrew text of the *Book of Asaph* is not a translation from another language. The text adduced in the *Book of Asaph* therefore reflects an early, but secondary, Hebrew version of the story.

[14] See pp. 146–154.

[15] As suggested by Dimant 1974: 48–49.

[16] García Martínez (1992: 1–44) reconstructed a substantial composition, based upon almost all of the stories in Second Temple literature that mention Noah (for a summary of his conclusions, see pp. 43–44). It is however preferable to view most of the sources that he combines as diverse traditions concerning an important, ancient biblical character.

[17] See pp. 158–163.

are distinguished from one another regarding the origin of evil in the world.

In his prayer, Noah refers to the origins of the spirits, who are leading his children astray:

> You know how your *Watchers, the fathers of these spirits*, have acted during my lifetime. As for these spirits who have remained alive, imprison them and hold them captive in the place of judgment. May they not cause destruction among your servant's sons, my God, for they are savage and were created for the purpose of destroying (10:5).

The descendants of the Watchers are also referred to as "spirits" in some of the traditions preserved in *1 Enoch* (10:15; 15:8–11; 16:1; 19:1).[18] These traditions from *1 Enoch* assert that the spirits, the Watchers' offspring, corrupted people, leading them to sin, and damaged and brought affliction upon the world and its inhabitants. The spirits will be active until the great day of judgment in the eschatological age. The traditions about the spirits in *1 Enoch* come to explain the existence of evil, suffering, and misery in this world, and they guarantee that these evils will disappear in the future. The mythological story of the sons of god and the women describes the mixing of the heavenly and earthly realms, a combination that led to changes in the world order and to the entry of evil into the universe. The intercourse between divine beings and people, which led to the creation of the spirits or demons, is perceived in these traditions as the point in history at which time all of humanity began to suffer due to the evil in the world. Prior to this, and similar to the period of time that will follow the "great day of judgment," the world existed without evil or suffering. In the eschatological age, the world will return to its pristine, original state.

According to *Jub.* 10:5, Noah's prayer in *Jub.* 10 seems to follow Enochic literature, which perceives the Watchers story as the primary reason for the existence of evil. In the beginning, during Noah's lifetime, the Watchers themselves corrupted mankind, leading to the flood; later, the spirits, the Watchers' offspring, continued to act as did their parents. According to the traditions from *1 Enoch* referred to above, the

---

[18] See VanderKam (1978) 2000: 324; García Martínez 1992: 37. The other traditions, of course, view the giants or Nephilim as the offspring of the Watchers (see the Watchers story in *Jubilees* 5 and Noah's testament in *Jub.* 7:20–39). As was suggested on pp. 146–154, *Jub.* 10:1–13 reflects a tradition distinct from the other passages in *Jubilees* regarding the Watchers story, and therefore, the differences between them should not be resolved by means of harmonistic interpretations.

Watchers' sin with the women, which occurred during Noah's lifetime, and which led to the coming of the flood, was the incident that led to the fundamental change in the world. The mythological story, which tells of the mixing of heaven and earth, explains the wretched state of this world, a world of misery and suffering. However, the identification of *Jub.* 10 as the direct continuation of the position outlined in *1 Enoch* regarding the origin of evil overlooks the second half of the story in *Jub.* 10. After the Lord acceded to Noah's request to imprison the spirits in the place of judgment, Mastema, "the leader of the spirits," appeared, and requested from God that he leave some of the spirits under his control (v. 8). Mastema himself is not one of the spirits, but rather, he is accorded a higher status, presumably that of an angel.[19] His senior status is expressed in a number of details in the story:

(1) Mastema can negotiate with God, similar to the role of Satan in the narrative framework of Job. In Job, Satan belongs to a divine council, composed of the sons of god (Job 1:6).[20]
(2) Mastema refers to the spirits as a crystallized group, to which he does not belong: "leave some of *them* before me; let *them* listen to me and do everything that I tell *them*..." (10:8).
(3) Mastema has his own agenda (v. 8: "the authority of my will among mankind"), which is not dependent upon the existence of the spirits. Mastema needs the spirits because of the quantity of the evil in the world: "because the evil of mankind is great."[21] If Mastema worked alone, he would be unable to reach each and every individual, because there are too many evil people. The spirits, who "are

---

[19] Cf. the role of "the Satan" in the narrative frame in Job, and Zech 3:1–2; in both of them, Satan faces off against an angel or son of god. In *Jub.* 10:11, Mastema is referred to as "the Satan," an identification which removes any doubt about the equation of the two epithets.

[20] Dimant (1994: 108–109) states that "according to the book of *Jubilees*, there are no individual angels with their own personality or role before the flood" [translation mine—MS], and therefore Mastema is not mentioned prior to Noah's lifetime. At the same time, Dimant notes that "there is an anomaly here, since from his first appearance, Mastema comes to argue with God with authority and status." I would suggest that Mastema's status is due to his being an angel, created at the beginning of time (despite that he is not mentioned explicitly in *Jub.* 2).

[21] This reason, attributed to Mastema, is based upon Gen 6:5: "The Lord saw how great was man's wickedness on earth." According to the interpretation in *Jub.* 10:8, the Watchers incident (Gen 6:1–4) led to the increase of evil, but not necessarily to its creation. The author of this passage thus attributed to Mastema that which God saw in the biblical story. This substitution is similar to the trend found elsewhere in the book, whereby in certain stories the Lord was replaced by Mastema (17:15–18:19; 48).

savage and were created for the purpose of destroying" (v. 5), easily integrate into Mastema's plots and plans. The jobs of the spirits and of Mastema are differentiated both in their character and in their sequence: the spirits are intended for the purpose of "destroying and misleading" humanity, while Mastema is responsible for their punishment (v. 8). Furthermore, in terms of the order of events, first the spirits act, with the goal of causing people to fail, and only afterwards Mastema comes to punish the wicked: "For they are meant for (the purposes of) destroying and misleading *before* my punishment."

One can therefore conclude that the author of *Jub.* 10 did not merely copy the Watchers story, which he inherited from *1 Enoch*. Rather, he incorporated this tradition about the Watchers and their offspring, the spirits, within a new framework, which obscures their significance. The spirits no longer act according to their own needs, and do not make any decisions for themselves, but rather implement the authority of Mastema's will. The connection between the Watchers story and Mastema is an innovation of *Jubilees*, as Mastema is absent from all of the strata and traditions in *1 Enoch*.[22]

What is the purpose of the connection between the Mastema tradition and the Watchers story, including the creation of the spirits as the result of the intercourse between divine and human beings? The character Mastema as the head of the divine forces of evil first appears in *Jubilees*.[23] Mastema's other appearances throughout the book do

---

[22] Dimant 1974: 102. In her opinion, the story in *Jub.* 10 serves to explain "the constant source for the existence of evil in the world," as it maintains that the spirits and the Satan will go unpunished until the great day of judgment. However, her claim that the existence of the spirits "provides an explanation for the existence of evil in our current world, but not in the prehistoric, antediluvian reality that passed from the world" is difficult. According to the analysis presented here, *Jub.* 10 does not assume a fundamental difference between the pre- and post-flood realities, except for: (1) the quantity of humanity's evil, and as a result, (2) the need for Mastema to punish more people.

[23] In addition to ch. 10, see 11:1–5, 11–13; 17:15–18:19; 19:26–28; 48; 49:2. As will become evident from the analysis of *Jub.* 17:15–18:19 (the Akedah) and 48 (bridegroom of blood and the Exodus), and specifically regarding the question of the relationship between the legal passages and the rewritten stories (see chs. 9 and 10), it seems likely that the rewritten versions of these stories, which include Mastema, were already extant, and the redactor of *Jubilees* included them in his new composition. Mastema appears in those two passages by himself, and in contrast to the rest of his appearances throughout *Jubilees*, there are no spirits assisting him (see the discussion of the text of *Jub.* 48:16 on pp. 219–220). This difference strengthens the argument that these texts

not limit his activity to a specific period of time (even though he only appears for the first time in ch. 10).[24] Mastema is presumably an angel, as can be discerned from his opposition to the angel of the presence (chs. 17–18 and 48), and against God (ch. 10). It can therefore be assumed that Mastema was created with the rest of the angels on the first day of creation.[25] *Jubilees* 48 contributes that Mastema acted as the patron of Egypt, in contrast to the angel of the presence and God, who protected the Israelites.[26]

According to the description of the creation of the world in *Jub.* 2, God chose Israel as his nation and his first-born son[27] from the beginning of time (ibid. 19–21):[28]

> 2:19 [He said to us: "I will now separate for myself] a people among my nations. And [they will keep sabbath. I will sanctify them as my people, and I will bless them. They will be my people and I will be their God.][29] 2:20 And he chose the descendants of Jacob among [all of those whom I have seen. I have recorded them as my first-born son and have sanctified them for myself] for all the age(s) of eternity. The [seventh] day [I will tell them so that they may keep sabbath on it from everything," 2:21 as he blessed them and sanctified them for himself as a special people] out of all the nations and to be [keeping sabbath] together [with us.]

The election of Israel from creation as the Lord's personal possession establishes a certain world order, including the nations, from the

---

were not composed by the redactor, but rather were already in existence (this claim is made in chs. 9 and 10 based upon other considerations).

[24] The role of Mastema in Qumran sectarian literature is similar to that found in *Jubilees*, but for methodological reasons I have refrained from comparing them until after the study of the *Jubilees* material by itself.

[25] *Jub.* 2:2 provides a long list of different angels that were created on the first day. Although there is no explicit reference to Mastema in this verse, it is reasonable to assume that he was included in "all the spirits who serve before him...the angel...of all the spirits of his creatures which are in the heavens, on earth, and in every (place)."

[26] The view that the each of the "sons of god" is in charge of one nation, while YHWH himself is responsible for Israel, first appears in Deut 32:8–9 (according to the original text, as preserved in 4QDeut[j] and LXX), and is also reflected in *Jub.* 15:31–32. The book of Daniel mentions "the prince of Greece" (10:20) and the "prince of Persia" (10:13, 20), terms which are similar to the epithet "Prince Mastema." On the contrast (in a dualistic context) between Egypt and Israel/Jerusalem, see Dimant 2003.

[27] For the motif of Israel as a firstborn son in Jewish literature of the Second Temple period, see Kugel 1998a: 122–134.

[28] According to 4QJubilees[a] (4Q216) VII, 9–13 (eds. VanderKam and Milik; DJD 13, pp. 19–20).

[29] As noted by VanderKam and Milik (ibid., p. 22), there is not enough space in this row to reconstruct the Ethiopic text in its entirety. In the reconstruction that they suggested (quoted here), the combination of the election of Israel with the Sabbath law does not occur until v. 20b (instead of v. 19).

beginning of history. The choice of Israel is meaningless without other nations, and therefore God chooses them from "among my nations." This hierarchy of nations demands a parallel heavenly hierarchy, which also distinguishes between Israel and the nations. *Jub.* 15:30–32 explicitly outlines the contrast between God's relationship with Israel and his connection to the other nations:[30]

> ...But he chose Israel to be his people. 15:31 He sanctified them and gathered (them) from all mankind. For there are many nations and many peoples and all belong to him. He made spirits rule over all in order to lead them astray from following him. 15:32 But over Israel he made no angel or spirit rule because he alone is their ruler. He will guard them and require them for himself from his angels, his spirits, and everyone...

The meaning of God's choice of Israel is his direct adoption of them as a nation. Other nations also belong to God, but lack this same unmediated connection. *Jub.* 15:31 describes the spirits which try to lead the other nations astray. The interpretation of that verse in light of *Jub.* 10:5 leads to the conclusion that these spirits are the descendants of the Watchers. But it is difficult to accept this interpretation in light of the interdependence of election and direct adoption, which are both mentioned together in the rewritten creation story. The separation of Israel from the other nations in the first week corresponds to the differentiation of the Sabbath from all of the other days of the week,[31] and at the same time corresponds to a heavenly-cosmological system, according to which God appointed an intermediary angel for each nation.

Jubilees 10:5 is the only place in the book which explicitly refers to a connection between spirits (or demons) and the Watchers.[32] In truth, it is difficult to connect the sons of god story, which refers to a one-time event in history (despite its drastic effects), and a system that sets the world order from creation. This system includes two axes: on one side, the Lord and Israel (and perhaps the angels of the presence), who were already chosen at creation (*Jub.* 2:19–21); on the other,

---

[30] For an extensive discussion of this passage, see ch. 11.
[31] See Kister 2005.
[32] Dimant (1974: 101, n. 288) and Eshel (1999: 52) both view the juxtaposition of the passages in Noah's testament (7:20–39), between the Watchers story and Noah's comment that his sons are guilty of bloodshed under the influence of the spirits, as a hint to the relationship (Dimant) or as the logical connection (Eshel) between the two traditions.

Mastema, the misleading spirits, and the other nations. There is no natural place within this approach for angels that sinned and were transformed into corrupting spirits. The connection between these two viewpoints is therefore a secondary development in the history of the traditions. Their combination is apparently the result of the author's wish to incorporate the "spirits" traditions from *1 Enoch* into a different theological framework: a dualistic worldview. Thus the earlier traditions were preserved, but were infused with a new meaning regarding the question of the origin of evil in the world.[33]

---

[33] The theological "advantage" of a dualistic system that was in effect from the beginning of time (in contrast to a system that arose due to a one-time, unexpected event) is that God controls the entire world, and is not limited by his own creations. God can create the world, and preserve it (while according to the other position, God cannot preserve the world order which he himself established).

CHAPTER EIGHT

THE ACTIONS OF NOAH'S SONS

The Relationship between the Description of Noah's Sons' Actions (11:1–6) and Other Passages in the Book

The story in *Jub.* 11 relates to the transitional period from the days of Noah and his sons to Abraham's lifetime. *Jubilees* 10 tells of Noah's concerns over his sons' behavior, and the continuation of this story (11:2–4a) describes their actions following his death: warfare, the taking of captives, bloodshed, the consumption of blood, the construction of fortified cities, the establishment of the first monarchy,[1] the capture of cities, and the sale of their inhabitants into slavery. Ur, the son of Kesed, built a city that he called Ur of Chaldees,[2] and all of its citizens began to fashion "statues, images, and unclean things" for themselves. *Jub.* 11:4b–5 explains the cause of these sins (apparently including those sins mentioned in vv. 2–4a):

> The savage spirits[3] were helping and misleading (them) so that they would commit sins, impurities, and transgression. Prince Mastema was exerting his power in effecting all these actions and he sent, by means of the spirits, who[4] were placed under his control, to commit every (kind of) error and sin and every (kind of) transgression; to corrupt, to destroy, and to shed blood on the earth.

The evil spirits are a group of divine beings that are responsible for the sins of humanity. They mislead people so that they will commit sins

---

[1] According to Gen 10:10, "And the beginning of his kingdom was Babylon…," in reference to Nimrod. It is possible that the negative perception of the monarchy here is the result of the interpretive tradition regarding the character Nimrod, which derives his name etymologically from the root מ-ר-ד, "rebel."

[2] The name of the character here is taken from the name of the city "Ur of Kasdim" mentioned in the Bible. According to *Jub.* 11:3, the process was reversed, and the city was named after the person.

[3] VanderKam (1989a–b) reads a construct form here, and translates "the spirits of the savage ones" (the difference between the two alternatives rests on a minor difference in the form of the final letter in the Geʿez). However, the parallel expression in 10:13 suggests that the spirits themselves were savage.

[4] The translation of this clause relative to the spirits follows Ethiopic mss 21 and 51, which read *ʾəlla* (relative pronoun "who"), instead of *la-ʾəlla* ("to those who").

and impurities, and as a result, the people are punished. The spirits are under the control of Prince Mastema, who sends them to cause the people to sin. The description of the forces of evil, the spirits under the command of a specific character (in this case, Mastema),[5] is identical to the picture presented in other passages surveyed until now. Here too, neither God nor the people are directly responsible for humanity's sins, and for the presence of evil in the world, but rather, divine beings, "savage spirits," whose purpose is to corrupt and destroy the people.

Jubilees 11:1–6 is literarily dependent upon two other passages in the book: Noah's testament (7:20–39, and specifically v. 27) and Noah's prayer (10:1–13). The dependence upon 10:1–13 can be recognized in the presentation of Mastema's control over the spirits, who sends them to cause the people to sin, and consequently, to be punished.[6] However, in contrast to *Jub.* 10, there is no reference in *Jub.* 11 to the story of the sons of god, nor to the Watchers as the fathers of the spirits. The only connection mentioned is between the spirits and Mastema. It is reasonable, however, to assume that the absence of any reference to this earlier story is the result of the proximity of ch. 11 to the previous passage, thus obviating the need to repeat this detail.

The events attributed to the spirits under the control of Mastema in *Jub.* 11:1–5 fulfill Noah's predictions from his testament in *Jub.* 7:[7]

(a) Noah expresses concern that his sons will commit bloodshed (7:27): "For I myself see that the demons have begun to lead you and your children astray; and now I fear regarding you that after I have died you will shed human blood on the earth and (that) you yourselves will be obliterated from the surface of the earth." *Jub.* 11:1–6 constructs the description of Noah's sons' behavior using Noah's own words:

---

[5] *Jub.* 1:20 and 15:31–33 both use the epithet Belial, but there does not appear to be a difference between Belial and Mastema in reference to the roles of the character and his status in heaven and on earth.

[6] Compare 10:8: "Leave some of them before me; let them listen to me and do everything that I tell them, because if none of them is left for me I shall not be able to exercise the authority of my will among mankind, for they are meant for (the purposes of) destroying and misleading before my punishment."

[7] Noah's other statement in the testament, "because you have begun to conduct yourselves in the way of destruction, to separate from one another, to be jealous of one another, and not to be together with one another, my sons" (7:26), refers to past events that were already mentioned in that chapter: "(14) He (Ham) built himself a city...(15) When Japheth saw (this), he was jealous of his brother. He, too, built himself a city...(16) But Shem remained with his father Noah. He built a city next to his father at the mountain...."

11:1...and he named him Serug...11:2...Noah's children began to fight one another, to take captives, *and to kill one another; to shed human blood on the earth, to consume blood;*...to go to war—people against people, nations against nations, city against city; *and everyone to do evil*, to acquire weapons, and to teach warfare to their sons...11:5 Prince Mastema was exerting his power in effecting all these actions and he sent, *by means of the spirits, who were placed under his control, to commit every (kind of) error and sin and every (kind of) transgression; to corrupt, to destroy, and to shed blood on the earth.* 11:6 For this reason Serug was named Serug: *because everyone turned to commit every (kind of) sin.*

(b) Following the description of Noah's concern that his sons will be guilty of bloodshed (7:27), the testament includes a passage that compares human bloodshed with the consumption of animal blood (7:28–32).[8] Just as Noah predicted, his concerns came true following his death. According to 11:2, his sons soon began both to commit murder and to consume blood. This latter charge was also leveled before Noah's testament. At the end of the flood story, *Jubilees* describes God's covenant with Noah, which serves as the source for the festival of Weeks (6:17),[9] and which includes Noah's and his sons' oath not to consume blood (6:7–14). Following the oath, the narrator notes that during Noah's lifetime, he and his sons observed this law prohibiting

---

[8] The passage, which compares the spilling of human blood to the consumption of animal blood, can be viewed as a parenthetical statement within the warning against bloodshed and its effects on the earth. This parenthetical statement interrupts the continuity from 7:27 to 7:33: "(27)...and now I fear regarding you that after I have died you will shed human blood on the earth and (that) you yourselves will be obliterated from the surface of the earth. (33) For the earth will not be purified of the blood which has been shed on it; but by the blood of the one who shed it the earth will be purified in all its generations." Verse 33 is based upon Num 35:33–34, which addresses the shedding of human blood. The author of the testament has inserted the warning against consumption of animal blood within an envelope of explicit prohibitions against bloodshed, and thus succeeded in equating the two.

[9] The derivation of this law is formulated using the terminology found throughout *Jubilees* in the legal passages juxtaposed to rewritten stories: "*(6:17) For this reason it has been ordained and written on the heavenly tablets* that they should celebrate the festival of weeks during this month—*once a year*—to renew the covenant *each and every year*...(20) Now you command the Israelites to keep this festival during all their generations as a commandment for them: *one day in the year*...." In light of the conclusions of the analyses in chs. 1–3, 5, 9–10, this unique terminology indicates that the passage was composed by the redactor, who emphasized the nomistic aspect of the stories. Therefore, *Jub.* 6:18, which describes the grave behavior of Noah's sons, belongs to the same editorial stratum.

blood consumption, but after Noah's death, "his sons corrupted (it) until Abraham's lifetime and were eating blood" (6:18).[10]

One can explain the correspondence between Noah's testament (7:20–39), Noah's prayer (10:1–13), and the description of Noah's sons' actions (11:1–6) in one of two ways:

(1) All three passages were composed by the same author. According to this explanation, it is unsurprising that Noah's dire forecast in his testament came true in ch. 11, and that the roles of Mastema and the spirits in ch. 11 match the description in ch. 10. From a literary perspective, Noah's testament would then serve as a foreshadowing for that which will befall his children in the future. The realization of Noah's predictions transforms Noah, viewed from a religious perspective, into a true prophet.

However, in the literary analysis of chapters 7 and 10,[11] it became apparent that these two passages reflect different traditions of the Watchers story, and that ch. 7, including Noah's testament in vv. 20–39, is an independent literary unit that was included in *Jubilees*. If these conclusions are correct, then one cannot claim that all three of the passages under discussion here are the work of the same author.

(2) *Jubilees* 11:1–6 and 10:1–13 present an identical approach to the status and tasks of Mastema and the spirits. If we assume that this identity between the two passages points to the same provenance, and we accept the conclusion that 7:20–39 originated in a different tradition, then we cannot attribute the description of Noah's sons' behavior in 11:1–6 to the author of the testament. It is preferable to presume that *Jub.* 11:1–6 was composed specifically in order to present the realization of Noah's predictions from the testament, an extant source known to the author of *Jub.* 11. The phenomenon of "completing" a prophecy by adding its fulfillment is known from "harmonistic" biblical textual witnesses,[12] and from internal processes involved in the literary development of the biblical books.[13] The literary and religious implications

---

[10] Kister (1986: 7, n. 26) and Werman (1994) suggested that the accusation that many Israelites were guilty of consuming blood refers to an internal, halakhic polemic regarding the laws of slaughter. According to this interpretation, the text does not refer to actual consumption of blood, but to the legal presumption of their action: due to the halakhic status of their slaughter, it was as if they had consumed blood.

[11] See pp. 146–154, 158–163.

[12] See Tov 1985; Eshel 1990.

[13] Von Rad (1953) was the first to note the Deuteronomistic view of the realization of the word of God which finds expression in the book of Kings. Rofé (1986:

already mentioned also apply to the process of literary development suggested here.

As suggested above, *Jub.* 7:27 presents a specific stance regarding the origin of evil in the world: evil was created as the result of the sin of the sons of god with women. The giants, the offspring of this intercourse, fought with each other, and then they killed the people. The descendants of the giants, the spirits in *Jub.* 7:27, continue to perpetrate this evil in the world. Evil thus began at a specific point in time in the history of the world, and was not part of the Lord's original plan. Mastema is not mentioned in Noah's testament as the leader of the forces of evil in the world. In contrast, he is the leader of the spirits in Noah's prayer (10:1–13), but is not counted among the spirits, but rather, has the status of an angel. The spirits are his envoys to perform the "authority of his will" (10:8). According to my suggestion, Noah's prayer reflects an attempt to reinterpret, within a new dualistic framework, the "evil spirits" tradition from *1 Enoch*. The misleading spirits are the descendants of the Watchers, as in the earlier traditions, but evil began before they were created, and is under the authority of Mastema.

If so, the cause of sins in 11:1–6 differs from that in 7:27, even though the former presents the realization of the latter. As noted, Noah's testament continues the traditions from *1 Enoch* that attribute the origin of evil in the world to the spirits, the giants' offspring, who are themselves the offspring of the Watchers. Noah was concerned that these spirits would negatively influence his sons, and cause them to commit murder and to consume blood (7:27). In *Jub.* 11:4b–5, the spirits are indeed responsible for this, but they do not act on their own, but rather at the behest of Mastema. Continuing the idea expressed in Noah's prayer in *Jub.* 10, the myth of the origin of evil in the time of the Watchers was reinterpreted, and here too, the spirits were included in a different tradition, which views evil as an integral part of the world from the time of creation. The spirits, the descendants of the Watchers, were added to the existing axis of evil in order to lead humanity astray, thus leading to their punishment.

85–91) expanded and further developed this notion in the Deuteronomistic corpus. Rofé (1977) also analyzed the phenomenon of realization of prophecies in the writings of Trito-Isaiah. Cf. the comprehensive survey presented by Fishbane 1985, ch. 4 (pp. 443–524).

The Sending of Ravens and Birds (11:11–13)

The theory that the sending of the spirits in vv. 4b–5 is the result of a theological realignment of Noah's forecast in 7:27 finds confirmation further on in ch. 11, in a story that has no parallel in the Bible nor in the Jewish literature of the Second Temple period known to us. *Jub.* 11:11–13 describes the condition of the land in the period immediately prior to the birth of Abraham:

> Then Prince Mastema sent ravens and birds to eat the seed which would be planted in the ground and to destroy the land in order to rob mankind of their labors... (v. 11).

Parallel to *Jub.* 11:5, Mastema sends emissaries to harm humanity. But in contrast to the previous description, the damage described here is not the sins of and consequent punishments for mankind, but rather monetary harm. The ravens and birds ate most of the fruit off the trees (v. 13), reducing the farmers to poverty. The human suffering caused by the birds is part of the problem of evil in the world—if the Lord is omnipotent and good, why does he allow for poverty to exist? The solution suggested here is similar to that suggested elsewhere in *Jubilees*: God was not the source of these agricultural-financial problems during the time of Terah and Abraham; rather, the people's failures were the result of the interference of another heavenly character, Prince Mastema.

A comparison of verses 5 and 11 will allow for a more precise understanding of the "spirits" in the former:

Jub. 11:5	*Jub.* 11:11
Prince Mastema was exerting his power in effecting all these actions and he *sent* by means of the spirits, who were placed under his control to commit every (kind of) error and sin and every (kind of) transgression; to corrupt, *to destroy*, and to shed blood on *the earth*.	Then *Prince Mastema* sent ravens and birds to eat the seed which would be planted in the ground and *to destroy the land*

Both verses describe Prince Mastema as the head of the forces of evil in the world, whose goal is to destroy the land and its inhabitants. The most prominent difference between the two descriptions refers to the identity of those sent by Mastema:[14] "the spirits, who were placed under his control" (v. 5) are parallel to the "ravens and birds" (v. 11). Mastema is responsible for the evil in the world, and he has different means at his disposal to achieve his will. He is not limited to only the spirits, the descendants of the Watchers. The birds and ravens, his agents in v. 11, were created during the first week of the world. Their existence is not related to a specific event in history, such as the Watchers' sin, but rather, God intentionally created them as one component of his larger plan. If they too can serve as agents of Mastema for perpetrating evil, then one cannot focus the origin of evil on the Watchers' sin. Evil is an integral component of the world from its creation.[15]

---

[14] The nations have a similar role in *Jub.* 1:19; see pp. 255–256.

[15] It is not clear from this short story if the ravens and birds are always acting as agents of Mastema, helping him realize the "authority of his will," or whether, as part of the animal kingdom, they are available to him when necessary.

CHAPTER NINE

THE AKEDAH AND THE FESTIVALS OF PASSOVER/
UNLEAVENED BREAD (17:15–18:19)

Theological Questions

The Akedah story (Gen 22) has raised numerous difficulties for interpreters throughout history, first and foremost of which was the question, how God could have tested Abraham with such a cruel ordeal, and what purpose it could possibly have served. These issues are interrelated with other, more general, theological questions. If God can create such a cruel test, which is fundamentally evil, one can then conclude that God is not completely good. One who wishes to defend the assumption that God is all-good by assigning evil to some other being (as is done in polytheistic religions) must then limit God's omnipotence. If another power is able to bring about events in the world, then that power controls certain areas that God does not. The existence of evil in the world thus leads to one of two possibilities according to a monotheistic worldview: God is limited either in his power (or knowledge), or he is the source of the evil.

God's desire to test Abraham raises another theological conundrum. If God did not know the results of the test in advance, and he therefore needed to put him through this ordeal in order to find out whether Abraham would obey or not, one can conclude that God is not omniscient. On the other hand, if God knew the results of the ordeal before Abraham passed, then one can conclude that Abraham lacked the free will to choose whether to observe his commandment or not. God's foreknowledge limits human freedom, and vice versa.

The Akedah story in Gen 22 perhaps addresses both of these theological issues, albeit only indirectly. Gen 22:1 states that "God tested Abraham," without mentioning any other power. According to the view of this story, God himself designed this harsh trial. In the more abstract terminology used above, according the view of Gen 22, God is the source of evil, and he decided to demand that Abraham offer his son as a sacrifice. This god is omnipotent, and no other being caused him to make this decision. But Gen 22 also assumes that God did not know the results of this test in advance, as can be demonstrated by God's response after Abraham successfully fulfilled his request: "For *now* I know that you fear God, since you did not withhold your son, your only one, from me" (Gen 22:12). The story therefore assumes that God did not know in advance that Abraham would obey him and offer his son. Only after he witnessed Abraham's willingness to fulfill the divine commandment was he able to declare that *"now"* he knows that Abraham is loyal to him. The biblical story limits God's knowledge in order to allow for Abraham's free will. God in Gen 22 is omnipotent, but not omniscient.

The rewritten version of the Akedah story in *Jub.* 17:15–18:19 describes that the idea of testing Abraham did not originate with God, but rather with another character, Mastema; the Lord only approved his idea (17:16–18).[1] This trial is parallel to the one found in the narrative framework of Job, with one important difference: Mastema appears here in the place of Satan (Job 1:9–11). There is no explicit reason offered for Mastema's animosity towards Abraham (nor for Satan's towards Job), and it is presumably the result of his being completely evil.[2] If God is not responsible for planning this test, he cannot be blamed for this evil act. In contrast to the biblical Akedah story, the rewritten version in *Jub.* 17–18 presents the Lord as completely good. At the same time, the inclusion of the character of Mastema in the story and his ability to influence God to test Abraham, detract from YHWH's power as the exclusive sovereign over all that takes place in the world.[3]

According to *Jub.* 17:17, the Lord, in contrast to Mastema, knew in advance that Abraham was loyal. After Abraham indeed obeyed the Lord, and was willing to offer his son Isaac as a sacrifice, God stated: "because I now have made known[4] that you are one who fears the Lord" (*Jub.* 18:11); "I have made known to everyone that you are faithful to me in everything that I have told you" (v. 16). The Lord is omniscient,

---

[1] Compare *Jub.* 48:2 (bridegroom of blood) and 48:3ff. (plagues and Exodus).

[2] Regarding the character of Mastema in literature of the Second Temple period, and especially in Qumran texts, see van Henten 1999; Mach 2000.

[3] Both *Jubilees* and Job leave unanswered the question why God agreed to Mastema's (or Satan's) proposal.

[4] According to Kugel (1997: 172), the verb should be vocalized as a *pi'el* form (similar in meaning to the *hiph'il*), based upon the Latin translation. The Geʻez reads "I know," in the *qal* conjugation. The verb *y-d-ʻ* appers in the *pi'el* in only one biblical text, the *qere* reading of Job 38:12. However, it is clear from *Jub.* 18:16 that the rewriter interpreted the biblical story in line with the Latin version of v. 11.

and he therefore does not need this test for himself, but rather in order to publicize Abraham's loyalty. One aim of the rewritten version of the Akedah story in *Jubilees*, therefore, is theological, in order to transform the Lord into an omniscient God, who is also completely good.

THE AKEDAH STORY AS A FORESHADOWING OF THE PASSOVER LAW[5]

A number of elements in the rewritten version express another purpose of the story. In the rewritten version, there are four components whose combination can be best explained based upon the assumption that they allude to the Passover law:

The Date of the Story. The Bible does not date the Akedah story. In contrast, *Jub.* 17:15 notes that the discussion concerning Abraham took place on the 12th of the 1st month (Nisan).[6] This date is not mentioned elsewhere in *Jubilees*, and therefore does not appear to have any independent significance; rather, it is only important for the dating of the subsequent events in the story. The narrator did not specify whether God appeared to Abraham at night or during the day. However, both Genesis and *Jubilees* describe that Abraham woke up in the morning,

---

[5] The next two sections develop an idea suggested to me by Professor Menahem Kister.
[6] The formulation of the date in *Jub.* 17:15 is uneven: "During the seventh week, in the first year during the first month—in this jubilee—on the twelfth of this month." The reference to the twelfth of the month is separated from the number of the month itself by the mention of the jubilee. This stands in contrast to the general practice throughout the chronological framework, in which the month and date of the month are juxtaposed (compare the date formulae of Jacob's children in *Jub.* 28). In VanderKam's translation (1989b: 105), he rearranged the different components, switching the places of the jubilee and the day of the month, and thus adapted the chronological notice to the general practice (VanderKam notes the abnormal order of the date formula).
As I will attempt to demonstrate, the rewritten Akedah story stands in tension with the legal passage in *Jub.* 18:18–19. The date on which this story begins, the twelfth of the first month, is an integral part of the rewritten story, and thus cannot be attributed to the same stratum as the legal layer. In light of the conclusion reached above (p. 83), that the chronological and halakhic redactions are both the work of the same person, the chronological note in 17:15 should correspond to the legal passage at the conclusion of the story. However, in this case, the awkward formulation of the chronological framework hints to its complexity: in the original story, only the month and day of the month appeared. When the chronological framework was superimposed upon this rewritten narrative as part of the chronological redaction, the new elements (week, year, jubilee) were added, but not all of them in their appropriate location, leading to the separation of the references to the month and the day of the month.

immediately after the commandment (Gen 22:1–2; *Jub.* 18:1–2), and saddled his donkey in preparation for travel (v. 3). This order of events seems to indicate that the revelation occurred at night.[7] The author of the passage in *Jubilees* did not indicate explicitly whether Abraham departed on his journey on the twelfth or the thirteenth of the month. This question is related to the larger issue of whether the 24-hour day was defined as beginning from the night or from the morning. If the day begins in the morning, the Abraham arose on the morning of the thirteenth of the first month. Alternatively, if the day begins at night, then the revelation to Abraham occurred on the night of the twelfth,[8] and when he woke up the next morning, the date was still the twelfth of the first month.

As demonstrated by Baumgarten, in other passages in *Jubilees*, the 24-hour day begins at night.[9] The Passover law in *Jub.* 49:1 is perhaps the best proof for this assertion:[10]

> Remember the commandments which the Lord gave you regarding the passover so that you may celebrate it at its time on the fourteenth of the first month, that you may sacrifice it before evening, and so that they may eat it at night on the evening of the fifteenth from the time of sunset.

The appropriate time for offering the Passover sacrifice is on the fourteenth of the first month, before evening. The proper time for its consumption, the night that immediately follows, is defined as a new day: the fifteenth of the first month. In the biblical law (Exod 12:1–20), the date for slaughtering the passover is also the fourteenth of the first month (v. 6), and one must eat it that night. However, there is no explicit specification of the date of that night, either as the continuation of the fourteenth or as the beginning of the fifteenth (vv. 8–10). By including this chronological detail, the fifteenth of the first month, *Jubilees* emphasizes that a new day begins at nightfall, a position reflected in the rabbinic calendar as well.

Abraham received the divine command on the twelfth of the first month at night, and departed on the same date in the morning. Gen

---

[7] See Radaq ad loc.; Maimonides, *Guide to the Perplexed* III, 24; Sarna 1989: 151.

[8] Even if one accepts that the 24-hour period begins at night, if the revelation occurred during the daytime hours (before nightfall) of the twelfth of the first month, then the next morning would already be the thirteenth of the month. However, it is more plausible that the revelation took place at night, because v. 3 explicitly states, "And Abraham got up in the morning."

[9] Baumgarten (1958) 1977, in contrast with previous scholars.

[10] Baumgarten (1958) 1977: 126.

22:4 tells: "On the third day Abraham looked up and saw the place from afar." The statement that he saw "the place" on the third day is repeated in *Jub.* 18:4. The third day for this journey would therefore fall on the fourteenth of the first month. According to the chronological data provided in (the narrative part of) this section, the Akedah took place on that very same day, on the date designated in the Bible for the festival of Passover.[11] The story does not convey that they remained for any period of time in the land of Moriah, the location of the Akedah. There is no explicit mention in the story of the time it took them to return to Beersheba, but there is no reason to assume that it lasted longer than the three-day journey needed to reach "the place."

The following chronology can be sketched based upon the temporal details included in the story, and the chronological details embedded therein. The twelfth of the first month falls out on a Sunday according to the *Jubilees* calendar:

Month 1

Sunday	Monday	Tuesday	Wednesday	Thursday	Friday	Sabbath
12	13	14	15	16	17	18

Abraham and Isaac arrived at the location of the Akedah on Tuesday, the fourteenth of the first month. Presumably, they returned to Beersheba three days later, on the seventeenth of the first month.[12]

Baumgarten objected to this interpretation for two reasons:[13]

(1) According to the conclusion of the passage in *Jub.* 18:18–19, the Akedah story serves as a precedent for the law of the feast of Unleavened Bread. The length of this festival is seven days, while according to the interpretation offered above, in which Abraham

---

[11] Exod 12:6; Lev 23:5; Num 28:16.
[12] This is similar to the chronology proposed by Goudoever 1961: 68; Jaubert 1963: 90, n. 5; Vermes 1973: 215, n. 3. Jaubert (1953: 252–263; 1965: 26 [translation of the 1957 book]) suggested that Abraham departed on the thirteenth of the first month, and arrived at Mount Zion on the fifteenth, but still dated his return to the seventeenth of the month. It is crucial for Jaubert that Abraham return prior to the eighteenth of the first month, which falls out on the Sabbath in the *Jubilees* calendar, for this supports her thesis that the patriarchs did not journey on Sabbath according to this book. Both Daly (1977: 55) and García Martínez (1997: 253) also date the Akedah to the fifteenth of the month, but the discussion above clarifies that the precise date is the fourteenth of the month.
[13] Baumgarten (1963) 1977: 103–104.

departed on the twelfth and returned on the seventeenth, his journey lasted only six days.¹⁴

(2) According to the etiology in *Jub.* 18:18–19, the journey began on the fifteenth of the first month and ended seven days later. Any other interpretation spoils the parallel between the narrative and the law.

Transferring the date of Abraham's departure to the fifteenth of the first month does indeed create a correspondence between the law and the narrative, but at the same time renders the explicit date of the revelation meaningless. Baumgarten does not explain why the commandment to Abraham was given on the twelfth of the month, if he was only to depart three days later. He also overlooked the order of events in the passage, according to which Abraham's awakening and departure (18:3) are mentioned immediately after the commandment (v. 2).¹⁵

Isaac as a firstborn son. When the Lord commanded Abraham to offer Isaac as a sacrifice, he described Isaac through a series of epithets: "your son, your only one (יחידך), whom you love, Isaac" (MT Gen 22:2). The description of Isaac as the "only" son did not truly fit Isaac, as Ishmael was also Abraham's son. According to *Jub.* 18:2, Abraham was commanded to "Take your son, your dear one whom you love—Isaac."¹⁶ In two other places in this chapter, the term "your only one" was replaced by a different epithet, "your firstborn":

---

¹⁴ Baumgarten ([1963] 1977) wrote his article in response to Jaubert's claim (1953; 1957) that the journey lasted five days. Jaubert (1963; 1965: 149, n. 18) changed her opinion, and came to the conclusion that it lasted for six days, from the twelfth of the first month until the seventeenth. Baumgarten's question though still remains.

¹⁵ VanderKam (1979: 393–394) also dates the events in the story according to the legal passage in 18:18–19, similar to Baumgarten's approach.

¹⁶ LXX translates יחידך here as τὸν ἀγαπητόν (and similarly in vv. 12, 16). Some (Zakovitch 1977: 106, n. 33; Salvesen 1991: 207) have suggested retroverting this translation into a Hebrew reading ידידך; for ἀγαπητός = ידיד, see Ps 45(44).tit; 60(59):7; 84(83):1; 108(107):7; 127(126):2 (cf. also Ps 68[67]:13, and Isa 5:1 [= דוד]). However, as noted by LSJ, p. 6, this Greek word carries the meaning "that wherewith one must be content..., *hence of only children*" (emphasis mine). As can be seen by the list of examples adduced in LSJ, this meaning is found already in classical Greek. The translation is thus appropriate to יחיד in Gen 22 (vv. 2, 12, 16), in addition to the same equivalence in Judg 11:34; Jer 6:26; Amos 8:10; Zech 12:10; Prov 4:3; cf. Wevers 1993: 316; Zipor 2005: 268. It is possible that the Geʿez translator misunderstood the special connotation of the term τὸν ἀγαπητόν in his *Vorlage*, and thus translated here "your dear one," from the Greek verb ἀγαπάω.

Gen 22:12	*Jub. 18:11*
because I now know that you are one who fears the Lord	because I now have made known that you are one who fears the Lord
and you did not withhold your son, your only one from me.	You have not refused me **your first-born son**
Gen 22:16	*Jub. 18:15*
because you have done this thing	because you have performed this command
and have not withheld from me your son, your only one	and have not refused me **your first-born son** whom you love

The interchange of "only son" and "first-born son" does not solve this problem completely, as Isaac was also not Abraham's first-born. It is possible that Isaac was legally considered the first-born son, since he was born to Abraham's official wife, while Ishmael was the son of his concubine Hagar.[17] However, it is unclear why the rewriter of the narrative felt the need to add this new element to the story specifically in these two verses, while leaving it out of v. 2. Is it possible that this detail is of significance beyond the immediate exegetical question of the meaning of the word יחיד?[18]

The Sheep. Both in Gen 22 and in *Jub.* 18, Isaac asks his father about the whereabouts of the sheep that is to be offered as a sacrifice (Gen 22:7; *Jub.* 18:6). In both works, Abraham responds that God will provide it (Gen 22:8; *Jub.* 18:7). This reply does indeed come to fruition at the end of the story: just as Abraham was ready to slaughter Isaac (and thus passed the test), God showed him a ram, and Abraham offered it as a sacrifice in place of his son (Gen 22:13; *Jub.* 18:12). The motif of the sheep is not the innovation of *Jub.* 18, but already appeared in its source, Gen 22, from which it was adopted almost word for word.

Mount Zion. The biblical story does not mention where the Akedah took place. In the beginning of the chapter, the Lord commands Abraham to journey to "the land of Moriah...on one of the mountains" (Gen 22:2), but the specific location is left unspecified. Following the Akedah, Abraham names the site "the Lord will See as is said today,

---

[17] Cf. Philo, *Abraham* §168, who raised a similar claim.
[18] The words בכור and יחיד appear in parallel in Zech 12:10, and thus might be related in meaning. However, the parallelism there more likely indicates the special status of these two kinds of children, the first-born and the only child, and not their equivalence. The use of the word בכור in our chapter fits a larger pattern throughout the story, as will be demonstrated.

'on the mountain the Lord appears'" (Gen 22:14), a reference to the Jerusalem temple. Many scholars have already noted that the second half of the verse was written at a time when the temple already stood on a mountain called "the mountain of the Lord" (cf. Isa 2:3; 30:29; Mic 4:2; Zech 8:3).[19] The tradition that the Akedah took place in Jerusalem was known to the author of 2 Chr 3:1, who referred to the Temple Mount as "Mount Moriah," similar to "the land of Moriah" in Gen 22:2.[20] Genesis 22 thus alludes to the location of the Akedah as the Temple Mount in Jerusalem, but *Jubilees* states this explicitly: "Abraham named that place 'The Lord Saw' so that it is named 'The Lord Saw.' *It is Mt. Zion.*" (*Jub.* 18:13).

The rewriting of the Akedah story in *Jubilees* combines all four of these motifs: (1) the Akedah is dated to the fourteenth of the first month; (2) Isaac is described as a first-born son; (3) the slaughter of a sheep/ram; (4) the identification of the location of the Akedah as Mount Zion. The combination of these four motifs appears in only one context in the Bible: the Passover law. Following the description of the plague of the firstborn in Exod 11:4–8, Exod 12 details the law of the Passover in Egypt, and describes the power of its blood to protect the Israelite firstborn. The law requires that each household take a lamb on the tenth of the first month (v. 3), keep it until the fourteenth of the month, and then slaughter it at twilight (v. 6). After the slaughter of the paschal lamb, the Israelites took its blood and placed some on the lintel and doorposts of their homes (v. 7), and thus the Israelite firstborn were protected (vv. 12–13). As emphasized twice in Exodus (11:5; 12:12), "every firstborn in the land of Egypt" was in danger, and only the slaughter of the lamb and the smearing of its blood at the entrance to their houses saved the Israelite firstborn.

The addition of Mount Zion transforms the allusion to Jerusalem to an explicit narrative detail. The emphasis on the Temple Mount as the location of the Akedah is related to the law of the Passover offering at the Jerusalem temple.[21] The law in Exod 12:3–4, 7 describes the Passover sacrifice as a family offering, offered by each household in its own home. In contrast, Deut 16:2 demands that it be offered "at the

---

[19] See the commentary of Ibn Ezra at the beginning of Deuteronomy. Sarna (1989: 154) and Zakovitch (1992: 30) both view the sentence "as is said today..." as a secondary element in the text.

[20] These are the only two instance of the word "Moriah" in the Bible.

[21] Daly 1977: 55.

place where the Lord will choose to establish his name," i.e., in the central temple. Following in the footsteps of the Deuteronomic law, 2 Chr 35, which describes the festival of Passover during Josiah's reign, tells that they brought their sacrifices to the Jerusalem temple. This is also explicitly established in *Jub.* 49:16–21:

> (16) It is no longer to be eaten outside of the Lord's sanctuary but before the Lord's sanctuary...(17) Every man who has come on its day, who is 20 years of age and above, is to eat it in the sanctuary of your God before the Lord, because this is the way it has been written and ordained—that they are to eat it in the Lord's sanctuary. (18)...until the time when the Lord's temple will be built in the land, they are to come and celebrate the passover in the Lord's tabernacle and sacrifice it before the Lord from year to year. (19) At the time when the house is built in the Lord's name in the land which they will possess, they are to go there and sacrifice the passover...(20)...and are to eat its meat roasted on a fire in the courtyard of the sanctuary in the name of the Lord. (21) They will not be able to celebrate the passover in their cities or in any places except before the Lord's tabernacle or otherwise before the house in which his name has resided...

In contrast to the other motifs, the idea of offering the Passover sacrifice specifically on Mount Zion does not appear in Exod 12, but rather in other biblical sources, and primarily Deut 16:2. The rewriter of the Akedah story clearly read all of the biblical Passover laws harmonistically, combining them together, similar to the approach reflected in 2 Chr 35 and *Jub.* 49. Therefore, even though the Jerusalem motif is absent from the law in Exod 12, the rewriter viewed it as part of the Passover law.

The revision in *Jubilees* fashions a parallelism between the Akedah story and the Passover law (mainly Exod 12): the life of Isaac "the firstborn" was in danger as a result of Mastema's provocation; Abraham almost slaughtered him on the fourteenth of the month at God's command; Isaac was saved at the last minute, and in his place, Abraham slaughtered and sacrificed a lamb on Mount Zion. Similarly in Egypt: the lives of the firstborn were in danger (according to *Jub.* 49:2, the "forces of Mastema" were the ones sent to kill them);[22] the firstborn were saved due to the offering of the paschal lamb on the fourteenth

---

[22] In addition to the desire to distance God from this cruel act, it is possible that the insertion of Mastema in that story reflects interpretation of the term המשחית in Exod 12:13.

of the month. The rewritten story should therefore be viewed as a foreshadowing of the pentateuchal Passover laws.[23]

The Legal Passage (18:18–19)

The rewritten story ends in v. 17 when Abraham and Isaac return to Beersheba (parallel to Gen 22:19). Following this, *Jubilees* presents a law derived from this story:

> (18) He used to celebrate this festival joyfully for seven days during all the years. He named it the festival of the Lord in accord with the seven days during which he went and returned safely. (19) This is the way it is ordained and written on the heavenly tablets regarding Israel and his descendants: (they are) to celebrate this festival for seven days with festal happiness.

Subsequent to their seven-day journey (to the location of the Akedah and back), Abraham joyously celebrated a "festival of the Lord" every year. Since the story took place during the first month (i.e., Nisan), it can be deduced that this seven-day celebration is the festival of Unleavened Bread.[24] *Jub.* 49:1–2 refers to the fifteenth of the first month as "the beginning of the festival and the beginning of joy," since the holiday begins on the fifteenth and continues until the twenty-first of the month.

Jub. 18:18 establishes this festival corresponding to the seven-day journey during which Abraham went and returned from the Akedah. The number seven does not appear in the rewritten story itself, and as noted above, from an analysis of the story alone, it appears that the journey lasted five or six days. However, even if one reads the story according to the halakhic passage at the end, and one adopts the reading that the journey lasted seven days, there is still a disagreement between the two sections. The story counts the seven days from the twelfth of the month until the eighteenth, while the legal passage refers to the period from the fifteenth to the twenty-first. If the author wished to connect the Akedah story to the festival of Unleavened Bread, one would expect complete

---

[23] Goudoever 1961: 68. See *Mek. RSB"Y, Pisha* 7; that source connects the blood placed on the doorposts with the blood spilled at the Akedah (Vermes 1973: 215–216). See also *Exod. Rab.* 15:11, which dates the Akedah to the month of Nisan (Spiegel 1967: 56).

[24] Exod 12:15–20; 34:17; Lev 23:6–8; Num 28:17–25; Deut 16:8.

agreement in reference to the dates of the journey, which serve as the source for the festival, and the dates of the festival itself.

Scholars have suggested two main approaches to solve this disparity between the rewritten story and the legal passage:

(1) Goudoever suggested that Abraham himself celebrated the festival for seven days, from the twelfth to the eighteenth.[25] This understanding is the result of the interpretation of *Jub.* 18:18 in light of the rewritten story: "He used to celebrate this festival joyfully for seven days during all the years... *in accord with the seven days during which he went and returned safely.*" Goudoever understood this to mean that he observed the festival on the same dates as the roundtrip journey. Verse 19 describes the seven-day festival which was observed by the Israelites for all generations, and therefore it certainly refers to the festival of Unleavened Bread known from the Pentateuch, which takes place from the fifteenth to the twenty-first. According to Goudoever, the legal passage needs to be interpreted in light of the rewritten story: Abraham observed the festival according to the dates of the story, and not the dates mentioned explicitly in the pentateuchal laws.

The difficulty in this solution is that the distinction between v. 18 (Abrahm's observance of the festival) and v. 19 (the eternal law for Israel) is uncharacteristic of the legal passages in *Jubilees*. The halakhic passages generally attempt to ground the pentateuchal laws in the actions of the forefathers. By and large, the formulation and style of these legal passages are based upon the following pattern: first the narrative details necessary for the legal precedent are reviewed,[26] and then the law for future generations is derived from them. For example,

> 3:8 [PRECEDENT:] In the first week Adam and his wife—the rib—were created, and in the second week he showed her to him. [LAW:] Therefore, a commandment was given to keep (women) in their defilement seven days for a male (child) and for a female two (units) of seven days. 3:9 [PRECEDENT:] After 40 days had come to an end for Adam in the land where he had been created, we brought him into the Garden of Eden to work and keep it. His wife was brought (there) on the eightieth day. After this she entered the Garden of Eden. 3:10 [LAW:] For this

---

[25] Goudoever 1961: 68–69.
[26] As I have attempted to show, the narrative elements within the legal passages that serve as the basis for the derivation of the laws do not always agree with the details of the rewritten narrative.

reason a commandment was written in the heavenly tablets for the one who gives birth to a child: if she gives birth to a male, she is to remain in her impurity for seven days like the first seven days; then for 33 days she is to remain in the blood of purification. She is not to touch any sacred thing nor to enter the sanctuary...3:11 As for a female she is to remain in her impurity for two weeks of days like the first two weeks and 66 days in the blood of her purification. Their total is 80 days...

The author of the legal passage in *Jub.* 3 summarizes the event or action upon which the law is based, and then quotes the law itself. In both sections, the precedent matches the derived law. In the case of postpartum impurity, the numbers recounted in the narrative precedents match the numbers in the law itself, because they have been added in order to justify the latter.

Jubilees 18:18–19 fits this pattern of the legal passages: "[PRECEDENT:] He used to celebrate this festival joyfully for seven days during all the years. He named it the festival of the Lord in accord with the seven days during which he went and returned safely. [LAW:] This is the way it is ordained and written on the heavenly tablets regarding Israel and his descendants: (they are) to celebrate this festival for seven days with festal happiness." As in the legal passage in *Jub.* 3, in which the precedent and the law match precisely, one should also interpret the precedent in 18:18, Abraham's celebration of the seven-day festival, as parallel or identical in its dates to the seven-day festival in the derived law (v. 19). If so, *Jub.* 18:18 assumes that Abraham's journey began on the fifteenth of the first month, and continued until the twenty-first, in contrast to Goudoever's suggestion to interpret it in light of the dates in the rewritten story.

(2) Baumgarten, and subsequently VanderKam,[27] interpreted the chronology in the rewritten story in light of the dates in the legal passage. According to them, if the festival of Unleavened Bread begins according to the pentateuchal laws on the fifteenth of the first month, then Abraham's departure to the Akedah took place on the same date. This approach ignores the explicit date in *Jub.* 17:15, the revelation to Abraham on the twelfth of the first month. If Abraham did not depart until the fifteenth of that month, one can conclude that he waited three days before leaving, even though there is no hint of

---

[27] Baumgarten (1963) 1977: 103–104; VanderKam 1979: 393–394. VanderKam agrees with Baumgarten regarding the dates of the journey, but not with his conclusion about whether Abraham traveled on the Sabbath or not.

such a delay in the story. If Abraham did not depart immediately, it is unclear why the date of the revelation was included at all in the story. In addition, Baumgarten's (and VanderKam's) solution eliminates the special connection in the rewritten narrative between the Akedah and the Passover law.

These two explanations both attempt to resolve the tension between the rewritten story and the legal passage: one interprets the legal passage according to the story, and the other reads the story according to the legal passage. However, in view of the difficulties created by the juxtaposition of the rewritten story and the legal passage, it seems preferable to let this tension stand. The attempts to blur the differences between the two sections have led scholars to interpret each of the passages against their plain meaning. If the two passages do not correspond to each other, or even contradict one another (as in this case), it is reasonable to assume that they are of different provenance.

From a literary perspective, the legal passage (vv. 18–19) is not an organic part of the story. It appears after Abraham and Isaac returned to Beersheba, which is the point at which the story in Gen 22 ends. One can also point to a certain unevenness at the seam between the rewritten story and the legal passage: "He used to celebrate *this festival* joyfully for seven days during all the years. He named it the festival of the Lord...." The author of this verse apparently assumed that this festival was already mentioned previously, and he therefore called it "this festival." But the rewritten narrative does not mention any festival, neither explicitly nor implicitly. This tension stands out in comparison with a parallel case, the establishment of the festival of Booths in ch. 16. *Jubilees* 16:20 reads: "There he [Abraham] built an altar for the Lord... he celebrated a joyful festival in this month—for seven days—near the altar which he had built at the well of the oath." The story there includes a detailed description of the first time Abraham celebrated the festival: "He constructed tents for himself and his servants during this festival. He was the first to celebrate the festival of tabernacles on the earth" (v. 21). In v. 20, the festival is still described indefinitely, "a joyful festival," since it had not yet been mentioned in the story. Only in v. 21, after the reader has already been informed of the festival's existence, does the author refer to it as "this festival" and the "festival of tabernacles."

Summary

The rewritten Akedah story in *Jubilees* foreshadows the pentateuchal Passover law by dating the event to the fourteenth of the first month, and by adding the motif of Isaac as a firstborn. In contrast, the legal passage dates Abraham's journey to the dates of the festival of Unleavened Bread. Despite the chronological proximity of these two holidays in the calendar, the different methods used to date the events surrounding the Akedah, and the literary relationship between the two sections, lead to the conclusion that the two passages were composed by different authors.

CHAPTER TEN

THE EXODUS (*JUBILEES* 48–49)

Replacing God with Mastema

The enslavement in and Exodus from Egypt are described in detail over the first fifteen chapters of the book of Exodus. In contrast, *Jubilees* drastically abridges this story, which extends from the end of ch. 46 through ch. 49.[1] This abbreviation is most pronounced in ch. 48, parallel to Exod 3–14, which includes the story of the burning bush, the bridegroom of blood, Moses and Aaron appearing before Pharaoh, the plagues, and the Exodus itself. This drastic reduction makes it difficult to analyze the rewritten narrative's interpretation of specific biblical verses or details. However, this abridged approach reveals how the rewriter understood the story as a whole, thus allowing for the identification of the general aims in this reworked version.

When Moses returned to Egypt from Midian,[2] he was confronted by Prince Mastema, who tried to prevent him from returning to Egypt in order to save Israel: "(2) You know... and what the prince of Mastema wanted to do to you while you were returning to Egypt—on the way at the lodging place.[3] (3) Did he not wish with all his strength to kill you and to save the Egyptians from your power because he saw that

---

[1] The rewritten story itself is in fact even shorter, from the end of ch. 46 through ch. 48, since ch. 49 contains the Passover laws (parallel to Exod 12–13).

[2] The Ethiopic translation does not explicitly mention Midian, neither in *Jub.* 47:12 (parallel to Exod 2:15) nor in *Jub.* 48:1 (*wanabarka **həyya***, "you lived **there**"). Charles translated according to the Latin version (*in terram madfiam]*, "in the land of Mid[ian]"). VanderKam (1989b: 309) suggested that the lack of detail reflected in the Geʿez translation is the result of the abridgment of the vast material from Exodus, and the Latin translation reflects, in his opinion, an exegetical expansion intended to make this verse correspond to Exod 2:15. Another "missing" detail in the rewritten story is the commissioning of Moses to return to Egypt in order to save the Israelites; the reader is only made aware of it when Mastema tries to prevent him from arriving there, although it is hinted at already in v. 2: "You know what was said to you at Mt. Sinai" (in contrast to VanderKam's translation, based upon the Latin text: "You know who spoke to you at Mt. Sinai").

[3] Most interpreters have had difficulty with the Ethiopian word *ba-ʾalāte*. The Latin translation reads: *in refectione*, and this version corresponds with the Hebrew במלון (lodging place, Exod 4:24).

you were sent to carry out punishment and revenge on the Egyptians?" (*Jub.* 48:2–3). This passage parallels the enigmatic episode in Exod 4:24 (MT): "And he was on the way to the lodging place, and YHWH encountered him and sought to kill him." Interpreters have already noted the problems raised by this verse:

(1) From an exegetical perspective, it is difficult to understand why God wanted to kill Moses,[4] if he commanded him to return to Egypt in v. 19.[5] Indeed, the passage in Exod 4:24–26 seems disconnected from its context: in the previous verses, God sends Moses back to Egypt armed with the signs and wonders to perform in front of Pharaoh, and this plot line continues in the subsequent verses (vv. 27ff.), which describe how Moses met Aaron and reported to him about his mission.[6] Most scholars view vv. 24–26 as an independent story (absent of names except for Zipporah), which was inserted into Exod 4 due to v. 23b, which relates to Pharaoh's son: "Behold, I will slay your first-born son."[7] The addition of the passage into the narrative sequence in Exod 3–4 created the tension between Moses' fulfillment of the mission, and God's desire to kill him.

In addition to this exegetical issue, two theological questions can also be raised:

---

[4] As interpreters have noted, the object of the infinitive "to kill *him*" can be either Moses or one of his sons. For the opinion that Moses was the one whose life was in danger, see *Exod. Rab.* 5:8; the position of R. Joshua b. Qarḥa in *b. Ned.* 31b; the position of R. Judah b. Bizna in *b. Ned.* 32a; Rashi and Ibn Ezra (in both the short and long commentaries) to Exod 4:24; Driver 1911: 32; Noth 1962: 49–50; Cassuto 1967: 58–60. For the opinion that the object of the verb is one of Moses' sons, see the position of R. Simeon b. Gamliel in *b. Ned.* 32a and *y. Ned.* 3:11 (38b). Some exegetes focus on his firstborn, Gershom (Luzzato; Greenberg 1969: 111–114; Sarna 1991: 25), while others posit that the object refers to his second son, Eliezer (R. Samuel b. Ḥofni [quoted in Ibn Ezra's long commentary]; Saadia Gaon; Nachmanides).

[5] For a response to this question, in the context of a different verse, see *Gen. Rab.* 76: "R. Huna in the name of R. Aḥa: 'And he said, 'I will be with you (Exod 3:12) and nothing bad will befall you'"; "And he was on the way to the lodging place" (Exod 4:24); from here that there is no promise to a righteous person in this world."

[6] Cassuto (1967: 59) identified linguistic links and connections in content between the bridegroom of blood story and the surrounding verses: "And he encountered him" (vv. 24, 27); "And he sought to kill him" (v. 24) and "that all those who sought to kill you (lit. who seek your soul) have died" (v. 19); "my son, my firstborn" (v. 22), "your son, your firstborn" (v. 23), and the circumcision of the son (v. 25).

[7] If this verse is actually the motive for the insertion of this story, then the author/editor who added it understood the object of "to kill *him*" as Moses' firstborn son, and not Moses himself.

(2) Why did God want to kill anyone at all, and Moses in particular, without an explicit motive? This question is even more pronounced in light of the exegetical problem just discussed. God's only request from Moses in the context of Exod 3–4 was to return to Egypt in order to deliver the Israelites. This is exactly what Moses did: "The Lord said to Moses in Midian: 'Go return to Egypt'...And Moses took his wife and his sons and mounted them on a donkey, and returned to the land of Egypt" (Exod 4:19–20), before God attacked him (v. 24). There is no description of any sin in the story, and Moses is described as one who obeys the word of God. If God attacks those who are loyal to him, the reader is left with the sneaking suspicion that God is unjust. The specific exegetical question leads therefore to a fundamental, theological question—the problem of theodicy: Did the Lord act unjustly? If God wished to kill Moses arbitrarily, then one can conclude that he has the potential for evil, a conclusion that contradicts the notion that God is completely good.[8]

(3) If God wished to kill Moses ("And YHWH encountered him and sought to kill him"),[9] how is it possible that he did not succeed? If the attack on Moses was justified, what prevented God from implementing his punishment? This problem is more acute in light of the story in Exod 2: after Moses struck and killed an Egyptian, Pharaoh wished to kill him, but was unsuccessful because Moses escaped to Midian: "When Pharaoh learned of the matter, *he sought to kill* Moses, and Moses fled from Pharaoh..." (Exod 2:15). Later on, God encouraged Moses to return from Midian to Egypt by using the argument that "all those

---

[8] In contrast with *Jubilees*, most Jewish sources from antiquity until the Middle Ages solve this exegetical and theological problem by assuming that Moses actually sinned. They generally deduce the nature of this sin from Zipporah's reaction in vv. 25–26: if the circumcision of their child saved Moses, then presumably the original problem was his lack of circumcision; see *m. Ned.* 3:11; *Mek. RSB"Y, Amaleq* 1; *b. Ned.* 31b–32a; *Exod. Rab.* 5:8; Ephrem's Syriac commentary to Exodus II, 8 (Tonneau 1955: 128–129), IV, 3 (ibid., 132); Rashi; Ibn Ezra. These interpreters thus justify God's (or the angel's) behavior; the attack was a punishment for Moses because he failed to perform the commandment of circumcision.

[9] This is a standard formulation used to express human intent—see Jer 26:21; Exod 2:15; 1 Sam 19:2; 2 Sam 20:19; 21:2; 1 Kgs 11:40; Esth 2:21; 3:6. (In Zech 12:9, the subject of the sentence is God. That verse raises a similar theological problem—does God need to request the assistance of others, and if so, is he unable to carry out his will? For rabbinic responses to the issues raised in that passage, see *b. 'Abod. Zar.* 4a; *Deut. Rab., 'Eqeb*; *Est. Rab.* 1:6.) For a similar meaning of ב-ק-ש + נפש (lit. seek + soul), see Exod 4:19; 1 Sam 20:1; 22:23; 23:15; 25:29; 2 Sam 4:8; 15:11; 1 Kgs 19:10, 14 et al.

who sought to kill you have died" (4:19). The biblical story in 4:24 uses an identical expression in order to describe God's desire to kill Moses, thus allowing for a potential comparison between God and Pharaoh: If Moses was able to flee from Pharaoh until the danger had passed, one can then also surmise that he was able to escape from God, who also "sought to kill him"; in fact, at the end of the story, Moses was not killed. The similar language regarding the two dangers that Moses faced therefore raises a theological question regarding God's omnipotence (in contrast to the limitations of a human king). From the description in Exod 4, one could theoretically conclude that YHWH wished to kill Moses, but similar to Pharaoh before him, he was unsuccessful in this matter due to Zipporah's quick reaction.

The rewritten version of this story solves all three problems at once, by replacing YHWH with Prince Mastema as the character that wished to kill Moses (or his son):

(1) The rewritten story distinguishes between God who commanded Moses to return to Egypt, and another character, Mastema, who tried to prevent Moses from arriving there. This eliminates the contradiction between Exod 4:19 (and Exod 3–4 in general) and 4:24. *Jubilees* explains that Mastema's motivation was his desire to prevent Moses from fulfilling the mission that God assigned to him. The rewriter thus transformed the independent story in Exod 4:24–26, which has no direct connection to the surrounding story, into an integral part of the general narrative sequence. In his attempt to prevent Moses from returning, Mastema acted against YHWH's wishes. This conflict of interests between God and Mastema is emphasized throughout ch. 48, whose main motif is the struggle of God and the angel of the presence against Mastema.[10] In particular, one should note *Jub.* 48:2–3, which juxtaposes God's command to Moses with Mastema's attempt to delay him: "You know what was said to you at Mt. Sinai and what the prince of Mastema wanted to do to you while you were returning to Egypt...Did he not wish with all his strength to kill you and to save the Egyptians from your power because he saw that you were sent to carry out punishment and revenge on the Egyptians?"

---

[10] Compare the struggle between Mastema and the angel of presence in the rewritten Akedah story in *Jub.* 17:15–18:19, as well as 4Qpseudo-Jubilees^a (4Q225), 2 II (DJD 13, pp. 149, 151).

(2) Since Mastema was the one who attacked Moses, and not YHWH, the question of theodicy is no longer relevant, because God was not involved at all. The theological tension that was created in the biblical story evaporates completely in *Jubilees*: in Exod 3–4, YHWH attacks Moses **even though** he is fulfilling his demand that he return to Egypt, while in *Jub.* 48:2–3, Mastema attacks Moses **because** he obeyed God's command. The attack itself demonstrates that Moses fulfilled the mission that he was given. The words of the angel of the presence at the beginning of *Jub.* 48:4, "I rescued you from his (Mastema's) power," turn this difficulty on its head: Moses, who obeyed God's command, was attacked by the head of the forces of evil in the world, while the angel of presence saved him as a reward for his loyalty to YHWH.

(3) God did not fail in his attempt to kill Moses, since he was not the one who attacked him; instead, Mastema failed to fulfill his machinations. This motif also appears in the rewritten Akedah story (*Jub.* 18:12: "The prince of Mastema was put to shame"),[11] which itself is based upon the narrative frame of the book of Job, which describes how the Satan failed in his attempts to cause Job to sin.

The solution of replacing God with Mastema in this story is not the exclusive invention of *Jubilees*. A similar interchange of God with another angelic character is found in all of the ancient translations: in place of the Tetragrammaton in MT of Exod 4:24, LXX reads "angel of the Lord" (ἄγγελος κυρίου),[12] and a similar translation is found in

---

[11] Cf. 4Q225 2 ii 5–8 (DJD 13, pp. 149, 151); according to this composition, the angels of Mastema were sure of Abraham's failure:
5 The angels of holiness were standing weeping above [
6 his sons from the earth. The angels of the Ma[stema
7 being happy and saying, "Now he will perish." And [
8 he would be found weak, and whether A[braham] would not be found faithful [

[12] It is difficult to determine whether this change is the work of the translator, or whether it was found in his Hebrew *Vorlage*. Wevers (1990: 54) and Tov (2001: 128) both view the translation here as exegesis of the MT reading. If the general tendency of this translator towards his Hebrew *Vorlage* is generally classified as free, then it seems reasonable to posit that this addition is an interpretive addition on his part. Aejmelaeus (1993: 84) views LXX Exodus as one of the freer translations within the Septauagint, but then qualifies this description: "…Genesis and Exodus…, even in free renderings mostly follows the original fairly faithfully, revealing reasonable consistency" (p. 85). Therefore, the character of the translation does not assist in arriving at an unambiguous, conclusive determination regarding Exod 4:24.

all of the extant Aramaic translations (*T. Onq.; T. Neof.*;¹³ *T. ps.-Jon.*¹⁴) to the verse.¹⁵ The use of an angel in place of God solves some of the exegetical and theological problems discussed above.¹⁶

The replacement of God by his angel is not limited to this passage, but is found elsewhere in the Bible as well. The interchange of the Tetragrammaton in MT and "angel of the Lord" in LXX is attested in only one other context:

Judges 6:14:
MT: ויפן אליו ה'—And **YHWH** turned to him
LXX: καί ἐπέβλεψεν (B ἐπέστρεψεν) πρὸς αὐτὸν ὁ ἄγγελος κυρίου
And the **angel of the Lord** looked (B turned) toward him
Judges 6:16:
MT: ויאמר אליו ה' כי אהיה עמך—And YHWH said to him, "I will be with you"
LXX: καί εἶπεν πρὸς αὐτὸν ὁ ἄγγελος κυρίου κύριος ἔσται μετὰ σοῦ
And the angel of the Lord said to him, "The Lord will be with you"

The modifications in vv. 14 and 16 express the tendency of the (Hebrew) author or the (Greek) translator to adapt them to the descriptions of the angel in the general context of the story in Judg 6 (vv. 11, 12, 20, 21 [twice], and especially v. 22, which tells how Gideon understood that he was in the presence of an angel). One can identify the signs

---

¹³ *Tg Neof.* also adds an angelic being later in the story: in v. 25, he translates the sentence "and cut off her son's foreskin and touched it to his legs," as "and she cut off her son's foreskin and brought it near the legs of *the Destroyer*"; in v. 26, the sentence "and when he let him go, then she said (he is a) bridegroom of blood of circumcision," as "and the *angel* [marginal gloss: *the angel of destruction*] let him go, and then Zipporah praised and said, 'How dear is the blood of this circumcision that delivered this bridegroom from the hands of the *angel of destruction*.'"

¹⁴ Cf. also the continuation in *Tg ps.-Jon.*: "(25)...and she brought the circumcised foreskin near the legs of the *angel of destruction*...(26) And the *angel of destruction* let him alone, then Zipporah praised and said...that saved the bridegroom from the hands of the *angel of destruction*."

¹⁵ The Fragment Targums (MSS P and V) also introduce an angel into the story (vv. 25–26), but not in v. 24, which is not represented in those manuscripts.

¹⁶ The replacement of God by an angel does not solve the contradiction between God's command to return to Egypt in Exod 4:19 and the attempt to delay Moses in Exod 4:24, unless one assumes that the angel acted against God's orders. This interpretation is expressed explicitly in the Palestinian Targums, which identify the angel as "the Destroyer" or "the angel of death" (cf. previous footnotes). This is not stated in LXX or *Tg Onq.*, and one wonders whether these translations had in mind the evil angel that appears in the Aramaic translations (and *Jubilees*), or perhaps they did not intend to solve all of the questions raised above.

of this process of harmonization in v. 16 in the doublet preserved in LXX: ὁ ἄγγελος κυρίου κύριος.[17]

These kinds of changes are attested many times within MT itself. Thus, for example, one can compare Exod 13:21, "and the Lord went before them by day in a pillar of cloud..." to the parallel passage in Exod 14:19, "the angel of God, who went before the Israelite camp...and the pillar of cloud...."[18] A similar interchange is found within the narrative of Exod 3: "(2) And an angel of the Lord appeared to him in a blazing flame out of the bush...(4) When the Lord saw that he had turned aside to look, God called to him out of the bush..." The alternation between Lord and "angel of the Lord" is characteristic of biblical literature, and therefore LXX and the Aramaic Targumim to Exod 4:24 should not be considered a major exegetical innovation. In contrast, the replacement of YHWH (MT) with Mastema (*Jubilees*) is a radical change that is hard to justify in and of itself.[19] Therefore, it is reasonable to assume that Mastema has entered the rewritten story at a second stage of the exegesis of the biblical passage: first YHWH

---

[17] It appears that the addition of "angel of YHWH" led to the transfer of God's words in the first person to the angel's in the third person. The particle כי appears 113 times in MT Judges, and LXX omits it only here and in four other instances: Judg 6:7 (the result of homoioteleuton); 11:16 (MS A); 12:5 (MS B); 20:41 (MS A).

[18] The example is adduced in Ibn Ezra's long commentary to Exod 4:24; Hacham 1991: 71. Regarding the overlap in meaning between YHWH and the "angel of YHWH" (or "angel of God"), see Focht 2002.

[19] Charles (1902: 250) and Vermes (1973: 185, n. 2) suggested that the replacement of YHWH by Mastema (or Satan) can be found already within the Bible itself, by comparing 2 Sam 24:1 and 1 Chr 21:1.

2 Sam 24:1: The anger of the Lord again flared up against Israel, and he incited David against them, saying, "Go, and number Israel and Judah".

1 Chr 21:1: Satan arose against Israel and incited David to number Israel.

However, this interchange can be explained in a slightly different, yet significant, way. The syntactical subject in the verse from Samuel is not the Lord himself, but "the anger of the Lord" (אף ה׳), and it is possible that the author responsible for 1 Chr 21 interpreted "the anger of the Lord" as an evil, divine entity, based upon Ps 78:49: "He sent against them *his burning anger* (חרון אפו), wrath, indignation, trouble, *a band of evil angels.*" According to this interpretation, the rewriting in 1 Chr 21 does not present evidence for a direct exchange of YHWH by Satan, but rather a reinterpretation of 2 Sam 24:1, in which one evil angel has been replaced by another destructive, heavenly entity. The understanding of "the anger of YHWH" as an evil angel is reinforced by a common tradition in rabbinic literature that takes "anger and wrath" as destructive angels in light of Deut 9:19 ("For I was in dread of the Lord's anger and wrath against you"); see *b. Ned.* 32a; *Exod. Rab.* 41:7; 44:8; *Num. Rab.* 11:3; *Qoh. Rab.* 4; 9:2; *Qoh. Zut.* 4; *Songs Rab.* 3; *Tanh. (Buber) Ki Tissa* 13; et al. I would like to thank Prof. Shlomo Naeh for calling my attention to the significance of this rabbinic tradition.

was replaced by "angel of YHWH," and then "angel of YHWH" was understood as Mastema.[20] On the basis of the evidence from LXX, we can reasonably surmise that the Hebrew *Vorlage* of Exod 4:24 used by the author of the rewritten story read "angel of YHWH," which then developed into the character of Mastema.[21]

Who Brought the Plague of the Firstborn?

The struggle between the angel of the presence and Mastema continues in *Jub.* 48:4ff., in which the angel describes how he assisted Moses and Israel while they were in Egypt: "I rescued you from his power. You performed the signs and miracles which you were sent to perform in Egypt against Pharaoh, all his house, his servants, and his nation." By rescuing Moses from Mastema's attack, the angel of the presence enabled him to reach Egypt in order to fulfill his mission. The nature of this mission was to precisely predict what was going to occur to the Egyptians: "(6) Everything was sent through you, before it was done, so that you should do (it). You were speaking with the king of Egypt and in front of all his servants and his people. (7) Everything happened by your word. Ten great and severe punishments came to the land of Egypt so that you could take revenge on it for Israel." The view reflected in this description does not assign an active role to Moses in Israel's liberation, but rather sees him as a messenger of God to reprove the Egyptians before the bringing of the plagues.[22]

---

[20] In rabbinic literature, one finds two close, but not identical, approaches as to the identity of the attacker: (1) an angel (*Mek. R. Išm., Amaleq* 1; *y. Ned.* 3:11 (38b); (2) Satan—a specific angel (*b. Ned.* 32a). The phenomenon of the appearance of Satan in rabbinic literature in the same place that Mastema appears in *Jubilees* is also attested in the context of the Akedah story: *b. Sanh.* 89b attributes the idea for the Akedah to Satan, just as *Jub.* 17:16 asserts that Mastema suggested this test (see Olyan 1993: 25–26; Kister 1994: 9; Bernstein 2000: 269–271).

[21] Prof. M. Kister has suggested to me that it is not necessary to assume that such a Hebrew reading was in his *Vorlage*. Since the exegetical tradition that identifies God with his angel was already well established, it is possible that this first interpretive stage (replacement of YHWH with angel of YHWH) occurred only in the rewriter's mind—his biblical text contained the reading YHWH, but he understood that this referred to an angel of YHWH.

[22] Loewenstamm (1992: 134–135) viewed *Jub.* 48:4 as an additional tradition that asserted that Moses brought the plagues, and not only foretold their arrival (as reflected in vv. 6–7). Loewenstamm suggested that the rewritten story in *Jubilees* was actually intended to emphasize Moses' role, and submerged under this tradition is one that posited that God himself brought the plagues. However, even if Loewenstamm is

All of the plagues were sent by God himself, in order to exact revenge on the Egyptians:[23]

> (5) **The Lord** effected a great revenge against them on account of Israel. He struck them and killed them with blood, frogs, gnats, dog flies, bad sores which break out in blisters; (and he struck) their cattle with death; and with hailstones—with these he annihilated everything that was growing for them; with locusts which ate whatever was left for them from the hail; with darkness; (and with the death of) their first-born of men and cattle. **The Lord** took revenge on all their gods and burned them up...(8) **The Lord did everything** for the sake of Israel and in accord with his covenant which he made with Abraham to take revenge on them just as they were enslaving them with force.

The plagues are God's reaction to the Israelites' enslavement at the hands of the Egyptians, and part of his promise to Abraham in the context of the Covenant of Pieces (Gen 15:14—"but I will pass judgment on the nation they shall serve"). Due to the brevity of the list of plagues, it is difficult to identify a specific biblical source for each one of them,[24] but in certain instances one can identify the verse upon which the rewriting is based: "bad sores which break out in blisters" is based upon Exod 9:9–10; "and with hailstones—with these he annihilated everything that was growing for them"—from Exod 9:25; "with locusts which ate whatever was left for them from the hail"—from Exod 10:12, 15.

The description of the plague of the firstborn is based upon Exod 12:12:[25]

---

correct in asserting that there is a tradition about Moses bringing the plagues, it has been combined into a story that emphasizes that God brought the plagues, and not vice versa.

[23] The rewriter continues the motif that God brought all of the plagues in v. 11 (the description of boils affecting the Egyptian magicians).

[24] In addition to the lengthy description in Exod 7–12, it is possible that Ps 78 and 105 were sources for the rewritten Exodus story in *Jubilees*. The number and order of the plagues follows the book of Exodus.

[25] There are other relevant verses, but they did not influence *Jubilees* at this point. Exod 11:5; 12:29; 13:15 all refer to the killing of the firstborn people and animals, but do not mention the Egyptian gods. In Exod 12:23, the firstborn are not mentioned at all. Similarly, Num 33:4, "And Egypt was burying those whom the Lord struck down from among them, every firstborn, and against their gods he meted out punishments," was not the direct source for the rewriting in *Jub.* 48:5, because it does not mention human firstborn and animal firstborn, but rather uses the more general term "every firstborn." In addition, this verse is located in the list of Israel's travels, far from the narrative context of Exod 11–12.

Exodus 12:12	Jubilees 48:5
I will strike down every *first-born* in the land of Egypt, both *man*	their *first-born of men*
and beast	*and cattle*
and *I will mete out punishments to all the gods of Egypt*	The *Lord took revenge*[26] on all their gods and burned them up[27]
I am YHWH	

Exod 12:12 is formulated in the first person ("I will go through...I will strike down...I will mete out...I am YHWH") in order to emphasize God's exclusive role in rescuing the Israelites from the hands of the Egyptians.[28] This tendency is emphasized in the Passover Haggadah, which quotes this verse in order to demonstrate that no other force was involved in this salvation:[29]

> "And the Lord took us out of Egypt" (Deut 26:8): Not by an angel, not by a seraph, and not by a messenger, but the Holy One, blessed be he, in his glory by himself, as it is said: "I will go through the land of Egypt that night and I will strike down every first-born in the land of Egypt, both man and beast; and I will mete out punishments to all the gods of Egypt, I am YHWH" (Exod 12:12). "I will go through the land of Egypt

---

[26] Goldmann translated the word in Geʿez, *baqal*, "revenge, take revenge, call to vengeance" by the Hebrew word נקמה. The expression "to exact revenge (לעשות נקמה)" appears in Ps 149:7. The verb from the same root, *baqqala*, means "punish, take vengeance...," and it is therefore more plausible to assume that the Geʿez translation reflects the Hebrew expression ע-ש-ה שפטים, parallel to Exod 12:12.

[27] The addition of the burning of the Egyptian gods is the result of exegesis of the expression ע-ש-ה שפטים in Exod 12:12. Cf. Ezek 30:14–19: "(14) I will lay Pathros to waste, and I will set fire to Zoan, and I will execute judgment on No...(16) I will set fire to Egypt...(19) Thus I will execute judgment on Egypt..."; 16:41: "And they will burn your houses with fire and execute punishments upon you...." The motif of fire in connection with the Egyptian gods appears in Jer 43:12–13: "And I will set fire to the temples of the gods of Egypt; he will burn them down and carry them off...he shall burn down the temples of the gods of Egypt." From the possibility of burning the Egyptian gods in fire, we can infer that this verse refers to idols or images. Compare 1QM XIV, 1: "Like the fire of his wrath upon the Egyptian idols"; *Mek. R. Išm., Pisḥa* 7; *Tg ps.-Jon.* to Exod 12:12; Rashi and Ibn Ezra ad loc.

[28] See Rofé 1979: 160.

[29] Bar-On (1999: 105, n. 252) takes the passage from the Haggadah as another example of the negation of the tradition of a destroying angel. Safrai and Safrai (1998: 11–12) contrast the perspective of the midrash to that expressed in *Jub.* 49:2 regarding God's direct intervention in the plague of the firstborn. Although they are correct regarding these two sources, they overlooked the description of the plague in *Jub.* 48:5, and therefore did not grasp the presence of both traditions side-by-side in *Jubilees* (see below).

that night"—I and not an angel; "I will strike down every first-born in the land of Egypt"—I and not a seraph; "I will mete out punishments to all the gods of Egypt"—I and not a messenger; "I am YHWH"—It is I, and not another.

In Exod 12 itself, one can identify two approaches to the question of who implemented the plague of the firstborn (vv. 12–13 and v. 23). The similarity between them leads to the conclusion that one of these rewrote the other, and it has already been suggested by scholars that vv. 12–13 are a reformulation of v. 23:[30]

vv. 12–13	*v. 23*
I will pass through	And YHWH will pass through
	to smite
the land of Egypt	Egypt
that night and I will smite every first-born in the land of Egypt, both man and beast and I will mete out punishments to all the gods of Egypt I am YHWH.	
And the blood will be for you a sign upon the houses where you are	
and when I see the blood	And He will see the blood
	on the lintel and on the two doorposts
I will pass over (ופסחתי) you	and YHWH will protect (ופסח) the door
and no blow (נגף) shall be upon you for destruction (למשחית)	and He will not allow the destroyer (המשחית) to enter your home to strike (לנגף).
when I smite the land of Egypt.	

The power that harms Egypt in v. 23 is not God, but rather "the (angel of) destruction,"[31] or "the destroyer". God's task was to prevent the destroyer from entering the houses upon which the Israelites had placed blood, on the lintel and the two doorposts. In contrast, according to vv. 12–13, God himself struck the land of Egypt, and there is no reference to an independent entity known as "the destroyer" (המשחית).[32]

---

[30] See Rofé 1979: 160–161 (and the extensive scholarly literature quoted there in n. 19). He assigns v. 23 to JE, and the reformulation in v. 13 to P. Bar-On (1999: 102–111) assigns both verses to priestly authors. This synoptic table appears there (in Hebrew, p. 103).

[31] Cf. 2 Sam 24:16: "the angel of destruction" (and the numerous studies quoted by Bar-On 1999: 104, n. 249).

[32] As noted by Bar-On (1999: 105, n. 250), לְמַשְׁחִית ("for destruction") in v. 13 is an abstract noun; cf. Joüon 1991: 259, §88Lm.

The inner-biblical reworking has removed this angel from the previous description. *Jubilees* 48:5 adopted Exod 12:12 as the source for its description of the plague of the firstborn, a choice which expresses a certain perspective of the circumstances of this event: God perpetrated this plague all by himself. *Jub.* 48:8 reemphasizes this view: "The Lord did everything...." In sum, *Jub.* 48 asserts that YHWH needed no assistance in the implementation of the plagues in general, and more specifically, that he brought about the plague of the firstborn by himself.

The Continuation of the Struggle between Mastema and the Angel of the Presence

Prince Mastema stood by the Egyptians, and assisted them in their struggle against Israel: "The prince of Mastema would stand up against you and wish to make you fall into the pharaoh's power; he would help the Egyptian magicians and they would oppose (you) and perform in front of you" (*Jub.* 48:9). Mastema did not desist from his attempts to stop Moses following his return to Egypt, as can be seen from the performance of the signs that accompanied the plagues. The plague narrative in the Priestly source of the Pentateuch includes a competition between Aaron and the Egyptian magicians (Exod 7:11–12, 22; 8:3, 14; 9:11). In the first three stages of this contest (transforming the staff into a serpent; blood; frogs), the magicians were able to copy Aaron, but were unable to rescind the plague.[33] The magicians' success in conjuring up these plagues troubled early exegetes: if the plagues were the work of God, and the biblical descriptions of the plagues emphasize their supernatural aspects, how were the magicians able to perform the same miracles themselves? Continuing the interpretive approach discussed above, *Jub.* 48:9 asserts that Mastema assisted the magicians in their achievements. Since the Torah itself describes that the magicians'

---

[33] The first two plagues, blood and frogs, raise an exegetical problem in the biblical story, because they both extended over the entire land of Egypt (Exod 7:21; 8:2). One would have expected the Egyptian magicians to remove or diminish the plague, and not to expand it by copying the plague. According to Loewenstamm (1992: 122–127), the replication of these plagues is the result the combination of an early tradition describing a competition between an Israelite (Aaron) and Egyptian priests, with the plagues tradition. The emphasis on the totality of the plagues is part of the general aim of the competition tradition, which describes spectacular signs.

powers were limited—they could bring the plagues (at least blood and frogs) but not eliminate them—*Jub.* 48:10 combines this detail into its description of the powers of Mastema: "We permitted them to do evil things, but we would not allow healings to be performed by them." Although Mastema is presented throughout this chapter as an independent entity, who has the ability to act contrary to God's interests, v. 10 acknowledges that the angels of presence limit his power: if they wish, he can bring a plague; if not, he is prevented from doing so. The angels' control over Mastema is emphasized in the description of the plague of boils in 48:11: "When the Lord struck them with bad sores, they were unable to oppose (you) because we deprived them of (their ability) to perform a single sign"; this, even though Exod 9:11 ascribes this inability to act against Moses to the effects of the plague itself: "And the magicians were unable to stand before Moses because of the boils, for the boils were upon the magicians and upon all of Egypt." *Jub.* 48:11 thus distinguishes between the physical results of the plague (caused by God), and the results of the angels' actions (who prevented the magicians from performing a single sign). By attributing the struggle against Mastema to the angels of presence, *Jub.* 48 places God on a higher plane than the other heavenly beings—both Mastema and the angels of presence are under his control. Mastema does not act directly against God; he attempted to act against Moses, but did not even succeed in eliciting a reaction from the deity. If Mastema represents the forces of evil in the world, he should be viewed as an independent, but limited, power. He has his own views and goals, but the angels of presence do not allow him to carry them out completely.

Mastema does not disappear, even though he fails time and time again: "Despite all the signs and miracles, the prince of Mastema was not[34] put to shame[35] until he gained strength and cried out to the Egyptians to pursue you with all the Egyptian army[36]—with their

---

[34] Thus in all the manuscripts. Charles (1895: 169) and Goldmann (1956: 309) omitted the word "not" without any textual support. As noted by VanderKam (1989b: 312), Charles (1902: 251) restored the word "not" to his translation.

[35] Compare *Jub.* 18:12, "The prince of Mastema was put to shame." In both verses, the Ge'ez translation uses the same verb, *ḥafara*.

[36] The expression "Egyptian army (חיל מצרים)" appears only in Deut 11:4, and in a similar context: "what he did *to the Egyptian army, to its horses, and to its chariots*, that he caused the water of the Sea of Reeds to flow over them when they were pursuing you."

chariots, their horses[37]—and with all the throng of the Egyptian people" (*Jub.* 48:12). The two halves of the verse are connected by the conjunction "until," which introduces the description of one instance in which Mastema did in fact regret his actions. The reader, of course, already knows the end of the story, including Mastema's failure and the drowning of the Egyptians in the sea. However, the characters themselves, including Mastema, are unaware of the impending events. Mastema continues to behave as he did previously—he encourages the Egyptians to pursue the Israelites, thinking that he is working at cross-purposes with God's will.

In the biblical story, God is responsible for encouraging Pharaoh to pursue the Israelites: "And I will stiffen Pharaoh's heart, and he will pursue them...and the Egyptians will know that I am the Lord..." (Exod 14:4); "And the Lord stiffened the heart of Pharaoh, king of Egypt, and he pursued the Israelites..." (ibid. 8). God forced Pharaoh and the Egyptians to chase the Israelites, in order to bring about their downfall. In *Jub.* 48:12, Mastema takes the place of God, and he encourages the Egyptians to pursue the Israelites. The rewriting in *Jub.* 48:12 assumes that God has no interest that Egypt chase after Israel, and clears him of any direct responsibility for Pharaoh's decision. The replacement of YHWH with Mastema is the result of the general tendency in ch. 48: Mastema is Egypt's heavenly representative, in opposition to YHWH and the angel of presence.

Furthermore, the substitution of God by Mastema solves a theological problem that the biblical story raises. The Torah repeatedly emphasizes that God prevented Pharaoh and the Egyptians from recanting their decision to force Israel to remain in Egypt (Exod 4:21; 9:12; 10:1, 20, 27; 11:10; 14:4, 8, 17). However, if God precluded Pharaoh from releasing the Israelites, how could he then punish him for this refusal? In order to solve this problem, biblical interpreters from antiquity until today have suggested possible reinterpretations of the expression "stiffen Pharaoh's heart."[38] *Jub.* 48 avoids the theological problem here by transferring this action to Mastema.

---

[37] The use of the terms "chariots," "horses, horsemen," and "army, force" (of Pharaoh) is taken from the description of the splitting of the sea and the death of the Egyptians in Exod 14:9, 17, 18, 23, 26, 28; 15:19.

[38] Kugel (1998: 548–551) surveyed the variety of solutions suggested in early exegesis for the problem of the hardening of Pharaoh's heart within the plagues narrative.

The struggle between Mastema and the angel of presence continues in v. 13: "I stood between you, the Egyptians, and the Israelites. We rescued the Israelites from his[39] power and from the power of the people. The Lord brought them out through the middle of the sea as if on dry ground." This account is constructed from verses further on in Exod 14: "(19) And the angel of God, who had been going ahead of the Israelite camp, moved and went behind them; and the pillar of cloud moved from in front of them and stood behind them. (20) And it came between the Egyptian camp and the Israelite camp...and one did not approach the other all night." The syntactical subject of Exod 14:19, "angel of God," was easily replaced in *Jubilees* by the "angel of the presence," the narrator throughout the book.[40] The final clause of *Jub.* 48:13 is based upon Exod 14:22: "And the Israelites went into the sea on dry ground...," and upon Exod 12:51: "And on that very day, the Lord brought the Israelites out of the land of Egypt...." Here too, the rewriter emphasizes God's direct intervention in order to save the Israelites.[41]

The Hardening of Egypt's Heart

As mentioned above, v. 12 solves the theological problem posed by the biblical story, that God hardened Egypt's heart and encouraged them to pursue the Israelites (Exod 14:4, 8, 17), thus bringing about their demise. *Jub.* 48:12 replaced God with Mastema, the head of the

---

[39] Thus Charles 1902: 251–252; VanderKam 1989a: 244; 1989b: 313. Goldmann (1956: 309), however, reads "*their* hand (or: power)". VanderKam (1989a: 244) cites in his critical apparatus a number of manuscripts that read the plural suffix, but the verb in v. 14 is in the singular, "All of the people whom *he* brought out to pursue the Israelites" (thus in all the manuscripts), which supports the reading of the singular suffix in v. 13. The transition to plural is apparently the influence of the view, which appears elsewhere in the book, that Mastema was the leader of the evil forces or spirits in the world; cf. below, n. 46 regarding v. 16.

[40] VanderKam (2000b) discusses the biblical sources for the angel of the presence, his roles in *Jubilees*, and the interchanges of YHWH or the angel of YHWH, and the angel of the presence.

[41] This view, that God himself took the Israelites out of Egypt, is repeated in other places in the Pentateuch (Exod 6:6, 7; 7:4, 5; 12:17; 13:3, 14, 16; 14:11; Deut 6:21; 26:8; Ps 105:37). A different approach appears in Num 20:16: "And he sent an angel and he took us out of Egypt"—God did not directly intervene in order to save the nation, but rather through the agency of an angel. The subject in the first part of *Jub.* 48:13 is the angel of the presence, while the subject of the final sentence is God.

forces of evil in the world, just as it switched them in the beginning of the chapter, in the bridegroom of blood story.[42] In both sections of the chapter, the rewriter wished to defend the notion that God is completely good.

The claim that Mastema encouraged the Egyptians to pursue the Israelites continues in vv. 13–14: "(13)...We rescued the Israelites from his power and from the power of the people. The Lord brought them out through the middle of the sea as if on dry ground. (14) All of the people whom *he brought out* to pursue the Israelites, the Lord our God threw into the sea...." Syntactically, one can interpret the subject of the verb "brought out" as either God or Mastema. However, because of the recurring motif of the competition between God and the angels of the presence (and Israel) versus Mastema (and Egypt), which appears at the beginning of the chapter, it is preferable to view vv. 13–14 as a contrast between God's and the angels' powers, and Mastema's lack thereof. From a literary perspective, vv. 13–14a presents a chisasmus, which emphasizes the contrast between them:

A We rescued the Israelites from his power and from the power of the people.
    B The Lord **brought them out** through the middle of the sea as if on dry ground.
    B' All of the people whom he **brought out** to pursue the Israelites,
A' the Lord our God threw into the sea

The angels saved their nation (A), whom the Lord brought out (B), from Mastema, while Mastema was not able to save his nation, whom he had brought out (B'), from the Lord (A').

As opposed to the view that Mastema hardened Pharaoh's heart, v. 17b offers a different explanation as to the cause of the Egyptians' pursuit of the Israelites until the sea: "They were made stubborn by the Lord our God so that he could strike the Egyptians and throw them into the sea." This explanation, similar to the biblical story itself, presupposes that God was responsible for the hardening the Egyptians' heart so that they pursued the Israelites. The encouragement of the

---

[42] Charles (1902: 252) also adduces *Jub.* 17:16 as an example of the replacement of God by Mastema.

Egyptians was intended to punish them more forcefully.[43] If so, v. 17b emphasizes and heightens the theological question that has troubled most interpreters.[44] Verse 17b does not seem concerned with the notion that God hardened Egypt's heart, and therefore contradicts vv. 12–14, both in its identification of who was responsible for the hardening of the heart, and regarding its treatment of the theological problem raised by the biblical story.

Moreover, v. 17b contradicts its immediate context regarding the same questions:

> (15) On the fourteenth day...and the eighteenth the prince of Mastema was bound and locked up behind the Israelites so that he could not accuse them.[45] (16) On the nineteenth day we released him/them[46] so that he/they could help[47] the Egyptians and pursue the Israelites.

---

[43] In Exod 14:4, God announced that he would harm Pharaoh and his forces, but in the end, the ultimate goal of his actions was that the Egyptians would acknowledge him: "I will stiffen Pharaoh's heart and he will pursue them, so that I may gain glory through Pharaoh and all his host; and the Egyptians shall know that I am the Lord" (similarly in the parallel verses, Exod 14:17–18). The goal of his actions is thus didactic, and not punitive. The expression "know that I am the Lord" appears a number of times throughout the plagues story in Exodus (6:7; 7:5, 12; 8:18; 10:2).

[44] Kugel (1997: 337–338) interprets *Jub.* 48:17b as the collection of a "final payment" from the Egyptians, in return for the enslavement of the Israelites and their cruelty towards them. This idea is expressed explicitly in another source that Kugel quotes, *Wis. Sol.* 19:4–5.

[45] The meaning of "so that he could not accuse them" in v. 15 is identical to that of v. 18 (the same translation, *'i-yāstawādəyyomu*, appears in both verses)—so that he would not accuse them in front of the Egyptians.

[46] Littman, Goldmann, and Hartom all translate "him," in the singular. Goldmann (1956: 310) observes in his notes that the Geʿez translation "mistakenly" translated "them," in the plural. Dillman (1859) and Charles both translated with the plural pronoun. According to Berger (1981: 545), the plural pronoun refers to the demons under Mastema's control. VanderKam (1989b: 314) adopted the plural reading (as reflected in all Ethiopic manuscripts, except for 42ᶜ and 58), and interpreted it as did Berger. However, it is difficult to accept their suggestion, because the story itself does not mention demons that assisted Mastema (comparable to the Akedah story [*Jub.* 17–18] which presents a similar portrait of Mastema), and Mastema alone is described as "bound and locked up" (v. 15). Admittedly, *Jubilees* (10:1–14; 11:5, 11) does include traditions about demons or spirits under Mastema's control, and it is possible that the interchange of the singular and plural pronouns here reflects an attempt to harmonize the story in *Jub.* 48 with these traditions. The abrupt transition (in the current form of the story) from singular to plural reveals the incongruity of the plural form (MSS 42ᶜ and 58 perhaps reflect either the original reading, or a secondary correction in order to resolve the tension between vv. 15 and 16, thus restoring the story to its original form). The "forces of Mastema" (*Jub.* 49:2), mentioned in the second story that describes the plague of the firstborn, follow God's commands (and not Mastema's), yet they could still theoretically have influenced the text of v. 16.

[47] The verb appears in the singular in only two manuscripts, 42ᶜ and 58, the same

(17) He stiffened their resolve and made them stubborn. They were made stubborn by the Lord our God so that he could strike the Egyptians and throw them into the sea.

The pronouns in v. 17a are ambiguous, and it is unclear who stiffened whose heart. Verse 15 refers only to Mastema; v. 16 presents either a plural object for the verb "released" and the plural verb "they could help," referring to demons, or both of these in the singular, referring to Mastema himself.[48] The continuation of the story in v. 17 is also ambiguous regarding the identity of the syntactical subjects in the sentence: "He stiffened their resolve and made them stubborn. They were made stubborn by the Lord our God so that he could strike the Egyptians and throw them into the sea." In the first half of the verse, the subject is masculine singular, and the only character from the previous verses that fits this pronoun is Mastema. This interpretation corresponds to *Jub.* 48:12–14, which credits Mastema with encouraging the Egyptians to pursue the Israelites. The plural forms in v. 17a (*"their* resolve... made *them"*) can refer to one of the two groups mentioned in v. 16, the Egyptians or Mastema's forces (although the latter are not referred to explicitly).[49]

If the interpretation of v. 17a is correct, and Mastema stiffened the Egyptians' resolve, then there is a clear contradiction between the two parts of the verse: according to the first half, "He (Mastema) stiffened their resolve and made them stubborn," while according to the second, "they were made stubborn by the Lord our God so that he could strike the Egyptians and throw them into the sea." In order to resolve this contradiction within v. 17, one can suggest that the subject of "He stiffened" is God, and not Mastema. This interpretation correlates both halves of v. 17, but simultaneously interrupts the continuity between vv. 15–16 and v. 17. God is not mentioned in the first two verses, and it is therefore difficult to claim that the subject of v. 17a, which is unspecified ("He stiffened"), refers to a new syntacti-

---

textual witnesses that preserve the objectival pronoun of the previous verb in the singular; see VanderKam 1989b ad loc.

[48] See notes 46, 47.

[49] According to the process of textual development suggested in n. 46, the demons, under the command of Mastema, were not part of the original story, and therefore the object of the verb "made *them* stubborn" refers to the Egyptians. The understanding that v. 17a refers to the Egyptians corresponds both to the biblical story and to the description in v. 12.

cal subject. This interpretation therefore leads to the assumption that the reader does not know the subject of v. 17a until he reaches 17b, "They were made stubborn by the Lord our God," an assumption that is difficult to sustain both syntactically and exegetically. However, even if we are to accept this possibility, and assume that God is responsible for the stiffening of Pharaoh's heart in both 17a and 17b, one can still not ignore the contradiction between v. 12 and v. 17: according to the former, Mastema urged the Egyptians to chase after the Israelites, while according to the latter (at least in the second half of the verse), God stiffened Egypt's heart.

One can suggest two possible solutions to this contradiction, both of which assume that the main thrust of the rewriting is to justify God's behavior by attributing his evil actions to a semi-independent, heavenly character:

(1) As noted above, v. 17b matches the biblical description: both claim that God encouraged the Egyptians to pursue the Israelites. It is possible that this verse is a vestige of the biblical text that survived in the rewritten text, which itself attributes the stiffening of the heart to Mastema. The problem with this explanation is that for this "accident" to occur in this reworking, the rewriter must have followed his biblical source text very closely. But as noted in the beginning of this discussion, *Jub.* 48 presents an abridged version of the Exodus story. Despite the biblical expressions that can be identified throughout the chapter, in contrast with the earlier sections of the book, one cannot describe ch. 48 as a close rewriting of the story from the book of Exodus, but rather as a thorough paraphrase of the story in its entirety. It is therefore difficult to claim that v. 17b survived in the reworked story, as a result of the author's negligence.

(2) If one rejects the conjecture that v. 17b was left over from the biblical source text, overlooked during the rewriting process, it is worth considering the reverse possibility, that v. 17b was added at a later stage to *Jubilees*.[50] What caused a later scribe to add v. 17b, thus creating tension with the rest of the chapter? At the beginning of ch. 48,

---

[50] The assumption that v. 17b is a secondary addition is more likely than the possibility that vv. 12 and 17a were added by a second scribe, because the latter two verses fit the overall tendency throughout the chapter, of transferring evil actions from God to Mastema in order to justify the former's behavior.

in the rewriting of the bridegroom of blood story, God was replaced by Mastema without any similar "remnant" of a task for God. The scribe who added v. 17b perhaps believed that there was a fundamental difference between the bridegroom of blood story, and the encouragement of the Egyptians to pursue the Israelites and their subsequent drowning. The first story raises the problem of the suffering of the righteous in its most extreme form: God commanded Moses to return to Egypt, but when he obeyed his command and returned to Egypt, he attacked him. As noted above, the invention of a sin for Moses in rabbinic literature and medieval bible commentaries, and especially the accusation that he did not circumcise his son,[51] emphasize that God acted unjustly in the biblical story. The discussion of the issue of theodicy above regarding the bridegroom of blood passage, addressed the difference between the rabbinic approach to solving this problem and the alternative proposed by *Jubilees*. *Jubilees* 48 admits that the attack on Moses was problematic, but manages to clear God of any guilt by claiming that Mastema was the assailant. Rabbinic literature refrains from viewing Moses as a completely righteous character, claiming that he indeed sinned, and thus justifies the punishment given to him. The goals of the different compositions are identical, but each one provides its own answer to the theological problem.

It is possible that these two approaches are presented side-by-side in ch. 48. Verse 17a justifies urging the Egyptians to pursue the Israelites, despite the disastrous results for the Egyptians, by claiming that Mastema, and not God, was the one offering this encouragement. Verse 17a thus expresses the same approach reflected at the beginning of ch. 48—transferring the guilt over God's injustice to another character. In contrast, v. 17b is closer in its approach to the rabbinic interpretation of the bridegroom of blood story: God himself urged the Egyptians, and hardened their hearts to chase after Israel, because their drowning in the sea was the appropriate punishment for their cruel behavior in the subjugation of the Israelites. Just as one cannot accuse God of acting unjustly if Moses sinned in the bridegroom of blood story, similarly one cannot attribute injustice to God if the Egyptians were worthy of punishment.[52]

---

[51] See above, n. 8, for sources that emphasize this approach.
[52] Kugel (1997: 337; 1998: 586) interpreted v. 17b in this manner, but did not discuss the contradictory tendencies within ch. 48. The idea that the Egyptians received a

The Plague of the Firstborn in the Legal Passage (Jubilees 49)

Following the rewritten Exodus story in *Jub.* 48 (parallel to Exod 3–14), ch. 49 presents a halakhic passage that contains the Passover laws. In all other instances throughout the book, the legal passages were juxtaposed to the rewritten stories without any reference in the biblical story to the legal import of the narrative. This is not the case in the Passover laws, as a legal passage already appears in Exod 12. The biblical description of the plague of the firstborn connects it to the observance of the Passover law in Egypt, through the blood of the lamb that was used in order to protect the Israelite firstborn.[53] This plague is mentioned both in the narrative sections of Exodus (ch. 11 [warning]; 12:29–30 [fulfillment]) and twice in the legal passage (12:12–13; 22–23).[54] An analysis of the biblical passages that were incorporated into *Jub.* 49 reveals the use of all of these verses:

Jubilees 49:2	
all the forces of Mastema[55] were sent to kill every first-born in the land of Egypt from Pharaoh's first-born to the first-born of the captive slave-girl at the millstone and to the cattle as well.	[Exod 12:23: "the destroyer"] Exod 11:5: And every firstborn in the land of Egypt shall die, from the firstborn of Pharaoh, who sits on his throne, to the firstborn of the slave-girl who is behind the millstones, and all the firstborn of the cattle.

deserved punishment does appear in two other verses in *Jub.* 48: (1) v. 14: "All of the people whom he brought out to pursue the Israelites, the Lord our God threw into the sea—to the depths of the abyss—in place of the Israelites, just as the Egyptians had thrown their sons into the river. He took revenge on 1,000,000 of them, 1000 men (who were) strong and also very brave perished for one infant of your people whom they had thrown into the river." This verse explains the drowning of the Egyptians as an instance of "measure for measure" (cf. *Jub.* 4:31), a motif that recurs in other compositions that address the story of the splitting of the sea (*Wisd. Sol.* 18:5; *Mek. R. Išm., Šīrta* 4; see Kugel 1997: 285–293). (2) v. 18: "...so that they could plunder the Egyptians in return for the fact that they were made to work when they enslaved them by force." Here too, the text attempts to solve a moral problem: how could God command Moses to instruct the Israelites to "borrow" the Egyptians' valuables (Exod 3:22; 11:2; 12:35–36)? The interpretation reflected in *Jub.* 48:18 asserts that these items were fair reimbursement for the many years of slavery; for other exegetical attempts to moderate this moral difficulty, see Kugel 1997: 322–326.

[53] Thus Exod 12:23; in v. 13, the blood serves as a sign, but without any magical force to protect the Israelites—see Fox 1980: 575; Bar-On 1999: 105–108.

[54] As noted above, Exod 12:13 rewrote 12:23, and removed "the destroyer" from the description of the plague. For the relationship between the two descriptions see above, in addition to Bar-On's (1999: 102–111) extensive discussion.

[55] For the significance of the epithet "forces of Mastema," and for their role relative to Prince Mastema, see the discussion below.

Jubilees 49:3	
This is the sign[56] which the Lord gave them	Exod 12:13: And the blood will be a sign for you on the houses
into each house on whose door they saw the blood	Exod 12:13: And when I see the blood…
	Exod 12:23: And he will see the blood on the lintel and on the two doorposts and YHWH will protect (ופסח) the door
of a year-old lamb,	Exod 12:5: A lamb without blemish, a yearling male
they were not to enter that house to kill	Exod 12:23: and he will not allow the destroyer to enter your home to smite
but were to pass over[57] (it)	Exod 12:13: I will pass over (ופסחתי) you [repetition of expressions]
in order to save all who were in the house because the sign of the blood was on its door.	
Jubilees 49:4	
The Lord's forces did everything that the Lord ordered them.	No Source
They passed over all the Israelites. The plague did not come on them to destroy any of them	Exod 12:13: I will pass over (ופסחתי) you and no plague shall be upon you for destruction when I smite in the land of Egypt
From cattle to mankind to dogs.	Exod 11:7: And against any of the Israelites no dog shall snarl (lit., sharpen its tongue), at man or beast
Jubilees 49:5	
The plague on Egypt was very great. There was no house in Egypt in which there was no corpse, crying, and mourning.	Exod 12:30: And there was a great cry in Egypt, for there was no house in which there was not someone dead

---

[56] VanderKam (1989b: 315) relied upon manuscripts that do not read the word "sign" (MSS 12 17 21 38 63), and translated: "This is that which the Lord gave them." In his opinion, the word *ta'əmərt* is an interpretive addition, influenced by the end of the verse (which itself is based upon Exod 12:13).

[57] The Ethiopic verb *'adawa*, "to pass," reflects exegesis of the Hebrew verb פ-ס-ח consonant with Exod 12:13 (and in contrast to Exod 12:23).

In order to unify these verses into one account, the author of *Jub.* 49 chose expressions from each one, and the final product is therefore different from any of its sources. In contrast with the narrative sections and the legal passage in Exod 12:12–13, God did not kill the firstborn himself, but rather sent the "forces of Mastema" (49:2) or his own forces (49:4) in order to accomplish this mission. This viewpoint is somewhat similar to Exod 12:23, "and he will not allow the **destroyer** to enter your home to smite," if we interpret "the destroyer" as the "angel of destruction."[58] However, the description in *Jub.* 49 also differs from Exod 12:23: in the biblical verse, God "protected"[59] or "hovered over"[60] (פסח) the houses upon which the Israelites had placed blood, so that the destroyer could not enter, while in *Jub.* 49, the forces of Mastema themselves "pass over" these houses. If one analyzes these sources regarding the division of labor between the different divine beings, who killed, who protected, and who passed over, then a single force is responsible for attacking and passing over in both Exod 12:13 (God) and *Jub.* 49:2–5 (forces of Mastema), while Exod 12:23 differentiates between the tasks: the destroyer killed and God protected the Israelites.

The attribution of the plague of the firstborn to the "forces of Mastema" could be the result of two different motivations:

(1) Exegetical motive:[61] The "destroyer" of Exod 12:23 was interpreted as God's messengers who were sent to perform his evil actions. If so, *Jub.* 49:2–5 asserts that God's forces accomplished this, against the reinterpretation of Exod 12:23 in Exod 12:13 described above, namely, the elimination of any active angelic agents in this story. The rewriting in *Jub.* 49 went even further than Exod 12:23—God is no longer an active participant in the story, and instead, the forces of Mastema are taken as the syntactical subject of the Hebrew verb פ-ס-ח (according to its new meaning in Exod 12:13). In addition, it is distinctly possible that *Jub.* 49:2 has been influenced by Ps 78:49, "He sent against them

---

[58] See above, n. 31.
[59] Thus according to *Tg. ps.-Jon.* to v. 23, ויגין (in v. 13 he uses the Aramaic verb ח-ו-ס), and LXX to v. 13, which uses the verb σκεπάζω, "cover, protect, shelter" (in v. 23 he translates with the verb παρέρχομαι, "go by, pass by," the same verb used to translate ועבר at the beginning of the verse). One can deduce this meaning from the parallelism in Isa 31:5 between ג-נ-ן and פ-ס-ח; see Weiss 1964.
[60] This meaning is perhaps found in Isa 31:5, which compares God's protection of Jerusalem to airborne birds protecting their fledglings (according to Deut 32:11, which describes God's protection of the Israelites using the same imagery).
[61] Cf. also Loewenstamm 1992: 211–212.

his burning anger, wrath, indignation, trouble, *a delegation of evil angels*," since this verse appears in the context of the plagues (although not specifically next to the firstborn plague), and which can be understood as a description of a group of evil angels, identified in *Jubilees* as "the forces of Mastema,"[62] who implemented this plague.

(2) Theological Motive: Attributing the plague of the firstborn to the forces of Mastema (as God's emissaries) is also of theological significance. God does not intervene directly in punishing the Egyptians, but rather appoints agents to act in his place. If God commanded his "troops" to perform this mission (v. 4), one should not conclude that the only aim of this rewriting is to distance God from evil or unethical actions, since he was in fact the one who decided that all of the Egyptian firstborn should die. It is possible instead that this reflects a general attempt to distance God from the world entirely—he is not directly involved in earthly matters, but sends agents, his "forces," in his place.

The transcendental nature of God in *Jub.* 49 emphasizes the glaring contradiction between chs. 48 and 49 regarding the plague of the firstborn. As we saw above, *Jub.* 48 emphasizes that the Lord himself killed the Egyptian firstborn (in addition to all of the other plagues that he brought; see 48:5–8: "The Lord effected a great revenge against them...He struck them and killed them...their first-born of men and cattle. The Lord took revenge on all their gods and burned them up...The Lord did everything for the sake of Israel..."). In contrast, ch. 49 asserts that God sent "the forces of Mastema" to fulfill this mission (49:2–5). One who wants to resolve the contradiction between the two chapters is likely to suggest that ch. 48, which describes how God brought the plagues, actually meant that he sent his agents on his behalf. However, it is difficult to accept this kind of harmonization in light of the fundamentally different descriptions as to the nature of Mastema. In ch. 48, Mastema is an independent entity with his own aims, even if God and the angel of the presence can thwart his specific plans. He decided to attack Moses when he was returning to Egypt from Midian, and he encouraged the Egyptians to pursue the children of Israel. Mastema therefore cannot be God's envoy, but rather often works against him. He is Egypt's patron, in contrast to the Lord and the angel of presence who are responsible for Israel. It is difficult to imagine

---

[62] As suggested to me by Prof. M. Kister.

that Mastema or his forces would knowingly work against Egypt's best interests. The picture is completely different in *Jub.* 49. The "forces of Mastema" (v. 2) are identified as the "forces of the Lord" (v. 4). God sent them and commanded them to kill the Egyptian firstborn. They are not the heavenly patrons of the Egyptians, but God's special forces for performing "dirty" operations on earth. God is responsible for their actions, because they function under his command; they are an integral part of the way God runs the world. The inclusion of Mastema in ch. 48 is intended to distance God from evil actions, while the goal of ch. 49 is to distance him from direct involvement in the world at all.

The contradiction between these two chapters regarding the identity of the perpetrator of the plague of the firstborn points to the different origins of the rewritten Exodus story and the juxtaposed passage of the Passover laws. The tension between the two descriptions is heightened by their divergent perspectives regarding the status of the forces of evil in the world, either as independent entities or as agents of God.

The Terminology of the Legal Passage

The differences between chs. 48 and 49 are not limited to the understanding of the plague of the firstborn or the heavenly hierarchy, but they also differ in their formulation. *Jubilees* 49 is marked by expressions and sentences that recur throughout *Jubilees*, specifically in the legal passages juxtaposed with the rewritten narratives:

> (7)...from year to year throughout all your lifetime...once a year on its day in accord with all of its law. Then you will not change a day from the day or from month to month.
> (8) For it is an eternal statute and it is engraved on the heavenly tablets regarding the Israelites that they are to celebrate it each and every year on its day, once a year, throughout their entire history. There is no temporal limit because it is ordained forever.
> (14)...from it there is to be no passing over a day from the day or a month from the month because it is to be celebrated on its festal day.
> (15) Now you order the Israelites to celebrate the passover each year during their times, once a year on its specific day...
> (17)...because this is the way it has been written and ordained...
> (22) Now you, Moses, order the Israelites to keep the statute of the passover as it was commanded to you so that you may tell them its year each year, the time of the days...

The vocabulary in these verses focuses on two central topics: the Heavenly Tablets and the correct calendar. These two topics are discussed together elsewhere in the book, and especially in the following two passages:

(1) 6:17, 20, 22 (the commandment of the festival of Weeks/Oaths): "(17) For this reason it has been ordained and written on the heavenly tablets that they should celebrate the festival of weeks during this month—once a year...(20) Now you command the Israelites to keep this festival...one day in the year...(22)...you should celebrate it at each of its times one day in a year...one day each year."

(2) 6:23–38: This passage contains a warning against the desecration of the festivals due to the adoption of the lunar calendar, which will lead to the celebration of the festivals on the incorrect dates. The 364-day calendar, including its special days, is recorded on the Heavenly Tablets.

The difference in terminology is not sufficient in and of itself to support the theory that chs. 48 and 49 were composed by different authors, because one could claim that this difference is the result of the difference in genre, narrative versus law. This division is confirmed, however, by the other arguments adduced above, and the distinction in terminology matches the theory developed here regarding the separate origins of the legal passages and the rewritten stories.[63] We can therefore differentiate between the passages on the basis of the "special terminology of the Heavenly Tablets."[64]

---

[63] Cf. chs. 1–3, 5, 9. Similar to the other examples of the juxtaposition of rewritten stories and legal passages, here too the legal passage first presents a short summary of the story (49:1–6) that contradicts the rewritten narrative (ch. 48).

[64] This was the expression suggested by Ravid (1999) to describe the vocabulary that appears in the halakhic passages. In her opinion, the terminology is a literary device used by the author to mark a passage as part of the Heavenly Tablets. As I suggested above, this terminology corresponds to the division of sources that was ascertained based upon independent considerations, and therefore, in other instances in *Jubilees*, the vocabulary itself can help determine the literary development of each passage.

CHAPTER ELEVEN

THE COMMANDMENT OF CIRCUMCISION AND THE ELECTION OF ISRAEL (15:25–34)

Israel's Special Relationship with YHWH

Jubilees 15:30–32 contrasts the Lord's treatment of Israel with his treatment of other nations:

> (30) For the Lord did not draw near to himself either Ishmael, his sons, his brothers, or Esau...But he chose Israel to be his people. (31) He sanctified them and gathered (them) from all mankind. For there are many nations and many peoples and all belong to him. He made spirits rule over all in order to lead them astray from following him. (32) But over Israel he made no angel or spirit rule because he alone is their ruler. He will guard them and require them for himself from his angels, his spirits, and everyone, and all his powers so that he may guard them and bless them and so that they may be his and he theirs from now and forever.

Israel's election signifies that the Lord has adopted them for himself. The other nations also belong to God, but they do not have the same direct relationship that Israel has.[1] The Lord "made spirits rule over" the nations and they attempt "to lead them astray from following him." The question of Israel's status, as opposed to that of the other nations, is discussed in this passage in the context of the law of circumcision (Gen 17; *Jub.* 15). The original commandment to Abraham (Gen 17:1–14) established that all of his descendants were required to undergo circumcision. Those circumcised belong to the covenant with the Lord; this seemingly applies to his son Ishmael as well (Gen 17:7, 9, 10; *Jub.* 15:9, 11, 12). However in the continuation of the chapter (Gen 17:15–22), the covenant is limited only to Isaac, excluding Ishmael. Although Ishmael was not considered part of this covenant, he received a blessing from God (Gen 17:19). The biblical story concludes with the circumcision of Ishmael and all the males in Abraham's house, in accordance with the original divine commandment (ibid., 23–27).

---

[1] This worldview is similar to that reflected in Deut 32:8–9; 4:19–20; Dan 10:13, 20; 12:1; Sir 17:17. Regarding Deut 32:8–9, see the discussion in the following chapter, pp. 250–251.

The limitation on those included in the covenant in vv. 15–22 creates a certain tension between the three sections that make up this story (vv. 1–14; 15–22; 23–27) regarding Ishmael's status. According to the first, all of Abraham's offspring were to be circumcised as a sign of the covenant, and this is explicitly expressed in the third section as well. In contrast, according to the second unit, circumcision by itself cannot be a sign of membership in the covenant, because Ishmael was indeed circumcised, yet he was left out of the covenant.

The rewriting of Gen 17 presented in *Jub.* 15:1–24 generally follows the biblical text. However, at the end of the passage there is a significant change concerning Ishmael's status.[2] As noted, the third unit in Gen 17 (vv. 23–27) recounts how Abraham fulfilled the commandment to circumcise his offspring and all the males in his household. The following is a synoptic table which compares this passage in Genesis with the parallel material in *Jub.* 15:23–24:

Genesis 17	*Jubilees 15*
	(23) Abraham did as the Lord told him
(23) And Abraham took Ishmael his son, and everyone who was born in his house	He took his son Ishmael, everyone who was born in his house
and all those who had been purchased with money	and who had been purchased with money
every male among the men of Abraham's household	every male who was in his house
and he circumcised the flesh of their foreskins	and circumcised the flesh of their foreskins.

---

[2] There is perhaps another difference in *Jub.* 15:14: "A male who has not been circumcised—the flesh of whose foreskin has not been circumcised *on the eighth day*—that person will be uprooted from his people because he has violated my covenant," while MT Gen 17:14 reads: "An uncircumcised male who has does not circumcise the flesh of his foreskin—such a person will be cut off from his kin; he has broken my covenant." However this addition in *Jubilees* is not the work of the reviser, but is already attested in textual witnesses of the Bible, including SP and LXX (see Hartom 1969: 58; VanderKam 1989b: 89). It is possible that this ancient change influenced the interpretation found in the legal passage appended to the end of the chapter; cf. Charles 1902: 108–109. Charles (1902: 110–111) translated v. 26 as "And every one that is born, the flesh of whose foreskin is not circumcised *on* the eighth day," even though all the Latin and Ethiopic manuscripts read "until" (ʾǝska; usque). In his opinion, v. 26 is an expansion of v. 14, which obligates circumcision specifically *on* the eighth day. However, the polemic in the legal passage is apparently directed against those who allowed for circumcision after the eighth day; see below, pp. 236–237, n. 22.

on that very day as God had spoken to him. (24) And Abraham was ninety-nine years old when he circumcised the flesh of his foreskin. (25) And Ishmael his son was thirteen years old when he circumcised the flesh of his foreskin.[3] (26) On that very day Abraham **and his son Ishmael** were circumcised; (27) and all the men of his household, those who were born in his house and those that had been purchased from outsiders, were circumcised with him.	(24) On the same day Abraham was circumcised and all the men of his household, and all those who had been purchased with money (even from foreigners) were circumcised with him.

According to Gen 17:23, 26–27, Abraham obeyed God's command on the very same day on which it was given, and immediately circumcised himself, Ishmael, and all of his servants. There are two small, but significant, differences between *Jub.* 15:23–24 and these verses from Genesis, and both are directed to the same purpose:

---

[3] It is possible that the passage "on that very day...the flesh of his foreskin" (Gen 17:23b–25) was omitted due to parablepsis, "(23)...on that very day...(26) On that very day Abraham...." However, v. 23b is not entirely absent from *Jubilees*, as the words "as God had spoken to him" are represented (albeit in a slightly different place) in *Jub.* 15:23: "Abraham did as the Lord told him" (as suggested to me by N. Mizrahi). It is possible therefore that these verses were omitted due to exegetical considerations: (1) The chronological framework of *Jubilees* dates the events of this chapter to A.M. 1986 (*Jub.* 15:1; 41/4/5). *Jub.* 14:24 sets the birth of Ishmael in A.M. 1965 (41/1/5), when Abraham was 86 years old (parallel to Gen 16:15–16). Therefore, according to the internal dating in *Jubilees*, Abraham was 107 years old and Ishmael 21 at the time of their circumcision, an explicit contradiction to Gen 17:24–25. This contradiction could possibly explain the omission of these two verses in *Jub.* 15. The problem of the relative date of Ishmael's birth does not arise in *Jubilees*, which offers no information regarding his age at the time he was circumcised. The problem of Abraham's birth though was not solved, because according to *Jub.* 15:17 (parallel to Gen 17:17), Abraham would be 100 years old the next year. Charles (1902: 105–106, following Dillman) suggested to correct the date in *Jub.* 15:1, and to read the "third week" instead of the "fourth week." This pushes the circumcision commandment to A.M. 1979, making Ishmael 14 years old at the time, almost equal to the age of 13 found in Gen 17:25. However, Charles' suggested correction also necessitates the emendation of *Jub.* 16:15 (the third week instead of the fourth) and 17:1 (the fourth week instead of the fifth), without any textual evidence for any of the three verses; cf. Wiesenberg 1961: 30–38; VanderKam 1989b: 87; (1995) 2000: 538–540. It should also be noted that even if the suggested corrections do indeed reflect the original text, it is possible that the omission of Gen 17:24–25 took place after the secondary readings had already entered the text. (2) Regarding the interpretive significance of the omission of the phrase "on that very day," see further in this chapter.

(1) *Jub.* 15:23 describes (parallel to Gen 17:23) the circumcision of Abraham, his son Ishamel, and all the males in his household, but omits the note that it occurred "on that very day."[4]

(2) *Jub.* 15:24 describes (parallel to Gen 17:26–27) the circumcision of Abraham and the members of his household "on that very day," but omits Ishmael from the list.

These two differences can be understood in light of the tension (discussed above) regarding Ishmael's status in Gen 17. The rewriter of *Jub.* 17:23–24 distinguished between the circumcision of Ishmael and that of Abraham and the members of his household: the latter underwent circumcision on the same day on which they were commanded, while Ishmael was circumcised, but not on that same day.

The aim of these "minor" changes in vv. 23–24 can be clarified in light of the juxtaposed legal passage, found at the end of *Jub.* 15 (vv. 25–34). *Jub.* 15:25 reads: "This law is (valid) for all history forever. There is no 'circumcising' of days, and no passing[5] of one day from the eight days because it is an eternal ordinance ordained and written on the heavenly tablets." Scholars have had difficulty interpreting the sentence "there is no circumcising of days," and have generally understood it in a figurative sense.[6] For example, Rabin rendered the sentence paraphrastically: "and there can be no reduction in the number of days."[7]

---

[4] As already suggested in the previous footnote, it is possible that "on that very day" was omitted due to a textual mishap (homoioteleuton), and was not the result of an intentional change. However, if one considers its absence together with the second difference (the omission of Ishmael's name from the list), it seems more likely that it reflects a specific interpretive tendency.

[5] In Ge'ez, *ta'adwa* (to pass over, transgress); in Latin, *praeterire* (to go past or by, to skip or pass over). These two translations together seem to reflect a Hebrew reading from the root ע-ב-ר, as translated by Goldmann and Hartom. Similarly, Wintermute translated "passing"; Littman—"übertretung"; Berger—"überschreiten." Charles, Rabin, and VanderKam all translated "omitting," thus changing the meaning of this sentence into a polemic against those people who circumcise their sons before the eighth day. Support for understanding this word as "passing" can be adduced from v. 26: "Anyone who is born, the flesh of whose private parts has not been circumcised by the eighth day...." This verse does not challenge those who circumcise their sons before the eighth day, but rather those who delay its implementation.

[6] These words are missing in the Latin translation, apparently due to homoioteleuton (this seems to be what VanderKam [1989b: 91] has in mind when he describes it as a case of haplography).

[7] Rabin 1984: 55. Rabin (ibid., 56, n. 10) notes that the literal translation is "and there is no circumcision of the days." Compare Charles (1902: 110 note), who understands the sentence as parallel to the following clause, which he translates as "and no omission of one day..."; see also Wintermute 1985: 87, note g.

VanderKam took the phrase "circumcising of days" as a metaphor for shortening the number of days, and therefore rejected Berger's suggestion to prefer a different Ethiopic reading.[8] However, in contrast with this interpretation, there is no indication further in the passage of people who reduce the number of days prior to circumcision.

Common to all interpretations proposed is the connection of the sentence "there is no circumcising of days" to that which follows:

> This law is (valid) for all history forever. (A)
> There is no circumcising of days, and no passing of one day from the eight days. (B + C)

The reason for this connection is probably the presence of the word "days" in both sentences B and C. The word "days" in the expression "eight days" in sentence C refers to the period before circumcision. Is this necessarily the meaning of the word "days" in sentence B as well? I would like to suggest a different division for the verse, which will allow for a new interpretation of the sentence "there is no circumcising of days":

> This law is (valid) for all history forever, and there is no circumcising of days. (A + B)
> And there is no passing of one day from the eight days. (C)

According to this proposed division, instead of connecting sentences B and C, it is suggested to join sentences A and B. Sentence A establishes that the law of circumcision is eternally valid, and will never cease to be in force. According to the division proposed here, the meaning of sentence B, "there is no circumcising of days," should also be related to the period during which the circumcision law is valid. A parallel passage in *Jubilees*, with similar terminology, can shed some light on this enigmatic phrase, "circumcising of days." Similar to the passage under discussion here, *Jub.* 33:16–17 is also part of a legal passage appended to a rewritten story,[9] and contains a similar cluster of expressions:

---

[8] VanderKam 1989b: 91–92. Berger (1981: 407) chose the Geʿez reading, *kətrata* (= *qətrata*), "locking, closing" (cf. the MSS listed in VanderKam 1989a: 90), instead of *kəsbata*, "circumcision." He too interprets it in parallel to the next clause (in note 25a).

[9] According to the conclusions of chs. 1–3, 5, 9–10, the legal passages juxtaposed to the rewritten stories are characterized by special nomistic terminology, and all belong to the same literary stratum in *Jubilees* (in contrast to the rewritten stories, which are based upon various traditions and sources). *Jub.* 15:25 contains some of the unique vocabulary of the legal passages, such as "this law is (valid) for all history forever" and

"(16)...but (only) in your time as a law of its particular time and as an eternal law for the history of eternity. (17) And there is no completion[10] of days for this law...." The parallelism between this passage and 15:25 can be aligned as follows:

Jubilees 15	Jubilees 33
This law is (valid) for all history forever	(16) and as an eternal law for the history of eternity
there is no **circumcising** of days	(17) there is no **completion** of days for this law

The construct "circumcising of days" parallels the phrase "completion of days" in 33:17. In the Bible, there are a number of possible ways to express the completion of a period of time. One common way is to use the Hebrew verb מ-ל-א ("fill, be full") juxtaposed with the period of time. The most common occurrences of this collocation in the Bible use the infinitive form of מ-ל-א: "completion of days," "completion of years."[11] For example:[12]

> Lev 12:4, 6: "...until her period of purification is completed (מלאת ימי טהרה)...At the completion of her period of purification..."
> Lev 25:30: "before a full year has been completed (עד מלאת לו שנה תמימה)"
> Num 6:5,13: "until the completion of his term (מלאת הימם) as a nazarite...On the day that his term as a nazarite is completed (ביום מלאת ימי נזרו)"
> Esth 1:5: "At the end of this period (ובמלואת הימים האלה)"

The use of the root מ-ל-א in all of these examples signifies the end of the period, and this meaning fits the Ge'ez translation of *Jub.* 33:17. It is possible therefore that the Ethiopic translation to that verse reflects a similar Hebrew *Vorlage*: ואין לחוק הזה מלאת ימים.

Jub. 33:16–17 addresses the prohibition of sexual intercourse with one's father's wife. The legal passage claims that the law only came into

---

"it is an eternal ordinance ordained and written on the heavenly tablets." As we will see in the following discussion, the specific usage of the word "days" in this context also belongs to this legal stratum, and is attested in the Qumran sectarian literature as well.

[10] The Ge'ez translation reads, *tawaddəʾa*, "completion, end, conclusion".

[11] The collocation of the Hebrew מ-ל-א with a period of time can also be found in finite forms of the verb; see Gen 25:24; 29:21, 27–28; 50:3; 2 Sam 7:12 (and the parallel verse in 1 Chr 17:11); Jer 25:34; Lam 4:18; Esth 2:12.

[12] Cf. also Lev 8:33; Jer 25:12; 29:10; Ezek 5:2; Dan 10:3.

force in the Mosaic era, but continues forever.[13] The author of the legal passage thus explains why Reuben and Bilhah were not punished for an act explicitly prohibited in the Pentateuch.[14] The eternal validity of the law is emphasized by a twofold expression—a positive formulation ("and as an eternal law for the history of eternity") and a negative one ("there is no completion of days for this law").

The Qumran Scrolls preserve a unique orthography for the infinitive form of מ-ל-א.[15] E. Qimron adduced this case as an example of the interchange between (proto-Semitic) short u and a sch^ewa (in Tiberian vocalization), in an open, unaccented syllable.[16] For example, instead of the form מְלֹאת in Tiberian orthography, 1QS VI, 17–21 preserves the form מולאת four times (lines 17, 18, 21 [twice]),[17] all of them juxtaposed with a specified period of time. In 4Q511, the *aleph* was replaced with a different *mater lectionis*: "You placed on my lips a fountain of praise and in my heart the secret of the beginning of all the works of man, and the fulfillment/completion (ומולות) of the deeds of the blameless..." (4Q511 63 III, 1–3).[18] The parallelism between "beginning" and "completion" confirms the meaning "conclusion, completion," which is semantically identical to the Hebrew forms מולאת or מלואת.[19]

The form מולות or מולאת (both presumably pronounced the same way), is remarkably similar to the biblical form מולֹת in Exod 4:26: חתן דמים למולֹת, which refers to circumcision.[20] These details allow us to suggest the following reconstructed original text of *Jub.* 15:25: "This law is (valid) for all history forever, and there is no *completion* (מולות or מולאת) of days. There is no passing of one day from the eight days." The structure of this verse parallels *Jub.* 33:16–17, and it too contains

---

[13] VanderKam 1989b: 222.
[14] See the extensive discussion in ch. 3 regarding the Reuben and Bilhah story of *Jub.* 33.
[15] The linguistic discussion here is based upon Qimron 1986:35–36 (esp. n. 42), 110, 117.
[16] Qimron (1986: 35–36, 117) emphasized the similarity between the Qumranic phenomenon and the Babylonian tradition.
[17] The form מלואת appears in 1QS VII, 20, 22. The phenomenon of inconsistent orthography is common in the Dead Sea Scrolls.
[18] The scroll was published by Baillet 1982 as "Cantiques du Sage (ii)." The translation here is based upon *DSSR* 6:190–193, in which the text was renamed 4QShir^b (eds. M. Wise, M. Abegg, E. Cook).
[19] The similar expression in 1QS III, 16, ימלאו פעולתם, explains the meaning of the phrase in 4Q511 (Baillet 1982: 249).
[20] Baillet (1982: 249) rightly rejects the possibility of interpreting the word ומולות in 4Q511 according to Exod 4:26.

a twofold formulation of the eternal nature of the law: positive ("This law is (valid) for all history forever") and negative ("there is no *completion* of days"). The general context of *Jub.* 15, the covenant of circumcision, led to a misunderstanding of the expression which originally referred to the everlasting status of the law. The beginning and end of v. 25 thus both refer to the same topic, the eternal nature of the commandment of circumcision: "This law is (valid) for all history forever, and there is no *completion* of days. (There is no passing of one day from the eight days) because it is an eternal ordinance ordained and written on the heavenly tablets."[21]

Verse 26 continues:

> Anyone who is born, the flesh of whose private parts has not been circumcised by the eighth day does not belong to the people of the pact which the Lord made with Abraham but to the people (meant for) destruction. Moreover, there is no sign on him that he belongs to the Lord, but (he is meant) for destruction, for being destroyed from the earth, and for being uprooted from the earth because he has violated the covenant of the Lord our God.

This verse builds upon the view, expressed in Gen 17:10–14 and *Jub.* 15:11–14, of circumcision as a sign of the covenant: one who is circumcised at *the proper time* belongs to the "people of the pact" and "belongs to the Lord," while one who is not circumcised by the eighth day is considered uncircumcised,[22] and is a member of the "people (meant

---

[21] One should note that it is also possible to interpret the text according to the expression found in the Ethiopic translation, "circumcision of days." The prohibition against having intercourse with one's father's wife (*Jub.* 33) began at a specific point in time in the history of the world, "a law of its particular time" (v. 16). Compare the similar expression in 1QS IX, 13–14: "according to what has been revealed for each period of history...as well as every statute applying to the time (חוק העת)". However, perhaps the law of circumcision has a different definition: "there is no circumcision of days." If the term "circumcision" refers to the law mandating this practice, it is possible that the sentence in question, "there is no circumcision of days," means that there was never a period during which the law was not in effect. This interpretation of v. 25 refers to the eternal nature of the law of circumcision, both in the past and in the future, and corresponds to the claim in v. 27 that the angels of the presence and the angels of holiness were created already circumcised.

[22] *Jub.* 15:25–26 is not directed against those who refrain from circumcising at all, but rather those who delay its performance until after the eighth day, Thus, for example, according to the rabbinic position expressed in m. *Šabb.* 19:5, circumcision can be performed in certain cases from the ninth to the twelfth day after birth. The legal passage in *Jub.* 15 claims that even though such children are physically circumcised, they are considered uncircumcised from the viewpoint of the halakhah. Kister (1986: 6–7, n. 26) suggested that the background for this harsh passage was the halakhic

for) destruction."²³ This dichotomy between the two extremes, those belonging to the covenant of the Lord and those destined for destruction, matches the dualistic approach found in other passages in *Jubilees*. Verse 26 describes the dualism in earthly terms: every person belongs to one of the two groups, either those who are part of the covenant with the Lord and who therefore benefit from his protection, or those who are destined for destruction because they do not.

Verse 27 asserts that the commandment of circumcision existed from the beginning of time: "For this is what the nature of all the angels of the presence and all the angels of holiness was like from the day of their creation. In front of the angels of the presence and the angels of holiness he sanctified Israel to be with him and his holy angels." Already on the first day of creation (compare the description of the creation of the spirits on the first day in *Jub.* 2:2), God chose the angels of the presence and angels of the holiness, and they became members of his covenant. The creation of these angels already circumcised (v. 27) not only illustrates the importance of this commandment at this early stage in history, but also expresses a dualistic worldview of heaven, parallel to the perspective of the human, earthy reality expressed in v. 26. Just as men who are circumcised at the appropriate time are considered members of God's pact, so too the angels of presence and holiness (in contrast with other heavenly beings) are part of that same covenant. Verses 25–27 therefore suppose a theological-cosmological scheme, according to which every creature, both in heaven and on earth, belongs to one and only one of these two camps. Verse 27 views circumcision as the symbol of affiliation with God's faction, and dates the beginnings of circumcision to the beginning of time. However, one cannot assign

---

polemic surrounding the appropriate time when to perform the circumcision, and not a specific historical setting in the Hellenistic period, before (or during) the reign of Antiochus Epiphanes (as suggested by Charles 1902: 108–109, and many scholars who adopted this position, based upon Judeo-Hellenistic sources, such as 1 Macc 1:15, 48, 60; 2:46; *As. Mos.* 8:3; Josephus, *Ant.*, XII, 241). Charles viewed the relationship between the severe demands of *Jub.* 15 and the more moderate rabbinic position as a linear development, from the stringent to the lenient, and did not raise the possibility that the position expressed in the Mishnah might reflect an earlier halakhic position from the Second Temple period.

²³ The Ge'ez translation reads *wəluda mussənnā* (children of destruction). Goldmann translated בני האבדון; Hartom suggested בני ההשמדה. Kister (1982: 125–126, n. 3) referred to this verse from *Jubilees* in a discussion of the ideological and linguistic background of the formulation of the blessing over circumcision, להציל ידידות שארנו משחת. In light of his analysis in that article, Kister suggested (oral communication) that the Hebrew *Vorlage* perhaps read בני השחת.

the heavenly or earthly beings to one camp without the assumption of the existence of an opposing side. Therefore, it can be concluded that the dualistic system that serves as the basis for vv. 25–27, which includes both those included and excluded from the covenant, was created by the Lord as in integral part of the world.

The theological perspective expressed in the legal passage in *Jub.* 15 is identical to that put forth in the description of the giving of the Sabbath laws to the same angels in *Jub.* 2:17–21 (according to 4QJubilees[a] [4Q216] VII, 5–13 [eds. VanderKam and Milik; DJD 13, pp. 19–20]):[24]

```
5                                                      ¹⁷He gave us a great sign the]
6    sabbath [day] on [which] he ceased[                                        ]²⁵
7    were made in six days. [                                                   ]
8    and that we should keep Sabbath on the se[venth] day [from all work. ¹⁸For
     we—all the angels of the presence and all the angels of holiness—]
9    these [two] kinds—he to[ld us to keep Sabbath with him in heaven and
     on earth. ¹⁹He said to us: "I will now separate for myself]
10   a people among my nations. And [they will keep Sabbath. I will sanctify
     them as my people, and I will bless them. They will be my people and
     I will be their God."]
```

---

[24] Chapter 2 contains a paraphrase of the creation story from Gen 1 (*Jub.* 2:1–24a), and a legal passage regarding the Sabbath laws (vv. 24b–33). In contrast to the other halakhic passages that have been analyzed here, the rewritten story and legal passage in *Jub.* 2 cannot be separated for the following reasons: First, the rewriting emphasizes the unique status of the Sabbath by transferring it to the beginning of the description of creation (v. 1), and by the sheer quantity of verses that describe the Sabbath day (vv. 16–24). Second, following the description of each day of the week, the rewriting summarizes the number of things created (v. 3: seven works on the first day; v. 4: one work on the second day, etc.). The total number of works created during the first six days, twenty-two, is mentioned explicitly in v. 15. This sum is the same number as the generations from Adam until Jacob/Israel, and thus the rewritten story draws a connection between Israel and the first Sabbath in history (v. 23). The rewriter describes both Sabbath and Israel as "blessed and holy" (vv. 23, 24). The roots ב-ר-ך and ק-ד-ש stand out even more in the legal passage (vv. 24b–33): "as it was sanctified and blessed on the seventh day" (v. 24b); "for it is a holy day; it is a blessed day" (v. 27); "everyone who observes...will be holy and blessed" (v. 28); "because it is more holy and more blessed" (v. 30); "the creator of all blessed but did not sanctify any people(s) and nations to keep sabbath on it except Israel alone" (v. 31); "created this day blessed it for (the purposes of) blessing, holiness..." (v. 32). *Jubilees* 2 is therefore one literary unit. The special terminology which appears in the legal passage, and especially "Torah and *te'udah*" in v. 24 (see 4QJub[a] VII, 17; DJD 13, p. 19) and v. 33, demonstrates therefore that the entire chapter is the work of the redactor responsible for adding the legal passages throughout the book. It is therefore possible to make use of the description of Israel's election at creation (2:19–21) in order to understand the worldview of the redactor.

[25] The Ge'ez translation of v. 17 reads: "He gave us the sabbath day as a great

11 ²⁰And he chose the descendants of Jacob among [all of those whom I have seen. I have recorded them as my first-born son and have sanctified them for myself]
12 for all the age(s) of eternity. The [seventh] day [I will tell them so that they may keep Sabbath on it from everything, ²¹as he blessed them and sanctified them for himself as a special people]
13 out of all the nations and to be [keeping Sabbath] together [with us.]

Sabbath and circumcision are the only two commandments that the angels of the presence and angels of holiness were given explicitly in *Jubilees*. One can also add the festival of *Shavuʿot*, the annual festival of covenant renewal, which the Lord and the angels celebrated in heaven (*Jub.* 6:17–18):[26]

> For this reason it has been ordained and written on the heavenly tablets that they should celebrate the festival of weeks during this month—once a year—to renew the covenant each and every year. This entire festival had been celebrated in heaven from the time of creation until the lifetime of Noah...

The common denominator of these three laws (Sabbath, circumcision, festival of Weeks/Oaths) is the motif of covenant.[27] Just as the Sabbath was given to the angels in the first week of creation, and *Shavuʿot* was observed from that time, so too circumcision began on the first day of creation, when the angels were created already circumcised. In the same way that Israel was chosen from among the nations to rest with the Lord (compare 2:19–21, 31: "The creator of all blessed but did not sanctify any people[s] and nations to keep sabbath on it except Israel alone"), and as the festival of weeks is the time in which the covenant between the Lord and Israel is remembered and renewed, so

---

sign so that we should perform work for six days and that we should keep sabbath from all work on the seventh day." As noted by VanderKam and Milik (1994: 21–22), there is too much space in lines 6–7 to merely retrovert this translation into Hebrew, and they therefore concluded that the scroll contained words not found in the Ethiopic version of v. 17.

[26] *Jub.* 6:17 is characterized by a concentration of the special legal terminology: "For this reason it has been ordained and written on the heavenly tablets," "once a year," "each and every year." Cf. also 6:20—"Now you command the Israelites...one day in the year, during this month, they are to celebrate the festival."

[27] Dimant 1994: 103–104. The Sabbath is referred to as a covenant between the Lord and Israel in Exod 31:13, 16–17. As Seeligmann (1992: 438–439) quoted in the name of Barthélemy, *Jub.* 6:21 derives the name of the festival *Shavuʿot*, as if it read *Shevuʿot*, "oaths," and therefore as the festival of the covenant.

too the Israelites were chosen from among the nations to observe the commandment of circumcision:

> (15:28) Now you command the Israelites to keep the sign of this covenant throughout their history as an eternal ordinance so that they may not be uprooted from the earth (29) because the command has been ordained as a covenant so that they should keep it forever on all the Israelites. (30) For the Lord did not draw near to himself either Ishmael, his sons, his brothers, or Esau. He did not choose them (simply) because[28] they were among Abraham's children, for he knew them. But he chose Israel to be his people.

The granting of the Sabbath and circumcision laws to Israel defines their relationship with the Lord (2:19; 15:30). *Jub.* 2:17–21 claims that the Lord's election of Israel, in contrast with the universalistic description of creation in Gen 1, occurred already at the dawn of time.[29] If so, both circumcision and *Shavu'ot*, which symbolize the special relationship between God and his covenantal partners, existed from the week of creation. The laws were in force for the angels of the presence and the angels of holiness, but were already set aside for the Israelites (in contrast to other nations), even if only theoretically.

Jubilees 2 (Sabbath) and 6 (Weeks/Oaths) emphasize only those chosen by the Lord: the angels of the presence, the angels of holiness, and the Israelites. But as mentioned above, *Jub.* 15:25–33 also refers to those rejected by God, those destined for destruction. Parallel to those who are included in the covenant of the Lord, in heaven and on earth, there are both heavenly and earthly creatures who are destined for "destruction." On the earth, this latter category includes all other nations: "For the Lord did not draw near to himself either Ishmael, his sons, his brothers, or Esau. He did not choose them (simply) because they were among Abraham's children, for he knew them. But he chose Israel to be his people" (v. 30). In the heavenly realm, corresponding to

---

[28] The Ge'ez: *əsma*; and Latin: *quoniam* both translate "because (כי)". Goldmann (1956: 254, note) suggests interpreting this כי as אף כי, "even though, despite"; VanderKam (1989b: 93) translates "(simply) because."

[29] In the Pentateuch, the Sabbath was given exclusively to Israel only in Exod 31:13–17, and not at the creation of the world. Doering (1997: 189–191) also noted rabbinic sources that express a similar, nationalistic approach to that of *Jubilees*, but they do not push backward the giving of the Sabbath law to the time of creation. According to the approach suggested here, the election of Israel and the giving of the Sabbath both result from the same comprehensive worldview, according to which a dualistic world order was established from creation.

the angels of the presence and the angels of holiness, God appointed spirits who rule over the nations, trying to lead them astray:

> (15:31) ...For there are many nations and many peoples and all belong to him. He made spirits rule over all in order to lead them astray from following him. (32) But over Israel he made no angel or spirit rule because he alone is their ruler. He will guard them and require them for himself from his angels, his spirits, and everyone, and all his powers so that he may guard them and bless them and so that they may be his and he theirs from now and forever.

The combination of these three passages (2:17–21; 6:17–20; 15:25–34), which share similar terminology, leads to a crystallized, dualistic system, which functions in heaven and on earth: those who are partners in God's covenant (angels of the presence, angels of holiness, and Israel) against those destined for destruction (the spirits and the other nations). This doctrine sees the latter group as the cause of evil in the world. This explanation for the origin of evil differs from the position underlying the various traditions found in the Enochic literature, which attributes evil to a one-time event—the intercourse between the sons of god and daughters of men and the resulting damage to the world order. The passages from *Jubilees* discussed here posit that from its inception, God planned a world which included both good and evil; the existence of evil is therefore not the result of some later defect in what he created, but is consistent with his original plan.

The worldview of the author of these passages in *Jubilees*, who posits that evil in the world is part of a dualistic system established at the beginning of time, and that the foreign nations are members of the group destined for destruction, perhaps explains the minor changes in *Jub.* 15:23–24 noted above. The legal passage adduces Ishmael as an example of one of the nations not chosen by God: "For the Lord did not draw near to himself either Ishmael, his sons, his brothers, or Esau" (v. 30). Instead, God chose Isaac for the establishment of the covenant with Abraham: "But my covenant I will establish with Isaac" (Gen 17:21; *Jub.* 15:21). Ishmael was not chosen to be part of the covenant, and he therefore should not receive the sign of the covenant, circumcision (Gen 17:10, 11, 13; *Jub.* 15:11, 13). Using the terminology of the dualistic approach reflected in *Jub.* 15:25–34, circumcision is the sign of membership on the side of those belonging to the covenant of the Lord (v. 26), and since Ishmael was not elected to this covenant, he therefore must belong to those destined for destruction (v. 30). The precise stipulation for affiliation with the Lord's covenant appears in v. 26:

Anyone who is born, the flesh of whose private parts has not been circumcised **by the eighth day** does not belong to the people of the pact which the Lord made with Abraham but to the people (meant for) destruction. Moreover, there is no sign on him that he belongs to the Lord, but (he is meant) for destruction...

As noted above, the demand to circumcise by the eighth day is probably part of a polemic against those (perhaps the Pharisees) who advocated a position, reflected later in rabbinic literature (*m. Šabb.* 19:5 et al.), which allowed for the circumcising of an infant after the eighth day under specific circumstances.[30] This specific stipulation, circumcision on the eighth day, could not of course apply to Abraham and his family, because they only received this law at a later stage in their lives (cf. Gen 17:24–25), but they fulfilled it immediately, "on that very day" (Gen 17:23, 26; *Jub.* 15:24), i.e. as soon as they were informed of this law and its importance for partnership in God's covenant. Both the original commandment to Abraham and his offspring, and the halakhah for future generations were time-bound; those who fail to fulfill them on time are destined for destruction, excluded from the Lord's covenant and under the control of the spirits.[31]

---

[30] See Kister 1986: 6–7, n. 26. It is possible that in the continuation of the legal passage, there is a polemic against another halakhic position reflected later in rabbinic literature. Verse 33 reads: "I am now telling you that the Israelites will prove false to this ordinance. They will not circumcise their sons in accord with this entire law because *they will leave some of the flesh of their circumcision* when they circumcise their sons." This verse is perhaps directed against a halakhic position similar to the one expressed in m. Šabb. 19:6, which defines "threads which invalidate the circumcision," i.e., threads of skin from the foreskin, which if not removed, the child is considered uncircumcised. The definition given there, "flesh that covers the majority of the corona," informs us that according to the opinion expressed there, there are threads of skin that can be left which do not prevent the children from being considered circumcised. The topic is discussed again in a *baraita* in *b. Šabb.* 133b, in the context of a discussion regarding circumcision on the Sabbath. The *baraita* notes that there are cases in which threads of skin remain and the child is still considered circumcised (and therefore one should not later cut those extra threads on the Sabbath). *Jub.* 15:33 is perhaps then reacting to the position that distinguishes between threads of the foreskin which need to be removed and those that can remain, and instead proposes a more stringent approach that demands the removal of the entire foreskin in order to be considered circumcised.

[31] Schechter (1910: lvi, and n. 5), Rabin (1954: 74–75), and Baumgarten and Schwartz (1995: 41) already noted the connection between *Jub.* 15:25–33 and CD XVI, 4–6, but one can expand this comparison to lines 1–6 in the scroll: "...with you a covenant and with all Israel. Therefore, a man shall take upon himself (an oath) to return to the Torah of Moses, for in it everything is specified...And on the day when a man takes upon himself (an oath) to return to the Torah of Moses, the angel Mastema shall turn aside from after him, if he fulfills his words. Therefore, Abraham

It is now possible to return to the question of Ishmael's status. If he fulfilled the commandment of circumcision, then according to the interpretation of the law found in vv. 25–34 he too should be a party to the covenant. The changes in vv. 23–24 can therefore be viewed as an attempt to resolve this tension regarding Ishmael. In the description of the circumcision of Abraham, Ishmael, and the other members of the household in v. 23 (parallel to Gen 17:23), the expression "on that very day" has been omitted. The phrase does indeed appear in v. 24 (parallel to Gen 17:26–27), but Ismael has been omitted from that list. If so, the story in *Jub.* 15 seeks to remove the possibility that Ishmael was circumcised immediately, and as a result he is not considered a member of the covenant.

The Provenance of the Legal Passage

The main interest of the legal passage is Israel's special status as compared to the other nations. However, the passage also includes a harsh polemic against people or groups from within Israel:

> Verse 26: Anyone who is born, the flesh of whose private parts has not been circumcised by the eighth day does not belong to the people of the pact which the Lord made with Abraham but to the people (meant for) destruction. Moreover, there is no sign on him that he belongs to the Lord, but (he is meant) for destruction...
>
> Verses 33–34: I am now telling you that the Israelites will prove false to this ordinance. They will not circumcise their sons in accord with this entire law because they will leave some of the flesh of their circumcision when they circumcise their sons. All the people of Belial will leave their

---

was circumcised on the day of his knowing" (translation according to Baumgarten and Schwartz 1995: 38–41). These lines also appear in the context of covenant, the special relationship between God and the sect, which is based upon the correct interpretation of the "Torah of Moses" (see also CD III, 12–14; VIII, 21). Abraham circumcised himself on the same day that he was informed of the covenantal significance of this act, and similarly those who join the special covenant of the sect will be considered members in that pact, and not under the influence of Mastema.

Kister (1999: 180–181) interpreted the special significance of circumcision in this *Damascus Document* passage as an example of a "new" commandment given to Abraham, and thus as a paradigm for the sect, which believed in gradual revelation of the laws. As Kister noted, the formulation of the idea of gradual revelation in 1QS I, 8–9 ("to be joined in God's council and *to walk blamelessly before him [according to] all that has been revealed in the appointed times*") is based upon the revelation to Abraham in Genesis 17:1: "walk before me and be blameless" (cf. also CD XV, 10, 13).

sons uncircumcised just as they were born. Then there will be great anger from the Lord against the Israelites because they neglected his covenant, departed from his word, provoked, and blasphemed in that they did not perform the ordinance of this sign. For they have made themselves like the nations so as to be removed and uprooted from the earth. They will no longer have forgiveness or pardon so that they should be pardoned and forgiven for every sin, for (their) violation of this eternal (ordinance).

These verses emphasize specifically inner-Jewish, halakhic polemics. The accusation that Jews who were not circumcised at the appropriate time do "not belong to the people of the pact which the Lord made with Abraham" and "have made themselves like the nations," informs us of the attitude of the author (and perhaps of the group to which he belonged) to other Jewish groups. According to the definition of the author of the passage, those who were not circumcised on time are outside the boundaries of the Jewish people. If the Pharisees are indeed the group against whom this polemic is directed (relying upon the evidence of *m. Šabb.* 19), then the author's caustic words were directed against a broad section of the Jewish population of his time.[32]

It is generally accepted in *Jubilees* scholarship to date the book prior to the separation of the Dead Sea sect from the rest of the nation, because it is claimed that it contains no hints or allusions to an internal split or division within Judaism.[33] However, the strict halakhic position expressed regarding circumcision, and its national-religious implications, call this consensus into question.[34] If the passage is directed against another group which advocated a halakhic approach similar to that attested later in rabbinic literature, it provides important evidence for

---

[32] Regarding the division of the nation into three sects, and the relationship between them, see Flusser 1970. Of course, not all males born to the Pharisees were circumcised after the eighth day; however, the severity of the claims against them still remains. Even if the passage is directed against a different group (and not the Pharisees), it would still attest to the inner-Jewish tensions regarding halakhic questions.

[33] See for example Wintermute 1985: 44—"The most significant difference between Jubilees and the writings from Qumran for the purpose of dating is the fact that Jubilees does not reflect any significant break with the larger national body, whereas the Qumran sect has broken with the establishment and its priesthood, which it judges apostate." VanderKam (2001: 21) recently summarized the consensus as follows: "It is also an established position among scholars today that *Jubilees* was an older, authoritative work inherited and cherished by the community associated with the Dead Sea Scrolls. *Jubilees* gives no indication that its author has separated from the Jewish community of his day, while a number of scrolls do express such a schism."

[34] Cf. Kister 1986. His analysis leads to the conclusion that the descriptions of the people's sins in *Jub.* 1 and 23 refer to a rupture or split that had already occurred.

some degree of a division within the nation, not necessarily physical or geographical, but a theological and halakhic separation. The extent of the divide between the groups (or sects) and its practical expressions are not fully clear. But the legal passage in *Jub.* 15 provides early evidence for the first stages of a split in the nation (over halakhic issues), and provides a theological justification for separation from the rest of the people. This position reached its full, radical expression in the sectarian literature discovered at Qumran.

CHAPTER TWELVE

THE PRAYER OF MOSES (1:19–21)

According to the narrative frame of *Jubilees* (which belongs to the redactional layer of the book),[1] Moses ascended Mount Sinai in order to receive additional tablets (which appear to overlap with *Jubilees* itself).[2] Prior to the giving of these tablets, God describes the Israelites' future sins (1:5–14), and envisions that only after a lengthy period of time, during which he will inflict various punishments upon them, will they repent and thus be rewarded (1:15–18). After Moses heard this dire prediction for Israel, he turned to God in prayer in order to save Israel from sinning:[3]

> (1:19) Then Moses fell prostrate and prayed and said: "Lord my God, do not allow your people and your inheritance to go along in the error of their minds, and do not deliver them into the control of the nations with the result that they rule over them lest they make them sin against you. (20) May your mercy, Lord, be lifted over your people. Create for them a just spirit. May the spirit of Belial[4] not rule over them so as to bring

---

[1] One can demonstrate that *Jub.* 1 belongs to the redactional layer based upon two arguments: (1) one cannot separate the narrative from the rest of the book, because it introduces the angel of the presence, and explains his role as the narrator throughout the book. (2) The expression "Torah and *te'udah*" appears repeatedly throughout the chapter (Prologue; vv. 4, 26, 29; possibly also v. 8 [according to the reconstruction suggested by Werman (1999) 2002: 95; 2001a: 242–243, accepted by Kister 2001: 297–298, n. 50]). This expression belongs to the vocabulary of the legal passages appended to the rewritten narratives (cf. 2:24, 33; 3:14; and see the discussion in ch. 14 regarding its meaning).

[2] Cf. van Ruiten 1995. The book opens with a rewriting of Exod 24:12–18, and dates his ascent to the sixteenth of the third month, the day **after** the giving of the Torah according to *Jubilees* and the Qumran Scrolls. The author of *Jub.* 1 therefore understands Exod 24:12–18 as a description of a second ascent to Sinai, and not the continuation of Exod 19; 24:1–11 (cf. the opinions of Rashi and Nachmanides to Exod 24:1,12). According to this scheme, Moses did not receive the "tablets of the covenant" and the content of the Heavenly Tablets, which contain "the divisions of times of the Torah and *te'udah*," at the same time (*contra* Werman [1999] 2002: 77–81, who posits that *Jubilees* describes one ascent, during which time Moses received both pairs of tablets).

[3] Kister (1999a: 352–354) identified Moses' prayer in *Jub.* 1:19–21 as an apotropaic prayer, according to the category and definition suggested by Flusser 1966.

[4] The Ge'ez translation reads *belḥor*; the *lamed/reš* interchange at the end of the

charges against them before you and to trap them away from every proper path so that they may be destroyed from your presence. (21) They are your people and your inheritance whom you have rescued from Egyptian control by your great power. Create for them a pure mind and a holy spirit. May they not be trapped in their sins from now to eternity."

The beginning and end of this prayer are based upon Moses' prayer in Deut 9:26–29, which he said following the sin of the golden calf:[5]

Jubilees 1	*Deuteronomy* 9
(19) Then Moses fell prostrate <u>and prayed and said: "Lord my God, do not</u> allow <u>your people and your inheritance</u> to go along in the error of their minds...	(26) <u>I prayed</u> to the Lord <u>and said:</u> "Lord YHWH <u>do not</u> annihilate <u>your people and your inheritance</u>...
(21) <u>They are your people and your inheritance whom you have rescued</u> from Egyptian control <u>by your great power</u>...	(29) <u>They are your people and your inheritance whom you have rescued by your great power</u> and your outstretched arm...

The prayer in Deut 9 addresses the Israelites' expected punishment for their previous misdeeds, and therefore Moses requests that God pardon them. In contrast, Moses' prayer in *Jub.* 1 is preventative: he refers to the future, and beseeches God to preclude Israel from sinning. The difference between the two prayers explains the replacement of "do not annihilate" (Deut 9:26) with "do not allow your people and your inheritance to go along in the error of their minds" (*Jub.* 1:19).

Both prayers attributed to Moses are intended to protect the Israelites from the punishments resulting from their sins, and both were said during a period of forty days and forty nights on Mount Sinai. Presumably, this connection between the two events led to the use of the prayer from Deut 9 in the composition of *Jub.* 1. Alternatively, it is possible that the specific formulation of the prayer in Deut 9:26–29, and the meaning embedded in its language, led to the adoption and rewriting

---

word reflects the form found in Greek: Βελιάρ. See Littman 1900: 40; VanderKam 1989b: 5.

[5] Moses' prayer in Deut 9:26–29 is based upon the prayer in Exod 32:11–14 (see Driver 1902: 116–117; Weinfeld 1991: 414). However, the point of departure in the version in *Jub.* 1 is the Deuteronomistic phrase "your people and your inheritance" (cf. Deut 4:20; 1 Kgs 8:51[, 53]), which appears twice in the prayer in Deuteronomy, and not in the Exodus version.

of this biblical passage in *Jub.* 1. The phrase "your people and your inheritance," which appears twice in each of the prayers, defines the relationship between God and his nation.[6] In the context of Deut 9, the collocation of the two nouns "your nation" and "your inheritance" is intended as a response to the God's statement to Moses in Deut 9:12:[7]

Deut 9:12	*Deut 9:26*
And the Lord said to me, "Hurry, go down from here at once, for <u>your people</u> <u>whom you freed</u> <u>from Egypt</u> have acted wickedly (שחת)...	I prayed to the Lord and said: "Lord YHWH do not <u>annihilate</u> (<u>תשחת</u>) <u>your people and your</u> <u>inheritance</u> whom you released in your greatness, <u>whom you freed</u> <u>from Egypt</u> with a mighty hand

Moses attempts to convince the Lord not to punish his nation, and responds to God's claim that Israel is Moses' nation ("your people"), which he led out of Egypt. Moses therefore emphasizes that they are God's nation, and even his "inheritance."[8] The idea that Israel is the "inheritance of the Lord" appears throughout the Bible,[9] and its meaning in Deut 9 is that they are the Lord's property. If the Israelites belong to God, then it is not in his best interest to harm them, as he would then be hurting himself.[10] Deut 9:26, 29 only refer to Israel's standing vis-à-vis God, and do not express a specific position regarding his relationship with other nations. Moreover, it does not seem as if these verses are even interested in the question of Israel's special status in light of YHWH's universal sovereignty.[11]

---

[6] The collocation "people" and "inheritance" also appears in Deut 4:20; 1 Kgs 8:36 (= 2 Chr 6:27), 51, 53; Joel 4:20; Ps 33:12. In 2 Sam 20:19–20, the wise woman from Abel-beth-maacah describes the Israelites as "the Lord's inheritance."

[7] God's statement to Moses in Deut 9:12 is based upon the formulation in Exod 32:7–8 (see Driver 1902: 113–114; Weinfeld 1991: 409).

[8] Tigay 1996: 103.

[9] See the important discussion by Loewenstamm 1986.

[10] Tigay, ibid. As he notes, the expression "to damage inheritance" originates in an economic context; cf. Ruth 4:6: "lest I damage my own inheritance."

[11] Loewenstamm (1986: 156–157) lists Deut 9:26, 29 amongst the verses that use the expression "inheritance of the Lord" as a term of endearment for the Israelites, but that do not address the theological questions regarding Israel's special status in the world. Moses' claim is actually based upon a specific understanding of Israel's status, and is not just an appeal to God's love, but Loewenstamm is correct that these verses do not address the theological ramifications of their unique standing.

In contrast, another passage in Deuteronomy employs the expression "inheritance of the Lord" in order to express a henotheistic worldview:

> When the Most High gave nations their *inheritance*, and set the divisions of man, he fixed the boundaries of *peoples* according to the number of the sons of god.[12] For YHWH's *portion* is *his people*; Jacob, the allotment of *his inheritance* (Deut 32:8–9).[13]

As opposed to strict monotheism, henotheism assumes the existence of more than one divine being in the world; however, in contrast to polytheistic religions, henotheism recognizes that one god (in this case YHWH) stands above all of the other divine entities. According to the approach expressed in these two verses, at the beginning of history, the "Most High" god divided all of humanity into nations and countries according to the number of divine, heavenly beings, or "sons of god."[14] Each nation is ruled by a specific "son of god," while the Lord adopted Israel as his portion and inheritance. YHWH therefore has a unique, direct relationship with Israel. The god who divided up the land is referred to as עליון, or "Most High." Some scholars have proposed identifying this god with Elyon or El, deities of the same name known from Canaanite sources, and therefore interpreted v. 9 as meaning that YHWH is merely one of the sons of god mentioned in v. 8.[15] However, as Rofé has argued, the emphasis in the Song that

---

[12] This is the reading of 4QDeut^j XII, 14 (DJD 14, p. 90) and LXX (ἀγγέλων θεοῦ = "angels of god" in most MSS [apparently to tone down the mythical tone of "sons of god"]), as opposed to "sons of Israel" in MT. The reading in MT is exegetically difficult, as there is no obvious connection between the number of nations and the number of Israelites. According to *Tg. ps.-Jon.*, the "number of sons of Israel" refers to the number of sons of Jacob who descended to Egypt, seventy (according to MT). But as noted by Rofé (1988: 219–221), there is no mention or hint in the entire song of the enslavement in Egypt, and it is therefore difficult to accept this interpretation. It is preferable to view the reading in MT Deut 32:8 as a theological correction, whose purpose was to remove any suggestion of a polytheistic (or henotheistic) notion from the biblical text. See the discussions of Skehan 1954; Rofé ibid.; Tigay 1996: 514–515.

[13] Compare also Deut 4:19–20 which contains the expression "people of inheritance (עם נחלה)," and expresses an outlook similar to that of Deut 32:8–9. For a description of the theological view that forms the basis of Deut 4:19–20, see Rofé 1979: 98–101; Knohl 1994: 5–7; Tigay 1996: 50.

[14] The status of the sons of god, the divine retinue surrounding YHWH, is described in Gen 6:1–4; 1 Kgs 22:19; Ps 29:1; 82:1; Job 1–2; 38:7.

[15] Budde 1920: 41–42; Eissfeldt 1958: 28–30; Loewenstamm 1986: 182–187; Tov 2001: 269. El and Elyon appear as a pair in an Aramaic inscription from Sefire. See Gibson 1975: 28–29, col. A i, line 11: "in the presence of El and Elyon (וקדם אל ועליון)." Cf. also Gen 14:18–20, 22 (according to LXX and Peshitta); Ps 78:35.

the Lord himself is responsible for Israel (v. 12: "The Lord alone did guide him, and there is no alien god at his side") is difficult to understand if he is responsible for only one nation. Each and every son of god is solely responsible for his own nation, and they too guide them by themselves. What makes YHWH's relationship with Israel unique is that he, who is responsible for the entire universe, rules directly over only one nation: Israel.[16] If so, Deut 32:8–9 establishes that YHWH stands at the head of a council of divine beings who are sovereign over the nations of the world, and simultaneously, he is directly responsible for the Israelites. The terminology that denotes this special relationship between the Lord and his nation includes: "portion (חלק)," "people (עם)," and "inheritance (נחלה)."

What is the meaning of the expression "your people and your inheritance" in *Jub.* 1:19–21? As noted, the use of the expression in Deut 9:26–29 was not intended to express a theological stance regarding God's relationship with Israel, in contrast with the other nations. However, the idea expressed by the terms "people" and "inheritance" in Deut 32:8–9 (and also Deut 4:19–20) allowed the author of *Jub.* 1:19–21 to transfer the focus of Moses' prayer in Deut 9:26–29 to a viewpoint similar to that expressed in the other verses: Israel is the Lord's special inheritance, and therefore his relationship with them is supposed to be direct, without the interference of any other divine power. This direct connection is emphasized in Moses' prayer in *Jubilees*, as he beseeches God to prevent Israel from sinning, and to protect them from "the spirit of Belial" so that he will "not rule over them" (v. 20); the dominion of "the spirit of Belial" over Israel is intended to "trap them away from every proper path," leading to their eventual punishment.

The Spirit of Belial

The collocation "spirit of Belial" is not found in the Hebrew Bible. The word "Belial" alone appears 27 times, with two possible meanings: (1) a mythical sense (2 Sam 22:5 || Ps 18:5), parallel to Sheol; (2) evil in general (e.g., 1 Sam 16:7; 30:22; Prov 6:12). In Jewish literature of the Second Temple period, and especially in the *Testaments of the Twelve Patriarchs*[17] and in the sectarian literature from Qumran, Belial was

---

[16] Rofé 1979: 229.
[17] Belial (Βελιάρ) is mentioned 29 (or 30) times in the *Testaments of the Twelve Patriarchs*:

transformed into a proper noun, as the personal name of the head of the demonic, evil forces in the world, who stands in opposition to God and the righteous heavenly forces. The viewpoint expressed in these compositions is dualistic: the evil axis in the world is in a constant struggle against justice and its adherents. Belial acts as an independent force who attempts to lead humanity astray, and to cause them to sin against God. For example, Benjamin warns his children in his testament (*T. Benj.* 3:3–4): "...and even though the spirits of Belial ask for you to be delivered up to every evil of tribulation, yet no evil of tribulation will have dominion over you, even as it had not over Joseph my brother...For he who fears God and loves his neighbor cannot be smitten by the spirit of the air of Belial because he is shielded by the fear of God."[18] In *T. Levi* 19:1, the actions of Belial are identified with darkness, while the Lord's Torah is associated with light: "And now, my children, you have heard all. Choose, therefore, for yourselves either darkness or light, either the law of the Lord or the works of Belial."[19] The author of *T. Iss.* mentions the "spirit of Belial" together with actions of evil people: "Do you also these things, my children, and every spirit of Belial will flee from you, and no deed of wicked men will rule over you..." (7:7).[20] But despite Belial's influence on humanity, the *Testaments of the Twelve Patriarchs* reflect the assumption that people always have the ability to choose between good and evil.[21] In some of the passages, Belial is presented as the embodiment of a negative characteristic, such as sexual impropriety, jealousy and arrogance, anger and deceit, or even the evil inclination itself,[22] and the purpose of the *Testaments* is to encourage readers to refrain from following these sinful paths.

Belial serves a similar function in the literature of the Qumran sect.[23] He causes people to sin: thus for example "You made Belial for the pit

---

T. Reu. 4:7, 11; 6:3; *T. Sim.* 5:3; *T. Levi* 3:3; 18:12; 19:1; *T. Jud.* 25:3; *T. Iss.* 6:1; 7:7; *T. Zeb.* 9:8; *T. Dan* 1:7; 4:7; 5:1, 10, 11; *T. Naph.* 2:6; 3:1; *T. Ash.* 1:8; 3:2; 6:4; *T. Jos.* 7:4; 20:2; *T. Benj.* 3:3, 4(, 8); 6:1, 7; 7:1, 2.

[18] Translation according to Hollander and de Jonge 1985: 417. In the next verse, (*T. Benj.* 3:5), the testament continues "Nor can he be ruled over by the plots of men or beasts...." The juxtaposition of spirits of Belial and people who try to rule over the righteous is reminiscent of *Jub.* 1:19–20, which mentions the spirit of Belial alongside the nations that prey on Israel.

[19] Hollander and de Jonge 1985: 182. See also *T. Iss.* 6:1, which contrasts the "commandments of the Lord" and "Belial."

[20] Hollander and de Jonge 1985: 250.

[21] Flusser 1971: 691.

[22] Eshel 1999: 121–123.

[23] For a compilation of all the sectarian sources which mention Belial, and for a

(or: destruction, לשחת), an angel of malevolence, his [ ] in darkne[ss] and his counsel is to condemn and convict. All the spirits of his lot—the angels of destruction—walk in accord with the rule of darkness, for it is their only [des]ire" (1QM XIII, 10–12);[24] "Every man who is ruled by the spirits of Belial and speaks apostasy..." (CD XII, 2–3).[25] Human beings are unable to choose between good and evil, and anybody who is under the "dominion of Belial," in other words under the control of the evil forces in the world, is by definition a sinner.[26] According to the dualistic approach of the Qumran sect, the world is divided into two camps, and the evildoers are under Belial's control: "all the people of the lot of Belial" (1QS II, 5), or "in the lot of the sons of darkness, in the army of Belial" (1QM I, 1 [,13]). Belial also assists the nations in their struggle against Israel: "For formerly Moses and Aaron stood by the hand of the Prince of Lights, and Belial raised up Jannes and his brother in his plotting, when he wrought evil (בהרשע)[27] against Israel in the beginning" (*Damascus Document* V, 17–19).[28]

At the same time, there are occurrences of the word "Belial" in the Qumran sectarian literature with the biblical meaning of "evil" in a general sense, and which do not possess this distinctive dualistic meaning. In particular, the *Hodayot* sometimes use the term with this biblical meaning (XII, 10: "They have plotted wickedness against me..."; XII, 12–13: "Because you, God, spurn every wicked thought [מחשבת בליעל]..."; *DSSR* 5:26–27), and in other cases in the sense of an

---

discussion of his status and position according to the sectarian foundational documents, see Yadin 1962: 232–234; Lewis 1992: 655–656; Sperling 1995; Eshel 1999: 123–130; Mach 2000.

[24] *DSSR* 1:232–233. Isolated words from this passage were preserved in 4QM[e] (4Q495) frg. 2, 3–4 (DJD 7, p. 55). The *War Scroll* does not distinguish between Belial and Mastema. This appears to be the case in *Jubilees* as well, as they both fill identical roles in the book. It is possible that the use of two different epithets is the result of two different traditions (which were eventually combined) about the head of the forces of evil in the world.

[25] Baumgarten and Schwartz 1995: 50–51. This version is almost identical to that preserved in 4QD[f] (4Q271) 5 I, 18–19 (DJD 18, p. 181).

[26] See 1QM XIV, 9; XVIII, 1; 1QS I, 18, 24; II, 18; III, 21–23 (regarding the angel of darkness and "his malevolent dominion [ממשלת משטמתו]").

[27] This is the reading of 4QD[a] (4Q266) 3 II, 5–7; 4QD[b] (4Q267) 2, 1–3 (DJD 18, pp. 41, 92). CD here reads "when Israel was first saved (בהושע)"

[28] A similar description is found in *Jub.* 48, but there Mastema, and not Belial, assists the Egyptians (Rabin 1954: 21; Eshel 1999: 124). The interchange between them points to the complete merger of the traditions regarding Belial and Mastema. The tradition about the magicians Jannes and Jambres, which is known from other Jewish and Christian sources, does not appear in *Jubilees*.

independent divine entity, so prevalent in the other sectarian scrolls (XIV, 21–22: "Belial is the counselor of their heart..."; XV, 3–4: "My heart is stupefied because of evil plotting, for Belial [is manifest] when the true nature of their being is revealed..."; *DSSR* 5:36–37).[29] Similarly, MMT C 29 contains the request: "and remove from you the plans of evil and the device of Belial...." Therefore, one cannot automatically assume that any instance of the term in sectarian literature (and in *Jubilees*) indicates a dualistic approach, i.e., an independent being named Belial, who stands at the head of the evil powers in the world.

What is the meaning of the expression "spirit of Belial" which appears in Moses' prayer in *Jub.* 1—evil and injustice or an independent entity? Kister noted the similarity between Moses' prayer and two other apotropaic prayers from Jewish literature of the Second Temple period: Levi's prayer in the *Aramaic Levi Document* and 4QMMT C 27–32. These three prayers all employ the same style in order to express the request to keep the one who prays from sinning:[30]

> ***Jub.* 1:20:** "May the spirit of Belial not rule over them so as to bring charges against them before you and to trap them away from every proper path"
>
> **Levi's Prayer:**[31] "And grant me all the paths of truth (ארחת קשט); make far (ארחק) from me, O Lord, the unrighteous spirit and evil thought... and let not any satan have power over me (אל תשלט בי כל שטן[ו]) to make me stray from your path"
>
> **MMT C 29:**[32] "And remove from you the plans of evil and the device of Belial"

The expression "spirit of Belial" in Moses' prayer is parallel to "unrighteous spirit" and "satan" in Levi's prayer, and "plans of evil" and "device

---

[29] Licht (1957: 245) claimed that in the *Hodayot*, Belial does not refer to the leader of the evil forces. In contrast, Eshel (1999: 128) noted that the word Belial appears a few times in the *Hodayot*, and that it does refer to an independent entity. Kister (1999a: 352, n. 159) and Steudel (2000: 338) both correctly identified both meanings within the scroll. Steudel's attempt to differentiate between the two usages in sectarian literature according to a linear, chronological progression, is unconvincing.

[30] Kister 1999a: 352–354.

[31] The Aramaic text from Qumran (4QLevi^b ar [4Q213a] 1–2; eds. M. Stone and J. Greenfield; DJD 22, pp. 27–33) is preserved in a fragmentary state, but can be reconstructed based upon MS *e* of the Greek *T. Levi*. For the reconstruction and analysis of the prayer, see Stone and Greenfield 1993 (the translation here is taken from their article, p. 259; the interspersed Aramaic text is found on p. 257).

[32] See Qimron and Strugnell 1994: 62–63.

of Belial" in 4QMMT, and it is not necessary to assume a dualistic background in any of them. According to Kister, one can identify the origins of these kinds of prayers in the combination of magical (the dichotomy of good and benefit versus evil and animosity, and of God versus the harmful forces which he overcomes) and religious (protection against the spiritual dominion of the demons by means of observing the commandments) assumptions, and not necessarily in a dualistic worldview. However, "it was convenient for those streams with a dualistic outlook to adopt these ideas, which were widespread in broad circles, and to give them a specific, sectarian garb."[33]

In the analysis of Moses' prayer in *Jub* 1, and the worldview expressed therein, it is crucial that one take into account all aspects of the prayer, and not just those in common with the apotropaic prayers adduced above. In the beginning of this chapter, we discussed the special meaning of the epithet "your people and your inheritance" in order to describe Israel, in contrast to all the other nations. Beyond this, one can infer about the nature of the relationship of those nations to Israel, and their status in the world, from the parallelism between verses 19 and 20. Moses' expression of concern regarding Belial contains three elements: (1) "May the spirit of Belial not rule over them";[34] (2) "so as to bring charges against them before you"; (3) "to trap them away from every proper path so that they may be destroyed from your presence." These three are indeed considered amongst Belial's tasks surveyed above. The same requests are articulated by Moses one verse earlier (v. 19) regarding the other nations:

---

[33] Translated from Kister 1999a: 354; and see more extensively in Kister 1999: 168–172.

[34] The collocation of Belial and the root מ-ש-ל is reminiscent of the expression "dominion of Belial (ממשלת בליעל)" common in the Qumran sectarian literature; this should also be compared to CD XII, 2–3: "Every man who is ruled by the spirits of Belial and speaks apostasy...." However, this request for protection from the control of any power is not necessarily dualistic nor sectarian, as it is based upon Ps 119:133b: "do not let iniquity have power over me." It does in fact appear in sectarian apotropaic prayers, but also in prayers that have been preserved in rabbinic literature (Flusser 1966; Kister 1999a: 352–354). One could therefore interpret Moses' prayer in *Jub.* 1 in a non-dualistic context. However, considering the similarity of this passage to other passages that belong to the redactional layer of the book and which express a dualistic perspective (especially 15:31–33 which also contains the epithet Belial), it is appropriate to interpret Moses' prayer accordingly.

Jub. 1:19	*Jub.* 1:20
Do not allow your people and your inheritance to go along in the error of their minds	Create for them a just spirit
and do not deliver them into the control of the nations with the result that they rule over them	May the spirit of Belial not rule over them
	so as to bring charges against them before you
lest they make them sin against you	and to trap them away from every proper path so that they may be destroyed from your presence.

The similarity between the two requests allows us to sketch a broader picture of the ideological worldview underlying the character of Belial in Moses' prayer. Parallel to Belial, "the nations" also torment Israel: they can both rule over Israel, and cause Israel to sin. The parallel between them, and their combination, corresponds to the viewpoint presented in *Jub.* 15:31–33,[35] according to which God appointed spirits to rule over the nations and lead them astray, but he took sole responsibility for Israel.[36] The nations are ruled by these spirits, and it is therefore understandable why the nations themselves try to cause the Israelites to sin. The one difference between the nations and the "spirit of Belial" in vv. 19–20 is the role of this spirit to "bring charges against them before" God. This distinction is the result of the disparity in status between the two—only Belial, who is a member of the heavenly pantheon, can instigate such claims before God.

---

[35] *Jub.* 1:20; 15:33 are the only verses in *Jubilees* that use the epithet Belial, which bolsters the connection between them.

[36] See the discussion above regarding Deut 32:8–9 (according to 4QDeut^j and LXX), upon which the viewpoint expressed in *Jub.* 15:31–33 is based. Compare also to the similar approach expressed in Sir 17:17 (LXX). According to Dan 10:13, 20, the "princes" of Persia and Greece were patron angels responsible for specific nations, while Dan 10:13, 21; 12:1 mention Michael, "the great prince," who was responsible for Israel. This outlook is slightly different from the one presented in *Jub.* 15:31–33.

CHAPTER THIRTEEN

ABRAHAM'S BLESSING AND PRAYER

Abraham's Blessing to Jacob (19:26–29)

Following the births of Jacob and Esau, Abraham noticed that Isaac preferred Esau over his brother, while Abraham himself and Rebecca loved Jacob more (19:15–16, 19, 21, 31). After observing Esau's behavior, Abraham decided that only Jacob would continue the covenant with the Lord, and that he would be chosen over Esau as the forefather of his special nation (ibid., 16–18). Abraham then blessed his grandson with a blessing that included a request from God to protect Jacob from the evil spirits in the world:

> (19:26) Then he (Abraham) summoned Jacob into the presence of his mother Rebecca, kissed him, blessed him, and said: (27) "My dear son Jacob whom I myself love, may God bless you from above the firmament. May he give you all the blessings with which he blessed Adam, Enoch, Noah, and Shem. Everything that he said to me and everything that he promised to give me may he attach to you and your descendants until eternity—like the days of heaven above the earth. (28) May the spirits of Mastema not rule over you and your descendants to remove you from following the Lord who is your God from now and forever. (29) May the Lord God become your father and you his first-born son and people for all time. Go in peace, my son."

Abraham's blessing to Jacob was given in the general context of the covenant between God and Abraham's offspring, and in the specific context of the election of Israel (Jacob) as opposed to other nations (Esau). Abraham appealed to God to prevent "the spirits of Mastema" from ruling over Jacob and his descendants, using terminology similar to that found in other passages in *Jubilees* that address the origin of evil.[1] Abraham blessed Jacob that he should be God's "first-born son" (v. 29). The motif of Israel as a first-born appears already in the Bible (Exod 4:22—"Thus says the Lord, Israel is my first-born son"), but its

---

[1] Cf. 1:20; 10:8; 11:5; 12:20.

precise meaning is unclear. In *Jubilees*, this motif received a specific theological meaning: "And he chose the descendants of Jacob among [all of those whom I have seen. I have recorded them as my first-born son and have sanctified them for myself] for all the age(s) of eternity" (2:20 according to 4Q216 VII, 11–12; DJD 13, pp. 19–20).[2] As noted above, according to the creation story in the redactional layer (*Jub.* 2), Israel was chosen from the beginning of time to be God's unique nation and his first-born son (so too in Moses' prayer in *Jub.* 1:19–21 and the legal passage in *Jub.* 15:25–34).[3] The connection between the creation of the world and the election of Jacob (Israel) forms the basis of the entire rewritten creation story in *Jubilees* 2: throughout the chapter, the rewriter counts the number of works created on each day (vv. 3, 4, 7, 11, 12, 14), for a total of twenty-two during the first week (v. 23). The number of works during the first week, at the end of which the holy and blessed Sabbath was observed, served the rewriter as a basis for comparison with the number of generations from the creation of the world. After twenty-two generations, a person (and a nation) will be chosen, and he too will be chosen and blessed, just like the Sabbath day (2:23–24a):[4]

14 [²³There were twenty-two heads of humanity]
15 from Adam until him; and twenty-two k[inds of work were made until the seventh day. The one is blessed and holy and the other is blessed]

---

[2] The special terminology of the legal passages ("Heavenly Tablets," "Torah and te'udah," etc.) is absent from Abraham's blessing to Jacob, and I therefore do not *a priori* assign it to the redactional stratum, which includes Moses' prayer (1:19–21), the creation story (ch. 2), and the legal passage on circumcision (15:25–34). However, since Abraham's blessing is similar to these passages in its motifs, in its theological notions, and in its vocabulary used to describe Israel's election, one can justifiably include it in the discussion of the origin of evil according to the redactional layer of *Jubilees*.

[3] 4QPrayer of Enosh (4Q369; ed. H. Attridge and J. Strugnell; DJD 13, pp. 353–362) is fragmentary, but 1 II, 6–7, preserves text that includes expressions that appear in a similar context to the passage in *Jubilees*: "...and you made him as a first-bo[rn] son to you [ ] like him for a prince and ruler in all your earthly land...." For the use of the first-born son motif in order to describe Israel in Jewish literature of the Second Temple period, see Kugel 1998a.

[4] Charles (1902: xxxix–xl; 17–18) claimed that there is an extensive omission between vv. 22 and 23, based upon the evidence of Epiphanius, Syncellus, Cedrenus, and *Midrash Tadshe*. In his opinion, the original text also mentioned the twenty-two letters of the alphabet and the twenty-two books of the Bible. However, the goal of this chapter is to connect Israel to the Sabbath law, and there is no place for or reference to the other two motifs (letters; biblical books). It is preferable to see these two traditions as later accretions, added due to the use of the number twenty-two.

16 and holy. This one with this one were made together for holiness [and for blessing. ²⁴It was given to this one to be for all times the blessed and holy ones.]⁵

The meaning of the election in this passage is the deity's direct dominion over Israel, without any other heavenly intermediary. In contrast, the other nations are under the control of spirits appointed by the Lord.[6] The spirits purposely lead the nations astray, causing them to sin. According to the redactional layer, the world is divided from the beginning of creation into two factions: YHWH, the angels of presence, angels of holiness, and Israel on one side, and the spirits and the nations on the other. This division exists from the beginning of time, and creates a dualistic system of good and evil forces in the world, similar to the worldview expressed in the Qumran sectarian literature. However, the evil spirits also attempt to cause Israel to sin (and according to 1:19, the nations do so as well). Therefore, in the prayers throughout *Jubilees* (Moses, 1:19–21; Noah, 10:1–13; Abraham, 12:19–20; and here), the speakers request protection from these spirits, and hope that the world will run according to the system established by God at the time of creation: the evil spirits should rule over the nations, and YHWH himself should look after Israel.

The election of Israel at the beginning of time finds expression in Abraham's list of those people who were blessed (v. 27): "May he give you all the blessings with which he blessed *Adam, Enoch, Noah, and Shem*. Everything that he said to me and everything that he promised to give me, may he attach to you and your descendants until eternity—like the days of heaven above the earth." The blessing given to Jacob is a continuation of the blessing given already to Adam. Abraham's blessing of Jacob is therefore part of the realization of God's blessing to Israel in the first week of creation.

Abraham's Prayer (12:19–20)

After Abraham recognized that God is sovereign over the universe, including the forces of nature and the heavenly omens, he concluded

---

[5] The translation is based upon 4QJubilees^a (4Q216) VII, 14–16 (DJD 13, pp. 19–20).

[6] The idea first appears in Deut 32:8–9; 4:19–20; and afterwards in Sir 17:17; *Jub.* 15:30–32. For an extensive discussion of the position adopted by the redactor of *Jubilees*, see ch. 11.

that observing the celestial bodies does not help in forecasting the anticipated precipitation for each year (12:16–18). If God controls the forces of nature, then the inspection of these heavenly signs cannot reveal the future, for he can change it as he desires: "If he wishes he will make it rain in the morning and evening; and if he wishes, he will not make it fall. Everything is under his control." The method of prediction based upon heavenly omens is mentioned in *Jub.* 11:8: Nahor, Abraham's grandfather, learned from his father "the studies of Chaldeans, to practice divination and to augur by the signs of the sky."[7] Abraham apparently learned to predict based upon these omens from his father in Ur of the Chaldees, and this knowledge provided the background for his astral observations in order to forecast the weather for the coming year.[8]

Once Abraham understood that God alone controls the world, and that he has the ability to change it at any moment, he expressed this insight in a prayer of supplication for protection from the forces of evil in the world (vv. 19–20):[9]

> (19) That night he prayed and said: My God, my God, God most High, You alone are my God. You have created everything: Everything that was and has been is the product of your hands. You and your lordship I have chosen. (20) Save me from the power of the evil spirits who rule the thoughts of people's minds. May they not mislead me from following you, my God. Do establish me and my posterity forever. May we not go astray from now until eternity.

Just as the celestial bodies are God's handiwork, and he controls them as he wishes, so too the "the evil spirits who rule the thoughts of people's minds" are under his sovereignty: if he wishes they will lead

---

[7] There is no explicit appraisal of the "studies of the Chaldeans." However, biblical verses, such as Exod 22:17; Lev 19:26; Deut 18:10 (ibid., v. 12: "For it is abhorrent to the Lord, anyone who does such things"), and the brief treatments in *Jub.* 8:3–4; 12:16–18 reflect a negative view of this knowledge.

[8] Chapter 11 offers no explanation as to how Serug, Nahor's father, acquired the knowledge of these destructive sciences. It is possible that the "wisdom of the Chaldeans" is identical to the "Watchers' teaching" (8:3). *Jub.* 8:1–4 tells how Kainan, son of Arpachshad, found these teachings, which included "the omens of the sun, moon, and stars and every heavenly sign" inscribed on a rock. According to what is told there, Kainan copied the writings from the stone, and "sinned on the basis of what was in it," apparently in an attempt to use the signs in order to predict the future.

[9] Lange (1997: 383) classified this prayer as a "hymnic exorcism" against the spirits, in addition to Noah's prayer in *Jub.* 10. One can also add Moses' prayer (1:19–21) and Abraham's blessing to Jacob (19:26–29) to his list.

Israel astray, and if he wishes they will be prevented from doing so. As part of his creation, he controls the spirits, just as he has power over the heavenly bodies, and he can therefore save each and every person from being led astray. Abraham describes them as part of a world in which God created everything (v. 19). It is therefore difficult to view the origins of these spirits as a byproduct of the story of the sons of god (Gen 6), the viewpoint reflected in the various traditions of *1 Enoch*. The worldview expressed in Abraham's prayer is similar to the dualistic approach known from the Qumran sectarian literature, such as in 1QS III, 25: "and he created the spirits of light and darkness, and founded every action upon them." The good and evil spirits are both an integral part of the administration of the world, and were created from the beginning.

The spirits in Abraham's prayer are described as divine beings, and therefore Abraham is unable to withstand their machinations without God's assistance. The "evil spirits" "rule the thoughts of people's minds," and therefore, human beings are unable to freely choose for themselves not to sin. The description of the actions of the spirits fits a dualistic worldview, but is still not a purely deterministic approach, because according to the story, Abraham's prayer is effective. According to pure determinism, anything that takes place in the world is predetermined, while the notion of supplicatory prayer assumes that God can change a given situation based upon a person's request, as Abraham does in this passage.

SUMMARY AND CONCLUSIONS

(1) From the analysis of all the passages in *Jubilees* that address the origin of evil in the world, a more complex picture emerges than has been described until today. According to the general scholarly consensus, *Jubilees* follows the various traditions in *1 Enoch*, and locates the origin of evil in the story of the sons of god and daughters of men in Gen 6:1–4;[1] alternatively it has been suggested that its origins are in the Garden of Eden story.[2] However the analysis here has revealed a third option: evil is not the result of a specific historical event, such as a sin in heaven or on earth, but rather, part of God's original plan when he created the world. As Deutero-Isaiah asserted earlier, at the beginning of creation God already created the dichotomy of good and evil: "I form light and create darkness, I make weal and create woe—I the Lord do all these things" (Isa 45:7).

The theological benefit of attributing evil to God rests in the recognition of his omnipotence: nothing exists in the universe against his will. According to the traditions that attribute evil to the sins of angels or human beings, the world in its current state exists against God's original intentions. The sad condition of the land would therefore attest to his limitations, as he is unable to extricate it from its misfortunes. If God created the universe, and included evil as an integral component, then the world, with all of its problems, is still perfect, and in consonance with his original plans. But the attribution of evil to God carries with it a heavy theological price, because if he is omnipotent, he is no longer completely good. As noted above, in light of the evil that is always present in the world, philosophers in monotheistic religions must assume one of two possibilities: either God is not completely good, or he is not omnipotent. This difficulty is the basis for the differences and tensions between the various traditions preserved in *Jubilees*.

The key to identifying the worldview of the redactor of *Jubilees* is a diachronic analysis of the book. *Jubilees* is one of the classic examples of the genre of Rewritten Bible, and therefore, scholars have generally

---

[1] See most recently Eshel 1999: 48–57.
[2] Collins 1995: 28–29.

assumed that any of its components that do not appear in the Bible itself are the work of the rewriter. However, a critical study of this composition leads to a different picture: the reviser or redactor relied upon extant, rewritten sources, and not just the Bible itself. His new composition therefore often includes earlier traditions, even if they are sometimes inconsistent with his own positions. The precise distinction between the sources included in *Jubilees* and the particular contribution of the redactor allows for a more precise definition of his own worldview. The literary-critical analysis of *Jubilees*, which was based primarily upon the examination of the connection between the rewritten narratives and the appended legal passages, is thus highly significant for the study of the ideology and theology of this book. The recognition of the complexity of this material allows for an accurate investigation of the redactor's perspective, in contrast to those expressed in his sources. Regarding the topic of the origin of evil, the book refers most often to Watchers traditions that were common in that period. On the one hand, the redactor included texts that attribute the origin of evil to a specific event in history (the Watchers [5:1–12; 7:20–39] or Garden of Eden [3:17] stories). But on the other hand, in the redactional layer, in the legal passages juxtaposed to the narratives, in the narrative frame of the book (ch. 1), and in prayers throughout the composition (12:19–20; 19:26–29), the author-redactor attributed evil to an external power (Belial or Mastema), without a link to a specific incident from the past. God created the heavens and the earth, including both good and evil (1:19–21; 2:17–24; 15:25–34).

(2) The redactor used different techniques to adapt the myths surrounding the sins of the Watchers and the Garden of Eden to his own perspective that God created evil at the beginning of time:

(a) At the point in the text parallel to Gen 6:1–4 (*Jub.* 5:1–12), the redactor included a long passage based upon *1 En.* 10–11; however, he added a legal passage to this section that transformed the Watchers story into a paradigm for reward and punishment (5:13–18). This view is similar to that expressed in *Jub.* 20:5, which mentions the "punishment of the giants and the punishment of Sodom." In the traditions with which *Jubilees* was acquainted (primarily from *1 Enoch*), the Watchers story functioned as a myth that explained the existence of evil in the world; in *Jub.* 5 and 20, the message of this story was changed in order to highlight God as a righteous judge. The reworking of the narrative is based upon the demythologization of the story, which no longer addresses the existence of evil in the world, but rather, describes an incident, which although exceptionally grievous, is only one of many such events throughout history.³

(b) The editor of *Jubilees* was not the original author of Noah's testament (7:20–39), and most importantly for the current discussion, not of the attribution of evil in the world to the Watchers and their offspring (ibid., 26–27). He adopted the extant testament from a text that also included the adjacent vineyard story (7:1–19). The different provenance of the testament was determined based upon editorial considerations, and especially its placement immediately after the vineyard story, in accordance with the order of events of Gen 9, and its date some 300 years prior to Noah's death. Signs of this reworking can be identified at the beginning (7:20–21) and end (v. 39) of the testament.⁴

(c) *Jubilees* 10:1–13 attests to another attempt at adapting the Enoch traditions to the dualistic worldview found in the redactional layer of *Jubilees*. According to this passage, the spirits, the offspring of the Watchers, are under the control of Mastema, the head of the forces of evil in the world. Scholars have tended to view Mastema as one of these spirits, but a careful analysis demonstrated that Mastema has a special status above the spirits. He is a member of the heavenly entourage, and can therefore negotiate with the Lord. He acts according to "the authority" of his own "will" (10:8), which includes independent goals and plans, and the spirits serve him. For this reason, it was suggested that Mastema was not one of the Watchers' offspring, but was considered, similar to the biblical Satan, one of the divine beings with access to YHWH, who was responsible both for causing people to sin and then for implementing their punishment. If Mastema had his own agenda, for which he then wanted the spirits to assist in its implementation, then evil existed in the world before the advent of these spirits, and also before the Watchers' sins. According to *Jubilees* and the sectarian literature, Mastema stood at the head of the heavenly forces of evil in a dualistic system that was established at creation, according to which the forces of good and evil struggle with each other in heaven and on earth. The spirits, offspring of the Watchers, were originally intended to explain the continued presence of evil in the world, but in the dualistic system—which offers a different solution to the problem—there is no natural place for spirits which were created at a later point in

---

³ See ch. 5.
⁴ See ch. 6.

history; their inclusion in the dualistic system attests to the secondary link between the two explanations.[5]

(d) The Sin in the Garden of Eden:[6] *Jub.* 3:17 dates the sin in the Garden to the seventeenth of the second month (exactly seven years after the entry into the Garden), which was the same date on which the flood later commenced. This tradition thus links the first sin in history to the cataclysmic punishment that was meted out due to the proliferation of evil in the world. *Jub.* 3:8–14 is a legal passage that derives the periods of impurity for the postpartum mother, detailed in the law in Lev 12, from the dates on which the first man and woman were created, and from those on which they entered the Garden. According to this halakhic passage, Adam entered the Garden forty days after he was created, namely the seventeenth of the second month. However, when the story is read in light of the *Jubilees* (and Qumran) calendar, it becomes clear that this date of entry does not match the periods of time recounted in the legal passage in *Jub.* 3:8–14. The tradition that explains the origin of evil from the sin in the Garden of Eden, and the derivation of the law of postpartum impurity from the Eden story, are therefore not of the same provenance, and cannot, and should not, be reconciled. The merger of the legal passage into the story is of special importance regarding the question of the origin of evil: the meaning of the date, the seventeenth of the second month, which originally offered an explanation for the origin of evil, has been transformed in the secondary, halakhic passage for a legal purpose, and serves as the source for the law which appears on the Heavenly Tablets.

(3) One can identify tensions between (and within) two of the traditions regarding the origin of evil: (i) the result of the Watchers story, and (ii) part of a dualistic system created from the dawn of time. The variety of the sources points to the many, different attempts in antiquity to address this difficult theological question, and simultaneously, informs us of the complexity of the material in *Jubilees*. The plurality

---

[5] See ch. 7. One could theoretically disagree with the claim that Mastema, who stands in charge of the forces of evil, was created at the dawn of time, as Mastema does not appear in *Jubilees* prior to ch. 10. However, the description of Mastema in *Jub.* 10 presents him as one who dares to disagree with God, and even succeeds at convincing him to leave some of the spirits for Mastema's use. The status of Mastema in ch. 10 is similar to that of Satan in the narrative frame of Job and in Zech 3:1–2. In Job 1–2, Satan is one of the sons of god (Job 1:6; 2:1), members of the divine retinue.

[6] See ch. 1.

of Watchers traditions is already evidenced in *1 Enoch*, and is expressed in *Jubilees* primarily regarding the connection between the Watchers and the spirits.[7] Regarding the attribution of evil to Mastema, in passages such as the Akedah story (17:15–18:19), he is portrayed as the equivalent of Satan, based upon his responsibilities and status known from Job 1–2 and Zech 3:1–2. In all of these instances, he acts alone, and provokes God into testing one of his loyal subjects. In *Jub.* 48, Mastema is still independent,[8] and he is even more autonomous than his biblical counterpart. He acts against God's will, and functions as the patron of Egypt, against the angel of presence, who protects Israel. In *Jub.* 10, Mastema has his own agenda, and he therefore requests the spirits as reinforcements; he still needs to ask God's permission to have the spirits under his control. *Jubilees* 10 perhaps hints that this demonic being, who stands at the head of all evil forces in the world, was created at the beginning of history,[9] and this view is emphasized in passages that can be attributed to the redactional layer of *Jubilees*. According to Moses' prayer in the narrative frame (1:19–21), the description of Israel's election in the first week of history (ch. 2), and the giving of the law of circumcision (15:25–34), God established the world order from the beginning of time: the forces of evil in heaven and on earth (Belial and the nations) against the forces of good (YHWH, the angels of presence and angels of holiness, and Israel).[10] God created the entire world, and rules over it, and he therefore rules over "the forces of Mastema" who perform his will (49:2).

(4) The theory proposed here regarding the literary development of *Jubilees* in light of the identification of the passages which belong to the redactional layer of the book, first in the legal passages appended to the rewritten narratives, and then in passages which contain similar

---

[7] As demonstrated in the analysis of *Jubilees* 5 (pp. 109–118), *Jubilees* was familiar with the *Book of Watchers* in its current literary form, after the combination of the Shemihazah and Asael traditions.

[8] Thus according to the original text of *Jub.* 48:16; see the textual analysis on pp. 219–220, nn. 46–49.

[9] It is not stated explicitly that Mastema was created at the beginning of the world, but this is apparently the assumption of *Jub.* 10; for the arguments in favor of this conclusion, see pp. 176–177. Prof. M. Kister suggested to me that the absence of Mastema in the creation story perhaps indicates that even the Mastema tradition, though dominant in this book, also comes from a different source, and is not the invention of *Jubilees*. See the analyses in chs. 9–10 which perhaps favor such a conclusion.

[10] According to *Jub.* 15:25–34, even some Israelites belong to the evil axis, and can be classified as "sons of Belial" (15:33).

terminology (e.g., ch. 1), is supported by this study of the origin of evil. One can identify different approaches to this question throughout the book; however, when the legal passages, and those sections that share similar terminology, are isolated, and this theological issue is then examined, one can identify a unified, crystallized approach to the origin of evil. This unity points to one editor, who intentionally included the traditions that he knew within a new theological construct.

(5) In light of the identification of the legal passages and those which contain similar terminology as a crystallized stratum in *Jubilees*, one can ask whether this redactional layer presents a comprehensive worldview, which includes other related ideas. According to the analysis here, the redactor attributed evil to God from the dawn of creation, and suggested a dualistic perspective according to which evil existed alongside good from the beginning of time. Is there a connection between the attribution of evil to the creation and the view of the redactional layer that the laws existed on the Heavenly Tablets, which were also in existence from the beginning of time?[11] One can also suggest a similar connection to the chronological system according to which all events are dated from creation until the entry to the Promised Land at the "jubilee of jubilees" (50:4).[12] The conclusion of the book at this important juncture expresses the idea of the cyclical nature of the world—one period of history is completed at the "jubilee of jubilees," and a new era is set to follow. This cyclical perspective is not the invention of *Jubilees*, and appears in earlier and contemporaneous compositions.[13] But the basic idea which underlies this outlook, that the world is administered based upon predetermined periods of time, also accords with the redactor's view of the origin of evil, as they both conceive of systems, chronological or theological, which were established from the dawn of creation. Therefore, law, evil, and chronology together form a well thought-out, comprehensive doctrine.

(6) The identification of the dualistic worldview in the redactional layer of *Jubilees* strengthens the connection between *Jubilees* and the Qumran sectarian literature. According to both of them, God created

---

[11] See the discussion on the origin of law in ch. 14.
[12] Cf. Wiesenberg 1961; VanderKam (1995) 2000.
[13] The dating of periods of time according to jubilees or weeks appears in the *Apocalypse of Weeks* (*1 Enoch* 93; 91); Daniel 9:24–27; 4Q180–181 (Pesher on the Periods); 11QMelchizedek; *T. Levi* 17; *Apocryphon of Jeremiah* (4Q383, 385a, 387, 387a, 388a, 389, 390).

evil at the dawn of history, opposite the forces of good in the world. According to both, the forces of good and evil exist in heaven and on earth, and the heavenly forces of evil are under the control of Mastema or Belial. In contrast to most other scholars, it has been suggested here that according to *Jubilees*, the earthly evil forces are not limited to the other nations, but also includes some Israelites as well; *Jub.* 15:25–34 thus describes those who do not undergo circumcision by the eighth day as "people (meant for) destruction" (v. 26). In light of the literary-critical analysis, the affiliation with the sectarian compositions is expressed specifically in the redactional layer of *Jubilees*, and not in its sources.

PART III

THE ORIGIN OF LAW

CHAPTER FOURTEEN

THE COMMANDMENTS, THE COVENANT, AND THE ELECTION OF ISRAEL

The Transmission of Laws Prior to the Sinaitic Revelation

One of the most prominent characteristics of *Jubilees* is the addition of legal passages, based upon laws known from the pentateuchal legal corpora, into the patriarchal narratives. As opposed to the Pentateuch, in which almost all of the laws first appear in collections of laws following the Sinaitic revelation, in *Jubilees* these statutes are introduced within the framework of stories from the preceding period. This difference in the "timing" of the giving of the laws has a dual significance, both chronological and literary. Regarding the time at which the laws were given, although certain laws in the Torah were presented in the patriarchal period, and were binding upon later generations,[1] the vast majority of the commandments were given at Sinai (Exod 20–23; Lev 25), during the wanderings in the desert (Leviticus, Numbers), or in the plains of Moab (Deuteronomy). These corpora are independent literary units that are presented against the backdrop of a narrative that describes their revelation, yet the laws themselves are not connected to a specific story. They are disconnected from external circumstances, and are presented without any context to explain their legislation. From a legal perspective, there is no meaning to all the events that occurred prior to the Sinaitic revelation.[2]

In contrast, *Jubilees* contains almost no collections of laws,[3] and the laws themselves are almost always quoted in the context of a story. In some of the cases, the stories serve as a precedent for the legislation:

---

[1] Gen 32:33 mentions the Israelite custom not to eat the sciatic nerve, but it is not formulated as a law. Only in early exegesis was this custom transformed into an actual prohibition, as a result of the formulation "*therefore* the Israelites do not eat...," and the presence of the story in the Torah (see Kister 2001: 292–293).

[2] This literary observation forms the basis of R. Isaac's famous question (*Tanhuma* [Buber] Gen 11), who wondered why the Pentateuch did not begin with Exod 12, the laws of Passover, instead of opening with narrative.

[3] Exceptions to this can be found in *Jub.* 49 (parallel to the Passover laws of Exod

the patriarchs acted in a certain way, and their behavior obligates future generations. For example, Adam entered the Garden of Eden after 40 days, and his wife at the end of 80. These dates serve as the basis in *Jub.* 3:8–14 for the derivation of the laws of the parturient mother known from Lev 12. In other instances, the patriarchs observed (or did not observe) the laws in the pre-Sinaitic period, and *Jubilees* therefore felt it necessary to justify their actions. In these cases, the story does not generate the law, but rather attempts to explain the lack of implementation of a law known to the reader from the Pentateuch itself. For example, *Jub.* 33 addresses the question of why Reuben and Bilhah were not punished, even though they violated an explicit pentateuchal proscription prohibiting intercourse with one's father's wife, and offers the justification that the law had not yet been publicized, and therefore could not be enforced (vv. 15–16). Judah was not punished for his problematic behavior with Tamar because he sinned unintentionally (he was unaware that he was having intercourse with his daughter-in-law), repented, and achieved atonement (41:23–26), or because Tamar was a virgin at the time of their intercourse (v. 27) and was therefore legally not considered his daughter-in-law.[4] The laws are recorded on the Heavenly Tablets, which attests to their existence from the beginning of time.

Why does *Jubilees* locate the giving of the laws within the patriarchal period? R.H. Charles suggested over a century ago that the primary purpose of *Jubilees* was to defend Judaism from Hellenistic influence.[5] One of the ways in which this was accomplished was the presentation of the laws as timeless and eternal; they have always existed and will continue to exist forever. The laws given to the patriarchs are the realization of these atemporal commandments. Charles adduced the laws of Sabbath and circumcision as examples of eternal laws: the angels observed both of these commandments from the time of creation, before they were observed by Israel (2:17–18; 15:27). If the laws are indeed timeless, observed from the dawn of creation by the angels, then they are also valid in the time of the readers of *Jubilees*. One can add the

---

12), and the section including the Sabbath laws at the end of the book (50:6–13a). Regarding the second passage, see Ravid 2000; Doering 2002; and Kister's position (quoted above in the Introduction, pp. 19–20).

[4] For the background of the double reason offered for Judah's non-punishment, see the discussion in ch. 2.

[5] Charles 1902: xlvii–liv.

festival of Oaths/Weeks (6:18), which was also observed in heaven from the time of creation as further evidence for this approach.

Building on this anti-assimilationist approach, some recent scholars[6] have even identified the group against which *Jubilees* allegedly polemicizes with the description in 1 Maccabees 1:11:

> In those days lawless men came forth from Israel, and misled many, saying "Let us go and make a covenant with the Gentiles around us, for since we separated from them, many evils have found us."

According to the claim of these "lawless men," there was an early period during which Israel was not separated from other nations, and therefore, assimilating into the Hellenistic world should be viewed as a return to this primary status. *Jubilees* thus counters that such an era never existed, because the commandments were given to Israel from the beginning of time, when Israel was separated from the nations (2:17–21).

This approach to the introduction of laws in the patriarchal period fits well with the three laws mentioned here: Sabbath, circumcision and the festival of Oaths/Weeks, and is certainly correct with regard to the worldview of *Jubilees* regarding the chosenness of Israel from creation. However, not all the laws given in this early period are reported to have been observed from the beginning of time, and thus it cannot be used to explain the phenomenon of the juxtaposition of law and narrative in its entirety. In fact, some of the laws, as noted, were specifically legislated as a response to actions of the forefathers. These laws would in fact support the view of the assimilationists of 1 Maccabees—there was indeed a period in which Israel did not observe laws (or certainly not all of them).

Gary Anderson offered an exegetical motive for the addition of laws in the pre-Sinaitic period.[7] In the Torah itself, there is a certain ambiguity as to the existence of laws in the pre-Sinaitic period. For example, the prohibition of eating blood (Gen 9:4–6) and the obligation of circumcision (Gen 17) were both given as part of pre-Sinaitic covenants. According to biblical scholars, the Priestly source proposed that laws were not given to Israel until Sinai (except for the two laws just mentioned which were given in the context of covenants),[8] while

---

[6] Schwarz 1982: 100; Endres 1987: 237–238; VanderKam 1997: 20–22.
[7] Anderson 1994.
[8] Wellhausen 1885: 34–38, 52–54, 336–342; Driver 1913: 141.

the J source assumed that the patriarchs knew certain laws: Noah distinguished between pure and impure animals (Gen 7:2–3), and knew how to properly offer a sacrifice (Gen 8:20–21). Abraham offered an appropriate sacrifice in place of his son Isaac (Gen 22:13). Judah's verdict to burn Tamar for licentious behavior (Gen 38:24) also indicates knowledge and practice of the laws of sexually inappropriate actions.[9] The existence of laws in the pre-Sinaitic period is thus not the creation of *Jubilees*, but was present already in some of the sources of the Pentateuch.

Anderson suggested that the tension between these sources, regarding the giving of the laws specifically at Sinai versus the awareness of some of the laws in the patriarchal period, when read together as a unified composition by the ancient exegete, created an interpretive problem. If the revelation at Sinai was the defining moment in Israelite history, and only then were the laws given exclusively to Israel, how is one supposed to relate to the stories in Genesis which suggest the observance of some of these commandments in an earlier period? Moreover, certain stories recognize the validity of some laws and the punishment for their nonobservance (e.g., Judah and Tamar), while others lack any penalty for the "violations" of the characters. Anderson posited that the tensions between these different traditions led to the approach offered in *Jubilees*: the revelation of the laws began in the patriarchal period, but only some of the laws, and only to select individuals. The Sinaitic theophany retained its significance as a national event, after which all individuals, men, women, adults and children alike, became legally liable for their actions. Prior to this event, however, God chose to reveal the laws, both partially and gradually. From a legal perspective, only those to whom the laws were revealed were obligated in their observance. One who transgressed unintentionally because he or she was unaware of the law,[10] could not be punished. For example, Judah knew of the punishment by fire for his daughter-in-law Tamar (*Jub.* 41), yet Reuben and Bilhah were unaware of the prohibition against intercourse with one's mother-in-law, and were thus spared punishment (*Jub.* 33:16).

---

[9] Ancient interpreters offered sundry suggestions as to the source of the death penalty by fire, and its relationship to biblical law; see Zakovitch and Shinan 1992: 149–159. Regarding *Jubilees* itself, see above, ch. 2.

[10] There is another kind of unintentionality: when one is aware of the existence of the law, but not that he or she is violating it through their actions; see *Jub.* 41:23–24, and my discussion above, pp. 69–70.

However, it is possible that this exegetical consideration, while significant, is not the basis for this legal outlook, but rather, this unique outlook, which accepts a partial pre-Sinaitic revelation of laws, was employed by the editor of *Jubilees* in order to solve the interpretive issue just described. This reversal of order in the presentation of the argument is due to the introduction of laws in *Jubilees*, even in those passages in which there is no interpretive difficulty in the biblical story which needs to be addressed. For example, there is no story in Genesis or Exodus in which the law of impurity of the parturient mother (Lev 12) is mentioned or implied, and certainly no passage in which a woman violates these statutes, yet *Jub.* 3:8–14 introduces this law into the story of the entry into the Garden of Eden. Similarly, the Sabbath laws appear twice in *Jubilees*, both near the beginning of the book (2:24b–33) and at its conclusion (50:6–13a),[11] without any "problem" of observance or nonobservance of the Sabbath prohibitions prior to the Sinaitic revelation. The only story which precedes Exod 20, in which there is a description of adherence to or violation of the Sabbath laws, is the Manna story in Exod 16. In that account, God explicitly states that the people will gather the manna each morning, and on Friday they will gather a double portion which will suffice for Friday and the Sabbath (vv. 5, 22–26). When certain individuals went out to gather on the Sabbath in violation of God's command (v. 27), he immediately rebuked them for their actions (vv. 28–30). There is therefore no question in this story of knowledge or ignorance of the law, for the prohibition against collecting the manna is explicitly expressed in the story itself. In most of the passages in *Jubilees* in which laws were attached to the narrative, there is no readily identifiable exegetical issue which needs to be solved by the addition of the laws. The exegetical approach suggested by Anderson is only relevant in a few instances, such as the stories of Reuben and Bilhah, and Judah and Tamar. It is therefore preferable to posit that the legal worldview found in *Jubilees*, that the laws were given gradually and to select individuals from the dawn of creation, logically precedes the application of this idea to solve some interpretive tensions in a small number of cases.

Instead, I prefer to posit a third possibility for understanding the placement of the laws in the patriarchal period, one which is the result

---

[11] See however, n. 3 above.

of inner-Jewish ideological developments,[12] and which can be related to some other fundamental notions in *Jubilees*. Throughout Jewish literature of the Second Temple period, one can identify the equation of Wisdom (as described in the Bible) with Torah. The earliest signs of this can perhaps be found in Psalm 119, which uses terminology from wisdom literature to describe and praise the Torah.[13] The clearest expression of this transition from Wisdom to Torah can be found in Ben Sira.[14] In the Bible itself, Wisdom is presented as existing from the time of creation (cf. especially Prov 3:19–20; 8:22–31; and Jer 10:12; Ps 104:24). If one combines the motif of Wisdom from creation, with the idea that Wisdom equals Torah, then one can conclude that the Torah also existed from creation. According to early Israelite Wisdom literature, universalistic Wisdom existed from the beginning of time: "The Lord created me (Wisdom) at the beginning of his course, as the first of his works of old. In the distant past I was fashioned, at the beginning, at the origin of earth" (Prov 8:22–23). In contrast, Sir 24 (Praise of Wisdom) offers a more particularistic notion of Wisdom, as the Torah and its commandments given specifically to Israel:

> (8)... He said "In Jacob make your (Wisdom's) dwelling, in Israel your inheritance. (9) Before the ages, from the beginning he created me, and forever I shall not cease...(12) I took root among the honored people, in the portion of the Lord is my inheritance...(23) All this is the book of the covenant of God Most High, the law which Moses commanded us, the heritage of the assemblies of Jacob.

This transformation of the earlier conception of Wisdom is also found in Rabbinic literature: "Six things preceded the creation of the world...the Torah, as it written 'The Lord created me at the beginning...' (Prov 8:22)..." (*Gen. Rab.* 1:6). This supposition is also the source for the widespread notion found in Rabbinic literature that the forefathers observed the commandments before the giving of the laws at Sinai (e.g., *m. Qidd.* 4:14 which mentions Abraham's observance of the laws of the Torah).

However, unlike the position expressed in this mishnah, the legal passages in *Jubilees* do not assume that all the laws of the Torah were

---

[12] Cf. Werman (1999) 2002: 93–94.
[13] See Amir 1982. Hurvitz (1972: 130–152) identified the linguistic elements in the psalm that can be dated to the Second Temple period.
[14] See Schnabel 1985.

given or observed prior to Sinai, but rather a select set of commandments: Shabbat, festivals, laws of sexual impropriety, impurity, murder, and agricultural regulations (fourth-year fruits; tithes). This limitation to specific laws is apparently a function of the biblical stories themselves—those laws which could be directly or indirectly related to the stories were adduced, while others were left out. The Sabbath is mentioned as the climax of the creation story in Gen 2:1–4, and therefore the laws of the Sabbath are discussed in *Jub.* 2:24b–33 at the end of the rewritten creation narrative; Reuben slept with his father's concubine in Gen 35:22, and therefore *Jub.* 33 presents a long legal passage on the prohibition of intercourse with one's father's spouse. The decision to append the pentateuchal laws to the narratives of Genesis and Exodus limited the selection of laws to those with a connection, whether direct or indirect, to those stories. The individual laws presented are therefore not uniquely significant, as their choice was determined by the specific story to which they were affixed, but rather, appear to be added as a whole to infuse the biblical narrative with a new dimension.

According to the redactional layer in *Jubilees*, God established the world order from the dawn of creation. This world order included the forces of nature in the world, but more significantly for this discussion, the division of divine and human beings into good and evil forces. As part of this dualistic approach which distinguishes between those who belong to the "covenant of the Lord" (15:26) as opposed to the "sons of Belial" (15:33), in the divine realm, those who belong to the covenant with God are the angels of presence and holiness, and were accordingly marked when they were created circumcised (2:2; 15:27).[15] Similarly, in the earthly realm, Israel was chosen from the first week of creation as a "noteworthy people" and as God's "firstborn-son":[16]

> (2:19) [He said to us: "I will now separate for myself] a people among my nations. And [they will keep Sabbath. I will sanctify them as my people, and I will bless them. They will be my people and I will be their God."] (20) And he chose the descendants of Jacob among [all of those whom I have seen. I have recorded them as my first-born son and have sanctified them for myself] for all the age(s) of eternity. The [seventh] day [I will tell them so that they may keep Sabbath on it from everything, (21) as he blessed them and sanctified them for himself as a special people] out of all the nations and to be [keeping Sabbath] together [with us.]

---

[15] For a more extensive discussion, see ch. 11.
[16] According to 4QJubilees[a] (4Q216) VII, 9–13 (eds. VanderKam and Milik; DJD 13, pp. 19–20).

What is the significance of this chosenness from amongst the nations? The expression "a noteworthy people" (v. 21) appears to reflect a Hebrew text עַם סְגֻלָּה. This designation is taken from the context of covenants in the ancient Near East in general, and biblical covenants in particular, reflecting Israel's special status relative to the other nations. As Loewenstamm demonstrated, the Hebrew term is similar to the Ugaritic political term *sig/kiltu*, used to denote a ruler's preferred vassal. In the Bible, the political term was adopted and adapted to a religious context, to describe Israel as the Lord's preferred vassal.[17] Out of its eight instances within the Bible, five of them refer explicitly to Israel's special status (Exod 19:5; Deut 7:6; 14:2; 26:18; Ps 135:4).[18] The four that appear in the Pentateuch all share three motifs:

(1) Israel's observance of the covenant through the performance of the commandments;
(2) Israel's status as the *segullah* nation vis-à-vis others;
(3) Israel as a holy nation.

Thus, for example, Exod 19:5–6 contains the following conditions and promise:

> Now then, if you will obey my voice and keep my covenant, you shall be a *segullah* from among all the peoples, for the entire earth is mine. And you shall be for me a kingdom of priests and a holy nation...

The special status of Israel in all of the verses is dependent upon the observance of the covenant, the fulfillment of the conditions of the בְּרִית, the laws of the Torah. The first occasion in the Pentateuch in which covenant, favored status, and holiness are combined, is this passage from Exod 19, immediately prior to the Sinaitic theophany, at which time the first set of laws was given to Israel.[19] According to the

---

[17] Loewenstamm 1983.

[18] Malachi 3:17 describes the righteous, presumably from Israel, as *segullah*, but there is no explicit identification of the righteous as Israelites. 1 Chr 29:3 and Qoh 2:8 both use the term with the meaning "treasure." Greenberg (1951), relying upon Mesopotamian and rabbinic sources, interpreted the word in the Bible as "treasure," a meaning appropriate to these two verses.

[19] As noted above, individual commandments were given prior to Sinai, such as the prohibitions against the consumption or spilling of blood (Gen 9:4), and the requirement of circumcision (Gen 17, parallel to *Jub.* 15). Both of these come in the contexts of covenants, the first with Noah (Gen 9:9–17; cf. *Jub.* 6:4) and the second with Abraham, in which circumcision functions as a "sign" of the covenant; see Fox 1980. The two

biblical conception, election to the covenant of the Lord demands the observance of the commandments (Exod 19:8; 24:7), and thus they appear together.[20] According to *Jubilees*, however, Israel was chosen from among the nations from the beginning of creation, as part of a broader worldview according to which the entire world order was established from that moment (*Jub.* 2:17–24a). Therefore, *Jub.* 2:24b–33 proceeds with the giving of the Sabbath laws to Israel, detailing the first covenantal conditions.

In line with this biblical notion of covenant, the election of Israel was meaningless without stipulations to the covenant, without commandments. If Israel was indeed a chosen nation from the first week of creation, then there was a need for laws from that same moment. In the pentateuchal version of the creation story, there were no laws given at that time; God rested on the seventh day (Gen 2:2), but there was no immediate, practical ramification for humanity as a result. God's actions did not serve as a precedent for human obligations at this early stage, because there was no covenant with humanity at this point. Moreover, there was no special relationship between Israel and this first Sabbath.[21] The obligation to rest on the seventh day in light of the precedent that God set in the first week is only first mentioned in the Decalogue (Exod 20:8–11) as part of the Sinaitic covenant:

> Remember the Sabbath day and keep it holy. Six days you shall labor and do all of your work, but the seventh day is a Sabbath of the Lord your God; you shall not do any work—you, your son or daughter, your slave, your maidservant, your cattle, and the stranger who is within your settlements. For in six days the Lord made heaven and earth and sea, and all that is in them, and on the seventh day he rested…

A similar transformation occurs elsewhere in the Pentateuch, also after the Sinaitic covenant. Exodus 31:16–17 reads:

> The Israelites shall keep the Sabbath, observing the Sabbath throughout the ages as a covenant for all time. It shall be a sign for all time between

---

passages, *Jub.* 6 and the legal passage at the conclusion of ch. 15, both belong to the halakhic redactional layer of the composition (as demonstrated above), and they reflect the worldview of the editor: the election of Israel and its subordination to the covenant obligate it in certain conditions, namely the commandments of the Torah.

[20] In Exod 19:4, the Exodus from Egypt serves as an argument to convince Israel to accept the conditions of the covenant. The motif of the Exodus in the context of God's choice of Israel appears again in Deut 7:8.

[21] See Doering 1997: 185–191, and the literature quoted there.

me and the people of Israel. For in six days the Lord made heaven and earth, and on the seventh day he ceased from work and was refreshed.

Covenant terminology is especially prominent in the formulation of the Sabbath law in Exod 31:12–17: "for this is a sign (אות) between me and you" (v. 13); "observing the Sabbath throughout the ages as a covenant for all time" (v. 16); "It shall be a sign for all time between me and the people of Israel" (v. 17). The formulation of the law using covenant terminology is appropriate to the particularistic perspective of the Sabbath expressed therein, a perspective expressed by the placement of the law following the election of Israel from among the nations. In contrast to the universalistic tone of the Creation story in Gen 1:1–2:4a, the Sabbath law in Exod 31:12–17 addresses Israel alone and its unique relationship with God.

The Sabbath law in *Jub.* 2 is presented within the context of its own rewritten creation story. Genesis 2:1–3, which includes a description of God's rest, and the sanctification and blessing of the day, was transformed in *Jub.* 2:24b–33 into a legal precedent obligating Israel in the observance of the Sabbath. The Sabbath of creation in Gen 2:1–3 was thus transformed from a universalistic day of rest into a particularistic day, reserved for Israel, as in Exod 20 and 31. The Sabbath of creation as a precedent for the earthly Sabbath is thus not the invention of *Jubilees*. Rather, its innovation lies in the retrojection of God's covenant with Israel to the beginning of time.

The Meaning of "Torah and Te'udah"

The laws of the Sabbath in *Jub.* 2 are defined as התעודה והתורה [הראש]ונה] (v. 24), "the fir[st] *te'udah* and Torah," the first laws to be given in the history of the world. In accordance with the explanation just offered, that the motive for the addition of laws in *Jubilees* prior to the Sinaitic revelation can be traced to the election of Israel from the dawn of creation, I would like to suggest that the covenantal motif is also of significance for the interpretation of the expression "Torah and *te'udah*."

In light of its presence in the (original) title of the composition,[22] and four (or five) times in the narrative framework of ch. 1, it can

---

[22] See the Introduction, p. 4.

be concluded that the expression "Torah and *te'udah*" is one of the keys for understanding *Jubilees* as a whole. It is based upon Isa 8: "(16) צור תעודה חתום תורה בלמדי, Bind up the message, seal the instruction with my disciples... (19) Now, should people say to you, 'Inquire of the ghosts and familiar spirits that chirp and moan; for a people may inquire of its divine beings—of the dead on behalf of the living—for תורה and תעודה....'" The verb צור in v. 16 is the imperative form of the root צ-ר-ר, meaning "to bind." The prophet employs this verb in parallel with חתום "seal," also vocalized as an imperative form. Sealing a document is an act that confirms its validity (Jer 32:9–15; Esth 3:13; 8:8; Neh 10:1).[23] The terms Torah and *te'udah* are presented in parallel, and appear to refer to the contents of Isaiah's prophecies. Torah in Isa 8 does not carry the connotation of laws;[24] Isaiah did not receive any laws until this point that he could transmit to the people. God commanded the prophet Isaiah to write down his prophecies and give them to his students (בלמדי[25]—v. 16) until a more appropriate time for their publication (v. 17). God warned Isaiah against behaving like the people, and related to Isaiah the punishment that they were to receive for their actions (vv. 11–15): God will hide his face from them (v. 17). The document that Isaiah was supposed to write and seal will attest to the truth of these prophecies at a later date.[26] It is difficult to arrive

---

[23] Williamson 1994: 100.
[24] See Jensen 1973; Williamson 1994: 88–89.
[25] For a similar meaning, see Isa 50:4; 54:13.
[26] Isa 30:8–11 also describes Isaiah writing for a future time (Williamson [1994, ch. 5] and Werman [2001a: 234] already noticed the connection between the two passages):
> Now, go, write it down on a tablet and inscribe it on a record, that it may be with them for future days *as a witness* (according to the reading reflected in the "Three," Vulgate, Peshitta, Targum) forever. For it is a rebellious people, faithless children, children who refused to heed the instruction of the Lord. Who said to the seers, "Do not see," to the prophets, "Do not prophesy truth to us; speak to us smooth things; prophesy delusions."

God commanded Isaiah to write his words on a tablet or to engrave them in a record, and they would serve as testimony "forever." The nation was not prepared to receive the Lord's instruction (i.e., the prophecies that God transmitted to Isaiah), and only wanted to hear "smooth things." In order to preserve the prophecies, Isaiah must write them for "future days." As Nitzan (1986: 138) noted, Isa 30:10 is the source for the epithet used by the Dead Sea sect for the Pharisees, "seekers of smooth things"; see CD 1:18: "since they sought after smooth things and chose delusions." It is possible that the sect had an implied *pesher* on this entire passage, according to which the Pharisees were unwilling to accept the hidden, esoteric Torah, and did not accept the "prophets" of the sect.

at a more precise definition of this expression in Isaiah because of the limited amount of material.[27] Kugel suggested that Isaiah's expression is employed in *Jubilees*' self-description, "the divisions of time for Torah and *te'udah*," in order to indicate that *Jubilees* itself contains God's words that were hidden away at the end of the First Temple period because of the nation's sins; they were preserved as evidence for later generations that this cycle of sin and punishment was predicted in advance by God.[28] This suggestion explains the choice of the relatively rare expression found in the Isaiah passage.

In order to fully understand the precise use and meaning of the expression תורה ותעודה in *Jubilees*, it is necessary to analyze each of its occurrences throughout the book. While these instances are limited to the first three chapters, the term תעודה/עדות, represented by the Geʿez *səmaʿ*, without the element תורה, is found throughout the book, almost exclusively within passages that can be attributed to the redactional layer.

The full expression first appears in the prologue of *Jubilees*, אלה דברי מחלקות העתים לתורה ולתעודה, and all together in four (or five)

---

[27] Two additional biblical passages in which the idea of writing as evidence for a future time, are Deut 31:7–30 and Hab 2:2–3. The first passage is one of the primary sources for *Jub.* 1, which combines it with Isa 8:1–16 (see Charles 1902: 2–10; Davenport 1971: 19–29; Berger 1981: 313–320; VanderKam and Milik 1994: 7, 10–11; Brooke 1997: 50–53; Werman (1999) 2002; VanderKam 2001: 269–273). The selection from Habakkuk serves as a source for the notion of pesher interpretation, as expressed in 1QpHab VI, 12 – VII, 14. These four passages can be viewed as a closed circle of verses that form the basis for the concept of pesher common to *Jubilees* and to the sectarian literature preserved at Qumran.

[27] A third verse that mentions *te'udah* is Ruth 4:7: "Now this was formerly done in Israel in cases of redemption or exchange: to validate any transaction, one man would take off his sandal and hand it to the other. And this was the *te'udah* in Israel." The context there allows for a number of possible translations of the term *te'udah*, all of them derived from the legal world. The removal of the shoe can be viewed: (1) as a symbolic act which provides legal *evidence* to the purchase (LXX; Vulgate; Rashi, Ibn Ezra); (2) as a *custom*, according to the Arabic *ʿādah* (Ibn Ezra quoting others; NJPS ["practice"]; Zakovitch 1990: 108); (3) in accordance with the meaning of *te'udah* in *Jubilees* suggested by Kister, Ruth 4:7 can also be understood as *law* (Kister 2001: 296, n. 43); (4) in accordance with the meaning of *te'udah* in *Jubilees* suggested below (*te'udah* = covenant), one can interpret it in Ruth 4:7 as signifying the entry of two parties into an agreement. According to the final interpretation, the sentence "And this was the *te'udah* in Israel" parallels the beginning of the verse, "Now this was formerly done in Israel in cases of redemption or exchange to validate any transaction," forming an *inclusio* around the act of acquisition, "one man would take off his sandal and hand it to the other" (cf. Zakovitch 1990: 108).

[28] Kugel 2000: 166–170.

instances throughout ch. 1 (prologue, vv. 4, 26, 29, and possibly in v. 8):

> Prologue: [These are the words regarding the divisions of the times **of the law and of the te'udah**, of the events of the years, of the weeks of their jubilees throughout all the years of eternity as he related (them) to Moses on Mt. Sinai when he went up to]re[ceive the stone tablets—the law and the commandments—]by the word of the Lord [as he had told him that he should come up] to the summit of the moun[tain] (4Q216 I, 1–4).
> 1:4—[Moses remained on the mountain for forty days and forty nights while the Lord told him the first and the last things and what will come. He related to him the di]visions of the times—for **the la[w and for the te'udah**] (4Q216 I, 9–12).
> 1:26—[Now you write all these words which I tell you on this mountain: the first and the] last thing[s and that which will come during all the divisions of the times for **the la]w and for the te'u[dah** and for the weeks of the jubilees forever, until I descend] and I live wi[th them for all the ages of eternity] (4Q216 IV, 1–6).
> 1:29 — The angel of the presence, who was going along in front of the Israelite camp, took the tablets (which told) of the divisions of the years from the time **the law and the te'udah** were created—for the weeks of their jubilees, year by year in their full number, and their jubilees from [*the time of the creation until*] the time of the new creation when the heavens, the earth, and all their creatures will be renewed like the powers of the sky and like all the creatures of the earth, until the time when the temple of the Lord will be created in Jerusalem on Mt. Zion.

As Charles already noted,[29] the Ge'ez translation of *Jub.* 1:29 is apparently corrupt. The reader here expects a starting point for the divisions of times, presumably the creation of the world, and an endpoint for the events that are described on the Tablets. According to *Jub.* 1:26, the Lord commanded Moses to write "the first and the] last thing[s and that which will come during all the divisions of the times for the la]w and for the te'u[dah and for the weeks of the jubilees forever, until I descend] and I live wi[th them for all the ages of eternity]." Afterwards, God turned to the angel of presence, and commanded him "to dictate[30] [to Moses from the beginning of the creation unti]l my sanctuary is built [among them for all the ages of eternity]" (1:27; according to 4Q216 IV, 6–8). The book of *Jubilees*, which constitutes that which the angel

---

[29] Charles 1902: 9.
[30] See VanderKam 1981.

dictated to Moses, opens this historical survey in ch. 2 with the creation of the world. Charles suggested that word "new (creation)" in v. 29 was a secondary addition in the Geʿez translation, and should therefore be deleted. Furthermore, he posited a corruption in the Greek *Vorlage* of the Geʿez translation, and conjectured emending "when (ὡς)" later in the sentence to "until (ἕως)." He thus reconstructed v. 29 to read: "from the time of the creation *until* the heavens, the earth, and all their creatures will be renewed...." Stone proposed a less radical textual solution, positing a case of parablepsis in the Geʿez version: "from [*the time of the creation until*] the time of the new creation."[31] Stone proposed this solution without being aware of the (as of then unpublished) scroll, 4Q225. 4Q225, frg. 1, line 7 preserves the reading, "] the creation until the day of the creation[," which supports his proposal.[32]

A version similar, but not identical, to the Ethiopic translation of 1:29, is found in another copy of *Jubilees* from Qumran (4Q217, frg. 2):[33]

1 [   ] the divisions of the times for the law and for the [*teʿudah*]
2 [   ] for all the ye[ars of] eternity, from the creatio[n   ]
3 [   ]*m* and all [that has been] created until the day wh[ich   ]
4 [   ]oo [Jer]usalem   ]

Although this version differs from the Geʿez translation to 1:29, the great similarity between them points to some degree of connection.[34] Line 1 contains the expression "the divisions of the times for the law and for the [*teʿudah*]," without the words "from the creation." This reading is almost identical to the other instances of the expression throughout ch. 1. In addition, the expression "from the creatio[n]" appears afterwards in line 2, as in the reconstructed reading of 1:29 proposed by

---

[31] Stone 1971: 125–126.

[32] VanderKam and Milik 1994: 143. This scroll is not a copy of *Jubilees* itself, but rather, a composition that uses similar terminology. This evidence is therefore not fully conclusive about the text of *Jub.* 1:29.

[33] According to the notes provided by VanderKam and Milik (1994: 26–27), the preserved lines are similar to some of the verses from *Jub.* 1, and especially *Jub.* 1:29. As they noted, one cannot reconstruct the missing parts of this fragment by retroverting the Geʿez translation into Hebrew. At the same time, they are aware of the textual problems present in 1:29, and accept Stone's suggested homoioteleuton; see also VanderKam 1989b: 6–7.

[34] "the divisions of the times for the law and for the [*teʿudah*]" (line 1); "for all the ye[ars of] eternity" (line 2) which is similar to *babba ʿāmat ba-kʷəllu ḥollaqomu*; "and all [that has been] created until the day wh[ich]" (line 3) which is similar to *wa-kʷəllu fəṭratomu... ʾəska ʾama*; "[Jer]usalem" (line 4).

Stone. It is possible that the phrase "from the creation," which appears in the Geʻez version as part of the larger expression "divisions of the times for the law and for the teʻudah," was mistakenly transferred from later in the verse, and there was therefore no "creation" of "Torah and teʻudah" in the original text of 1:29.

1:8—According to Werman's reconstruction,[35] the expression also appears in v. 8 (the verse is partially preserved in 4Q216 II, 3–5; DJD 13, pp. 8–9): "And this [law and] teʻudah will respond." However, the Ethiopic translation preserves a different reading: "And the [teʻudah] will respond [to] this teʻudah," and VanderKam and Milik reconstructed the Hebrew text accordingly. As noted by Kister, the proposed reconstruction is highly unlikely in Hebrew; however, it still remains the only attested reading to this verse. The word התעודה is the first word in line 5, and is close to the right margin. Because of a hole in this fragment, the end of line 4 and the beginning of line 5 are missing (see Plate I, frg. 5), and it is therefore impossible to ascertain whether the missing words are "[teʻudah to]" as suggested by the editors, or "[law and]" as posited by Werman, or any other reading.

The verses in ch. 1 do not help us ascertain the meaning of the expression "Torah and teʻudah," as in each instance, the fuller expression מחלקות העתים לתורה ולתעודה (divisions of the times of the Torah and teʻudah), is employed to describe the book of *Jubilees* as a whole. This name is known from some sectarian scrolls, and also functions there as the title of a composition, presumably *Jubilees* itself;[36] however, the context of each of these instances does not assist in the analysis of the meaning of the expression. Kister noted that the key to its interpretation is actually to be found elsewhere in the book.[37] If we limit

---

[35] Werman (1999) 2002: 94–95; 2001a: 242–243. Kister (2001: 298, n. 50) accepted her suggestion.

[36] See CD 16:2–4: "And the explication of their times, when Israel was blind to all these; behold it is specified in *the Book of the Divisions of the Times in their Jubilees and in their Weeks*." The text has been partially preserved in 4Q271 4 II, 5 (Baumgarten 1996; DJD 18, p. 178). In addition, the title has been (partially preserved) in two other scrolls: 4Q228 1 I, 9 (VanderKam and Milik 1994; DJD 13, pp. 178–180): "For thus it is written in the Divisions[" (and three additional times in the same column [lines 2, 4, 7]); 4Q384, frg. 9, line 2 (Smith 1995; DJD 19, p. 144): "[In the Book of the Di]visions of the Tim[es]." The word "book" in this final source is a reasonable reconstruction proposed by the editor. The phrase "Torah and teʻudah" does not appear (or at least is not preserved) as part of the title of the work.

[37] Kister 2001: 294–295. Ravid (1999: 468) observed that the expression appears only in the Prologue, and not in the body of the work. Apparently, Ravid understood

the investigation of this phrase to those cases in which both elements, Torah and te'udah, appear together, then the three instances in chs. 2–3 point to a general legal context:

2:24—"And this is the *te'udah* and the fir[st] law [" (4Q216 VII, 17). This is the only instance in which the combination of the two elements is preserved in a Qumran Hebrew text. In the Ethiopic translation, the pair appears in construct with the "the blessed and holy ones (of the testimony and of the first law)." However the Qumran version opens with "and this" (וזאת) before the phrase, demonstrating that this is the beginning of a new sentence.[38] This sentence serves as an introduction to the Sabbath laws presented at the end of the creation story.[39] The formulation of this verse is similar to Priestly formulations associated with legal sections: "And this is the law of . . .,"[40] with the additional expansion of the element *te'udah* from the expression in Isa 8:16, 20.

2:33—"This law and *te'udah* were given to the Israelites as an eternal law throughout their history." This verse completes the Sabbath laws, and closes the section that opened in v. 24.[41]

3:14—"These are the law and *te'udah* that were written for Israel to keep for all times." This verse refers to the law of the parturient mother of Lev 12, which, according to the legal passage in *Jub.* 3:8–14, is based upon certain chronological details of the story of the entrance to the Garden of Eden. This verse concludes the derivation of the law from the narrative, and parallels *Jub.* 2:33 in its formulation.

The formulation of the phrase in 2:24, according to 4Q216 VII, 17, וזאת התעודה והתורה הראש[ונה], uses the singular demonstrative adjective, indicating that the author of this passage understood the pair תורה ותעודה as a hendiadys.[42] As with other such biblical word

---

the term Prologue to include all of ch. 1 of the book (even though this term usually refers to the opening sentence which appears before 1:1). However, she herself (p. 467) quotes a counter-example to this claim, *Jub.* 2:24: "This is the *te'udah* and the fir[st] law" (4Q216 VII, 17). The expression also appears in *Jub.* 2:33; 3:14.

[38] VanderKam and Milik (1994: 22) suggested that the Ge'ez text *za-* which creates the construct, is actually a textual error for *ze-* ("this").

[39] Doering 1997: 186–187, especially n. 35.

[40] Lev 6:2, 7, 18; 7:1, 11; 11:46; 12:7; 13:59; 14:2, 32, 57; 15:32; Num 5:29; 6:13, 21; 19:14; Ezek 43:12 (2x).

[41] Similarly, the Priestly source in the Pentateuch sometimes opens and closes a legal unit with the phrase: "this is the law of . . ." (Lev 14:2, 32, 57; Num 6:13, 21).

[42] For a definition and study of the concept, see Melamed 1945. Melamed adduced (p. 176) the example of תושב ושכיר, which functions grammatically as a singular unit

pairs, both words together express one single idea, with one element modifying the other. I would thus suggest that the phrase תורה ותעודה should also be understood as one concept, with one element modifying the other: תורת התעודה, the Torah of *teʿudah*.[43] Scholars agree that the element Torah refers to the many legal passages in the book (as demonstrated by the usage in 2:24, 33; 3:14 to frame the laws). There is no consensus, however, regarding the second, and more obscure, element, תעודה. Most, but not all, of the passages that contain this term refer either to laws or the calendar. A number of studies of the word *teʿudah* in *Jubilees* have recently been published:

(1) Brooke translated the word as "testimony" (based upon the Geʿez *samaʿ*), and thus explained its meaning:[44]

> The testimony is in effect to be understood as another way of talking about the secrets of the heavenly realm which are disclosed only to the chosen few. In particular they are the "signs of heaven," "the ordained times." Since the use of Isa 8:12–16 allows for the understanding that the תעודה is synonymous with the תורה (Isa 8:20), the extended meaning of the term allows the author to imply what is the prime content of the Law itself as it is now being dictated to Moses by the angel of presence: it has to do with the knowledge of the calendar and the periodisation of history.

Brooke's interpretation fits some of the instances of תעודה or עדות that do appear in the context of a fixed chronological system. However, it is not appropriate for most of the verses, and in particular 2:24, 33; 3:14, which address legal issues. In addition, his suggestion regarding "the periodisation of history" does not accord with most of the verses.

(2) Werman suggested that the term *teʿudah* in its various contexts refers to the process of history, and to the events that occur therein. In her estimation, "It would seem that the phrase תורה ותעודה itself designates the march of history… התורה והתעודה is the historical

---

in Exod 12:45 and Lev 22:10, and noted (pp. 178, 189) that other than these two verses, in the overwhelming majority of cases of hendiadys in the Bible, the verb attached to the word-pair is in the plural. The use here of a demonstrative pronoun in singular form is therefore even more striking.

[43] Avishur (1977) focused on those examples of hendiadys in the Bible and in post-biblical literature that appear in a construct relationship. The vast amount of material that he assembled exemplifies and emphasizes the relationship between the two elements of the expression, with one modifying the other.

[44] Brooke 1997: 52.

sequence of events from beginning to end... Thus, while תעודה is the preordained march of history, תורה comprises the laws and commandments inserted in the תעודה."⁴⁵ This interpretation is based upon Werman's understanding of תעודה in Isaiah,⁴⁶ but it is also influenced by the general outlook of *Jubilees* regarding the gradual revelation of the commandments throughout the generations. However, this suggested meaning does not fit most of the occurrences of the word *səmaʿ*.⁴⁷

These problems were recognized by both Kugel and Kister, who each offered an interpretation based upon a philological analysis of the word:

(3) Kugel suggested an interpretation for the word תעודה in *Jubilees*, based upon the meaning of the root ע-ו-ד in the *hiphil* conjugation.⁴⁸ Alongside the meaning "testify, bear witness,"⁴⁹ in many cases in biblical Hebrew the appropriate translation for this form is "protest, warn, exhort solemnly, admonish, charge."⁵⁰ This is apparently the meaning of the term *səmaʿ* in 30:17: "For this reason I have ordered you: 'Proclaim this *warning (səmaʿ)* to Israel—See how it turned out for the Shechemites and their children....'" *Jubilees*, which is equivalent to the *teʿudah*, refers often to the "*teʿudah* of the Heavenly Tablets," which according to Kugel is "the solemn warning contained in the tablets, the same warning that is being transmitted by the book of *Jubilees* itself." The *teʿudah* contains the warnings against specific prohibited actions, without which punishment cannot be meted out.⁵¹ One cannot be punished for an action without the prior knowledge that the specific behavior is prohibited and punishable. Kugel suggests that this is the reason why *Jubilees* contains

---

⁴⁵ Werman (1999) 2002: 82–85.
⁴⁶ Werman 2001a.
⁴⁷ As Kister noted (2001: 298, n. 49): "I do not see how this suggestion can be integrated into most of the verses quoted..." (translation—M.S.).
⁴⁸ Kugel 2000: 169–170.
⁴⁹ 1 Kgs 21:10, 13; Mal 2:14; Job 29:11. Similarly, there are cases in which one can identify a causative meaning, "cause to testify, take or call as witness, invoke" (Deut 4:26; 30:19; 31:28; Isa 8:2; Jer 32:10, 25, 44); see BDB, 729–730.
⁵⁰ So too Gen 43:3; Exod 19:21, 23; 21:29 (*hophal*); Deut 8:19; 32:46; 1 Sam 8:9; 1 Kgs 2:42; 2 Kgs 17:13, 15; Jer 6:10; 11:7; 42:19; Amos 3:13; Zech 3:6; Ps 50:7; 81:9; 2 Chr 24:19; Neh 9:26, 29, 30, 34; 13:15, 21; see BDB, 729–730.
⁵¹ Japhet (1989: 184–191) identified the importance of the concept of warning, well documented in rabbinic literature, in order to understand the worldview of the Chronicler regarding the punishment of sinners. Kugel (1990: 223–231) traced this idea in early Jewish exegesis; see also Anderson (1994) regarding *Jubilees* and the *Damascus Document*, and the discussion above (ch. 3) regarding the Reuben and Bilhah story.

numerous "warnings" not found in the Pentateuch.[52] This interpretation has the advantage that it is both philologically justifiable, and is also appropriate to the general worldview of *Jubilees*. However, at the same time, there are a number of instances where this interpretation is not appropriate to the context; in many of the usages there is no reference to warnings or exhortations, but rather to the laws themselves. In two cases (30:19; 31:32), Kugel himself notes that תעודה cannot refer to a warning, but rather to the fate of Jacob's children, Levi and Judah.[53]

(4) Alternatively, Kister suggested that in many of the contexts, the meaning of תעודה seems to be "law, commandment," with either legal or astronomical meaning (such as 6:32).[54] In his opinion, the word תעודה acquired the meaning of the first element, תורה, as part of a semantic shift in the Second Temple period of the word עדות, from "warning" to "law." The parallelism of the terms Torah and *te'udah* in Isa 8:16, 20 also contributed to this usage in *Jubilees*.[55] This suggested sense fits almost all the instances of *səmə'* in *Jubilees*, but this interpretation does not fit two passages (the same two left unexplained by Kugel's approach), which address the status and fate of Levi and Judah (30:19–23; 31:32). Kister suggested that those two aberrations are the result of *Jubilees*' dependence upon other traditions.[56]

---

[52] Kugel (2000: 169–170) adduced 7:20: "He (Noah) testified to his sons that they should do what is right…," as an example of an admonition. According to the analysis offered above, ch. 6, Noah's testament in *Jub.* 7:20–39 was not written by the redactor of *Jubilees*, but was an already-existing written source that was included by this editor in his composition. Kugel does not enumerate the verses in which these admonitions appear. However, from the one example that he quotes, Noah's testament, it appears that he intended to refer to the numerous testaments throughout the composition. There were many testaments composed in the Second Temple period (for a description of the genre, see Collins 1984), and the purpose of their admonition sections is generally moral-didactic. It is therefore questionable whether these elements of the testaments in *Jubilees* are actually different in their aims from the contemporaneous testamentary literature.

[53] Kugel 2000: 170, n. 8. Similarly, both verses do not fit the interpretation proposed by Kister 2001 (see below).

[54] Kister 2001: 295, and ibid., n. 34.

[55] Kister 2001: 295–296.

[56] "This is not surprising, since, as we saw above, the term 'Heavenly Tablets' in *Jubilees* also has meanings and different shades of meaning, which have been absorbed from different traditions" (ibid., 298) (translation—M.S.). Regarding the different functions of the Heavenly Tablets, see below, pp. 313–316.

Teʿudah/ʿĒdut as Covenant

In contrast to the previous suggestions, I would like to suggest that the two passages mentioned above, which include the word *səmaʿ* and neither of which fits the interpretations suggested by Kugel and Kister, in fact hold the key to the interpretation of this word in *Jubilees*, and to the important phrase "Torah and *teʿudah*."

> *Jub.* 30:18–23: (18) Levi's descendants were chosen for the priesthood and as levites to serve before the Lord as we (do) for all time. Levi and his sons will be blessed forever because he was eager to carry out justice, punishment, and revenge on all who rise against Israel. (19) So are entered for him **as a *teʿudah* on the heavenly tablets** blessing and justice before the God of all. (20) We ourselves remember the justice which the man performed during his lifetime at all times of the year. As far as 1000 generations will they enter (it). It will come to him and his family after him. <u>He has been recorded on the heavenly tablets as a friend</u> and a just man. (21) I have written this entire message for you and have ordered you to tell the Israelites not to sin or transgress the statutes or violate the <u>covenant</u> which was established for them so that they should perform it and be <u>recorded as friends</u>. (22) But if they transgress and behave in any impure ways, they will be recorded on the heavenly tablets as enemies. They will be erased from the book of the living and will be recorded in the book of those who will be destroyed and with those who will be uprooted from the earth. (23) On the day that Jacob's sons killed (the people of) Shechem, a written notice was entered in heaven for them (to the effect) that they had carried out what was right, justice, and revenge against the sinners. It was recorded as a blessing.

This passage appears after the story of the rape of Dinah (*Jub.* 30 || Gen 34), and focuses on Levi's (and Simeon's) reaction to this act. In contrast to the critical tone against their behavior in Gen 49:5–7, which condemns their anger and act of retaliation, *Jub.* 30 actually praises them, and specifically Levi, for their swift and unambiguous reaction to their sister's rape. The story as a whole is presented in *Jubilees* as a paradigm against intermarriage.[57] Following a discussion of intermarriage, characterized by the terminology of the legal passages in *Jubilees*, the text turns in vv. 18–23 to the election of Levi, as a reward for his zeal which he demonstrated in the story of Shechem and Dinah. In addition to its dependence on Gen 34, the description

---

[57] Endres 1987: 133–147; Werman 1997.

of Levi's elevation to priesthood is based upon the biblical story of the sin of Baal-peor (Num 25:1–15).[58] In that narrative, Phineas the priest, Aaron's grandson, acted zealously to defend (or punish) the Israelites from fornication and idol worship with the Midianite women. Endres identified three common motifs between this pentateuchal narrative and the portrayal of Levi's reaction to the rape of Dinah according to this legal passage in *Jubilees*:

(1) Intercourse with a Gentile
(2) Praise for zealousness (Num 25:11, 13; *Jub.* 30:18)
(3) Reward of Eternal Priesthood (Num 25:13; *Jub.* 30:18)

Another significant theme of the Baal-peor story is the covenant given to Phineas as a reward for his swift and decisive action: "I grant him my covenant of peace" (Num 25:12), "and it shall be for him and his descendants after him an eternal covenant of priesthood" (v. 13).[59] At first glance, this aspect appears to be absent from *Jubilees*; however a careful comparison between *Jub.* 30:18–20 and Num 25 allows for its identification in the *Jubilees* story:

Jubilees 30	Numbers 25
(18) Levi's descendants were chosen for the priesthood and as levites to serve before the Lord as we (do) for all time. Levi and his sons will be blessed forever	(13) And it shall be for him and his descendants after him an eternal covenant of priesthood
because he was eager to carry out justice, punishment, and revenge on all who rise against Israel.	because he was zealous for his God…
(19) So are entered for him **as a teu'dah on the heavenly tablets** *blessing and justice* before the God of all.	(12) Therefore say, "I grant him my **covenant** *of peace*."
(20) We ourselves remember the justice which the man performed during his lifetime at all times of the year.	

---

[58] Hengel (1976) 1989: 178–179; Collins 1980: 96, n. 14; Endres 1987: 150–151.
[59] The covenant motif is also mentioned in 1 Macc 2:24–27, which describes Mattathias' actions, shaped according to the model of Phineas' zealotry in the story of Baal-peor.

As far as 1000 generations will they enter (it). It will come to him and his family after him. He has been recorded on the heavenly tablets as a friend and a just man.	(13) And it shall be for him and his descendants after him an eternal covenant of priesthood

(1) The covenant mentioned in Num 25:13, "an eternal covenant of priesthood," the reward for Phineas' zeal, has been adopted in *Jub.* 30:18 in order to describe the election of Levi and his sons as priests and levites forever.

(2) *Jub.* 30:20–22 connects the promise of the eternal covenant for Phineas to God's promise to observe his covenant with "those who love him and keep his commandments" in Deut 7:9–10:

> Know, therefore, that the Lord your God is God, the steadfast God *who keeps the covenant and the steadfast love with those who love him and keep his commandments to a thousand generations*. But who immediately requites with destruction those who reject (or: hate) him—never slow with those who reject him, but requiting them instantly.

The use of term "friend" (אוהב) for Levi in *Jub.* 30:20 is based upon its use in Deut 7, with the meaning "loyalty to the covenant." This is the term used throughout Deuteronomy (6:5; 10:12–13; 11:1, 22; 30:16–20), and is based upon ancient Near Eastern treaty terminology.[60] Similarly, CD III, 2–4 records: "Abraham did not walk in it and he was ente[red as a lo]ver (ויע]ל או[הב), for he kept God's ordinances, and did not choose (that which) his (own) spirit desired. And he transmitted (his way) to Isaac and Jacob; and they observed (them) and were registered as lovers of God and parties to (his) covenant forever (ויכתבו אוהבים לאל ובעלי ברית לעולם)."[61] The dependence upon Deut 7 explains the continuation in *Jub.* 30:21–22, which includes a warning to those who violate the covenant, and are therefore defined as "enemies" in the Tablets of Heaven. This detail in *Jubilees* interprets Deut 7:10, and has no direct connection to the status and election of Levi, who specifically obeyed the Lord's command.

(3) "Covenant of peace" in Num 25:12 is parallel to "*səma'* on the heavenly tablets blessing and justice before the God of all." The word שלום (peace) is found in parallel to both "blessing" and "justice" in

---

[60] Cf. Moran 1963; Weinfeld 1991: 351–352.
[61] Translation according to Baumgarten and Schwartz 1995: 16–17.

the Bible,[62] leaving the remaining element, ברית (covenant) parallel to "səmaʿ on the heavenly tablets."

In light of this parallel, and the context of this passage in general, I would like to suggest that the term תעודה/עדות in *Jubilees* can be equated with the biblical ברית, "covenant." The interchange of עדות and ברית is well attested in the Bible: note especially the alternative expressions לוחות העדות/הברית[63] and ארון העדות/הברית[64] in the Priestly and Deuteronomic literature, as well as the use of these terms in parallelism or in proximity of one another in some biblical passages (Ps 25:10; 132:12; 2 Kgs 17:15; 23:3).[65] In addition, the words עדות, עדוות, עדת are often used in Deuteronomistic literature in combination with other legal terms, such as חוקים, משפטים, מצוות (Deut 4:45; 6:17, 20; 1 Kgs 2:3; 2 Kgs 23:3; Jer 44:23). In Psalm 119, the term עדות is used frequently in conjunction with a wider group of legal terms. Based upon these considerations, scholars have suggested that the words עדות, עדת, עדוות in biblical Hebrew mean "covenant" or the laws that are "stipulations of the covenant."[66] The cognate legal terms in

---

[62] The expression "covenant of peace" also appears in Isa 54:10; Ezek 34:25; 37:25. In Ezek 34:25–26, as part of the "covenant of peace" established between the Lord and Israel, God promises: "And I will make them and the environs of my hill a *blessing*... rains that bring *blessing*." Similarly, שלום appears as the object of the verb ב-ר-ך "bless" in Ps 29:11. "Justice" (צדק/צדקה) and "peace" (שלום) appear in parallelism in Isa 32:17; 60:17; Ps 72:3; 85:18.

[63] **Tablets of the ʿĒdut**: Exod 31:18; 32:15; 34:29. **Tablets of the Covenant**: Deut 9:9, 11, 15.

[64] **Ark of the ʿĒdut**: Exod 25:22; 26:33, 34; 30:6, 26; 39:35; 40:3, 5, 21; Num 4:5; 7:89; Jos 4:16. **Ark of the Covenant**: Num 10:33; 14:44; Deut 10:8; 31:9, 25, 26; Jos 3:3, 6, 8, 11; 4:7, 9, 18; 6:6, 8; 8:33; Judg 20:27; 1 Sam 4:3, 4, 5; 2 Sam 15:24; 1 Kgs 3:15; 6:19; 8:1, 6; Jer 3:16; 1 Chr 15:25, 26, 28, 29; 16:6, 37; 17:1; 22:19; 28:2, 18; 2 Chr 5:2, 7.

[65] Shalom Paul called my attention to another parallel of similar terms. Isa 33:8, which reads הפר ברית מאס ערים ("a covenant has been renounced, *cities* rejected") in the MT, should be read with the more original reading, מאס עדים in 1QIsaᵃ, reflecting the same covenantal context.

[66] Cross 1973: 300; Parnas 1975; Veijola 1976; Seow 1984: 192–193. There is not complete agreement amongst scholars regarding the meaning of this term. For example, Loewenstamm (1971) understood the ʿēdut as the tablets on which the Decalogue was written or a general expression of divine law, and claimed vehemently: "In the Bible, the word ʿēdut does not even once serve to signify a covenant" (trans.—M.S.). Similarly, Schwartz (1996: 126, n. 52) emphasized that according to the Priestly source, ʿēdut is an object given by God to Moses to commemorate their meeting on Mount Sinai. Knohl (1995: 137–148) distinguished between the meaning of *bərît* (a two-sided commitment) and ʿēdut (a one-sided obligation [according to the meaning of the Assyrian *adê*; see below]) in the Priestly source, and viewed the two terms as expressions of different

other Semitic languages bear the same meaning. In the Aramaic Sefire inscriptions, the plural form עדיא (from the root ע-ד-י) is used with the sense of "covenant."[67] The word always appears in plural form, and it is possible that this refers to the stipulations and obligations of the covenant.[68] The same is true for the Akkadian *adê*, which also always appears in plural form,[69] and refers to the commitment made by a vassal to his Assyrian master.[70] The term in *Jubilees* should be understood similarly: "covenant," but also "stipulations of the covenant."

Another passage, 31:31–32, supports this interpretation of תעודה. In the context of a long addition to the biblical text (*Jub.* 31:1–3a parallels Gen 35:1–7, 14; *Jub.* 32:30 parallels Gen 35:8), *Jub.* 31:3b–32 describes how Jacob brought Judah and Levi to visit his father Isaac. During their stay, Isaac blessed his grandchildren, and then his son Jacob. The blessings to Levi and Judah promise them specific roles that they and their descendants will fill in the future: Levi is promised the priesthood[71] (vv. 14, 16), and Judah the kingship (vv. 18, 20). *Jub.* 31:31–32 describes Jacob's reaction to the blessings after he returned to Bethel:

---

perceptions of the relationship between God and his people, in the patriarchal period (*bərit*) and in the Mosaic period (*'ēdut*). However, even if one accepts the reservations expressed by scholars regarding the various biblical occurrences, the understanding of *te'udah/'ēdut* in *Jubilees* as "covenant" can reflect later exegesis of the word according to its parallels (and especially the identification of the Tablets of the Covenant with the Tablets of the *'ēdut*) and its contexts.

[67] Fitzmyer (1967) 1995: 57–59; Greenfield 1964: 308; Volkwein 1969: 34–37; Parnas 1975: 239–240.

[68] Weinfeld 1972: 87, n. 17.

[69] Tadmor (1982: 165, n. 76) noted that the form *adû* listed in *CAD* does not actually exist, and is a theoretical form, reconstructed by the editors of the dictionary.

[70] Tadmor, ibid. See also Gelb 1962; Weinfeld 1972: 95; Parnas 1975: 240–244. *CAD* (1A: 133) explains: "The agreement called *adû* was drawn up in writing between a partner of higher status (god, king, member of the royal family) and servants or subjects."

[71] According to the blessing, the descendants of Levi are not limited to service in the temple, but also serve as "princes, judges, and leaders" (v. 15). Charles (1902: 187) posited a connection between the dual responsibilities of Levi's blessing in *Jub.* 31 and the political-religious leadership during the Maccabean period. But as Davenport (1971: 63) noted, there is no need to assume that the blessing represents a historical reality, and it might rather reflect the different roles of Levi and the Levites mentioned in the Bible. Davenport also claimed that *Jub.* 31:14 (a description of the Levites' service in the temple) was a secondary addition to the text. However, in light of the multiple tasks assigned to Levi's descendants in Moses' blessing to Levi (Deut 33:8–11), there is no basis for the removal of v. 14 from the text.

> When Jacob recalled the prayer with which his father had blessed him and his two sons—Levi and Judah—he was very happy and blessed the God of his fathers Abraham and Isaac. He said: "Now I know that I and my sons, too, have an eternal hope before the God of all." This is the way it is ordained regarding the two of them, and it is entered for them as an **eternal te'udah** on the heavenly tablets just as Isaac blessed them.

Most commentators understand the "entering of an eternal *səmaʿ* on the Heavenly Tablets" as the recording of their blessings, a heavenly register of their future fate.[72] However, in light of the analysis of the previous example, v. 32 can be better understood as "an eternal covenant." The descendants of both Judah and Levi were given eternal covenants in the Bible. As we just saw, Phineas was given an "eternal priestly covenant" (Num 25:12–13). In Moses' blessing to the tribe of Levi in Deut 33, they are praised "for they observed your precepts and kept your covenant" (v. 9). The prophet Malachi chastises the priests for violating "the covenant of the Levites" (Mal 2:8). Similarly, Judah's descendant King David was promised an eternal covenant on a number of occasions in the Bible (2 Sam 23:1–5; Isa 55:1–5; Ps 89:4–5, 29–30). Isaac's promise to Judah, "Be a prince—you and one of your sons" (*Jub.* 31:18), creates the link between Judah, the tribal ancestor, and David (and his descendants), who received an eternal covenant with the Lord.[73]

> 23:32—"Now you, Moses, write down these words because this is how it is written and entered in the **te'udah/'ēdut** of the heavenly tablets for the history of eternity."

This verse concludes an eschatological passage (23:11–31),[74] which explains the dismal state of humanity (including their short lifespan) as the result of their sins. It is worth noting that the entire passage emphasizes the nation's need to observe the covenant. Violation of this covenant results in drastic consequences:

> (14) All of this will happen to the evil generation which makes the earth commit sin through sexual impurity, contamination, and their

---

[72] García Martínez 1997: 249–250.
[73] Thus Testuz 1960: 68. Davenport (1971: 64–65) surveyed the various suggested interpretations of "and one of your sons," most of them with a messianic tone (Jewish or Christian). However, in light of the interpretation suggested here for the term *te'udah/'ēdut*, and the connection to the covenant with the Davidic line, it is difficult to accept them.
[74] See Davenport 1971: 32–46.

detestable actions...(16)...because of sin and injustice, because of what they say and the great evils that they commit, and *because of their abandoning the covenant which the Lord had made between them and himself so that they should observe and perform all his commands, ordinances, and all his laws without deviating to the left or right.*

Only when "the children will begin to study the laws, to seek out the commands, and to return to the right way" (v. 26) will the world be transformed into a utopia, where there is neither old age nor evil, only peace, happiness, and blessing (vv. 27–30). When they turn "to seek out the commands," they will learn that *"that the Lord is one who executes judgment but shows kindness to hundreds and thousands and to all who love him"* (v. 31). As noted above, the verbal root "love" in Deuteronomy (influenced by Mesopotamian covenant terminology) signifies loyalty, and especially loyalty to the covenant with God. This apocalypse expands the covenant between God and Israel until the eschatological age.

According to the version of v. 32 quoted above (based upon the base text in VanderKam's edition), the meaning of the verse itself ("and entered in the *te'udah/'ēdut* of the heavenly tablets") is still not fully clear. However, Ethiopic MS 12[75] (according to VanderKam's apparatus) preserves a different word order: "and entered in the heavenly tablets as a *te'udah/'ēdut* for the history of eternity."[76] Support for this reordering can be adduced from another verse that refers to the Heavenly Tablets, "(This is the way it is ordained regarding the two of them,) and it is entered for them as an eternal *te'udah/'ēdut* on the heavenly tablets..." (31:32), which also describes eternal covenants, for Levi and Judah. The order in that verse matches the suggested meaning of *te'udah/'ēdut* in 23:32: the covenant with the Lord is eternally valid

---

[75] Despite belonging to an inferior textual family, VanderKam (1989b: XIX–XX) still considers MS 12 an important manuscript due to its age (15th century) and also for specific readings contained therein. I would suggest that the current verse exemplifies the importance of these readings.

[76] Thus translated by Charles 1902: "and they record (them) *on the heavenly tables for a testimony for the generations for ever*"; Rabin 1984: "and recorded *on the heavenly tablets as a testimony for each generation for ever*." Goldmann (1956) does not include the word *te'udah/'ēdut* at all (but notes that Charles added it). He apparently relied upon MS 38 (according to the sigla of VanderKam 1989 = MS D in Charles 1895) and MS 51 (VanderKam 1989a notes MS 58, but it seems that it should be MS 51 = MS C in Charles 1895), in which the word *səmaʿ* is absent. Berger (1981: 446) offers a translation similar to VanderKam's text, but also mentions the possibility suggested here (ibid., note c).

and recorded on the Heavenly Tablets. The eternality of the covenant in *Jub.* 23 is expressed by the requirement to observe the commandments forever, and by the description of the utopian world during the eschatological era, without aging or war, which Israel will receive as a reward for their behavior.

"Torah and Te'udah"—The Stipulations of the Covenant

In two passages (2:24b–33; 3:8–14), the laws are defined by the expression "Torah and *te'udah*." As noted above, the biblical source for this expression (Isa 8:16) does not refer specifically to laws; however, elsewhere in the Bible the term תורה certainly carries this connotation.[77] The sources above demonstrated the usage of the expression in *Jubilees* in reference to laws. The context of 2:24, 33, verses that open and conclude a list of laws, lends support to Kister's suggestion that the meaning of *te'udah* is laws or halakhot. However, the foregoing analysis demonstrated that one can replace the term *te'udah/'ēdut* with the legal term "covenant." Similarly, both according to biblical usage, and the forms and contexts of cognate terms in Aramaic and Akkadian, the meaning of the term can be extended to "stipulations of the covenant" as well. Does this suggested meaning match the abovementioned verses? In principle, the commandments and halakhot given to Israel are stipulations to the covenant between God and Israel. Moreover, the topic of *Jub.* 2:17–24a is the covenant established between them from the dawn of creation. This covenant regulates both parties—in exchange for the election of Israel as his preferred nation, they are obligated to observe the stipulations of the covenant, God's commandments. In the Pentateuch itself, this election occurs only at a later stage. But in *Jubilees*, according to which Israel was chosen from creation, God needed to present them with the conditions for their special status at that point in time. As suggested above, this is the reason for transferring the laws to the patriarchal period, beginning with the Sabbath laws at the end of the first week. It seems therefore that there are three factors which assist in the correct interpretation of the expression "Torah and *te'udah*":

---

[77] See BDB, 435–436: "direction, instruction, law," and the many examples adduced there.

(1) The recognition that the notion of covenant forms the framework of *Jub.* 2;
(2) The philological analysis of the word *te'udah/'edut*;
(3) The syntactical-stylistic understanding of the idiom "Torah and *te'udah*" as a hendiadys.

If one exchanges each of the two elements with parallel terms, the expression can be taken as "law and covenant," or in construct form, "law(s) of the covenant." "Torah and *te'udah*" according to *Jubilees* denotes the stipulations of the covenant, those commandments which God already established from the first week in history.

The opening of the Sabbath halakhot with the sentence, "And this is the **firs[t]** Torah and *te'udah*" conveys that the giving of these laws is not a one-time event, but rather the first time that Israel received conditions to their covenant with the Lord. The law of the parturient mother, which is connected to the story of the entrance to the Garden of Eden, is also defined as "Torah and *te'udah*" (3:14). Other laws presented in the patriarchal period are referred to as *te'udah/'edut*, without the first element, "Torah." However, as noted above, the biblical term *'edut* can be understood as either "covenant" or "stipulations of the covenant." This interpretation can be applied to the following passage:

> (6:10) Noah and his sons swore an oath not to consume any blood that was in any animate being. During this month he made a covenant before the Lord God forever throughout all the history of the earth. (11) For this reason he told you, too, to make a covenant—accompanied by an oath...because of all the words of the covenant which the Lord was making with them for all times. (12) This **te'udah** has been written regarding you to keep it for all times so that you may not at any time eat any blood...

After Noah emerged from the ark, he offered a whole-burnt sacrifice to God from the pure animals, following which God decided not to destroy the entire world ever again (Gen 8:15–22). In the postdiluvian world, God permitted the eating of animals, but continued to prohibit the consumption of their blood. Alongside this proscription, it was also prohibited to murder another human being (9:1–7). The prohibitions against murder and consumption of animal blood are mentioned before the covenant between God and Noah, in which he promised never again to bring a flood upon the earth (9:8–17). It is unclear in the biblical story whether these proscriptions are stipulations of the covenant, or whether God's commitment was not conditional upon human behavior.[78] However, in the rewritten version of events in *Jub.* 6 there is no doubt that these prohibitions are explicit conditions of the covenant: the description of the covenant was transferred immediately after Noah's offering of the sacrifice (*Jub.* 6:4), and Noah and his sons swore not to consume blood as part of the covenant (v. 10). The ban on eating blood in v. 12, which was explicitly transformed into a covenantal stipulation, is called *te'udah/'ēdut*, consonant with the meaning suggested here.

The Constancy of the Celestial Bodies

In addition to those cases of *te'udah/'ēdut* which can be interpreted as "covenant" or "stipulations of the covenant," there are also a number of instances of this word in *Jubilees* which refer to the chronological system established by God, consisting of the correct calendar and the dates determined therein. What is the meaning of *te'udah* which allows for its usage in the context of a divine temporal system? According to Kister, who suggested that *te'udah* refers to laws and commandments, one can take its usage in the chronological context as the rules governing the orbits of the luminaries. However, one can point to an explicit connection in *Jubilees* between covenant and chronology.

At the conclusion of the biblical flood story, subsequent to Noah's sacrifice, God promised not to bring another cataclysmic punishment upon the earth, neither to destroy all living creatures, nor to suspend the natural order, especially the celestial bodies:

> The Lord smelled the pleasing odor, and the Lord said to himself: "Never again will I doom the world because of man, since the devisings of man's mind are evil from his youth; nor will I ever again destroy every living being, as I have done. So long as the earth endures, seedtime and harvest, cold and heat, summer and winter, day and night, shall not cease." (Gen 8:21–22)

At this stage in the story, there is no explicit reference to the covenant between God and Noah. This covenant is first mentioned in Gen 9:8–17, following the permission granted to eat animals, and the

---

[78] Werman 1995b: 191–196. Skinner (1930: 173–174) and Knohl (1995: 138, 141–142) take the prohibitions in Gen 9, against consumption of animal blood and spilling of human blood, as stipulations of the covenant.

prohibitions against blood consumption and murder (ibid., 1–7). The Lord's covenantal promise, "never again shall all flesh be cut off by the waters of a flood, and never again shall there be a flood to destroy the earth" (v. 11), displays some similarity to his words (quoted above) at the end of Gen 8. On the one hand, the Lord's promise not to bring another flood was delivered in two stages, first in response to Noah's sacrifice, and then in the covenant. On the other hand, there is no clear reference in the covenant in Genesis to the constancy of the heavenly bodies. In the rewritten story of *Jub.* 6, one can identify two differences relevant to the discussion at hand, which were introduced into the Genesis story:[79]

(1) The covenant between the Lord and Noah is mentioned already in *Jub.* 6:4 (parallel to Gen 8:21–22):

> 6:4 The Lord smelled the pleasant fragrance **and made a covenant with him** that there would be no flood waters which would destroy the earth; (that) throughout all the days of the earth seedtime and harvest would not cease; (that) cold and heat, summer and winter, day and night would not change their prescribed pattern and would never cease.

According to the *Jubilees* account of Gen 8–9, the constancy of the luminaries is part of the "eternal covenant" (Gen 9:16) that was promised to Noah.

(2) At the end of Gen 8:22, a lyrical list which describes the forces of nature which will never again cease, *Jub.* 6:4 adds a short sentence: "day and night *would not change their prescribed pattern* (śərʿātomu) and would never cease." The term "prescribed pattern" refers to the preordained chronological system that, according to God's promise, will never again change following the flood. The term śərʿat appears twice more at the end of ch. 6, in the description of the proper calendar: "...all of them will disturb their times...they will transgress their prescribed pattern (śərʿātomu)" (v. 33); "they will forget the first of the month, the season, and the sabbath; they will err with respect to the entire prescribed pattern (śərʿāta) of the years" (v. 34). The context there is a polemic against those who subscribe to an "errant," lunar calendar, instead of a solar one (v. 36). The adherence to the correct, 364-day calendar will prevent the disruption of the festivals, "because everything will happen in harmony with their **teʿudah**" (v. 32). One can therefore identify the "prescribed

---

[79] See VanderKam 2000a.

pattern" of the celestial bodies with the *te'udah/'ēdut*, both of which are anchored in the covenant between God and Noah in *Jub.* 6:4.

The temporal system, according to which the world functions, was established following the flood as part of the covenant with God.[80] The use of the term *te'udah/'ēdut*, whose meaning is "covenant," is therefore appropriate to a description of the calendar that is based upon the covenant with Noah, as well as for the various festival days that appear throughout the calendar. The following verses belong to the category of *te'udah/'ēdut* in reference to the divine temporal system, whose status was covenantally confirmed:

> 6:23 On the first of the first month, the first of the fourth month, the first of the seventh month, and the first of the tenth month are memorial days and days of the seasons (*gize*).[81] They are written down and ordained at the four divisions of the year as an **eternal *te'udah***.

---

[80] The prophet Jeremiah (33:19–26) compares God's covenant with the celestial bodies to his covenants with the House of David and Levi's descendants (Jer 33:14–26 is not represented in LXX, and many scholars have already suggested that this prophecy was written in the Exile or post-Exilic period):

> (20) Thus said the Lord: If you could break my covenant with the day and my covenant with the night, so that day and night should not come at their proper time, (21) then also my covenant with my servant David could be broken—so that he would not have a descendant reigning upon his throne—or with my ministrants, the levitical priests...(25) Thus said the Lord: If I have not established my covenant with day and night—the laws of heaven and earth—(26) then I will reject the offspring of Jacob and my servant David...

Just as the regulation of the heavenly luminaries (based upon which the sun and moon come at their proper times) is guaranteed in a covenant with God and exists forever, so too the covenants between God and the House of David and the tribe of Levi are eternal. This idea is also found in Jer 31:34–36 (without the explicit use of the term "covenant"). Rashi (commentary to Jer 33:20) identified the covenant mentioned in Jeremiah's prophecy with the covenant established with Noah and his sons, fixing the times and seasons.

The constancy of the celestial bodies functioned in Jewish literature of the Second Temple period as a hortatory paradigm, serving as the basis for Israel's recognition of the need to observe the commandments—see *1 En.* 2–5; Sir 16:26–28; *T. Naph.* 3:2–5; *Sifre Deut.* 306; and the studies of Stone 1987; Kister 1991: 190–199 (esp. 196–199); Fraade 1991: 153–154. The use in *Jubilees* of one term (*te'udah/'ēdut*), both for the commandments and for the divinely sanctioned calendar, seems to point to a similar idea. From the interpretation suggested here for the word *te'udah/'ēdut*, it can be concluded that the common denominator between these two groups, Israel and the celestial bodies, is the covenant that each shares with God.

[81] Perhaps this term should be retroverted into Hebrew as ימי תקופה. The word *gize* translates תקופה in *Jub.* 2:9: "and for all the cy[cles (תק[ופות]) of the years]" (4Q216 VI, 8; DJD 13, p. 17). The expression יום (ה)תקופה is known from rabbinic literature as a chronological term; cf. *S. 'Olam* 11; *b. San.* 13a–b. In the passage in Sanhedrin, the question arises as to whether these days open or conclude these periods of time; the calendar of *Jubilees* lends support to the former option.

The four days which divide the year into quarters are referred to as "memorial days" in commemoration of past events from the flood story (cf. vv. 24–28), and at the same time "days of the seasons," fixed days in the calendar as an "eternal te'udah/'ēdut." The dates are part of the divine temporal system, by which the world functions.

> 6:37 Therefore years will come about for them when they will disturb (the year) and make a day of **te'udah** something worthless and a profane day a festival…

According to the contrasting parallelism in this verse, "day of te'udah/'ēdut" is equivalent to "festival." According to *Jub.* 6:23, the four days at the beginning of the quarters are ordained as an "eternal te'udah/'ēdut." A "day of te'udah/'ēdut" apparently refers to a special date in the 364-day calendar, which was established as part of the divine chronological system, and as part of the te'udah.

> 16:28 We blessed him eternally and all the descendants who would follow him throughout all the history of the earth because he had celebrated this festival at its time in accord with the **te'udah** of the heavenly tablets.

After the angels returned to Abraham in the seventh month and saw that their previous promise (16:15–16) had been realized when Sarah became pregnant, they blessed Abraham,[82] Isaac (who was soon to be born), and Jacob, who was destined to be chosen from among the nations (ibid., 16–18). They then reported this blessing to Sarah.[83] Abraham and Sarah rejoiced at hearing their message, and he built an altar, and "celebrated a joyful festival in this month—for seven days" (ibid. 20).

---

[82] Most Ethiopic MSS read here "and we blessed her," but the content of the blessing (six additional sons for Abraham) and the announcement to Sarah in v. 19 support the originality of the Latin translation: *benediximus eum* ("and we blessed him"); see Charles 1902: 115; Berger 1981: 412; VanderKam 1989b: 97.

[83] It is difficult to understand the order of events in *Jub.* 16. Verses 1–15 describe the promise that Isaac will be born, his actual birth, and circumcision. Following this (vv. 16–31), the story returns to the period before Isaac's birth, when the angels return to Sarah in the seventh month after she had conceived (v. 16; Goldmann translates "the fourth month," but this is not found in any of the textual witnesses). Charles (1902: 115) suggested that vv. 15b–16a are a gloss that disturb the context. The only mention of the seventh month in the story appears in v. 16a, and this date functions as a precedent for the law of Sukkot at the end of the chapter. It is therefore possible that vv. 15b–16a were inserted into the narrative along with the juxtaposition of the legal passage. This proposed literary development corresponds to the process suggested elsewhere in this study.

The passage continues with a detailed description of Abraham's actions during this festival (vv. 21–27, 31), as a precedent for the observance of the festival of Tabernacles throughout history (vv. 29–30).[84]

In v. 28, the angels blessed Abraham for observing the festival "at its time in accord with the *te'udah/'edut* of the heavenly tablets."

---

[84] *Jub.* 16:12–14 parallels Gen 21:1–4; *Jub.* 17:1ff. parallels Gen 22:1ff. Presumably, there is no representation of Gen 21:5–7 in *Jubilees*. However, the connection between the story of Isaac's birth and the law of the festival of Sukkot is based upon exegesis of Gen 21:6 – "And Sarah said: 'God has brought me laughter (צחק); everyone who hears will laugh (יצחק) for me.'" According to the story in Gen 18:9–15 (and the summary in *Jub.* 16:2), after Sarah heard God's promise for children in her old age, she laughed at the possibility that a woman so advanced in years could conceive a child (v. 12). God immediately accused Sarah that her laughter was an expression of her denial of his ability to perform this task (vv. 13–14). Sarah denied laughing, but God insisted that she had. The denial of her laughter in Gen 18:5 raises a double exegetical problem in Gen 21:6 following the birth of Isaac: (1) if God rebuked Sarah for her laughter in response to his promise, how could she now mention it after the birth? (2) If Sarah denied laughing, how can she refer to it now? The root צ-ח-ק in biblical Hebrew carries with it a tone of mockery and derision (Gen 18:13, 15; 19:14; 21:9; 39:14, 17; Judg 16:25; Ezek 23:32). However, according to an interpretive tradition attested in the Aramaic Targumim as well as in rabbinic literature (Peshitta; *Onqelos*; *Neofiti* [also in the marginal note]; *Gen. Rab.* 53:8), the meaning of the verb צ-ח-ק in Gen 21:6 is "rejoice," and not an expression of mockery (see Maori 1995:114–115; Kugel 1998: 311–312). Similarly, LXX translates the word יצחק with the verb συγχαίρω "rejoice" (although this specific Greek verb is only used here to translate a Hebrew text, the related verb χαίρω translates verbs from the root ש-מ-ח 15 times in the Bible—Exod 4:14; 1 Sam 19:5; 1 Kgs 4:20 [A]; 5:21; 8:66; 2 Kgs 11:14, 20; Jer 7:34; 31 (LXX 38):13; Ezek 7:12; Hos 9:1; Jon 4:6; Zech 4:10; 10:7; Esth 8:15). *Targum pseudo-Jonathan* translates the Hebrew root צ-ח-ק with the Aramaic ת-מ-ה "be amazed, astonished," another verb with a positive meaning. All of these interpreters understood that Sarah did not repeat her mocking laughter, but rather expressed her joy at the birth of her son.

Abraham also laughed when he heard the promise of progeny for Sarah (Gen 17:17), but God refrained from rebuking him. There too, early exegetes understood the verb צ-ח-ק as an expression of joy, and thus resolved the tension between this verse and the description of Sarah's laughter; see *Jub.* 15:17 and *Targum Onqelos*. *Targum Neofiti* and *Targ. pseudo-Jonathan* both translate ותמה, similar to *Targ. ps.-Jon.* to Gen 21:6.

In the legal passage in *Jub.* 16:15–31 that connects the birth of Isaac to the observance of Sukkot, the verb ש-מ-ח functions as a *leitwort*: "(19)…The two of them were extremely happy. (20)…and who was making him so happy… He celebrated a joyful festival in this month…(25) He celebrated this festival for seven days, being happy with his whole heart and all his being…(27) He gave a blessing and was very happy….a joy acceptable to the most high God. (29)…joyfully for seven days…(31)…he would give praise and joyfully offer humble thanks to his God for everything." The motif of joy on Sukkot appears twice in the laws of Feast of Tabernacles in the Torah: "You shall take on the first day…and you shall rejoice (ושמחתם) before the Lord your God seven days" (Lev 23:40); "You shall make for yourself the festival of Booths for seven days…And you shall rejoice (ושמחת) in your festival…" (Deut 16:13–14). The exegetical tradition of Gen 21:6 as a description of Sarah's joy is therefore the basis for the connection in *Jub.* 16 to the Feast of Booths, which is the festival of joy.

Syntactically, the clause "in accord with the *teʿudah*/*ʿedut* of the heavenly tablets" can modify one of two possible elements in the verse: either "he had celebrated this festival" or "at its time (*ba-gizehu*)." According to the first possibility, the law itself is part of the "*teʿudah*/*ʿedut* of the heavenly tablets"; this fits the interpretation of *teʿudah*/*ʿedut* as covenant or stipulations of the covenant. According to the second possibility, "*teʿudah*/*ʿedut* of the heavenly tablets" refers to the preordained temporal system of the divinely sanctioned calendar, and the date of the festival of Tabernacles was established in the *teʿudah*/*ʿedut*.[85]

> 6:32 Now you command the Israelites to keep the years in this number—364 days. Then the year will be complete and it will not disturb its time from its days or from its festivals because everything will happen in harmony with their **teʿudah**. They will neither omit a day nor disturb a festival.

The length of every year is unambiguously set at 364 days, and the calendar is based upon the sun (cf. 2:8–9). A 364-day calendar contains exactly 52 weeks, and therefore the festivals fall out every year on the same days of the week.[86] There are no shifts in the calendar from year to year, and it is eternally fixed. The author of 6:23–38 warns against those who use a different calendar (specifically a lunar system—see v. 36), according to which the days of the week on which the festivals occur shift annually. The calendrical scheme, which is based upon a fixed, unique number of days in a year, is referred to as *teʿudah*/*ʿedut*—"everything will happen in harmony with their *teʿudah*/*ʿedut*."

> 32:29:[87] It was called Addition because of the fact that it is entered in the **teʿudah/ʿedut** of the festal days in accord with the number of days in the year.

After Jacob celebrated a seven-day festival (in the seventh month) in Bethel (32:7), he remained there for an extra day, during which he con-

---

[85] Kister (2001: 295) quotes this verse as an example of *teʿudah* meaning "law, commandment," a sense close to "stipulations of the covenant" that I have suggested. He also raised the possibility (ibid., n. 34) that *ʿedut* can refer to the "heavenly, chronological law," but did not cite 16:28 as an example.

[86] Jaubert 1953, 1957; Talmon (1958) 1989; VanderKam 1998.

[87] The Latin translation reflects a different reading in two details: et uocatum est nomen eius retentatio propter quod **addita** est in **dies** dierum festorum secundum numerum dierum anni ("and it was called ʾAṣeret because it was **added** in **the days of** the days of the festival according to the number of days of the year"). Regarding the reading *dies* (which Charles [1902: 196] and Rabin [1984: 101] both took to be the original text), VanderKam (1989b: 216) commented that: (1) the word *teʿudah*/*ʿedut*

tinued to celebrate and offer sacrifices as he did on the first seven days (v. 27). His actions served as a precedent for the *'aṣeret* on the eighth day of the festival of Tabernacles (v. 28; cf. Lev 23:36; Num 29:35; Neh 8:18; 2 Chr 7:9), which follows the first seven (Lev 23:34, 39, 41–42; Num 29:12; Deut 16:13, 15), and whose status vis-à-vis the first week of the holiday is unclear.[88] According to the Ethiopic translation, the eighth day is called "Addition (*tosāk*) because that day was added (*tawassakat*)" (*Jub.* 32:27). The name of the day reflects its status relative to the other days of the festival—it was not originally part of them, but rather was added to the seven central days. Assuming that the eighth day was named *'aṣeret* as it is in the biblical laws (as well as in the later historiographical books—Neh 8:18; 2 Chr 7:9), it is presumed that Hebrew *Vorlage* (of the Greek *Vorlage*) of the Ethiopic translation read *'aṣeret* (and not a Hebrew word for "Addition"). The etymology found in the Latin translation is clearer: "He named it Detaining (*retentatio*) because he was detained (*retentus est*) there one day." The name of the festival is based upon the details of the story—Jacob was detained for one extra day in Bethel, and the festival was established to commemorate this delay. The motif of the additional day continues in v. 28 (in both translations): "For this reason it was revealed to him that he should celebrate it and add it (*yəwassək* = *adicere*) to the seven days of the festival." The law of Sukkot appeared already in the legal passage in *Jub.* 16:20–31, following Abraham's celebration of the festival, and it is therefore unnecessary to interpret the story about Jacob as a legal precedent for both the festival of Tabernacles and the additional eighth day. The legal passage in *Jub.* 32 therefore only addresses the eighth day, which was transformed from a regular day into a special one following the story of Jacob in Bethel.

The interpretation in v. 27, regarding the nature of the extra day that serves as a memorial for Jacob's delay (according to the Latin

---

is more appropriate in the context of the Heavenly Tablets; (2) the word *dies* seems to have entered the text through dittography of the adjacent word *dierum* (the textual argument is even more convincing when the Latin is retroverted into Hebrew: בימי ימי). If one adopts the version found in the Latin translation, this example does not belong to the discussion of the meaning of *te'udah*/*'ēdut*. Regarding the word *addita*, see n. 90 below.

[88] According to Num 29:36, only one bull was offered on *'Aṣeret*, in contrast to the descending number of bulls over the seven days of the festival of Sukkot (Num 29:12–34), until seven on the seventh day (all together 70); cf. *Num. Rab.* 21:24; *Pesiq. R. Kah.* 28.

translation), is significant for the understanding of v. 29, which opens similarly: "It was called Addition because...."[89] The reason offered in v. 29, "because of the fact that it is entered in the *teʿudah/ʿēdut* of the festal days," indicates that this festival was added to the heavenly calendar. Prior to this story in *Jub.* 32, only the first seven days of Sukkot were festal days; subsequently the eighth day was recorded on the Heavenly Tablets as part of the *teʿudah/ʿēdut*, the divine chronological system by which the world functions.[90]

The final sentence "in accord (*bakama; secundum*) with the number of days in the year" apparently reflects the Hebrew reading במספר ימי השנה. Charles suggested that the preposition *ke-* is an error created in the process of textual transmission, and that the original version was *be-* (במספר ימי השנה), and interpreted the verse as meaning that the *ʿaṣeret* day was added to the "festal days" within the days of the year.[91] The verse addresses therefore the fixing of the dates of the festivals within the framework of the calendar. However, this interpretation is based upon a reordering of the elements in the verse: the element "number" is attached to the "festal days" and not to the "days of the year." This suggestion understands the verse as if it was ordered as follows: "it is entered...in the number of festal days in the days of the year."

Berger interpreted the two sentences in the second half of the verse differently. His explanation is based upon the Geʿez translation, as opposed to the Latin version and Charles' corrections. He read:

(a) because of the fact that it is entered in the *teʿudah/ʿēdut* of the festal days
(b) in accord with the number of days in the year.

---

[89] Charles (1902: 196) suggested that the Greek translator misunderstood the use of the word כי in v. 29, meaning "when" (which should have been ὅτε and not διότι). According to Charles, v. 29 does not relate to the source of the name of the festival *ʿAṣeret*, because that information was already provided in v. 27.

[90] VanderKam (1989b: 216) noted that the verb "is entered" is the standard verb used to record data on the Heavenly Tablets. It is interesting that specifically in the Latin translation, which derives the name of the festival *ʿAṣeret* from Jacob's delay there (*retentus est*) in v. 27, records here the reason given for the name in the Ethiopic translation of v. 27.

[91] Charles (1902: 195–196) suggested a series of corrections to v. 29, but most of them are difficult to accept. Charles did not note that MS 38 reads *ba-* instead of *bakama*, a reading that would textually support his suggestion mentioned above (despite the fact that Dillman relied upon MSS 38 and 51 in his 1859 edition, and Charles should therefore have been aware of this reading; see VanderKam 1989a: XIV, 180; 1989b: 216). Hartom (1969: 101) also translates "in the days of the year" and offers a similar interpretation.

According to Berger, the word *teʿudah/ʿēdut* in sentence (a) carries the meaning "law" (as also suggested by Kister), but the laws of the festival, and not the laws governing the celestial bodies. The recording on the Heavenly Tablets thus does not refer to the fixing of the calendar. Sentence (b), which seemingly refers to calendrical issues, relates to the fixed time of *ʿaṣeret* within the calendar (as part of the law).[92] But this interpretation does not fit the phrase "the number of days in the year," which does not refer to the set date within the calendar. In addition, *Jub.* 16:28 does refer to the fixing of a specific date for the festival, but formulates it differently: "because he had celebrated this festival (of Booths) **at its time** in accord with the *teʿudah/ʿēdut* of the heavenly tablets."

It is possible to suggest an alternative interpretation based upon a parallel passage, *Jub.* 6:32, which appears within the context of a halakhic polemic surrounding the calendar:

> Now you command the Israelites to keep **the years in this number—364 days**. Then the year will be complete and it will not disturb its time **from its days or from its festivals**[93] because everything will happen in harmony with their **teʿudah/ʿēdut**. They will neither omit a day nor disturb a festival.

The expression "the number of days in the year" in 32:29 has a precise definition in the legal passage quoted here, a period of 364 days. The observance of the correct calendar guarantees that the festivals will fall out on the dates that were fixed for them in the *teʿudah/ʿēdut*. The solar calendar, which consists of 364 days, is the key to the occurrence of all of the days of the year in their proper place and time. Any deviation from the chronological scheme underlying this calendar (and especially changes due to lunar observations, v. 36) will lead to the shifting of all the calendar days from their proper place, and will thus cause confusion between festal and non-festal days. The course of the year that was established in advance is referred to as *teʿudah/ʿēdut*, because it refers either to the laws that govern the orbits of the luminaries (Kister) or to the covenant according to which the chronological system was established.

---

[92] Berger 1981: 485, n. 29c (and then VanderKam 1989b: 216).
[93] Perhaps one should read here a construct form, "the festal days," similar to the formulation in *Jub.* 32:29. According to the final sentence in the verse, "they will neither omit a day nor disturb a festival," the concern expressed here is desecration of the festal days.

If one interprets *Jub.* 32:29, "It was called *ʿAṣeret* because of the fact that it is entered in the *teʿudah/ʿēdut* of the festal days in accord with the number of days in the year," according to 6:32, then the final clause "in accord with the number of days in the year" can be understood as a definition of the *teʿudah/ʿēdut*, the divine chronological plan. The *ʿaṣeret* day was added to the authoritative calendar, as a festival whose place and time within the calendar are fixed forever.

> 4:30—He lacked 70 years from 1000 years because 1000 years are one day in the *teʿudah/ʿēdut* of heaven. For this reason it was written regarding the tree of knowledge: "On the day that you eat from it you will die." Therefore he did not complete the years of this day because he died during it.

This verse addresses an exegetical problem in Gen 2:17.[94] According to that verse, God commanded the man not to eat from the Tree of Knowledge, and threatened him "for on the day you eat from it you shall surely die."[95] Soon after, the snake promised the man and the woman that they would not die if they ate from the fruits of the Garden, and accused God of deception: "And the serpent said to the woman, 'you are not going to die. For God knows that on the day on which you eat from it your eyes will be opened and you will be like gods, who know good and evil" (Gen 3:4–5). The result of their eating from the fruits of the tree actually matched the snake's prediction, and not God's threat: "And the eyes of both of them were opened and they knew that they were naked, and they sewed fig leaves and made for themselves loincloths" (ibid., v. 7). The punishments meted out to the man and woman are detailed in the curses against them (vv. 16–19), and they were exiled from the Garden at the end of the story (vv. 23–24), but there was no penalty of death as promised by God at the beginning of the story. A straightforward reading of the story thus leads to the conclusion that the snake was actually truthful, while God was the one who spoke falsely.

Jubilees 4:30 solves this problem by a reinterpretation of the word "day" in Gen 2:17, "for on *the day* you eat from it you shall surely

---

[94] Kugel 1998: 94–95.
[95] The verbs are in the singular in MT and SP. LXX (and subsequently the Vetus Latina and the Ethiopic translation of the Bible) read plural forms, and so too *Jub.* 4:30. In the biblical story, the woman was not yet created (Gen 2:18–25), so the singular form is presumably original.

die," not as 24 hours, but rather as a 1000-year period. The first man, who died at the age of 930 (Gen 5:5), therefore did indeed die on the same "day" on which he ate, during the same 1000-year period.[96] The identification of "one day" with "1000 years" is based upon Ps 90:4, which equates the two "in the eyes of God": "because 1000 years in your eyes are like one day/yesterday that has passed."[97] *Jubilees* 4:30 quotes Ps 90:4 with one significant difference:

Psalms 90:4	***Jubilees* 4:30**
because 1000 years	because 1000 years
in your eyes	are one day
are like one day	in the *te'udah*/*'edut* of heaven

The "*te'udah*/*'edut* of heaven"[98] describes, therefore, the divine chronological framework for the world, the temporal system by which the universe is run. If according to the divine temporal system one year equals 1000 years, then God's words in Gen 2:17 were not an empty threat, but rather a warning which actually came true.

One passage that does not accord with the meaning suggested here for *te'udah*/*'edut* is *Jub.* 4:18–19 (and the parallel context in 10:17), a description of Enoch's actions:[99]

---

[96] See also Justin Martyr, *Dialogue with Trypho* 81; *Gen. Rab.* 19:8 (without quoting Ps 90:4 explicitly); *Pesiq. Rab.* 40; *Num. Rab.* 14 (see Kugel 1998: 94–95). Kugel (ibid., 96–97) quotes other early exegetes who resolved this difficulty by interpreting the expression "you shall surely die" not as a reference to death, but as the transformation of human beings into mortals.

[97] MT and LXX read "like yesterday (כיום אתמול)." By itself, *Jub.* 4:30 would not be enough to use as a basis for positing a reading "like one day" in Ps 90:4, but a similar reading is attested in 2 Pet 3:8: ὅτι μία ἡμέρα παρὰ κυρίῳ ὡς χίλια ἔτη καὶ χίλια ἔτη ἡμέρα μία, and *Ep. Barnabas* 15:4, which offer independent confirmation of this reading.

[98] The meaning of the expression "*te'udah* of heaven" in 4Q300 (4QMysteries), 1a II, 2 (ed. L. Schiffman; DJD 20, 1997; p. 100) is not clear, and the context is not preserved. Schiffman translated "the signs of the heavens" without explaining this interpretation.

[99] *Jubilees* 10:17 is based upon the description of Enoch's actions in 4:17–26, and thus the use of *sama'* there does not constitute independent evidence. In my survey of sources, I only addressed nominal forms of *te'udah* or *'edut*, but not the verb העיד (hiphil). One can identify two different meanings of this verb (reconstructed from the Ge'ez) throughout *Jubilees*. The verb generally means "to warn" (1:12; 6:38; 7:20, 31, 39; 20:7; 30:11, 17; 36:11). In the description of Enoch's actions, the verb appears to mean "to testify" (4:22, 24; 10:17), but this different meaning perhaps reflects literary dependence upon sources from Enochic literature.

> He was the first to write a *te'udah/'ēdut*. He testified to mankind in the generations of the earth: The weeks of the jubilees he related, and made known the days of the years; the months he arranged, and related the sabbaths of the years, as we had told him. 4:19 While he slept he saw in a vision what has happened and what will occur—how things will happen for mankind during their history until the day of judgment. He saw everything and understood. He wrote a *te'udah/'ēdut* for himself and placed it upon the earth against all mankind and for their history.

Enoch was the first person in history to write a *te'udah/'ēdut*, which included the history of mankind, the weeks of jubilees, the months and the Sabbath-years. This description includes much broader areas than the definition suggested above, especially the recording of future events. The difference in the semantic range of the word *te'udah/'ēdut* in *Jub.* 4 from other places in the book is apparently due to the dependence of this passage upon earlier sources. VanderKam analyzed these verses (4:16–25) and showed that they were based upon Enochic traditions that preceded *Jubilees*.[100] Dimant demonstrated that the tradition reflected in 4:21 was not the creation of the "author" of *Jubilees*, basing her argument upon the difference in the length of a jubilee period in this verse (50 years) as opposed to the rest of the book (49 years).[101] She concluded from this example that *Jubilees* adopted some earlier sources, often without resolving the contradictions and tensions that resulted from their different provenance. One can similarly view the difference regarding the semantic range of *te'udah/'ēdut* in 4:18–19 (not with the meaning of "covenant, stipulations of the covenant," but "testimony" for or about future generations) as another manifestation of the different origins of *Jub.* 4:16–25.

From the survey of passages in which the word *te'udah/'ēdut* appears, one can conclude that it connotes "covenant, covenantal conditions," and the meaning of the phrase "Torah and *te'udah*" is therefore "stipulations of the covenant." The "first *te'udah* and Torah" (2:24), the Sabbath laws, were given right after the election of Israel, in line with the biblical notion of covenant described above, according to which the making of a covenant is accompanied by the acceptance of its conditions. The transmission and observance of commandments in the patriarchal period are a direct result of the special relationship between God and

---

[100] VanderKam (1978) 2000; 1984.
[101] Dimant 1983: 21, especially n. 17; see also the discussion above, pp. 16–17.

Israel already from the dawn of time, as part of a covenant between them.[102] In contrast to the suggestion of R.H. Charles noted above, the notion of the election of Israel from the dawn of time is fundamental to the general worldview of the redactional layer in *Jubilees*, and therefore should not be viewed as a direct reaction to Hellenistic influences and claims. Furthermore, this worldview exists without any reference to an exegetical problem in the biblical text, as posited by Anderson, and should therefore be viewed as part of the broader *Weltanschauung* of *Jubilees*.

The "Heavenly Tablets" Containing the "Torah and Teʿudah"

The concept of Heavenly Tablets is attested prior to *Jubilees* in Mesopotamian literature,[103] in the Bible, and in Jewish literature of the Second Temple period,[104] and is therefore clearly not the creation of *Jubilees*. The innovation in *Jubilees* can be found in the new tasks assigned to the Tablets, which do not appear in prior or contemporaneous literature. García Martínez identified five distinct categories of functions of the Tablets:[105]

(1) Tablets of the Law (*Jub*. 3:9–11; 4:5; 16:3–4; 33:10–12)
(2) Heavenly Register of Good and Evil (19:9; 30:19–22)
(3) Book of Destiny (5:13–14; 16:9; 23:32; 24:33; 31:32b; 32:21–22)
(4) Calendar and Festivals (6:17, 28–29a, 30–35; 16:28–29; 18:19; 32:27–29; 49:8)
(5) New Halakhot (3:31; 4:32; 15:25; 28:6; 30:9; 32:10–15)

Of these five categories, one can distinguish between categories (2) and (3), which already appear in literature prior to *Jubilees*, and the other functions, which can be considered innovative. The motif of a heavenly register of good and evil actions can already be found in the Bible

---

[102] VanderKam (1997: 18) comments: "The laws that are found in the book and revealed to the ancestors are stipulations that are parts of the ongoing, frequently renewed covenant between God and members of the chosen line, from Adam to Moses."
[103] Paul (1973) assembled sources from the ancient Near East, the Bible, Jewish literature from the Second Temple period, and rabbinic literature.
[104] Charles 1912: 91–92.
[105] García Martínez 1997. The categorization of the verses is according to his analysis, and does not necessarily reflect my interpretation of each verse.

(Exod 32:32–33; Isa 4:3; 65:6; Jer 22:30; Mal 3:16; Ps 139:16; Dan 7:10; 10:21; 12:1),[106] and is prominent in *1 Enoch* (81:4; 89:61–64, 68, 70, 71, 76, 77; 90:17, 20; 98:7, 8; 104:7). A book of destiny (category 3), based upon a deterministic worldview according to which all actions are recorded before they occur, is also reflected in the central role of the Tablets in *1 Enoch* (81:1, 2; 93:1–3; 103:2–3; 106:19; 107:1). The inclusion of these two functions in *Jubilees*' conception of the Heavenly Tablets does not therefore inform us about the worldview of the author/editor of this book, but rather of the literary dependence of this author on previous works, primarily Enochic literature.[107]

The opinions of the redactor are reflected specifically in the new functions assigned to the Heavenly Tablets, namely García Martínez's categories (1), (4), and (5). Instead of analyzing each of these categories separately, it is more beneficial to identify their common denominator: commandments and covenant. The distinction between categories (1) and (5)—old and new commandments—is the result of a diachronic view of *Jubilees*; those laws that appeared in the Pentateuch were assigned to category (1), and those "non-biblical" commandments were assigned by García Martínez to the category of "new halakhot."[108] However, *Jubilees* itself makes no such distinction between "old" and "new," employing the same terminology to describe both kinds, and apparently intending to equate them. "Calendar and festivals" (category 4) are also inherently connected to both laws and covenant, as demonstrated above.[109] The redactor of *Jubilees* merged these concepts in a number of passages: "They will forget all my law, all my commandments, and all my verdicts. They will err regarding the beginning of the month, the sabbath, the festival, the jubilee, and the decree"

---

[106] Paul 1973: 346–348.

[107] The references are according to Charles 1912: 91–92. Milik (1978: 103–104) noticed that in a fragment from an Aramaic composition from Qumran Cave 4 (4Q537, which he named "Visions de Jacob"), Jacob saw into the future on Heavenly Tablets, shown to him by an angel, as is also found in *Jub.* 32:21–22; see now Puech's publication of this scroll, under the title "4QTestament de Jacob? ar" and his comments there (Puech 2001; DJD 31, pp. 171–177). Similar to the dependence of *Jubilees* upon *1 Enoch* mentioned above, it is reasonable to assume that *Jub.* 32 is directly dependent on the "Testament of Jacob" in attributing the task of a "book of destiny" to the Heavenly Tablets in the story of Jacob at Bethel.

[108] García Martínez (1997: 251): "Of a completely different character than the previous categories of the HT are the last two categories presented below."

[109] The festivals are connected on the one hand to the calendar (and the covenant), and on the other to the pentateuchal commandments.

(1:14); "All the Israelites will forget and will not find the way of the years. They will forget the first of the month, the season, and the sabbath; they will err with respect to the entire prescribed pattern of the years… lest they forget the covenantal festivals and walk in the festivals of the nations…" (6:34–35); "regarding the law and the covenant; for they have forgotten commandment, covenant, festival, month, sabbath, jubilee, and every verdict" (23:19).[110]

The new function of the Heavenly Tablets in *Jubilees*, Tablets of the Covenant and Commandments, corresponds to the worldview of the redactional layer described above: Israel was chosen at the dawn of time as the preferred nation and God's firstborn son, and this chosenness necessitated the giving of laws as the stipulations of the covenant between God and his nation. The stipulations of the covenant, the "Torah and *te'udah*," began already in the first week of time, parallel to Israel's election. The retrojection of laws into the pre-Sinaitic period created a problem, however, for there was no "Book of the Covenant" (Exod 24:7; 2 Kgs 23:2, 21; 2 Chr 34:30) in which the stipulations were recorded, nor any "Tablets of *'Edut*" (Exod 31:18; 32:15; 34:29), nor any "Tablets of the Covenant" (Deut 9:9, 11, 15), which could attest to the special relationship between God and Israel. According to the worldview of *Jubilees* (that the stipulations of the covenant began prior to Sinai), the need arose for a different medium that could function in this earlier period in a similar fashion to the earthly Tablets. The concept of Heavenly Tablets from *1 Enoch*, a heavenly object that records earthly information, was therefore adopted for this task. The extensive use of the concept of Heavenly Tablets throughout *Jubilees* therefore stems from the centrality of covenant in the worldview of this author/redactor.

Regarding the terminology employed by *Jubilees*, the eternal "Tablets of Heaven" parallel the "Tablets of *'Edut*" or "Tablets of Covenant" given at Sinai. One can point to the identification between them in the order of events in *Jub.* 1, the narrative framework of the book. In Exod 24:12–18, God commands Moses to ascend Mount Sinai in order to receive the "Tablets of stone (and) the Torah and the commandment." Following the description of the Tabernacle (Exod 25–31:11) and the giving of the Sabbath law (Exod 31:12–17), God presents

---

[110] All of these passages can be attributed to the redactional layer of *Jubilees* based upon their special terminology.

Moses with the "two tablets of *'Edut*" (ibid. v. 18). In *Jub.* 1, God commands Moses to ascend Mount Sinai in order to receive "the tablets of stone, the Torah and the commandment" (Prologue; 1:1; parallel to Exod 24:12), and at the end of the chapter, the angel of the presence brings the "Tablets of the Divisions of the Times[111] of the Torah and *Te'udah*"[112] to Moses, and begins to tell him the stories of Genesis and Exodus in the following chapter. The parallel between "Tablets of *'Edut*" in Exod 31:18 and "Tablets of the Divisions of the Times of the Torah and *Te'udah*" in *Jub.* 1:29 bolsters the claim that similar to the former tablets, the latter ones are also "tablets of the covenant," albeit in the heavenly realm.

The new role of the Heavenly Tablets as tablets of the "Torah and *te'udah*" attests to the centrality of the notion of covenant and commandments in the worldview of the redactor of *Jubilees*. The combination of all the motifs discussed in this chapter—the election of Israel from the dawn of time as God's preferred nation, the covenant between the Lord and Israel, the laws as "Torah and *te'udah*" from the time of creation, and the Heavenly Tablets that contain them—reveals a unified, comprehensive worldview regarding the origin of law in the redactional layer of *Jubilees*.

---

[111] For the identification of the Heavenly Tablets with the "Tablets of the Divisions of Times," see Werman 1999 (2002): 85–90.

[112] For the text of *Jub.* 1:29, see above, pp. 285–287.

CONCLUSION

The Literary Question

The consensus opinion in the study of *Jubilees* views the book as a unified composition written by a single author. But as I have tried to show throughout this study, there are many contradictions within the work, both in biblical exegesis and in details of the plot (including chronological data). The contradictions often create an incomprehensible story, which cannot be easily resolved. It is difficult to attribute an illogical story to one author even if that author relied on multiple traditions. The contradictory elements in the book are always differentiated by their genres, either between the rewritten stories and the appended legal passages, or between the rewritten stories and the chronological framework. The legal passages and the chronological framework are each characterized by their own special terminology, which points to the unity of the passages within each of these two literary genres.

On the basis of these difficulties, a new approach was suggested in this study regarding the literary development of the book: the redactor of *Jubilees* adopted written sources,[1] usually rewritten stories (but sometimes other texts as well, such as testaments; see for example Noah's testament in *Jub.* 7:20–39). However, the redactor did not limit himself to copying and joining existing sources, but also integrated them within the framework of a new literary composition. The contribution of this editor can be recognized in two elements throughout the book: the chronological framework based upon the system of jubilees and weeks of years, and the legal passages juxtaposed with the rewritten narratives (as well as in other passages in the book which bear the stamp of the

---

[1] In accordance with the definition provided in the Introduction (p. 14, n. 36), the term "source" refers to a written passage, which the redactor relied upon in the composition of the book. (One should not connect this term to its use in pentateuchal source criticism, in which scholars are of the opinion that one can isolate and reconstruct lengthy, continuous sources.) The redactor's direct dependence upon a source text can be demonstrated if there are three shared characteristics between them: content, order and terminology. If the content in *Jubilees* is similar to earlier material, but they do not share common order or language, then I have defined the earlier material as a "tradition" relied upon by the editor.

terminology of the legal passages, such as the narrative frame [ch. 1; 50:1–5,13b]; chs. 2; 6; 23:9–32).

It is also possible to identify the editor's intervention within his sources. For example, in the Watchers story in *Jub.* 5,[2] the names of the angels that appear in *1 Enoch* have been removed, in accordance with a general trend in *Jubilees*. The description in *Jub.* 5:1–12 is indeed shorter than *1 En.* 10–11, and it is difficult to know whether the redactor of *Jubilees* relied upon an abridged rewritten story of *1 Enoch*, or whether he himself was responsible for the shortening. However, despite the differences between *Jub.* 5:1–12 and *1 En.* 10–11, the editor left the content, order, and formulation as he found them before him, and in line with the story in *1 En.* 10–11. As I demonstrated in the discussion of *Jub.* 5, the reliance upon *1 En.* 10–11 led to a contradiction between the rewritten story (vv. 7–9) and the chronological framework (v. 1) regarding the interpretation of Gen 6:3.[3] In the case of the Watchers story, it is possible to adduce solid, textual evidence for the literary-critical theory proposed here, and it also allows us to learn how this redactor worked. The redactor did not quote his sources word for word as he found them, but rather inserted certain changes into them. At the same time, he did not alter his sources drastically, nor did he smooth over the various contradictions between them and his own positions. The model of the Watchers story explains the presence of the many contradictions in other sections of the book, even though in those other cases there is no independent evidence for the sources used by the editor. The redactor did indeed intervene in his sources, but as the contradictions themselves attest, he did not attempt to resolve the difficulties, which were unavoidably created when he relied upon other sources.

The theory proposed here solves all of the problems that were raised in the Introduction, and which were discussed extensively throughout this study. The internal contradictions—between the rewritten stories and the legal passages and between the rewritten stories and the chronological framework—are a direct result of the literary development of the composition. If the contradictory details are differentiated by their provenance, there is no reason to expect conceptual or exegetical uniformity between them. For example, one can thus explain the two reasons offered for sentencing Tamar to death by fire (41:25–26 and

---

[2] For an extensive discussion of this passage, see ch. 5.
[3] See pp. 91–93, 119–125.

28) or the two answers given to the question whether Judah sinned (ibid., vv. 23–24; v. 27). The first rationale offered for her punishment appears in the legal passage (vv. 23–26), which posits that Judah sinned but was forgiven; the second reason given for burning Tamar appears in the rewritten story (vv. 1–21, 27–28), which assumes that Judah did not sin, because Tamar was not legally his daughter-in-law. The doublet regarding the source for her punishment and the internal contradiction in *Jub.* 41 were created because the halakhic redactor relied upon a rewritten story of Judah and Tamar.[4] The same is true for the story of the births of Jacob's children (*Jub.* 28). According to the chronological framework, the birth of Bilhah's son Dan preceded the birth of Judah, and Dan was conceived prior to the birth of Levi (vv. 14, 15, 18). But the rewritten story (v. 17) states that Bilhah was only presented to Jacob after Leah's first four sons (including Levi and Judah) were born. Instead of correcting the text of the dates in the chronological framework, as suggested by Rönsch, it is preferable to view the rewritten story as an existing source, which the editor fixed within the chronological framework.[5] The direct literary dependence upon the rewritten story, and its insertion within a new chronological framework are what caused the explicit contradiction between the different verses.

These two cases exemplify the two aspects of the redaction, halakhic and chronological. The two areas are combined together in the narrative frame of the book: the expression "divisions of the times of the Torah and the *teʿudah*" appears four times at the beginning of the book (Prologue; 1:4, 26, 29), and the motif reappears in the concluding verse of the work: "so that I could write for you the laws of each specific time in every division of its times" (50:13). The combination of these concepts appears in passages that are characterized by the special terminology of the legal redactional layer. One can therefore conclude that the halakhic redaction and the chronological redaction were the work of the same editor.

The Date of the Redactional Layer

In addressing the question of the date of composition of *Jubilees*, it is necessary to take into account the literary complexity of the book. The

---

[4] See ch. 2.
[5] See ch. 4.

conclusion of this study, that *Jubilees* is made up of various texts which were collected and edited together in a comprehensive framework, forces us to readdress the question of the date of the book, at least in general terms. There are no signs within the rewritten narratives (or the other sources used by the redactor, such as the testament in ch. 7) that suggest that they form a unified stratum. Moreover, there are no unambiguous references in these passages to specific historical periods or events. We are therefore unable to suggest a date for the composition of the various passages which do not belong to the redactional layer.

However, we can identify the general climate in which the redactional layer was composed, and thus offer an approximate date for its formation. As a number of scholars have already noted,[6] the key for dating of the book can be found in the apocalypse in *Jub.* 23:9–32. The terminology in this passage attests to its belonging to the redactional layer. Since it does not mention Antiochus' decrees, this passage should be dated either prior to these edicts (as suggested by Finkelstein, Goldstein, and Nickelsburg) or following them (as suggested by Kister, and adopted by Werman).[7]

The main difference between these two approaches, before or after the decrees, revolves around the identification of the address of the criticism leveled throughout the book. According to the former opinion, *Jubilees* focuses on an external polemic against Hellenism and Hellenizers, as reflected both in passages which relate to the nations and in the sharp criticism concerning two behaviors characteristic of the period of Hellenization (nudity [3:31; 7:20] and abstention from the performance of circumcision [15:25–34]). These scholars therefore date the entire composition between Antiochus' Hellenistic reform (175 B.C.E.) and his decrees (167 B.C.E.).

According to the second opinion, the polemic is directed inwards, within Israel. The apocalypse in *Jub.* 23 does not refer to the nations, but rather to an inner-Jewish polemic. The accusations leveled at the elders of the nation are similar in their content and terminology to *Jub.* 1:14 and 6:34 (both chapters belong to the redactional layer), which polemicize against those Jews who employ a lunar-solar calendar. We have no evidence whatsoever of a polemic against Hellenizers regard-

---

[6] See pp. 37–38.
[7] See the studies of Finkelstein, Goldstein, Nickelsburg, Kister, and Werman quoted on pp. 37–38, nn. 96–97, in contrast to the date proposed by VanderKam, which is generally accepted (see above, pp. 36–37).

ing the calendar. In contrast, assuming that the 364-day calendar promoted in *Jubilees* is identical to that used by the Qumran sect, it seems likely that this calendar served as the cause of a schism within Judaism.[8] Similarly, in the passage concerned with circumcision in *Jub.* 15:25–34, the argument is directed against those who do not circumcise their children by the eighth day, i.e., Jews who perform circumcision but according to a different halakhic system, and not towards those who refrained from this commandment completely. Likewise, similar prohibitions against nudity also appear in sectarian compositions from Qumran, and are therefore not necessarily connected to the period of Hellenization.[9] Kister therefore concluded that *Jub.* 23 (in addition to *Damascus Document* I, 8–11 and the *Apocalypse of Weeks* from *1 Enoch*) describes an Essene rebellion on *halakhic* grounds against the Jewish establishment, and not specifically against Hellenizers.

In this study, I have reached the following conclusions that support Kister's approach:

(1) All the passages relevant to Kister's claim (1:1–29; 6:32–38; 15:25–34; 23:9–32) belong to the redactional layer of *Jubilees*.
(2) The analysis of *Jub.* 15:25–34 led to the conclusion that it is indeed an inner-Jewish halakhic polemic regarding the possibility of circumcising after the eighth day. Moreover, the extreme position expressed in that passage (any male child not circumcised by the eighth day belongs to the "sons of Belial" instead of the covenant of the Lord) supplies a theological basis for a rift with the nation, even if this split did not yet reach its full historical manifestation.[10]
(3) Scholars have already identified various connections between *Jubilees* and the sectarian literature from Qumran, and we can now add two additional links, one in the area of ideology and theology, and the other regarding principles of halakhic exegesis:
   a) According to the redactional layer, God created evil from the dawn of time, as part of a dualistic system of good and evil, in heaven and on earth. This approach is very close to the perspective expressed in the sectarian literature (see especially 1QS III, 15–IV, 26).

---

[8] See Talmon (1951) 1989; (1958) 1989; VanderKam 1998.
[9] See Kister 1986: 6–7, n. 26, and the analysis above, ch. 11.
[10] See ch. 11.

b) In the area of legal interpretation, we noted that the justification offered for Tamar's punishment in the legal passage in 41:23–26 is based upon an interpretive principle identical to that expressed explicitly in the *Damascus Document* in order to prohibit marriage with one's niece.

Similarity does not imply identity, and I therefore am not claiming that *Jubilees* was composed by a member of the Qumran sect. However, as more similarities between *Jubilees* and this literature are identified, the probability grows accordingly that *Jubilees* was redacted within the same stream of Judaism within which one can locate the Qumran sect, and in a similar ideological climate.

Based upon these considerations, *Jub.* 23:9–32 and the other passages that belong to the redactional layer should be interpreted against the background of inner-Jewish halakhic polemics. *Jubilees* was therefore redacted following the formation of the Essene sect or stream, and it reflects the beginnings of the internal rift in the nation, which reached its full expression in the sectarian literature preserved at Qumran.

Ideology and Theology

One can identify many internal tensions in *Jubilees* in the area of ideology and theology, and specifically regarding the question of the origin of evil in the world. The literary-critical method proposed in this study provides a reason for these tensions: the views expressed in the sources adopted by the redactor are not necessarily identical to his own perspective. One can only expect uniformity between those passages that belong to the redactional layer. As noted in the Introduction, the study of ideology and theology has double significance: on the one hand, the distinction between the redaction and the sources incorporated therein allows for a new, more precise understanding of the redactor's worldview; on the other hand, the study of the ideas expressed in *Jubilees* functions as a control for the entire theory—if the proposed redactional layer represents a homogeneous stratum, then the passages that belong to this layer must present a unified approach to the issues at hand. The analysis of the perspectives expressed regarding the origin of evil in *Jubilees* confirmed this approach: the redactor was aware of various sources that address this theological issue, and integrated them into his composition. The sections identified as belonging to the redcational layer, however, express a single, crystallized perspective regarding this question: evil was created from the beginning of the world as part of a dualistic system of good and evil, in heaven and on earth.

The analysis of the ideology and theology of *Jubilees* by means of the literary-critical approach proposed here uncovered a fully developed, unified worldview in the redactional layer. This worldview is expressed in three different areas: law, evil, and chronology. The perspectives expressed in each of these realms can be reduced to one fundamental notion: God established the entire world order from the beginning of time.

The Origin of Law:[11] God chose Israel as a favored nation at the end of the first week in history (2:17–21). Israel's special status carries both certain special rights, but also responsibilities. The covenant between God and his nation is reciprocal, and includes conditions (the commandments of the Torah) that Israel is required to fulfill. According to the Pentateuch, the covenant between God and Israel was established at the theophany at Mount Sinai, and therefore the commandments were given from that point in time and onwards. *Jubilees* brought the election of Israel backward to the week of creation, and therefore the stipulations of the covenant (called "Torah and te'udah") were also brought backward to the pre-Sinaitic period. This explains the widespread phenomenon in (the redactional layer of) *Jubilees* of the juxtaposition of legal passages to the rewritten stories of Genesis and Exodus, which took place prior to the giving of the Torah at Sinai.[12] The stories were transformed into etiologies, and the gradual transmission of laws throughout the pre-Sinaitic era is in essence a series of covenants between God and Israel. The Heavenly Tablets, which include a register of laws given to Israel before Sinai, are intended to stand in place of "Tablets of the Covenant" or "Tablets of *Ēdut*," which contain a record of the laws given at Sinai and beyond.

The Origin of Evil:[13] In contrast to previous studies of *Jubilees*, which associated the origin of evil in this book with the Eden or Watchers stories, it was suggested here that according to the redactional layer, evil was created by God himself at the dawn of time, as part of a dualistic system of good and evil. The "good" domain, those who

---

[11] See ch. 14.
[12] The transfer of the laws to the earlier period is therefore the result of theological considerations, and not historical (as suggested by Charles, VanderKam and others) or exegetical (Anderson) factors.
[13] See Part II.

are part of the covenant with the Lord, includes the angels of presence and holiness in heaven, and Israel on earth. The "evil" domain includes Belial and his spirits in heaven, and on earth, both the other nations and those Israelites who did not enter the covenant with the Lord within the appropriate time (1:19–21; 2:17–21; 15:25–34). The view that God created both good and evil appears already in Second Isaiah (Isa 45:7), but is only fully developed as a dualistic system in *Jubilees* and the sectarian literature from Qumran.

The Chronological Conception:[14] The chronological redaction is based upon a system of jubilees (49 years) and weeks of years (7 years). *Jubilees* concludes in the "jubilee of jubilees" (the 50th jubilee), when Israel was released from the bondage of Egypt and returned to their promised inheritance (in accord with the jubilee law of Lev 25). This chronological system is known from other contemporaneous compositions, but the systematic, detailed application of this system to the numerous events in Genesis and Exodus is unparalleled. This chronological system expresses the idea of the cyclical nature of events in the world—at the end of one period of predetermined length, the world returns to its prior condition. One can therefore divide history into measured periods.

These three primary areas of the theology of *Jubilees* all express the same fundamental notion: God created and determined all aspects of the universe. As noted above, the literary-critical approach suggested here has allowed for a precise analysis of the worldview of the redactional layer of *Jubilees*. The results of this investigation, which demonstrated the ideological unity and homogeneity of this stratum, thus confirm and support the proposed theory for the literary development of this book.

---

[14] See VanderKam (1995) 2000; and above, pp. 83–84.

BIBLIOGRAPHY

Adams and Adams
  1990   Marilyn M. Adams and Robert M. Adams (eds.), *The Problem of Evil* (Oxford Readings in Philosophy; Oxford: Oxford University Press, 1990)
Aejmelaeus
  1993   Anneli Aejmelaeus, *On the Trail of the Septuagint Translators: Collected Essays* (Kampen: Koh Pharos, 1993)
Albeck
  1930   Chanoch Albeck, *Das Buch der Jubiläen und die Halacha* (Hochschule für die Wissenschaft des Judentums 27; Berlin: Siegfried Scholem, 1930) 3–60
Alexander
  1988   Phillip Alexander, "Retelling the Old Testament," in *It is Written: Scripture Citing Scripture* (ed. D.A. Carson and H.G.M. Williamson; Cambridge: Cambridge University Press, 1988) 99–121
Amir
  1982   Yoshua Amir, "The Place of Psalm cxix in the History of Jewish Religion," *Te'uda* 2 (1982) 57–81 (Heb.)
Anderson
  1989   Gary Anderson, "Celibacy or Consummation in the Garden? Reflections on Early Jewish and Christian Interpretations of the Garden of Eden," *HTR* 82 (1989) 121–148
Anderson
  1994   Gary Anderson, "The Status of the Torah Before Sinai: The Retelling of the Bible in the Damascus Covenant and the Book of Jubilees," *DSD* 1 (1994) 1–29
Attridge and Strugnell
  1994   Harold Attridge and John Strugnell, "369. 4QPrayer of Enosh," in *Qumran Cave 4.VIII Parabiblical Texts, Part 1* (ed. H.W. Attridge et al.; DJD XIII; Oxford: Clarendon Press, 1994) 353–362
Avishur
  1977   Yitshak Avishur, *The Construct State of Synonyms in Biblical Rhetoric* (Jerusalem: Kiryat-Sepher, 1977) (Heb.)
Baillet
  1982   Maurice Baillet (ed.), "511. Cantiques du Sage (ii)," in *Qumrân Grotte 4.III (4Q482–4Q520)* (DJD VII; ed. M. Baillet; Oxford: Clarendon, 1982) 219–262
Barker
  1987   Margaret Barker, *The Older Testament: The Survival of Themes from the Ancient Royal Cult in Sectarian Judaism and Early Christianity* (London: Society for Promoting Christian Knowledge, 1987)
Bar-On (Gesundheit)
  1999   Shimon Bar-On (Gesundheit), *Festival Legislation in the Torah: A Literary-Historical Study of Exodus 12:1–20, 21–28; 23:14–19; 34:18–26; Deuteronomy 16:1–8* (Ph.D. diss., Hebrew University of Jerusalem, 1999) (Heb.)
Baumgarten (1958)
  1977   Joseph M. Baumgarten, "The Beginning of the Day in the Calendar of Jubilees," *JBL* 77 (1958) 355–360; repr. in J. Baumgarten, *Studies in Qumran Law* (Leiden: E.J. Brill, 1977) 124–130

Baumgarten (1963)
1977 Joseph M. Baumgarten, "The Calendar of the Book of Jubilees and the Bible," in idem, *Studies in Qumran Law* (Leiden: E.J. Brill, 1977) 101–114; trans. of idem, *Tarbiz* 32 (1963) 317–328 (Heb.)
Baumgarten
1982 Joseph M. Baumgarten, "Some Problems of the Jubilees Calendar in Current Research," *VT* 32 (1982) 485–489
Baumgarten
1987 Joseph M. Baumgarten, "The Laws of 'Orlah and First Fruits in Light of Jubilees, the Qumran Writings, and Targum Ps. Jonathan," *JJS* 38 (1987) 195–202
Baumgarten
1994 Joseph M. Baumgarten, "Purification after Childbirth and the Sacred Garden in 4Q265 and *Jubilees*," in *New Qumran Texts and Studies: Proceedings of the First Meeting of the International Organization for Qumran Studies, Paris 1992* (ed. George Brooke and Florentino García Martínez; STDJ 15; Leiden: Brill, 1994) 3–10
Baumgarten
1996 Joseph M. Baumgarten (ed.), *Qumran Cave 4.XIII: The Damascus Document (4Q266–273)* (DJD XVIII; Oxford: Clarendon, 1996).
Baumgarten
1999 Joseph M. Baumgarten (ed.), "265. 4QMiscellaneous Rules," in *Qumran Cave 4.XXV: Halakhic Texts* (DJD XXXV; Oxford: Clarendon, 1999) 57–78
Baumgarten and Schwartz
1995 Joseph M. Baumgarten and Daniel R. Schwartz, "Damascus Document (CD)," in *The Dead Sea Scrolls: Hebrew, Aramaic, and Greek Texts with English Translations*. Vol. 2: *Damascus Document, War Scroll, and Related Documents* (ed. J.H. Charlesworth; Tübingen: J.C.B. Mohr [Paul Siebeck] and Louisville: Westminster John Knox, 1995) 4–57
Beer
1856 Bernhard Beer, *Das Buch der Jubiläen und sein Verhältnis zu den Midraschim* (Leipzig: Wolfgang Gerhhard, 1856)
Beer
1900 Georg Beer, "Das Buch Henoch," in *Die Apokryphen und Pseudepigraphen des Alten Testaments* (ed. E. Kautzsch; 2 vols.; Tübingen, Freiburg and Leipzig: J.C.B. Mohr [Paul Siebeck], 1900) 2:217–310
Ben-Dov and Horowitz
2003 Jonathan Ben-Dov and Wayne Horowitz, "The 364-Day Year in Mesopotamia and Qumran," *Meghillot* 1 (2003) 3–26 (Heb.)
Berger
1981 Klaus Berger, *Das Buch der Jubiläen* (JSHRZ 2/3; Gütersloh: G. Mohn, 1981)
Bernstein
1994 Moshe J. Bernstein, "4Q252: From Re-Written Bible to Biblical Commentary," *JJS* 45 (1994) 1–27
Bernstein
1996 Moshe J. Bernstein, "Rearrangement, Anticipation and Harmonizations as Exegetical Features in the Genesis Apocryphon," *DSD* 3 (1996) 37–57
Bernstein
2000 Moshe J. Bernstein, "Angels at the Aqedah: A Study in the Development of a Midrashic Motif," *DSD* 7 (2000) 263–291
Bernstein
2005 Moshe J. Bernstein, " 'Rewritten Bible': A Generic Category which has Outlived its Usefulness?," *Textus* 22 (2005) 169–196

BIBLIOGRAPHY

Bhayro
2005   Siam Bhayro, *The Shemihazah and Asael Narrative of 1 Enoch 6–11: Introduction, Text, Translation and Commentary with Reference to Ancient Near Eastern and Biblical Antecedents* (AOAT 322; Münster: Ugarit-Verlag, 2005)

Black
1970   Matthew Black (ed.), *Apocalypsis Henochi Graece* (Leiden: E.J. Brill, 1970)

Black
1985   Matthew Black, *The Book of Enoch or I Enoch: A New English Edition with Commentary and Textual Notes* (in consultation with J.C. VanderKam; SVTP 7; Leiden: E.J. Brill, 1985)

Böttrich
1997   Christfried Böttrich, "Gottesprädikationen im Jubiläenbuch," in *Studies in the Book of Jubilees* (ed. M. Albani, J. Frey and A. Lange; TSAJ 65; Tübingen: J.C.B. Mohr [Paul Siebeck], 1997) 221–241

Brooke
1996   George J. Brooke (ed.), "252. 4QCommentary on Genesis A," in *Qumran Cave 4.XVII: Parabiblical Texts, Part 3* (ed. G.J. Brooke et al.; DJD XXII; Oxford: Clarendon, 1996) 185–207

Brooke
1997   George J. Brooke, "Exegetical Strategies in *Jubilees* 1–2: New Light from 4QJubilees^a," in *Studies in the Book of Jubilees* (ed. M. Albani, J. Frey, and A. Lange; TSAJ 65; Tübingen: J.C.B. Mohr [Paul Siebeck], 1997) 39–57

Broshi et al.
1995   M. Broshi et al. (ed.), *Qumran Cave 4.XIV: Parabiblical Texts, Part 2* (DJD XIX; Oxford: Clarendon, 1995)

Büchler
1930   Adolph Büchler, "Traces des idées et des coutumes hellénistques dans le livre des Jubilés," *REJ* 89 (1930) 321–48

Budde
1920   Karl Budde, *Das Lied Moses, Deut. 32* (Tübingen: J.C. Mohr, 1920)

Cassuto (1943)
1973   Umberto Cassuto, "The Episode of the Sons of God and the Daughters of Men," in idem, *Biblical and Oriental Studies* (2 vols.; trans. from Hebrew [1943] by I. Abrahams; Jerusalem: Magnes, 1973) 1:17–28

Cassuto
1967   Umberto Cassuto, *A Commentary on the Book of Exodus* (trans. from Hebrew by I. Abrahams; Jerusalem: Magnes, 1967)

Charles
1895   R.H. Charles, *maṣḥafa kufālē or the Ethiopic Version of the Hebrew Book of Jubilees* (Oxford: Clarendon, 1895)

Charles
1902   R.H. Charles, *The Book of Jubilees or the Little Genesis* (London: Adam and Charles Black, 1902)

Charles
1912   R.H. Charles, *The Book of Enoch or 1 Enoch* (Oxford: Clarendon, 1912)

Chazon
1997   Esther G. Chazon, "The Creation and Fall of Adam in the Dead Sea Scrolls," in *The Book of Genesis in Jewish and Oriental Christian Interpretation* (ed. J. Frishman and L. Van Rompay; Louvain: Peeters, 1997) 13–24

Collins
1980   John J. Collins, "The Epic of Theodotus and the Hellenism of the Hasmoneans," *HTR* 73 (1980) 91–104

Collins
1984   John J. Collins, "Testaments," in *Jewish Writings of the Second Temple Period*

(ed. M. Stone; CRINT; Assen/Philadelphia: Van Gorcum/Fortress, 1984) 325–355

Collins
1995 John J. Collins, "The Origin of Evil in Apocalyptic Literature and the Dead Sea Scrolls," in *Congress Volume, Paris 1992* (ed. J.A. Emerton; VTSup 61; Leiden, New York and Köln: E.J. Brill, 1995) 25–38

Cross
1973 Frank Moore Cross, Jr., *Canaanite Myth and Hebrew Epic* (Cambridge, Mass., 1973)

Daly
1977 Robert J. Daly, "The Soteriological Significance of the Sacrifice of Isaac," *CBQ* 39 (1977) 45–75

Davenport
1971 Gene L. Davenport, *The Eschatology of the Book of Jubilees* (Leiden: E.J. Brill, 1971)

De Jonge
1978 Marinus de Jonge, *The Testaments of the Twelve Patriarchs: A Critical Edition of the Greek Text* (PVTG vol. 1, pt. 2; Leiden: E.J. Brill, 1978)

Dillman
1850, August Dillman, "Das Buch der Jubiläen oder die kleine Genesis," *Jahrbuch
1851 der biblischen Wissenschaft* 2 (1850) 230–256; 3 (1851) 1–96

Dillman
1859 August Dillman, *maṣḥafa kufālē sive Liber Jubilaeorum* (Kiel and London: C.G.L. van Maack and Williams & Norgate, 1859)

Dillman
1907 August Dillman, *Ethiopic Grammar* (2nd ed.; enlarged by C. Bezold; trans. J.A. Crichton; London: Williams & Norgate, 1907)

Dimant
1974 Devorah Dimant, *"The Fallen Angels" in the Dead Sea Scrolls and in the Apocryphal and Pseudepigraphic Books Related to Them* (Ph.D. diss., Hebrew University of Jerusalem, 1974) (Heb.)

Dimant
1983 Devorah Dimant, "The Biography of Enoch and the Books of Enoch," *VT* 33 (1983) 14–29

Dimant
1994 Devorah Dimant, "Sons of Heaven—Angelology in the Book of Jubilees in Light of the Qumran Sectarian Writings," in *Tribute to Sara: Studies in Jewish Philosophy and Kabbala Presented to Prof. Sara Heller Wilensky* (eds. M. Idel, D. Dimant and S. Rosenberg; Jerusalem: Magnes, 1994) 97–118 (Heb.)

Dimant
2001 Devorah Dimant (ed.), *Qumran Cave 4.XXI. Parabiblical Texts, Part 4: Pseudo-Prophetic Texts* (DJD XXX; Oxford: Clarendon, 2001)

Dimant
2002 Devorah Dimant, "1 Enoch 6–11: A Fragment of a Parabiblical Work," *JJS* 53, 2 (2002) 223–237

Dimant
2003 Devorah Dimant, "Egypt and Jerusalem in Light of the Dualistic Doctrine at Qumran (4Q462)," *Meghillot* 1 (2003) 27–58 (Heb.)

Dods
1977 Marcus Dods (trans.), "St. Augustin's City of God," in *A Select Library of the Nicene and Post-Nicene Fathers of the Christian Church*, II (Grand Rapids: Eerdmans, 1977) 1–511

Doering 1997	Lutz Doering, "The Concept of the Sabbath in the Book of Jubilees," in *Studies in the Book of Jubilees* (ed. M. Albani, J. Frey and A. Lange; TSAJ 65; Tübingen: J.C.B. Mohr [Paul Siebeck], 1997) 179–205
Doering 2002	Lutz Doering, "Jub 50:6–13 als Schlussabschnitt des *Jubiläenbuchs*: Nachtrag aus Qumran oder unsprünglicher Bestandteil des Werks?" *RevQ* 20 (2002) 359–387
Doran 1989	Robert Doran, "The Non-Dating of Jubilees: Jub 34–38; 23:14–32 in Narrative Context," *JSJ* 20 (1989) 1–11
Driver 1902	Samuel R. Driver, *A Critical and Exegetical Commentary on Deuteronomy* (ICC; 3rd ed.; Edinburgh: T. & T. Clark, 1902)
Driver 1911	Samuel R. Driver, *The Book of Exodus with Introduction and Notes* (Cambridge: Cambridge University, 1911)
Driver 1913	Samuel R. Driver, *An Introduction to the Literature of the Old Testament* (Edinburgh: T. & T. Clark, 1913)
Ego 1997	Beate Ego, "Heilige Zeit—heiliger Raum—heiliger Mensch: Beobachtungen zur Struktur der Gesetzbegründung in der Schöpfungs- und Paradiesgeschichte des Jubiläenbuches," in *Studies in the Book of Jubilees* (ed. M. Albani, J. Frey, A. Lange; TSAJ 65; Tübingen: J.C.B. Mohr [Paul Siebeck], 1997) 207–219
Eissfeldt 1958	Otto Eissfeldt, *Das Lied Moses, Deut. 32,1–43 und das Lehrgedicht Asaphs Psalm 78 samt einer Analyse der Umgebung des Mose-Liedes* (Berlin: Akademie-Verlag, 1958)
Elior 2004	Rachel Elior, *The Three Temples: On the Emergence of Jewish Mysticism* (Oxford/Portland: Littman, 2004)
Emerton 1987	John A. Emerton, "Sheol and the Sons of Belial," *VT* 37 (1987) 214–217
Endres 1987	John Endres, *Biblical Interpretation in the Book of Jubilees* (CBQMS 18; Washington, D.C.: Catholic Bible Association of America, 1987)
Eshel 1990	Esther Eshel, *Harmonistic Editing of the Penteateuch in the Second Temple Period* (M.A. thesis, Hebrew University of Jerusalem, 1990) (Heb.)
Eshel 1999	Esther Eshel, *Demonology in Palestine during the Second Temple Period* (Ph.D. diss., Hebrew University of Jerusalem, 1999) (Heb.)
Feldman 1998	Louis H. Feldman, *Studies in Josephus' Rewritten Bible* (JSJSup 58; Leiden: Brill, 1998)
Finkelstein 1923	Louis Finkelstein, "The Book of Jubilees and the Rabbinic Halakha," *HTR* 16 (1923) 39–61
Finkelstein 1943	Louis Finkelstein, "The Date of the Book of Jubilees," *HTR* 36 (1943) 19–24

Fishbane
1985   Michael Fishbane, *Biblical Interpretation in Ancient Israel* (Oxford: Clarendon, 1985)

Fitzmyer (1967)
1995   Joseph A. Fitzmyer, S.J., *The Aramaic Inscriptions of Sefire* (2nd rev. ed. [1st ed. 1967]; Biblica et Orientalia 19A; Rome: Editrice Pontificio Istituto Biblico, 1995)

Fitzmyer
2004   Joseph A. Fitzmyer, S.J., *The Genesis Apocryphon of Qumran Cave I (1Q20): A Commentary* (3rd ed.; Biblica et Orientalia 18B; Rome: Pontifical Biblical Institute, 2004)

Flemming and Radermacher
1901   Johannes Flemming and Ludwig Radermacher (eds.), *Das Buch Henoch* (Die griechischen christlichen Schriftsteller der ersten drei Jahrhunderte 5; Leipzig: J.C. Hinrichs, 1901)

Flusser
1966   David Flusser, "Qumran and Jewish 'Apotropaic' Prayers," *IEJ* 16 (1966) 194–205

Flusser
1970   David Flusser, "Pharisees, Sadducees, and Essenes in Pesher Nahum," in *Essays in Jewish History and Philology in Memory of Gedaliahu Alon* (eds. M. Dorman, S. Safrai, and M. Stern; Tel Aviv: Hakibbutz Hameuchad, 1970) 133–168 (Heb.)

Flusser
1971   David Flusser, "צוואת בני יעקב," *Encyclopedia Biblica*, vol. 6 (Jerusalem: Bialik Institute, 1971) 689–692 (Heb.)

Flusser
1972   David Flusser, "Mastema," in *Encyclopedia Judaica* (1972) 11:1119–1120

Focht
2002   Adam Focht, *מלאך ה'* *of the Early Narratives in Light of the Biblical Messenger Style* (M.A. thesis, Hebrew University of Jerusalem Rothberg International School, 2002)

Fox
1980   Michael V. Fox, "The Sign of the Covenant," *RB* 87 (1980) 557–596

Fraade
1991   Steven D. Fraade, *From Tradition to Commentary: Torah and its Interpretation in the Midrash Sifre to Deuteronomy* (Albany: SUNY Press, 1991)

García Martínez
1992   Florentino García Martínez, *Qumran and Apocalyptic: Studies on the Aramaic Texts from Qumran* (STDJ 9; Leiden: E.J. Brill, 1992)

García Martínez
1997   Florentino García Martínez, "The Heavenly Tablets in the Book of Jubilees," in *Studies in the Book of Jubilees* (ed. M. Albani, J. Frey, and A. Lange; TSAJ 65; Tübingen: J.C.B. Mohr [Paul Siebeck], 1997) 243–260; trans. from Spanish: "Las Tablas Celestes en el Libro de los Jubileos," *Palabry y Vida: Homenaje a José Alonso Díaz en su 70 cumpleaños* (ed. A. Vargas Machuca and G. Ruiz; Publicationes de la Universidad Pontifica Comillas Madrid, Series 1, Estudios 58; Madrid: Ediciones Universidad de Comillas, 1984) 333–349

Gelb
1962   I.J. Gelb, "Review of D.J. Wiseman, 'The Vassal-Treaties of Esarhaddon' (Reprint from *Iraq* 20)," *BiOr* 19 (1962) 159–162

Gibson
1975   John C.L. Gibson, *Textbook of Syrian Semitic Inscriptions. Volume II: Aramaic Inscriptions* (Oxford: Clarendon, 1975)

Glatt
1992   David A. Glatt, *Chronological Displacement in Biblical and Related Literatures* (Ph.D. diss., University of Pennsylvania, 1991; Ann Arbor: UMI, 1992)

Goldmann
1956   Moshe Goldmann, "The Book of Jubilees," in *The Apocryphal Books* (ed. A. Kahana; 2 vols.; Tel-Aviv: Masada, 1956) 1:216–313 (Heb.)

Goldstein
1983   Jonathan A. Goldstein, "The Date of the Book of Jubilees," *PAAJR* 50 (1983) 63–86

Goudoever
1961   J. van Goudoever, *Biblical Calendars* (2nd ed.; Leiden: Brill, 1961)

Greenberg
1951   Moshe Greenberg, "Hebrew *segulla*: Akkadian *sikiltu*," *JAOS* 71 (1951) 172–174

Greenberg
1969   Moshe Greenberg, *Understanding Exodus* (New York: Berman, 1969)

Greenfield
1964   Jonas C. Greenfield, "Linguistic Criteria in the Sefire Inscriptions," *Leš* (1964) 303–313 (Heb.)

Greenfield and Qimron
1992   Jonas C. Greenfield and Elisha Qimron, "The Genesis Apocryphon Col. XII," AbrNSup 3 (1992) 70–77

Grintz
1969   Yehoshua M. Grintz, *Chapters in the History of the Second Temple Times* (Jerusalem: Y. Marcus, 1969) (Heb.)

Hacham
1991   Amos Hacham, *Exodus (Shemoth-Jethro)* (Daat Mikra; Jerusalem: Mossad HaRav Kook, 1991) (Heb.)

Halpern-Amaru
1994   Betsy Halpern-Amaru, "The First Woman, Wives and Mothers in Jubilees," *JBL* 113 (1994) 609–626

Halpern-Amaru
1999   Betsy Halpern-Amaru, *The Empowerment of Women in the Book of Jubilees* (Leiden: Brill, 1999)

Harrington
1986   Daniel J. Harrington, "The Bible Rewritten," in *Early Judaism and Its Modern Interpreters* (ed. R.A. Kraft and G.W.E. Nickelsburg; Atlanta: Scholars, 1986) 239–247

Hartom
1969   Eliyahu S. Hartom, "The Book of Jubilees," in *The Apocryphal Literature* (7 vols.; 3rd ed.; Tel-Aviv: Yavneh, 1969) 5b:7–147.

Hayward
1992   Charles T.R. Hayward, "The Figure of Adam in Pseudo-Philo's Biblical Antiquities," *JSJ* 23 (1992) 1–20

Hayward
1995   Charles T.R. Hayward, *Saint Jerome's Hebrew Questions on Genesis: Translated with Introduction and Commentary* (Oxford: Clarendon, 1995)

Heinemann
1954   Yitshak Heinemann, *Darkhe ha-Agadah* (Jerusalem: Magnes, 1954) (Heb.)

Hendel
1995   Ronald S. Hendel, "4Q252 and the Flood Chronology of Genesis 7–8: A Text-Critical Solution," *DSD* 2 (1995) 72–79

Hengel (1976)
- 1989 Martin Hengel, *The Zealots: Investigations into the Jewish Freedom Movement in the Period from Herod I until 70 A.D.* (trans. D. Smith; Edinburgh: T. & T. Clark, 1989); trans. of *Die Zeloten: Untersuchungen zur Jüdischen Freiheitsbewegung in der Zeit von Herodes I. bis 70 n. Chr.* (2nd impr. and enlar. ed.; Leiden: E.J. Brill, 1976)

Himmelfarb
- 1994 Martha Himmelfarb, "Some Echoes of *Jubilees* in Medieval Hebrew Literature," in *Tracing the Threads: Studies in the Vitality of Jewish Pseudepigrapha* (ed. J.C. Reeves; SBLEJL 6; Atlanta: Scholars Press, 1994) 115–141

Hollander and de Jonge
- 1985 H. W. Hollander and M. de Jonge, *The Testaments of the Twelve Patriarchs: A Commentary* (SVTP 8; Leiden: E.J. Brill, 1985)

Hurvitz
- 1972 Avi Hurvitz, *The Transition Period in Biblical Hebrew: A Study in Post-Exilic Hebrew and its Implications for the Dating of Psalms* (Jerusalem: Bialik Institute, 1972) (Heb.)

Japhet
- 1989 Sara Japhet, *The Ideology of the Book of Chronicles and its Place in Biblical Thought* (BEATAJ; Frankfurt am Main: Peter Lang, 1989)

Jaubert
- 1953 Annie Jaubert, "Le calendrier des Jubilés et la secte de Qumrân. Ses origines bibliques," *VT* 3 (1953) 250–264

Jaubert
- 1957 Annie Jaubert, *La date de la cène: calendrier biblique et liturgie chrétienne* (Paris: J. Gabalda, 1957)

Jaubert
- 1963 Annie Jaubert, *La notion d'alliance dans le judaisme aux abords de l'ere chrétienne* (Paris: Le Seuil, 1963)

Jaubert
- 1965 Annie Jaubert, *The Date of the Last Supper* (trans. I. Rafferty; Staten Island, N.Y.: Alba House, 1965); trans. of Jaubert 1957

Jellenik
- 1938 Aaron Jellenik, *Bêt ha-Midraš* (2nd ed.; 6 vols.; Jerusalem: Bamberger and Wahrman, 1938) (Heb.)

Jensen
- 1973 Joseph Jensen, *The Use of tôrâ by Isaiah: His Debate with the Wisdom Tradition* (CBQMS 3; Washington: Catholic Bible Association of America, 1973)

Joüon
- 1991 Paul Joüon, *A Grammar of Biblical Hebrew* (trans. and rev. by T. Muraoka; 2 vols.; Subsidia biblica 14/1–2; Rome: Editrice Pontificio Instituto Biblico, 1991)

Kahana
- 1956 Abraham Kahana (ed.), *The Apocryphal Books* (2 vols.; Tel-Aviv: Masada, 1956) (Heb.)

Kahana
- 1969 Abraham Kahana, *Torah, Nevi'im, and Ketubim with a Critical Commentary: Genesis* (Jerusalem: Makor, 1969) (Heb.)

Kister
- 1982 Menahem Kister, "Notes on the Book of Ben-Sira," *Leš* 47 (1982) 125–146 (Heb.)

Kister
- 1986 Menahem Kister, "Concerning the History of the Essenes: A Study of the *Animal Apocalypse*, the *Book of Jubilees*, and the *Damascus Covenant*," *Tarbiz* 56 (1986) 1–18 (Heb.)

Kister
1988   Menahem Kister, "Marginalia Qumranica," *Tarbiz* 57 (1988) 315–325 (Heb.)

Kister
1991   Menahem Kister, "Metamorphoses of Aggadic Traditions," *Tarbiz* 60 (1991) 179–224 (Heb.)

Kister
1992   Menahem Kister, "Some Aspects of Qumranic Halakhah," in *The Madrid Qumran Congress: Proceedings of the International Congress on the Dead Sea Scrolls. Madrid 18-21 March 1991* (ed. J. Trebolle Barrera and L. Vegas Montaner; STDJ 11; 2 vols.; Leiden: E.J. Brill, 1992) 571–588

Kister
1994   Menahem Kister, "Observations on Aspects of Exegesis, Tradition, and Theology in Midrash, Pseudepigrapha, and Other Jewish Writings," in *Tracing the Threads: Studies in the Vitality of Jewish Pseudepigrapha* (ed. J.C. Reeves; SBLEJL 6; Atlanta: Scholars Press, 1994) 1–34

Kister
1995   Menahem Kister, "Commentary to 4Q298," *JQR* 85 (1995) 237–249

Kister
1999   Menahem Kister, "Demons, Theology and Abraham's Covenant (CD 16:4–6 and Related Texts)," in *The Dead Sea Scrolls at Fifty: Proceedings of the 1997 Society of Biblical Literature Qumran Section Meetings* (ed. R.A. Kugler and E.M. Schuller; Atlanta: Scholars, 1999) 167–184

Kister
1999a   Menahem Kister, "Studies in 4QMiqṣat Maʿaśé Ha-Torah and Related Texts: Law, Theology, Language and Calendar," *Tarbiz* 68 (1999) 317–371 (Heb.)

Kister
2001   Menahem Kister, "Two Formulae in the Book of Jubilees," *Tarbiz* 70 (2001) 289–300 (Heb.)

Kister
2003   Menahem Kister, "Syncellus and the Sources of *Jubilees* 3: A Note on M. Segal's Article," *Meghillot* 1 (2003) 127–133.

Kister
2005   Menahem Kister, "Physical and Metaphysical Measurements Ordained by God in the Literature of the Second Temple Period," in *Reworking the Bible: Apocryphal and Related Texts at Qumran* (eds. E. Chazon, D. Dimant, and R. Clements; STDJ 58; Leiden: Brill, 2005) 153–176

Knibb
1984   Michael A. Knibb, "1 Enoch," in *The Apocryphal Old Testament* (ed. H.F.D. Sparks; Oxford: Clarendon, 1984) 169–319

Knohl
1994   Israel Knohl, "Biblical Attitudes to Gentile Idolatry," *Tarbiz* 64 (1994) 5–12 (Heb.)

Knohl
1995   Israel Knohl, *The Sanctuary of Silence: The Priestly Torah and the Holiness School* (Minneapolis: Fortress, 1995)

Knohl
2003   Israel Knohl, *The Divine Symphony: The Bible's Many Voices* (Philadelphia: Jewish Publication Society, 2003)

Kugel
1983   James L. Kugel, "Two Introductions to Midrash," *Prooftexts* 3 (1983) 131–155

Kugel
1990　James L. Kugel, *In Potiphar's House: The Interpretive Life of Biblical Texts* (San Francisco: Harper, 1990)

Kugel
1993　James L. Kugel, "Levi's Election to the Priesthood in Second Temple Writings," *HTR* 86 (1993) 1–64

Kugel
1994　James L. Kugel, "The Jubilees Apocalypse," *DSD* 1 (1994) 322–337

Kugel
1995　James L. Kugel, "Reuben's Sin with Bilhah in the Testament of Reuben," in *Pomegranates and Golden Bells: Studies in Biblical, Jewish, and Near Eastern Ritual, Law, and Literature in Honor of Jacob Milgrom* (ed. D.P. Wright et al.; Winona Lake, Ind.: Eisenbrauns, 1995) 525–554

Kugel
1997　James L. Kugel, *The Bible as It Was* (Cambridge, Mass.: Harvard University Press, 1997)

Kugel
1998　James L. Kugel, *Traditions of the Bible* (Cambridge, Mass./London: Harvard University Press, 1998)

Kugel
1998a　James L. Kugel, "4Q369 'Prayer of Enosh' and Ancient Biblical Interpretation," *DSD* 5 (1998) 119–148

Kugel
2000　James L. Kugel, "Biblical Apocrypha and Pseudepigrapha and the Hebrew of the Second Temple Period," in *Diggers at the Well: Proceedings of the Third International Symposium on the Hebrew of the Dead Sea Scrolls and Ben Sira* (ed. T. Muraoka and J.F. Elwolde; STDJ 36; Leiden: Brill, 2000) 166–177

Kugel and Ravid
2001　James L. Kugel and Leora Ravid, "A Reexamination of the Calendar in the Book of Jubilees," Appendix in Ravid 2001, 1*–27*

Lambdin
1978　Thomas O. Lambdin, *Introduction to Classical Ethiopic (Ge'ez)* (HSS 24; Atlanta: Scholars Press, 1978)

Lambert
2004　David Lambert, "Last Testaments in the Book of Jubilees," *DSD* 11 (2004) 82–107

Lange
1997　Armin Lange, "The Essene Position on Magic and Divination," in *Legal Texts and Legal Issues: Proceedings of the Second Meeting of the International Organization for Qumran Studies, Cambridge 1995* (ed. M. Bernstein, F. García Martínez and J. Kampen; STDJ 23; Leiden, New York and Köln: Brill, 1997) 377–435

Leslau
1987　Wolf Leslau, *Comparative Dictionary of Ge'ez* (Wiesbaden: Harrassowitz, 1987)

Lewis
1992　Theodore J. Lewis, "Belial," in *Anchor Bible Dictionary* (1992) 1:654–656

Licht
1957　Jacob Licht, *The Thanksgiving Scroll: A Scroll from the Wilderness of Judea* (Jerusalem: Bialik Institute, 1957) (Heb.)

Licht
1961　Jacob Licht, "The Plant Eternal and the People of Divine Deliverance," in *Essays on the Dead Sea Scrolls in Memory of E.L. Sukenik* (eds. C. Rabin and Y. Yadin; Jerusalem: Shrine of the Book, 1961) 49–75 (Heb.)

Licht
  1965　Jacob Licht, *The Rule Scroll: A Scroll from the Wilderness of Judea* (Jerusalem: Bialik Institute, 1965) (Heb.)
Lim
  1992　Timothy H. Lim, "The Chronology of the Flood Story in a Qumran Text (4Q252)," *JJS* 43 (1992) 288–298
Lim
  1993　Timothy H. Lim, "Notes on 4Q252, fr. 1, cols. i–ii," *JJS* 44 (1993) 121–126
Littman
  1900　Enno Littman, "Das Buch der Jubiläen," in *Die Apokryphen und Pseudepigraphen des Alten Testaments* (ed. E. Kautzsch; 2 vols.; Tübingen, Freiburg and Leipzig: J.C.B. Mohr [Paul Siebeck], 1900) 2:31–119
Littré
  1851　Emile Littré (ed.), *Oeuvres complètes d'Hippocrate: traduction nouvelle avec le texte grec en regard*, vol. VII (10 vols. [1839–1861]; Paris: J.B. Baillière, 1851)
Lloyd
  1978　G.E.R. Lloyd (ed.), *Hippocratic Writings* (trans. from Greek by J. Chadwick, W.N. Mann et al.; Harmondsworth/New York: Penguin, 1978)
Loewenstamm
  1971　Samuel E. Loewenstamm, "עדות," *Encyclopedia Biblica*, vol. 6 (Jerusalem: Bialik Institute, 1971) 89 (Heb.)
Loewenstamm
  1983　Samuel E. Loewenstamm, "*'am segulla*," in *Hebrew Language Studies Presented to Professor Zeev Ben-Hayyim* (eds. M. Bar-Asher et al.; Jerusalem: Magnes, 1983) 321–328 (Heb.)
Loewenstamm
  1986　Samuel E. Loewenstamm, "נחלת ה'," in *Studies in Bible* (ed. S. Japhet; ScrHier 31; Jerusalem: Magnes, 1986) 155–192
Loewenstamm
  1992　Samuel E. Loewenstamm, *The Evolution of the Exodus Tradition* (trans. by B.J. Schwartz; Jerusalem: Magnes, 1992)
Mach
  2000　Michael Mach, "Demons," in *Encyclopedia of the Dead Sea Scrolls* (ed. L. Schiffman and J. VanderKam; Oxford: Oxford University Press, 2000) 189–192
Mackie (1955)
  1990　J.L. Mackie, "Evil and Omnipotence," *Mind* 64 (1955) 200–212; repr. in *The Problem of Evil* (Oxford Readings in Philosophy; ed. M.M. Adams and R.M. Adams; Oxford: Oxford University Press, 1990) 25–37
Maori
  1995　Yeshayahu Maori, *The Peshitta Version of the Pentateuch and Early Exegesis* (Jerusalem: Magnes, 1995) (Heb.)
Marcus
  1953　Ralph Marcus (ed.), *Philo: Questions and Answers on Genesis* (London: W. Heinemann, 1953); supplementary vol. 1 in *Philo of Alexandria: Collected Works* (LCL; 12 vols.; London: W. Heinemann, 1929–1962)
Martin
  1911　Francois Martin, "Le livre des Jubilés. But et procédés de l'auter. Ses doctrines," *RB* 8 (1911) 321–44; 503–33
Matthews and Amar
  1994　E.G. Matthews and J.P. Amar (trans.), *St. Ephrem the Syrian: Selected Prose Works* (The Fathers of the Church 91; Washington, D.C.: Catholic University of America Press, 1994)

Mazor
- 2002 Lea Mazor, "The Correlation between the Garden of Eden and the Temple," *Shnaton* 13 (2002) 5–42 (Heb.)

Melamed
- 1945 Ezra Zion Melamed, "Hendiadys (ἕν διὰ δυοῖν) in the Bible," *Tarbiz* 16 (1945) 173–189 (Heb.)

Mendels
- 1987 Doron Mendels, *The Land of Israel as a Political Concept in Hasmonean Literature* (Tübingen: J.C.B. Mohr [Paul Siebeck], 1987)

Menn
- 1997 Esther M. Menn, *Judah and Tamar (Genesis 38) in Ancient Jewish Exegesis: Studies in Literary Form and Hermeneutics* (Leiden: Brill, 1997)

Milgrom
- 1991 Jacob Milgrom, *Leviticus 1–16: A New Translation with Introduction and Commentary* (AB 3; New York: Doubleday, 1991)

Milgrom
- 1993 Jacob Milgrom, "The Concept of Impurity in *Jubilees* and the *Temple Scroll*," *RevQ* 16 (1993) 277–284

Milgrom
- 2000 Jacob Milgrom, *Leviticus 17–22: A New Translation with Introduction and Commentary* (AB 3A; New York: Doubleday, 2000)

Milik
- 1976 Jozef T. Milik, *The Books of Enoch: Aramaic Fragments of Qumran Cave 4* (with collaboration of M. Black; Oxford: Clarendon, 1976)

Milik
- 1978 Jozef T. Milik, "Écrits prééssèniens de Qumrân: d'Hénoch à Amram," in *Qumrân: sa pieté, sa theologie et son milieu* (ed. M. Delcor; Paris/Leuven: Duculot/University, 1978) 91–106

Miller
- 1977 Frank J. Miller (ed.), *Ovid in Six Volumes: III. Metamorphoses I* (LCL; 6 vols.; 3rd ed.; Cambridge, Mass./London: Harvard and William Heinemann, 1977)

Moran
- 1963 William L. Moran, "The Ancient Near Eastern Background of the Love of God in Deuteronomy," *CBQ* 25 (1963) 77–87

Mosshammer
- 1984 Alden A. Mosshammer (ed.), *Georgii Syncelli Ecloga Chronographica* (Bibliotheca Scriptorum Graecorum et Romanorum Teubneriana; Leipzig: BSB B.G. Teubner, 1984)

Muntner
- 1957 Suessman Muntner, *Introduction to the Book of Asaph the Physician* (Jerusalem: Geniza, 1957) (Heb.)

Muntner
- 1972 Suessman Muntner, "Asaph Ha-Rofe," in *Encyclopedia Judaica* (1972) 3:673–676

Naeh
- 1997 Shlomo Naeh, "On Two Hippocratic Concepts in Rabbinic Literature," *Tarbiz* 66 (1997) 169–185 (Heb.)

Najman
- 1999 Hindy Najman, "Interpretation as Primordial Writing: Jubilees and its Authority Conferring Strategies," *JSJ* 30 (1999) 379–410

Nickelsburg
- 1977 George W.E. Nickelsburg, "Apocalyptic and Myth in Enoch 6–11," *JBL* 96 (1977) 383–405

Nickelsburg
  1984   George W.E. Nickelsburg, "The Bible Rewritten and Expanded," in *Jewish Writings of the Second Temple Period* (ed. M. Stone; CRINT; Assen/Philadelphia: Van Gorcum/ Fortress, 1984) 89–156
Nickelsburg
  2001   George W.E. Nickelsburg, *1 Enoch: A Commentary on the Book of 1 Enoch, Chapters 1–36, 81–108* (Hermeneia; Minneapolis: Fortress, 2001)
Nitzan
  1986   Bilhah Nitzan, *Pesher Habakkuk: A Scroll from the Wilderness of Judea (1QpHab)* (Jerusalem: Bialik Institute, 1986) (Heb.)
Noth
  1962   Martin Noth, *Exodus: A Commentary* (OTL; trans. J. Bowden; Philadelphia: Westminster, 1962)
Olyan
  1993   Saul Olyan, *A Thousand Thousands Served Him: Exegesis and the Naming of Angels in Ancient Judaism* (TSAJ 36; Tübingen: J.C.B. Mohr [Paul Siebeck], 1993)
Parnas
  1975   Moshe Parnas, "'Ēdūt, 'Ēdōt, 'Ēdwōt in the Bible against the Background of Ancient Near Eastern Documents," *Shnaton* 1 (1975) 235–246 (Heb.)
Paul
  1973   Shalom M. Paul, "Heavenly Tablets and the Book of Life," *JANES* 5 (1973) 345–352
Puech
  2001   Émile Puech (ed.), "537. 4QTestament de Jacob? ar (4QTJa? ar)," in *Qumrân Grotte 4.XXII. Textes Araméens, Première Partie (4Q529–549)* (ed. E. Puech; DJD XXXI; Oxford: Clarendon, 2001) 171–190
Qimron
  1986   Elisha Qimron, *The Hebrew of the Dead Sea Scrolls* (HSS 29; Atlanta: Scholars, 1986)
Qimron and Strugnell
  1994   Elisha Qimron and John Strugnell, *Qumran Cave 4.V: Miqsat Maʿase ha-Torah* (DJD X; Oxford: Clarendon, 1994)
Rabin
  1954   Chaim Rabin, *The Zadokite Documents: I. The Admonition, II. The Laws* (Oxford: Clarendon, 1954)
Rabin
  1984   Chaim Rabin, "Jubilees," in *The Apocryphal Old Testament* (ed. H.F.D. Sparks; revision of R.H. Charles, *The Book of Jubilees*; Oxford: Clarendon, 1984) 1–139
Ravid
  1999   Liora Ravid, "The Special Terminology of the Heavenly Tablets in the Book of Jubilees," *Tarbiz* 68 (1999) 463–471 (Heb.)
Ravid
  2000   Liora Ravid, "The Relationship of the Sabbath Laws in *Jubilees* 50:6–13 to the Rest of the Book," *Tarbiz* 69 (2000) 161–166 (Heb.)
Ravid
  2001   Liora Ravid, *Issues in the Book of Jubilees* (Ph.D. diss., Bar Ilan University, 2001) (Heb.)
Ravid
  2003   Liora Ravid, "The Book of Jubilees and its Calendar: A Reexamination," *DSD* 10 (2003) 371–394

Rofé
1977 Alexander Rofé, "Isaiah 55:6–11: The Problems of the Fulfillment of Prophecies and Trito-Isaiah," *Proceedings of the Sixth World Congress of Jewish Studies* (1977) 1:213–221 (Heb.)

Rofé
1979 Alexander Rofé, *The Belief in Angels in the Bible and in Early Israel* (2 vols.; Jerusalem: Makor, 1979) (Heb.)

Rofé
1986 Alexander Rofé, *The Prophetical Stories: The Narratives about the Prophets in the Hebrew Bible – Their Literary Types and History* (Jerusalem: Magnes, 1986) (Heb.)

Rofé
1988 Alexander Rofé, *Introduction to Deuteronomy: Part I and Further Chapters* (Jerusalem: Akademon, 1988) (Heb.)

Rönsch
1874 Hermann Rönsch, *Das Buch der Jubiläen oder die kleine Genesis* (Leipzig: Fues's Verlag, 1874)

Rosenthal
1993 Abraham Rosenthal, "Oral Torah and Torah from Sinai: Halakha and Praxis," in *Mehqerei Talmud 2* (eds. M. Bar-Asher and D. Rosenthal; Jerusalem: Magnes, 1993) 448–487 (Heb.)

Rothstein
2004 David Rothstein, "Sexual Union and Sexual Offences in Jubilees," *JSJ* 35 (2004) 363–384

Rubenstein
1999 Jeffrey Rubenstein, "Nominalism and Realism in Qumranic and Rabbinic Law: A Reassessment," *DSD* 6 (1999) 157–183

Safrai and Safrai
1998 Shmuel Safrai and Ze'ev Safrai, *Haggadah of the Sages: The Passover Haggadah* (Jerusalem: Carta, 1998) (Heb.)

Salvesen
1991 Alison Salvesen, *Symmachus in the Pentateuch* (JSSMS 15; Manchester: University of Manchester Press, 1991)

Sarna
1989 Nahum Sarna, *Genesis: The Traditional Hebrew Text with the New JPS Translation* (JPS Torah Commentary; Philadelphia: Jewish Publication Society, 1989)

Sarna
1991 Nahum Sarna, *Exodus: The Traditional Hebrew Text with the New JPS Translation* (JPS Torah Commentary; Philadelphia: Jewish Publication Society, 1991)

Schechter
1910 Solomon Schechter, *Documents of Jewish Sectaries: Fragments of a Zadokite Work* (Cambridge: Cambridge University Press, 1910)

Schiffman
1975 Lawrence H. Schiffman, *The Halakhah at Qumran* (SJLA 16; Leiden: E.J. Brill, 1975)

Schnabel
1985 Eckhard Schnabel, *Law and Wisdom from Ben Sira to Paul: A Traditional Historical Inquiry into the Relation of Law, Wisdom and Ethics* (WUNT Reihe 2, 16; Tübingen; J.C.B. Mohr [Paul Siebeck], 1985)

Schwartz
1990a Daniel R. Schwartz, *Agrippa I: The Last King of Judea* (Tübingen: Mohr, 1990)

Schwartz
1990b   Daniel R. Schwartz, "On Two Aspects of a Priestly View of Descent at Qumran," in *Archaeology and History in the Dead Sea Scrolls* (ed. L.H. Schiffman; JSPSup 8; Sheffield: JSOT, 1990) 157–179

Schwartz
1992a   Daniel R. Schwartz, "Law and Truth: On Qumran-Sadducean and Rabbinic Views of the Law," *The Dead Sea Scrolls: Forty Years of Research* (ed. D. Dimant and U. Rappaport; STDJ 10; Leiden/Jerusalem: Brill/Magnes and Yad Izhak Ben Zvi, 1992) 229–240

Schwartz
1992b   Daniel R. Schwartz, "Kingdom of Priests: A Pharisaic Slogan?," in *Studies in the Jewish Background of Christianity* (Tübingen: J.C.B. Mohr [Paul Siebeck], 1992) 57–80

Schwartz
1996   Baruch J. Schwartz, "The Priestly Account of the Theophany and Lawgiving at Sinai," in *Texts, Temples and Traditions: A Tribue to Menahem Haran* (ed. M.V. Fox et al.; Winona Lake: Eisenbrauns, 1996) 103–134

Schwartz
1999   Baruch J. Schwartz, *The Holiness Legislation: Studies in the Priestly Code* (Jerusalem: Magnes Press, 1999) (Heb.)

Schwarz
1982   Eberhard Schwarz, *Identität durch Abgrenzung: Abgrenzungsprozesse in Israel im 2. vorchristlichen Jahr- hundert und ihre traditionsgeschichtlichen Voraussetzungen. Zugleich ein Beitrag zur Erforschung des Jubiläenbuches* (Europäische Hochschulschriften 23/162; Frankfurt/Bern: Peter Lang, 1982)

Scott
2005   James M. Scott, *On Earth as in Heaven: The Restoration of Sacred Time and Sacred Space in the Book of Jubilees* (JSJSup 91; Leiden/Boston: Brill, 2005)

Seeligmann
1992   Isac L. Seeligmann, *Studies in Biblical Literature* (eds. A. Hurvitz, S. Japhet, and E. Tov; Jerusalem: Magnes, 1992) (Heb.)

Segal
2003   Michael Segal, "Law and Narrative in *Jubilees*: The Story of the Entrance into the Garden of Eden Revisited," *Meghillot* 1 (2003) 111–125 (Heb.)

Segal
2004   Michael Segal, *The Book of Jubilees: Rewritten Bible, Redaction, Ideology and Thology* (Ph.D. diss., Hebrew University of Jerusalem, 2004) (Heb.)

Segal
2005   Michael Segal, "Between Bible and Rewritten Bible," in *Biblical Interpretation at Qumran* (ed. M. Henze; Studies in the Dead Sea Scrolls and Related Literature; Grand Rapids: Eerdmans, 2005) 10–28

Seow
1984   C.L. Seow, "The Designation of the Ark in Priestly Theology," *HAR* 8 (1984) 185–198

Shemesh
2002   Aharon Shemesh, "How Many Forms of Capital Punishment and Why did the Rabbis Create the Penalty of Death by Strangulation?," *Bar Ilan Law Studies* 17 (2002) 509–529 (Heb.)

Skehan
1954   Patrick W. Skehan, "A Fragment of the 'Song of Moses' (Deut. 32) from Qumran," *BASOR* 136 (1954) 12–15

Skinner
1930   John Skinner, *A Critical and Exegetical Commentary on Genesis* (ICC; 2nd ed.; Edinburgh: Clark, 1930)

Smith
1995   Mark Smith (ed.), "384. 4QApocryphon of Jeremiah B?," in *Qumran Cave 4.XIV. Parabiblical Texts, Part 2* (ed. M. Broshi et al.; DJD 19; Oxford: Clarendon, 1995) 137–152

Smyth
1922   Herbert W. Smyth (ed.), "Prometheus Bound," in *Aeschylus with an English Translation* (LCL; 2 vols.; Cambridge, Mass./London: Harvard and William Heinemann, 1922) 1:214–315

Speiser
1964   E.A. Speiser, *Genesis: Introduction, Translation, and Notes* (AB 1; Garden City, N.Y.: Doubleday, 1964)

Sperling
1995   S.D. Sperling, "Belial בליעל," in *Dictionary of Deities and Demons in the Bible* (ed. K. van der Toorn, B. Becking, and P.W. van der Horst; Leiden, New York and Köln: E.J. Brill, 1995) 169–171

Spiegel
1967   Shalom Spiegel, *The Last Trial: On the Legends and the Lore of the Command to Abraham to Offer Isaac as a Sacrifice: The Akedah* (trans. from Hebrew by J. Goldin; New York: Pantheon, 1967)

Steck
1977   Odil H. Steck, "Die Aufnahme von Genesis 1 in Jubiläen 2 und 4 Esra 6," *JSJ* 8 (1977) 154–182

Steiner
1995   Richard C. Steiner, "The Heading of the Book of the Words of Noah on a Fragment of the Genesis Apocryphon: New Light on a 'Lost' Work," *DSD* 2 (1995) 66–71

Steudel
2000   Annette Steudel, "God and Belial," in *The Dead Sea Scrolls Fifty Years after their Discovery: Proceedings of the Jerusalem Congress, July 20-25, 1997* (ed. L.H. Schiffman, E. Tov, J.C. VanderKam; Jerusalem: Israel Exploration Society in cooper. with The Shrine of the Book, 2000) 332–340

Stone
1971   Michael E. Stone, "Apocryphal Notes and Readings," *IOS* 1 (1971) 123–131

Stone
1972   Michael E. Stone, "Noah, Books of," in *Encyclopedia Judaica* (1972) 12:1198

Stone
1987   Michael E. Stone, "The Parabolic Use of Natural Order in Judaism of the Second Temple Age," in *Gilgul: Essays on Transformation, Revolution and Permanence in the History of Religions dedicated to R.I. Zwi Werblowsky* (ed. S. Shaked, D. Shulman, and G.G. Stroumsa; Leiden: E.J. Brill, 1987) 298–308

Stone
1999   Michael E. Stone, "The Axis of History at Qumran," in *Pseudepigraphic Perspectives: The Apocrypha and Pseudepigrapha in Light of the Dead Sea Scrolls. Proceedings of the International Symposium of the Orion Center, 12-14 January 1997* (ed. E.G. Chazon and M.E. Stone; STDJ 31; Leiden: Brill, 1999) 133–149

Stone and Greenfield
1993   Michael E. Stone and Jonas C. Greenfield, "The Prayer of Levi," *JBL* 112 (1993) 247–266

Stone and Greenfield
1996   Michael E. Stone and Jonas C. Greenfield, "Aramaic Levi Document," in *Qumran Cave IV.XVII: Parabiblical Texts, Part 3* (DJD XXII; ed. G. Brooke et al.; Oxford: Clarendon, 1996) 1–72

Tadmor
1982 Hayim Tadmor, "Treaty and Oath in the Ancient Near East: A Historian's Approach," *Shnaton* 5–6 (1982) 149–173 (Heb.)
Talmon (1951)
1989 Shemaryahu Talmon, "Yom Hakippurim in the Habakkuk Scroll," *Biblica* 32 (1951) 549–563; repr. in *The World of Qumran from Within* (Jerusalem/Leiden: Magnes/E.J. Brill, 1989) 186–199
Talmon (1958)
1989 Shemaryahu Talmon, "The Calendar of the Covenanters of the Judean Desert," in *Aspects of the Dead Sea Scrolls* (ed. C. Rabin and Y. Yadin; ScrHier 4; Jerusalem: Magnes, 1958) 162–199; repr. in *The World of Qumran from Within* (Jerusalem/Leiden: Magnes/E.J. Brill, 1989) 147–185
Talmon
1978 Shemaryahu Talmon, "The Presentation of Synchroneity and Simultaneity in Biblical Narratives," in *Studies in Hebrew Narrative Art Throughout the Ages* (ed. J. Heinemann and S. Werses; ScrHier 27; Jerusalem: Magnes, 1978) 9–26
Testuz
1960 Michel Testuz, *Les idées religieuses du livre des Jubilés* (Genève/Paris: Droz/Minard, 1960)
Tigay
1996 Jeffrey H. Tigay, *Deuteronomy: The Traditional Hebrew Text with the New JPS Translation* (JPS Torah Commentary; Philadelphia: JPS, 1996)
Tonneau
1955 Raymond M. Tonneau (ed.), *Sancti Ephraem Syri in Genesim et in Exodum: Commentarii* (CSCO 152; Scriptores Syri 71; Louvain: Peeters, 1955)
Tov
1985 Emanuel Tov, "The Nature and Background of Harmonizations in Biblical Manuscripts," *JSOT* 31 (1985) 3–29
Tov
2001 Emanuel Tov, *Textual Criticism of the Hebrew Bible* (rev. ed.; Minneapolis/Assen: Fortress/Van Gorcum, 2001)
Tur-Sinai
1954 Naphtali H. Tur-Sinai, "בליעל," *Encyclopedia Biblica*, vol. 2 (Jerusalem: Bialik Institute, 1954) 132–133 (Heb.)
Van Henten
1999 J.W. van Henten, "Mastemah משטמה," in *Dictionary of Deities and Demons in the Bible* (ed. K. van der Toorn, B. Becking, P. W. van der Horst; Leiden: Brill, 1999) 553–554
Van Ruiten
1995 Jacques T.A.G.M. van Ruiten, "The Rewriting of Exodus 24:12–18 in Jubilees 1:1–4," *BN* 79 (1995) 25–29
Van Ruiten
1997 Jacques T.A.G.M. van Ruiten, "The Interpretation of Genesis 6:1–12 in Jubilees 5:1–19," in *Studies in the Book of Jubilees* (ed. M. Albani, J. Frey, and A. Lange; TSAJ 65; Tübingen: J.C.B. Mohr [Paul Siebeck], 1997) 59–75
Van Ruiten
2000 Jacques T.A.G.M. van Ruiten, *Primaeval History Interpreted: The Rewriting of Genesis 1–11 in the Book of Jubilees* (JSJSup 66; Leiden: Brill, 2000)
VanderKam
1977 James C. VanderKam, *Textual and Historical Studies in the Book of Jubilees* (HSM 14; Missoula, Mont.: Scholars Press, 1977)
VanderKam (1978)
2000 James C. VanderKam, "Enoch Traditions in Jubilees and Other Second-Century Sources," *SBLSP* (1978) 229–251; repr. in *From Revelation to Canon* (2000) 305–331

VanderKam
1979   James C. VanderKam, "The Origin, Character, and Early History of the 364–Day Calendar: A Reassessment of Jaubert's Hypothesis," *CBQ* 41 (1979) 390–411
VanderKam
1981   James C. VanderKam, "The Putative Author of the Book of Jubilees," *JJS* 26 (1981) 209–217
VanderKam
1984   James C. VanderKam, *Enoch and the Growth of an Apocalyptic Tradition* (Washington, D.C.: The Catholic Biblical Association of America, 1984)
VanderKam
1989   James C. VanderKam, *The Book of Jubilees* (2 vols.; CSCO 510–511; Scriptores
a–b   Aethiopici 87–88; Leuven: Peeters, 1989)
VanderKam
1992   James C. VanderKam, "The Jubilees Fragments from Qumran Cave 4," in *The Madrid Qumran Congress* (STDJ 11; ed. J. Trebolla Barrera and L. Vegas Montaner; 2 vols.; Leiden, New York and Köln: Brill, 1992) 635–648
VanderKam
1994   James C. VanderKam, "Genesis 1 in Jubilees 2," *DSD* 1 (1994) 300–321
VanderKam (1995)
2000   James C. VanderKam, "Studies in the Chronology of the Book of Jubilees," in *From Revelation to Canon* (2000) 522–544; trans. of "Das chronologische Konzept des Jubiläenbuches," *ZAW* 107 (1995) 80–100
VanderKam
1997   James C. VanderKam, "The Origins and Purposes of the *Book of Jubilees*," in *Studies in the Book of Jubilees* (ed. M. Albani, J. Frey, and A. Lange; TSAJ 65; Tübingen: J.C.B. Mohr [Paul Siebeck], 1997) 3–24
VanderKam
1998   James C. VanderKam, *Calendars in the Dead Sea Scrolls: Measuring Time* (London: Routledge, 1998)
VanderKam
1999   James C. VanderKam, "The Angel Story in the Book of Jubilees," in *Pseudepigraphic Perspectives: The Apocrypha and Pseudepigrapha in Light of the Dead Sea Scrolls. Proceedings of the International Symposium of the Orion Center, 12–14 January 1997* (ed. E.G. Chazon and M.E. Stone; STDJ 31; Leiden: Brill, 1999) 151–170
VanderKam
2000   James C. VanderKam, *From Revelation to Canon: Studies in Hebrew Bible and Second Temple Literature* (JSJSup 62; Leiden: Brill, 2000)
VanderKam
2000a James C. VanderKam, "Covenant and Biblical Interpretation in Jubilees 6," in *The Dead Sea Scrolls Fifty Years after their Discovery: Proceedings of the Jerusalem Congress, July 20–25, 1997* (ed. L.H. Schiffman, E. Tov, J.C. VanderKam; Jerusalem: Israel Exploration Society in cooper. with The Shrine of the Book, 2000) 92–104
VanderKam
2000b James C. VanderKam, "The Angel of the Presence in the Book of Jubilees," *DSD* 7 (2000) 378–393
VanderKam
2000c James C. VanderKam, "Studies on the Prologue and Jubilees 1," in *For a Later Generation: The Transformation of Tradition in Israel, Early Judaism, and Early Christianity* (ed. R.A. Argall, B.A. Bow and R.A. Werline; Harrisburg: Trinity, 2000) 266–279

VanderKam
2001   James C. VanderKam, *The Book of Jubilees* (Guides to Apocrypha and Pseudepigrapha; Sheffield: Sheffield Academic Press, 2001)

VanderKam and Milik
1994   James C. VanderKam and Jozef T. Milik, "Jubilees," in *Qumran Cave 4.VIII: Parabiblical Texts, Part 1* (ed. H.W. Attridge et al.; DJD XIII; Oxford: Clarendon Press, 1994) 1–185

Veijola
1976   Timo Veijola, "Zu Ableitung und Bedeutung von *hē'īd* I im Hebräischen: Ein Beitrag zur Bundesterminologie," *UF* 8 (1976) 343–351

Vermes
1973   Geza Vermes, *Scripture and Tradition in Judaism: Haggadic Studies* (2nd rev. ed.; Leiden: E.J. Brill, 1973)

Volkwein
1969   Bruno Volkwein, "Masoretiches *'ēdût, 'ēdwôt, 'ēdôt*—'Zeugnis' oder 'Bundesbestimmungen'?," *BZ* 13 (1969) 18–40

Von Rad
1953   Gerhard von Rad, "The Deuteronomistic Theology of History in the Books of Kings," in *Studies in Deuteronomy* (trans. D. Stalker; SBT 9; London: SCM Press, 1953) 74–91

Von Rad (1953)
1972   Gerhard von Rad, *Genesis: A Commentary* (trans. J.H. Marks; Philadelphia: Westminster, 1972); trans. of *Das erste Buch Moses* (Göttingen: Vandenhoeck & Ruprecht, 1953)

Weinfeld
1972   Moshe Weinfeld, "הברית והחסד: The Terms and the Shifts of their Development in Israel and the Ancient World," *Leš* 36 (1972) 85–105 (Heb.)

Weinfeld
1991   Moshe Weinfeld, *Deuteronomy 1–11: A New Translation with Introduction and Commentary* (AB 5; New York: Doubleday, 1991)

Weiss
1964   Raphael Weiss, "פסח—חמל, חוס," *Leš* 27–28 (1964) 127–130 (Heb.)

Wellhausen
1885   Julius Wellhausen, *Prolegomena to the History of Israel* (trans. from German by J.S. Black and A. Menzies; Edinburgh: Adam and Charles Black, 1885)

Werman
1994   Cana Werman, "Consumption of Blood and its Covering in the Priestly and Rabbinic Traditions," *Tarbiz* 63 (1994) 173–183 (Heb.)

Werman
1995a Cana Werman, *The Attitude Towards Gentiles in the Book of Jubilees and Qumran Literature Compared with Early Tanaaic Halakha and Contemporary Pseudepigrapha* (Ph.D. diss., Hebrew University of Jerusalem, 1995) (Heb.)

Werman
1995b Cana Werman, "The Story of the Flood in the Book of Jubilees," *Tarbiz* 64 (1995) 183–202 (Heb.)

Werman
1997   Cana Werman, "*Jubilees* 30: Building a Paradigm for the Ban on Intermarriage," *HTR* 90 (1997) 1–22

Werman
1999   Cana Werman, "Qumran and the Book of Noah," in *Pseudepigraphic Perspectives: The Apocrypha and Pseudepigrapha in Light of the Dead Sea Scrolls. Proceedings of the International Symposium of the Orion Center, 12–14 January 1997* (ed. E.G. Chazon and M.E. Stone; STDJ 31; Leiden: Brill, 1999) 171–181

Werman 1999	(1999)
Werman 2002	Cana Werman, "'The תורה and the תעודה' Engraved on the Tablets," *DSD* 9 (2002) 75–103; trans. of idem, *Tarbiz* 68 (1999) 473–492
Werman 2001a	Cana Werman, "Teʿudah: On the Meaning of the Term," in *Fifty Years of Dead Sea Scrolls Research* (eds. G. Brin and B. Nitzan; Jerusalem: Yad Ben-Zvi, 2001) 231–243 (Heb.)
Werman 2001b	Cana Werman, "The Book of Jubilees in Hellenistic Context," *Zion* 66 (2001) 275–296 (Heb.)
Werman 2004	Cana Werman, "The *Book of Jubilees* and the Qumran Community," *Meghillot* 2 (2004) 37–55 (Heb.)
Wevers 1990	John W. Wevers, *Notes on the Greek Text of Exodus* (SBLSCS 30; Atlanta: Scholars, 1990)
Wevers 1993	John W. Wevers, *Notes on the Greek Text of Genesis* (SBLSCS 35; Atlanta: Scholars, 1993)
Wiesenberg 1961	Ernest Wiesenberg, "The Jubilee of Jubilees," *RevQ* 3 (1961) 3–40
Williamson 1994	Hugh G.M. Williamson, *The Book Called Isaiah: Deutero-Isaiah's Role in Composition and Redaction* (Oxford: Clarendon, 1994)
Wintermute 1985	O.S. Wintermute, "Jubilees: A New Translation and Introduction," in *The Old Testament Pseudepigrapha* (ed. J.H. Charlesworth; 2 vols.; New York: Doubleday, 1985) 35–142
Yadin 1962	Yigael Yadin, *The Scroll of the War of the Sons of Light Against the Sons of Darkness* (Oxford: Oxford University, 1962)
Zakovitch 1977	Yair Zakovitch, "The Synonymous Word and the Synonymous Name in Name-Midrashim," *Shnaton* 2 (1977) 100–115 (Heb.)
Zakovitch 1990	Yair Zakovitch, *Ruth: Introduction and Commentary* (Mikra le-Yisrael; Tel Aviv/Jerusalem: Am Oved/Magnes, 1990) (Heb.)
Zakovitch 1992	Yair Zakovitch, *An Introduction to Inner-Biblical Exegesis* (Even-Yehuda: Reches, 1992) (Heb.)
Zakovitch and Shinan 1992	Yair Zakovitch and Avigdor Shinan, *The Story of Judah and Tamar* (Research Projects of the Institute of Jewish Studies Monograph Series 15; Jerusalem: Hebrew University of Jerusalem, 1992) (Heb.)
Zeitlin 1939–40	Solomon Zeitlin, "The Book of Jubilees: Its Character and its Significance," *JQR* 30 (1939–40) 1–31
Zipor 1997	Moshe A. Zipor, "The Flood Chronology: Too Many an Accident," *DSD* 4 (1997) 207–210
Zipor 2005	Moshe A. Zipor, *The Septuagint Version of the Book of Genesis* (Ramat-Gan: Bar-Ilan University, 2005) (Heb.)

ABBREVIATIONS

AB	Anchor Bible
AbrNSup	Abr-Nahrain: Supplement Series
AOAT	Alter Orient und Altes Testament
BASOR	*Bulletin of the American Schools of Oriental Research*
BDB	F. Brown, S.R. Driver, and C.A. Briggs, *A Hebrew and English Lexicon of the Old Testament* (Oxford: Clarendon, 1907)
BEATAJ	Beiträge zur Erforschung des Alten Testaments und des antiken Judentum
BiOr	*Bibliotheca orientalis*
BN	*Biblische Notizen*
BZ	*Biblische Zeitschrift*
CAD	*The Assyrian Dictionary of the Oriental Institute of the University of Chicago* (Chicago, 1956–)
CBQ	*Catholic Biblical Quarterly*
CBQMS	Catholic Biblical Quarterly Monograph Series
CRINT	Compendia rerum iudaicarum ad Novum Testamentum
CSCO	Corpus scriptorum christianorum orientalium
DJD	Discoveries in the Judaean Desert
DSD	*Dead Sea Discoveries*
DSSR	Donald W. Parry and Emanuel Tov (eds.), *The Dead Sea Scrolls Reader* (6 vols.; Leiden/Boston: Brill, 2004–2005)
HAR	*Hebrew Annual Review*
HSM	Harvard Semitic Monographs
HSS	Harvard Semitic Studies
HTR	*Harvard Theological Review*
ICC	International Critical Commentary
IEJ	*Israel Exploration Journal*
IOS	*Israel Oriental Studies*
JANES	*Journal of the Ancient Near Eastern Society*
JAOS	*Journal of the American Oriental Society*
JBL	*Journal of Biblical Literature*
JJS	*Journal of Jewish Studies*
JPS	Jewish Publication Society
JQR	*Jewish Quarterly Review*
JSHRZ	Jüdische Schriften aus hellenistisch-römischer Zeit
JSJ	*Journal for the Study of Judaism in the Persian, Hellenistic and Roman Periods*
JSJSup	Journal for the Study of Judaism in the Persian, Hellenistic and Roman Periods: Supplement Series
JSOT	*Journal for the Study of the Old Testament*
JSPSup	Journal for the Study of the Pseudepigrapha: Supplement Series
JSSMS	Journal of Semitic Studies Monograph Series
LCL	Loeb Classical Library
Leš	*Lešonénu*
Meghillot	*Meghillot: Studies in the Dead Sea Scrolls*
OTL	Old Testament Library
PAAJR	*Proceedings of the American Academy for Jewish Research*
PVTG	Pseudepigrapha Veteris Testamenti Graece

RB	*Revue biblique*
REJ	*Revue des études juives*
RevQ	*Revue de Qumran*
RHR	*Revue de l'histoire des religions*
SBLDS	Society of Biblical Literature Dissertation Series
SBLEJL	Society of Biblical Literature Early Judaism and Its Literature
SBLSCS	Society of Biblical Literature Septuagint and Cognate Studies
SBLSP	*Society of Biblical Literature Seminar Papers*
SBT	Studies in Biblical Theology
ScrHier	Scripta hierosolymitana
Shnaton	*Shnaton: An Annual for Biblical and Ancient Near Eastern Studies*
SJLA	Studies in Judaism in Late Antiquity
STDJ	Studies on the Texts of the Desert of Judah
SVTP	*Studia in Veteris Testamenti pseudepigaphica*
TSAJ	Texte und Studien zum antiken Judentum
UF	*Ugarit-Forschungen*
VT	*Vetus Testamentum*
VTSup	Supplements to Vetus Testamentum
WBC	Word Biblical Commentary
WUNT	Wissenschaftliche Untersuchungen zum Neuen Testament
ZAW	*Zeitschrift für die alttestamentliche Wissenschaft*

INDEX OF MODERN AUTHORS

Abegg, M. 235
Aejmelaeus, A. 207
Albeck, C. 13, 17, 18, 27, 79, 145, 156
Alexander, P. 4
Amar, J.P. 77
Amir, Y. 278
Anderson, G. 13, 17, 21, 49, 60, 65, 74, 80–81, 141, 146, 275–277, 290, 323
Attridge, H. 258
Avishur, Y. 289

Baillet, M. 235
Barker, M. 110
Bar-On (Gesundheit), S. 212, 213, 223
Barthélemy, D. 239
Baumgarten, J.M. 4, 13, 17, 18, 27, 49, 55, 56, 57, 68, 145, 156, 192–194, 242–243, 253, 287, 294
Beer, G. 111
Ben-Dov, J. 8
Berger, K. 10, 13, 79, 121, 123, 132, 134, 150, 219, 232, 233, 284, 298, 304, 308–309
Bernstein, M.J. 4, 84, 120, 210
Bhayro, S. 110
Black, M. 110, 135
Böttrich, C. 13
Brooke, G.J. 53, 107, 284, 289
Büchler, A. 13
Budde, K. 250

Cassuto, U. 104, 110, 169, 204
Charles, R.H. 10, 13, 15, 17, 35, 39, 62, 78, 79, 86, 89, 115, 117, 121, 123, 127, 132, 134, 148, 150, 152, 155, 156, 161, 170–171, 173, 203, 209, 215, 217, 218, 219, 230, 231, 232, 237, 258, 274, 284, 285–286, 296, 298, 304, 306, 308, 313, 314, 323
Chazon, E.G. 139
Collins, J.J. 93, 145, 159, 263, 291, 293
Cook, E. 235
Cross, F.M. 295

Daly, R.J. 193, 196
Davenport, G.L. 12, 13, 14, 15, 16, 40, 134, 140, 284, 296, 297

Dillman, A. 15, 36, 79, 123, 159, 219, 231, 308
Dimant, D. 3, 9, 13, 16, 17, 21, 25, 84–85, 94, 99, 110–111, 113–114, 117, 118, 125, 127, 148, 150, 151, 154, 171, 174, 176, 177, 178, 179, 239, 312
Doering, L. 19, 20, 83, 240, 274, 281
Doran, R. 36
Driver, S.R. 204, 248, 249, 275

Ego, B. 49
Eissfeldt, O. 250
Elgvin, T. 139
Elior, R. 7
Endres, J. 5, 10, 14, 275, 292, 293
Eshel, E. 13, 100, 132, 150, 151, 153, 179, 184, 252, 253, 254, 263

Feldman, L. 134
Finkelstein, L. 11, 37, 67, 320
Fishbane, M. 185
Fitzmyer, J.A. 127, 296
Flemming, J. 135
Flusser, D. 170, 244, 247, 252, 255
Focht, A. 209
Fox, M.V. 223, 280
Fraade, S.D. 303

García Martínez, F. 6, 13, 26, 115, 138, 139, 152, 170, 174, 175, 193, 297, 313–314
Gelb, I.J. 296
Gibson, J.C.L. 250
Glatt, D.A. 84
Goldmann, M. 52, 62, 66–67, 79, 121, 123, 132, 212, 215, 217, 219, 232, 237, 240, 298, 304
Goldstein, J.A. 36, 37, 320
Goudoever, J. van 193, 198–201
Greenberg, M. 204, 280
Greenfield, J.C. 18, 254, 296
Grintz, Y.M. 174

Hacham, A. 209
Halpern-Amaru, B. 5, 10, 11, 14, 27, 49, 61, 62, 64, 74, 75

Harrington, D.J. 4
Hartom. E.S. 52, 66–67, 219, 230, 232, 237, 308
Hayward, C.T.R. 49, 120
Heinemann, Y. 74
Hendel, R.S. 55
Hengel, M. 293
Henten, J.W. van 190
Himmelfarb, M. 170, 171
Hollander, H.W. 252
Horowitz, W. 8
Hurvitz, A. 278

Japhet, S. 290
Jaubert, A, 8, 13, 53, 54, 193, 194, 306
Jellenik, A. 170
Jensen, J. 283
Jonge, M. de 252
Joüon, P. 213

Kahana, A. 128, 148
Kister, M. 6, 16, 17, 18, 19, 20, 21, 26, 27, 35, 37, 38, 46, 55, 57, 81, 83, 145, 147, 156, 163, 164, 179, 184, 191, 210, 226, 236–237, 242, 243, 244, 247, 254, 255, 267, 273, 274, 284, 287, 290–291, 292, 299, 301, 303, 306, 309, 320, 321–322
Knibb, M.A. 135, 139, 151
Knohl, I. 64, 98, 100, 250, 295, 301
Kugel, J.L. 5, 9, 10, 28–29, 38, 55, 71, 74, 75, 76, 120, 164, 178, 190, 216, 219, 222–223, 258, 284, 290–291, 292, 305, 310, 311

Lambert, D. 147
Lange, A. 260
Leslau, W. 62
Lewis, T.J. 253
Licht, J. 100, 155, 254
Lim, T.H. 55
Littman, E. 66, 121, 123, 219, 248
Littré, E. 49
Lloyd, G.E.R. 49
Loewenstamm, S.E. 210–211, 214, 225, 249, 250, 280, 295

Mach, M. 190, 253
Mackie, J.L. 97
Maori, Y. 305
Marcus, R. 51
Martin, F. 13, 134
Matthews, E.G. 77
Mazor, L. 49

Melamed, E.Z. 288
Mendels, D. 36
Menn, E.M. 60, 62–63
Milgrom, J. 48, 49, 75, 78
Milik, J.T. 6, 15, 16, 36, 80, 100, 112, 124, 126, 127, 135, 139, 147, 178, 238, 239, 279, 284, 286, 287, 288, 314
Milikowski, C. 128
Mizrahi, N. 231
Moran, W.L. 294
Mosshammer, A.A. 114, 121
Mulgatta, M. 79
Muntner, S. 170

Naeh, S. 49–50, 209
Najman, H. 14, 157, 165
Newsom, C. 139
Nickelsburg, G.W.E. 4, 36, 37, 39, 110–113, 115, 124, 127, 148, 320
Nitzan, B. 283
Noth, M. 204

Olyan, S. 210

Parnas, M. 295, 296
Paul, S. 295, 313, 314
Puech, E. 314

Qimron, E. 18, 235, 254

Rabin, C. 62, 78, 79–81, 134, 232, 242, 253, 298, 306
Rad, G. von 104, 184
Radermacher, L. 135
Ravid, L. 19, 20, 21, 31, 35, 38, 39, 55, 77, 83, 138, 140–141, 228, 274, 287–288
Rofé, A. 9, 184–185, 212, 213, 250, 251
Rönsch, H. 27, 88–91, 319
Rosenthal, A. 68
Rothstein, D. 64, 68
Rubenstein, J. 69
Ruiten, J.T.A.G.M. van 2, 14, 49, 105, 106, 115, 116, 117, 134, 150, 156, 159, 161, 165, 172, 173, 247

Safrai, S. and Z. 212
Salvesen, A. 106, 194
Sarna, N. 74, 128, 133, 192, 196, 204
Schechter, S. 242
Schiffman, L. 311
Schnabel, E. 278
Schwartz, B. 295

Schwartz, D.   4, 11, 68, 69, 242–243, 253, 294
Schwarz, E.   10, 13, 275
Scott, J.M.   13, 17
Seeligmann, I.L.   157, 239
Segal, M.   4, 57
Seow, C.L.   295
Shemesh, A.   68
Shinan, A.   27, 61, 65, 66, 276
Skehan, P.W.   250
Skinner, J.   103, 301
Smith, M.   287
Speiser, E.A.   103, 110
Sperling, S.D.   253
Spiegel, S.   198
Steiner, R.C.   152
Steudel, A.   254
Stone, M.   56, 99–100, 152, 170, 171, 173, 254, 286–287, 303
Strugnell, J.   254, 258

Tadmor, H.   296
Talmon, S.   9, 13, 54, 59, 306, 321
Testuz, M.   5, 10, 13, 15, 39, 297
Tigay, J.   249, 250
Tonneau, R.M.   205
Tov, E.   139, 184, 207, 250

VanderKam, J.C.   3, 5, 6, 7, 8, 9, 10, 12, 13, 15, 16, 17, 35, 36, 37, 40, 53, 54, 62, 78, 79, 80, 84, 92, 107, 121, 122–127, 129, 130, 134, 147, 156, 161, 165, 172, 173, 175, 178, 181, 191, 194, 200–201, 203, 215, 217, 219, 220, 224, 230, 231, 232, 233, 235, 238, 239, 240, 244, 248, 269, 275, 279, 284, 285, 286, 287, 288, 298, 302, 304, 306, 308, 309, 312, 313, 320, 321, 323, 324
Veijola, T.   295
Vermes, G.   4, 193, 198, 209
Volkwein, B.   296

Weinfeld, M.   248, 249, 294, 296
Weiss, R.   225
Wellhausen, J.   275
Werman, C.   4, 6, 13, 31, 35, 38, 107, 138, 140, 141, 145, 152, 156, 163, 170–171, 172, 184, 247, 278, 283, 284, 287, 289–290, 292, 301, 316, 320
Wevers, J.W.   194, 207
Wiesenberg, E.   8, 12, 13, 14, 15, 231, 269
Williamson, H.G.M.   283
Wintermute, O.S.   10, 13, 121, 123, 232, 244
Wise, M.   235

Yadin, Y.   253

Zakovitch, Y.   27, 61, 65, 66, 194, 196, 276, 284
Zeitlin, S.   38
Zipor, M.   55, 194

INDEX OF ANCIENT JEWISH SOURCES

I. Jubilees

1	2, 3, 31, 32, 83, 141, 244, 247, 254, 264, 284, 286, 315–317, 321	2:14	258
		2:15	238
		2:16–24	238
1:1–4	2	2:17–24	264, 281, 299
1:1	2, 288, 316	2:17–21	9, 238, 240, 241, 275, 323, 324
1:4	2, 4, 83, 247, 285, 319		
1:5–14	247	2:17–18	9, 274
1:5	15, 62	2:17	9, 239
1:6	77, 141	2:18	9
1:7–25	15	2:19–24	100
1:7	15	2:19–21	7, 178, 179, 238, 239, 279
1:8	247, 285, 287	2:19	6, 178, 240
1:12	311	2:20–21	7
1:14–15	37	2:20	178, 258
1:14	314, 320	2:21	147
1:15–18	247	2:22	258
1:15	155	2:23–24	258, 259
1:16	155	2:23	238, 258
1:19–21	247–256, 259, 260, 264, 267, 324	2:24–33	19, 24, 238, 277, 279, 281, 282, 299
1:19–20	247	2:24	238, 247, 282, 288, 289, 299
1:19	187, 248, 255, 256, 259		
1:20–21	248	2:27	238
1:20	10, 150, 182, 251, 254–257	2:28	238
1:21	248	2:29	286
1:26–29	39	2:30	238
1:26	4, 15, 83, 247, 285, 319	2:31	83, 238, 239
1:27–29	20	2:32	238
1:27	3, 15, 16, 19, 285	2:33	238, 247, 288, 289, 299
1:28	15	3	47–58, 72, 142, 200
1:29	3, 4, 83, 247, 285, 287, 316, 319	3:1–7	47
		3:1	9, 49
2–10	3, 14	3:4–5	9
2	20, 31, 47, 176, 178, 238, 240, 258, 267, 282, 286, 300, 318	3:5–6	49
		3:8–14	6, 22, 24, 34, 47–52, 267, 274, 277, 288, 299
2:1–24	238	3:8–13	47
2:1	3, 15, 238	3:8–10	199
2:2	9, 178, 237, 279	3:8	48, 57
2:3	147, 238, 258	3:9–11	313
2:4	238, 258	3:9	6, 22, 48
2:7	258	3:10–13	49
2:8–9	8, 306	3:10–11	48, 51, 200
2:9	303	3:10	57
2:11	258	3:12	9, 48, 49
2:12	258	3:13–14	48

INDEX OF ANCIENT JEWISH SOURCES

3:13	48, 57	5:5	106, 135
3:14	57, 247, 288, 289, 300	5:6–7	135
3:15	9, 132	5:6	9, 108, 109, 115, 117, 119, 123, 125, 153
3:17	22, 34, 52, 53, 55, 56, 83, 100, 264, 266	5:7–9	25, 33, 92, 108, 115, 120, 124, 318
3:27	10, 173	5:8	109, 112, 124, 125
3:30–31	24, 147	5:9	153
3:31	313, 320	5:10	108, 109, 116, 119, 132–135, 139, 153
3:32	56, 83	5:11–12	108, 122, 134, 135
4–5	120	5:11	116, 132, 136
4	160, 312	5:12	116, 132, 137
4:2	121	5:13–18	32, 77, 108, 137–142, 264
4:5–6	24	5:13–14	139, 313
4:5	313	5:13	137, 140
4:6	9	5:14	140
4:14	127	5:17	75, 140
4:15	9, 100, 117, 125–127, 129–130, 132	5:18	140
4:16–25	312	5:19	108, 136, 149
4:16–24	165	5:20	83, 108, 136
4:16	127	5:22–23	25, 92
4:17–26	311	5:22	92, 123
4:18–19	311	5:23	9, 55, 83, 93, 123
4:19	36, 133	5:24–27	136
4:21	16, 17, 84, 85, 312	5:25	56
4:22	311	5:29	56, 83
4:23	164	5:31	123
4:24	164, 311	6–7	163
4:25	10	6	31, 38, 240, 281, 301, 302, 318
4:28–33	90		
4:28	123, 130, 158	6:4	107, 280, 301, 302, 303
4:29	90	6:17–22	24
4:30	310–311	6:17–20	241
4:31–32	24	6:7–14	183
4:31	223	6:10–12	300
4:32	313	6:10	301
4:33	25, 86, 90, 92, 121–123	6:17–18	239
5	34, 57, 72, 92, 93, 99, 103–143, 146–148, 150, 153, 169, 264, 266, 318	6:17	183, 228, 239, 313
		6:18	9, 123, 183–184, 275
5:1–18	32, 100	6:20	183, 228, 239
5:1–12	32, 33, 137, 141, 264, 318	6:21	239
5:1–6	107	6:22	228
5:1–3	115	6:23–38	8, 24, 228, 306
5:1	25, 33, 92, 105, 107, 108, 120–123, 318	6:23	303, 304
		6:24–28	304
5:2–5	105	6:25	83
5:2–3	135, 139	6:26	56, 83
5:2	105, 107, 109, 118, 124, 132, 148	6:27–28	75
		6:28–29	313
5:3	105, 106	6:29	53
5:4–5	115	6:30–35	313
5:4	106, 124, 136	6:30	8, 52, 53

6:32-38	321	7:34	146, 154-158
6:32	8, 39, 52, 53, 55, 291, 302, 306, 309, 310	7:35-37	18, 24, 146, 156-158, 163
6:33	302	7:36	18
6:34-36	37	7:37	156
6:34-35	315	7:38-39	146, 156-158, 165, 173
6:34	107, 302, 320	7:38	157, 158
6:36	8, 53, 302, 306	7:39	162, 165, 166, 265, 311
6:37	304	8-11	129
6:38	8, 39, 53, 55, 311	8:1-10:13	160
7	40, 145-148, 152-154, 158, 162, 163, 167, 169, 170, 174, 182, 184, 320	8-9	160-162
		8:1-8	162
		8:1-7	160
7:1-19	26, 265	8:1-4	100, 260
7:1-6	18, 24, 156	8:1	160, 161
7:1-2	161	8:3-4	260
7:1	160	8:3	260
7:2-7	160	8:5-8	160
7:2	83	8:6	129
7:3-6	18	8:8-9:15	128, 162
7:8-9	160	8:8	128-130
7:7-13	147	8:10	9, 128
7:7-9	147	8:19	49
7:10-19	160	9:15	133
7:14-19	149	10	27, 77, 94, 130, 150, 152, 153, 158, 163, 170, 172, 174-178, 181, 182, 184, 260, 265, 267
7:14	182		
7:15	147, 149, 182		
7:16	182		
7:18	123	10:1-15	150, 170
7:20-39	3, 26, 34, 93-94, 100, 138, 145-167, 170, 175, 179, 182, 184, 264, 291, 317	10:1-14	100, 171-172, 219
		10:1-13	10, 152, 153, 160, 161, 169-180, 182, 184, 185, 259, 265
7:20-34	155		
7:20-26	145	10:1-2	172
7:20-25	150	10:1	158, 169
7:20-21	147, 162, 265	10:2	169-170
7:20	26, 93, 146, 147, 149, 150, 155, 158, 161, 166, 169, 291, 311, 320	10:3-7	170
		10:5	10, 150, 152, 153, 175-177, 179
7:21	149	10:7	9
7:22-25	117, 153	10:8	101, 176, 177, 182, 185, 257, 265
7:22	148		
7:23-24	149	10:9	153
7:26-33	145	10:10-13	9
7:26-27	264	10:10	172
7:26	149, 150, 155, 182	10:11	10, 176
7:27-28	149	10:12-13	10, 172
7:27	10, 26, 93, 145, 150, 152, 153, 159, 161, 167, 169, 170, 182, 183, 185, 186	10:12	172
		10:13	172, 173, 181
		10:14	10, 157, 160, 172, 173
7:28-32	183	10:15-17	26
7:30-32	11	10:15-16	158, 160, 161
7:31	311	10:15	145, 173
7:33	183	10:16-17	93

INDEX OF ANCIENT JEWISH SOURCES

10:16	158	15:25-33	240, 242
10:17	133, 164, 311	15:25-27	237, 238
10:18-19	129	15:25-26	236
10:18	129, 130	15:25	232, 234-236, 313
10:20-21	129	15:26	230, 232, 236, 237, 241, 243, 269, 279
10:20	130		
10:21	130	15:27	9, 236, 237, 274, 279
10:22	133	15:28-30	240
10:27	130	15:30	240, 241
11-23:8	3	15:30-32	229, 259
11	181, 182, 184, 260	15:31-33	182, 255, 256
11:1-6	181-185	15:31-32	10, 101, 178, 179, 241
11:1-5	177, 182	15:33-34	243-244
11:1	130, 183	15:33	10, 242, 256, 267, 279
11:2-4	181	16	201, 305
11:2	183	16:1-15	304
11:3	181	16:1	83
11:4-5	181, 185, 186	16:2	305
11:5	10, 152, 183, 186-187, 219, 257	16:3-4	313
		16:9	313
11:8	260	16:12-14	305
11:11	10, 186-187, 219	16:12	305
11:11-13	177, 186-187	16:13-14	305
11:15	15	16:14	83
12	77	16:15-31	305
12:15	56	16:15-16	304
12:16-18	260	16:15	231
12:19-20	259-261, 264	16:16-31	304
12:19	261	16:16-18	304
12:20	10, 257	16:16	304
12:27	157, 173	16:19	304, 305
13	77	16:20-31	24, 307
13:8	83	16:20	201, 304, 305
13:25-27	19, 24	16:21-27	305
14:10	83	16:21	201
14:24	231	16:25	305
15	229, 236-238, 247, 280, 281	16:27	305
		16:28	304-306, 309
15:1-24	230	16:28-29	313
15:1	83, 231	16:29-30	305
15:9	229	16:29	305
15:11-14	236	16:31	305
15:11	229, 241	17-18	72, 99, 101, 126, 142, 178, 190
15:12	229		
15:13	241	17	305
15:14	230	17:1	231
15:17	231, 305	17:15-18:19	10, 176, 177, 189-202, 206, 267
15:21	241, 280		
15:23-24	230, 231, 243	17:15-18:17	23
15:23	230-232, 243	17:15	23, 191, 200
15:24	231, 232, 242, 243	17:16	210, 218
15:25-34	24, 37, 39, 101, 229-245, 258, 264, 267, 269, 320, 321, 324	17:17	190
		17:23-24	232
		18	77

18:1–2	192	22:10–30	3
18:2	194, 195	22:21	133
18:3	23, 192, 194	23	12, 244, 299, 320, 321
18:4	193	23:8	15, 16
18:6	195	23:9–32	3, 31, 37–39, 318, 320–322
18:7	195	23:11–32	15
18:9	9	23:11–31	297
18:11	190, 195	23:11	133
18:12	195, 207, 215	23:14	297–298
18:13	196	23:16	298
18:15	195	23:19	315
18:16	190	23:26	298
18:17	198	23:27–30	298
18:18–19	23, 24, 191, 193, 194, 198–201	23:31	298
		23:32	15, 297, 298, 313
18:18	198, 199	24–45	3
18:19	199, 313	24:12	56
19:1	56	24:22	83
19:9	313	24:28–30	15
19:12	56	24:30	133
19:15–16	257	24:33	133, 313
19:16–18	257	25:11–23	3
19:19	257	27:19	83, 86
19:21	257	28	30, 85–91, 191, 319
19:26–29	257–259, 260, 264	28:2	86
19:26–28	177	28:6–7	24
19:26	10	28:6	313
19:27	259	28:11	86, 87, 89, 90
19:28	10, 101	28:13	86, 87, 89, 90
19:29	257	28:14–15	25
19:31	257	28:14	83, 86–90, 319
20	3, 72, 154, 264	28:15	83, 86, 87, 89, 90, 91, 319
20:1–2	166	28:17	25, 88, 89, 319
20:1	159	28:18	25, 86–91, 319
20:2–10	147	28:19	86, 90, 91
20:4	11, 23, 64, 65, 67, 71, 72, 80	28:20	86, 88, 89
		28:21	86, 88, 89
20:5–6	154	28:22	86, 88, 89
20:5	100, 138, 146, 264	28:24	83, 86
20:7	311	29:5	86
21	3, 12, 155, 158	29:7	83
21:1	159, 166	30–32	10
21:4	141	30	17, 24, 292
21:5–20	24	30:9	313
21:5–10	157–158	30:11	311
21:5–8	11	30:12	15, 17
21:6	158	30:17	290, 311
21:7	158	30:18–23	292
21:10	157, 173	30:18–20	293
21:24	62, 155	30:18	293, 294
21:25	62	30:19–23	291
22	12	30:19–22	313
22:1	15	30:19	291
22:7	15	30:20–22	294

INDEX OF ANCIENT JEWISH SOURCES

30:20	294	35:1–8	3
30:21–22	294	35:1	159, 166
30:21	15	35:6	159
31	296	35:13	105, 106
31:1–3	296	35:27	159
31:3–32	296	36:1–3	166
31:12–17	10	36:1	159
31:14	296	36:3–4	147
31:16	296	36:11	311
31:18	296, 297	36:18	3, 84, 121
31:20	296	36:20	81
31:31–32	296, 297	37–38	36
31:32	291, 297, 298, 313	39:2	86
32	307, 308, 314	39:6–7	157
32:1–9	19	39:6	80, 173
32:1–8	18, 19	41	17, 22, 59–72, 80, 84, 142, 276, 319
32:1	39		
32:7	306	41:1–21	59, 60–65, 66, 71, 319
32:8	18	41:1	59
32:9–15	18, 24	41:2	22, 61
32:9	18, 19	41:3	61
32:10–15	18, 313	41:4	62
32:15	18	41:5	22, 62
32:20	296	41:6–7	61
32:21–22	313, 314	41:19–20	65
32:27	307, 308	41:19	65, 71
32:27–29	24, 313	41:21	59
32:28	307	41:22	59
32:29	306, 308–310	41:23–28	59
32:36	309	41:23–26	22–24, 65–71, 274, 319, 322
33	6, 72, 73–82, 142, 235, 274, 279		
		41:23–24	69, 70, 276, 319
33:1–9	24, 73–77, 142	41:23	70
33:1	75	41:24–25	68
33:2	74	41:24	71
33:4	74, 76	41:25–26	67, 68, 69, 318
33:4–5	74–75	41:25	66, 67
33:7	75, 76	41:26	67
33:9–20	24, 77–81	41:27–28	60–65, 66, 71, 319
33:10–12	313	41:27	22, 62–64, 66, 274, 319
33:10	78, 79	41:28	22, 64, 65, 67, 71, 72, 80, 157, 319
33:15–16	77–79, 141, 274		
33:15	78, 79	45:15–16	173
33:16–17	233–235	45:16	10, 157, 173
33:16	24, 69, 79–81, 236, 276	46–49	3, 203
33:17	79, 234	46:3	86
33:18	15, 141	47:9	56
33:20	11	47:10	56
34–41	84, 94	47:12	203
34–38	39	48–49	72, 142, 203–228
34	3, 36, 84	48	10, 23, 99, 101, 126, 176–178, 203, 206, 214–216, 219, 221, 253, 276
34:10	86, 121		
34:18–19	24		
34:20	60	48:1	203

355

48:2–3	204, 206, 207	49:1–2	198
48:2	190, 203	49:1	192
48:3	190, 203	49:2–5	225, 226
48:4	207, 210	49:2	10, 23, 177, 197, 212, 219, 223–225, 227, 267
48:5–8	226		
48:5	211, 212, 214	49:3	224
48:6	210	49:4	224–227
48:7	210	49:5	224
48:8	211, 214	49:7	227
48:9	214	49:8	227, 313
48:10	215	49:14	227
48:11	9, 211, 215	49:15	227
48:12–14	219, 220	49:16–21	197
48:12	215–217, 220, 221	49:17	227
48:13–14	218	49:22	227
48:13	9, 217	50	3, 20
48:14	217, 223	50:1–5	20, 31, 32, 318
48:15–17	219	50:1	20
48:15–16	9, 220	50:4	7, 84, 122, 269
48:15	219, 220	50:5	19, 39
48:16	177, 219, 220, 267	50:6–13	6, 19, 20, 24, 83, 274, 277
48:17	218–222	50:6	15
48:18	219, 223	50:7	19
49	6, 20, 24, 197, 203, 223–227, 274	50:8	20
		50:12	20
49:1–6	228	50:13	19, 20, 31, 32, 83, 318, 319

II. HEBREW BIBLE

Genesis

1–11	14	5:18	127
1–2	49	5:22	16, 17, 164
1	2, 3, 238, 240	5:24	164, 165
1:1–2:4	98, 282	5:28	130
1:14–19	9, 54	5:32	128
1:14–18	8	6	104, 105–109, 131, 261
1:25	51	6:1–9:17	162
1:26–28	49	6:1–4	32, 91, 92, 99, 103, 104, 110, 111, 119, 147, 148, 152, 154, 176, 250, 263, 264
2:1–4	279		
2:2	281		
2:17	310, 311		
2:18–25	310	6:1–2	105
2:18–24	47	6:3	25, 33, 91–93, 103, 108, 112, 119–125, 152, 318
2:18–20	47		
2:18	47	6:4	62, 103–105, 148
3:4–5	310	6:5–8	105, 106
3:7	310	6:5	92, 104–106, 133, 176
3:16–19	310	6:6	106, 130
3:22	103	6:7	105–107, 136
3:23–24	310	6:8–10	149
5	17, 127, 160, 164	6:8	106, 135
5:5	311	6:9–12	105, 106
5:15	125, 126	6:9	132, 147

6:11–12	104, 111, 135	14:22	250
6:11	34, 105, 106	15:14	211
6:12	105–107, 133, 139	16:2	62
6:19	135	16:15–16	231
6:23	56	17	229, 230, 232, 275, 280
7:1	147	17:1–14	229, 230
7:2–3	276	17:1	243
7:6	123	17:7	229
7:11	55	17:9	229
7:12	56	17:10–14	236
8–9	302	17:10	229, 241
8	302	17:11	241
8:15–22	300	17:13	241
8:20–21	276	17:14	230
8:21–22	107, 301, 302	17:15–22	229, 230
8:21	133	17:17	231, 305
8:22	107, 302	17:19	229
9	145, 161, 162, 265, 301	17:21	241
9:1–7	300, 302	17:23–27	229, 230
9:4–6	275	17:23–25	231
9:4	118, 280	17:23	230–232, 242, 243
9:8–17	300, 301	17:24–25	231, 242
9:9–17	280	17:24	231
9:11	302	17:25	231
9:16	302	17:26–27	231, 232, 243
9:18–29	94	17:26	231, 242
9:18–27	26	17:27	231
9:20–29	145, 159–160, 161	18:5	305
9:20	160	18:9–15	305
9:21–23	147	18:13	305
9:21	160	18:15	305
9:22–23	147, 160	18:18–19	147
9:24–27	160	18:19	147
9:28–29	94, 160	19:14	305
9:28	93, 162	19:31	62
9:29	158	21:1–4	305
10–11	162	21:5–7	305
10	161, 162	21:6	305
10:10	181	21:9	305
10:21	128	22	189, 190, 196, 201, 305
10:25–32	128	22:1–19	23
10:25	128, 129	22:1–2	192
10:26–32	129	22:1	189
10:32	129	22:2	194–196
11	119, 129, 160, 162	22:4	192–193
11:1–9	104, 162	22:7	195
11:9	128	22:8	195
11:10–32	129	22:12	190, 194, 195
11:10	123	22:13	195, 276
11:26	162	22:14	195–196
11:32	162	22:16	194, 195
12	162	22:19	198
12:4	162	24:10	61
14:18–20	250	25:7	15

25:20	61	*Exodus*	
25:24	234	2	205
25:26	121	2:2	85
28:2	61	2:15	203, 205
28:5	61	3–14	203, 223
28:6	61	3–4	204–207
29–31	85	3:2	209
29–30	25, 29, 85, 86	3:4	209
29:18	85	3:12	204
29:20	85	3:22	223
29:21	234	4	206
29:27–28	234	4:14	305
29:27	85	4:19–20	205
29:30	85	4:19	204–208
29:32–35	87	4:21	216
30:1–4	87	4:22	204, 257
30:3	62	4:23	204
30:4	73	4:24–26	204, 206
30:5–6	87	4:24	126, 203–210
30:23	85	4:25–26	205
31:38	85	4:25	204, 208
31:41	25, 85, 86	4:26	208, 235
32:33	273	4:27	204
34	292	6:6	217
35:1–7	296	6:7	217, 219
35:8	296	7–12	211
35:14	296	7:4	217
35:22	23, 73, 76, 279	7:5	217, 219
35:28	121	7:11–12	214
35:29	3, 121	7:12	219
37	3, 59, 121	7:21	214
37:2	73, 86, 121	7:22	214
38	59, 60, 61, 63, 67	8:2	214
38:1	59	8:3	214
38:2	60	8:14	214
38:8	62	8:18	219
38:9	62	9:9–10	211
38:10	61	9:11	214, 215
38:11	61	9:12	216
38:24	22, 64, 276	9:25	211
38:25	70	10:1	216
38:26	64, 70–72	10:2	219
39	59, 75	10:12	211
39:1	59	10:15	211
39:14	305	10:20	216
39:17	305	10:27	216
41:46	121	11–12	211
43:3	290	11	223
45:6	121	11:2	223
47:9	121	11:4–8	196
49:3–4	24	11:5	196, 211, 224
49:4	73, 74, 77	11:7	224
49:5–7	292	11:10	216
50:3	234	12	6, 11, 20, 196, 197, 223, 273, 274

INDEX OF ANCIENT JEWISH SOURCES

12:1–20	192	20	20, 277, 282
12:3–4	196	20:8–11	281
12:3	196	21:29	290
12:5	224	22:17	260
12:6	192, 193, 196	23:1	137
12:7	196	23:8	138
12:8–10	192	24:1–11	247
12:12–13	196, 213, 223, 225	24:7	281, 315
12:12	196, 211–214	24:12–18	2, 247, 315
12:13	197, 213, 223, 224	24:12	316
12:15–20	198	25–31:11	315
12:17	217	25:22	295
12:22–23	223	26:33	295
12:23	211, 213, 224, 225	26:34	295
12:29–30	223	30:6	295
12:29	211	30:26	295
12:30	224	31	282
12:35–36	223	31:12–17	282, 315
12:45	289	31:13–17	240
12:51	217	31:13	239, 282
13:3	217	31:16–17	239, 281–82
13:14	217	31:16	282
13:15	211	31:17	282
13:16	217	31:18	295, 315, 316
13:21	209	32:7–8	249
14:4	216, 217, 219	32:11–14	248
14:8	216, 217	32:15	295, 315
14:9	216	32:32–33	314
14:11	217	34:17	198
14:17–18	219	34:29	295, 315
14:17	216, 217	39:35	295
14:18	216	40:3	295
14:19	209, 217	40:5	295
14:20	217	40:21	295
14:22	217		
14:23	216	*Leviticus*	
14:26	216	6:2	288
14:28	216	6:7	288
15:19	216	6:18	288
16	20, 277	7:1	288
16:5	20, 277	7:11	288
16:20–22	20	8:33	234
16:22–26	277	11:46	288
16:28–30	277	12	6, 22, 34, 47, 49, 51, 52, 267, 274, 277, 288
16:27	277	12:1–2	48
19–20	20	12:4–5	48
19	247	12:4	48, 234
19:4	281	12:6	234
19:5–6	6, 11, 280	12:7	288
19:5	280	13:59	288
19:8	281	14:2	288
19:21	290	14:32	288
19:23	290	14:57	288
20–23	273		

15:19-33	48	25:1-15	293
15:32	288	25:11	293
16	98	25:12-13	297
18	60, 63	25:12	293, 294
18:8	24, 65, 73, 78	25:13	293, 294
18:13	68	26:19-22	64
18:15	22, 23, 63-65	28:16	193
18:16	63, 65, 66	28:17-25	198
18:18	78	29:12-34	307
18:24-30	75, 78	29:35	307
18:29	63	29:36	307
19:15	138	33:4	211
19:23-25	17, 156	35:33-34	183
19:23	17		
19:24	17, 18, 156	*Deuteronomy*	
19:25	17	1:17	138
19:26	260	4:19-20	229, 250, 251, 259
20	60, 63	4:20	248, 249
20:11	24, 65, 73, 78, 79	4:26	290
20:12	22, 23, 63-68	4:45	295
20:14	22, 23, 67, 68	5	20
20:21	63, 65	6:5	294
21:9	11, 22, 23, 64, 67	6:17	295
22:10	289	6:20	295
23:5	193	6:21	217
23:6-8	198	7	294
23:15-16	53	7:6	280
23:34	307	7:8	281
23:36	307	7:9-10	294
23:39	307	7:10	294
23:40	305	8:19	290
23:41-42	307	9:9	295, 315
25	7, 84, 273, 324	9:11	295, 315
25:10	84, 122	9:12	249
25:13	84	9:15	295, 315
25:30	52, 234	9:19	209
26:16	172	9:26-29	248, 251
		9:26	248, 249
Numbers		9:29	248, 249
4:5	295	10:8	295
5:29	288	10:12-13	294
6:5	234	10:17	138
6:13	234, 288	11:1	294
6:21	288	11:4	215
7:89	295	11:22	294
10:33	295	14:2	280
12:10-11	172	16:2	196-197
13:33	104	16:8	198
14:44	295	16:13-14	305
19:4	288	16:19	138
20:16	217	18:10	260
22:18	138	18:12	260
24:13	138	19:16	137
25	293	22:13	62

INDEX OF ANCIENT JEWISH SOURCES

22:23–27	74	11:16	209
23:1	24, 66, 73, 78	11:34	194
25:5–6	63	12:5	209
25:5	62, 63	16:25	305
25:7–10	63	20:27	295
25:9–10	63	20:41	209
26:8	212, 217		
26:18	280	*1 Samuel*	
27:20	24, 66, 73, 78	4:3	295
27:25	138	4:4	295
28:22	172	4:5	295
28:27	172	8:3	138
28:35	172	8:9	290
30:16–20	294	16:7	251
30:19	290	19:2	205
31	37	19:5	305
31:7–30	284	20:1	205
31:9	295	22:23	205
31:25	295	23:15	205
31:26	295	25:29	205
31:28	290	30:22	251
32:8–9	101, 178, 229, 250, 251, 256, 259	*2 Samuel*	
32:8	250	3:7	74
32:11	225	4:8	205
32:12	251	7:12	234
32:46	290	11	74
33:6	77	15:11	205
33:8–11	296	15:24	295
33:9	297	16:21–22	74
		16:21	62
Joshua		20:3	62
3:3	295	20:19–20	249
3:6	295	20:19	205
3:8	295	21:2	205
3:11	295	22:5	251
4:7	295	23:1–5	297
4:9	295	24:1	209
4:16	295	24:16	213
4:18	295		
6:6	295	*1 Kings*	
6:8	295	2:3	295
8:33	295	2:42	290
10:13	53	3:15	295
		4:20	305
Judges		5:21	305
6:7	209	6:19	295
6:11	208	8:1	295
6:12	208	8:6	295
6:14	208	8:36	249
6:16	208, 209	8:51	248, 249
6:20	208	8:53	248, 249
6:21	208	8:66	305
6:22	208	11:40	205

19:10	205	22:30	314
19:14	205	25:12	234
21:10	290	25:34	234
21:13	290	26:21	205
22:19	250	29:10	234
		31:13	305

2 Kings

11:14	305	31:34–36	303
11:20	305	32:9–15	283
17:13	290	32:10	290
17:15	290, 295	32:25	290
23:2	315	32:44	290
23:3	295	33:19–26	303
23:21	315	33:20	303
		33:21	303
		33:25	303

Isaiah

1:23	138	33:26	303
2:3	196	42:19	290
4:3	314	43:12–13	212
5:1	194	44:23	295
5:23	138		

Ezekiel

8	283	5:2	234
8:1–16	284	7:12	305
8:2	290	16:41	212
8:11–15	283	22:12	138
8:12–16	289	23:32	305
8:16	283, 288, 291, 299	23:44	62
8:17	283	30:14–19	212
8:19	283	30:14	212
8:20	288, 289, 291	30:16	212
30:8–11	283	30:19	212
30:10	283	32:27	104, 110
30:29	196	34:25–26	295
31:5	225	34:25	295
32:17	295	37:25	295
33:8	295	43:12	288
33:15	138		
45:7	98, 263, 324	*Hosea*	
50:4	283	9:1	305
54:10	295		
54:13	283	*Joel*	
55:1–5	297	4:20	249
60:17	295		
60:21	155	*Amos*	
65:6	314	3:13	290
		8:10	194
		9:15	155

Jeremiah

3:16	295	*Jonah*	
6:10	290	4:6	305
6:26	194		
7:34	305	*Habakkuk*	
10:12	278	2:2–3	284
11:7	290		
11:17	155		

Micah
3:11	138
4:2	196

Zechariah
3:1–2	101, 176, 265, 266
3:6	290
4:10	305
8:3	196
10:7	305
12:9	205
12:10	194, 195

Malachi
2:8	297
2:14	290
3:16	314
3:17	280

Psalms
15:5	138
18:5	251
25:10	295
26:10	138
27:12	137
29:1	250
29:11	295
33:12	249
35:11	137
45:1	194
50:7	290
55:10	128
60:7	194
68:13	194
72:3	295
78	211
78:35	250
78:49	209, 225–226
81:9	290
82:1	250
82:2	138
84:1–2	194
85:18	295
89:4–5	297
89:29–30	297
90:4	311
104:24	278
105	211
105:37	217
108:7	194
119	278, 295
119:133	255
127:2	194
132:12	295
135:4	280
139:16	314
149:7	212

Proverbs
3:19–20	278
4:3	194
6:12	251
6:29	62
6:35	138
8:22–31	278
8:22–23	278
8:22	278
17:23	138
18:5	138
21:14	138

Job
1–2	101, 250, 265, 266
1:9–11	190
1:6	176, 265
2:1	265
29:11	290
38:7	250
38:12	190

Song of Songs
8:7	138

Ruth
4:6	249
4:7	284

Lamentations
4:18	234

Qohelet
2:8	280

Esther
1:5	234
2:12	234
2:21	205
3:6	205
3:13	283
8:8	283
8:15	305

Daniel
7:10	314
9:24–27	7, 269
10:3	234
10:13	178, 229, 256
10:20	178, 229

10:21	256, 314	15:29	295
12:1	256, 314	16:6	295
		16:37	295
Nehemiah		17:1	295
8:18	307	17:11	234
9:26	290	21	209
9:29	290	21:1	209
9:30	290	22:19	295
9:34	290	28:2	295
10:1	283	28:18	295
13:15	290	29:3	280
13:21	290		
		2 Chronicles	
1 Chronicles		3:1	196
1:19	128	5:2	295
5:1–2	24	5:7	295
5:1	73, 76, 77	6:27	249
6:13	10	7:9	307
6:18	10	19:7	138
15:25	295	24:19	290
15:26	295	34:30	315
15:28	295	35	197

III. Apocrypha

Sirach		*Wisdom of Solomon*	
16:26–28	303	18:5	223
17:17	229, 256, 259	19:4–5	219
24	278		
24:8	278	*1 Maccabees*	
24:9	278	1:11	275
24:12	278	1:15	237
24:23	278	1:48	237
46:4	53	1:60	237
49:14	164	2:24–27	293
		2:46	237

IV. Pseudepigrapha

Assumption of Moses		6–8	112
1:2	84	6	114
8:3	237	6:2–8	111
		6:6	126, 127
1 Enoch		7:1	111, 114
1–36	32, 110, 148	7:2–6	114
2–5	303	7:2	148
5:8–11	175	7:3–6	111, 118
6–11	109–115, 118, 119, 124, 130, 136, 148, 150, 151, 152	7:4–5	148
		7:4	118
		8:1–3	111
6:1–10:14	114	8:1–2	114
6–9	115	8:3	111, 114

INDEX OF ANCIENT JEWISH SOURCES

4	111, 114	86–89	110
-11	112	86:4	148
1–5	111, 114	88:2	148
1	112	89:61–64	314
6–8	111	89:68	314
6	114	89:70	314
7–8	114	89:71	314
8	111, 114	89:76	314
9–11	111, 114	89:77	314
9–10	112	90:17	314
)–11	32, 33, 93, 112, 115–118, 119, 135, 136, 137, 141, 264, 318	90:20	314
		91	7, 269
		93	7, 269
)	33, 111, 113, 115, 117, 136, 139	93:1–3	314
		93:5	155
):1–6	114	93:10	155
):1–3	111, 112, 113, 115, 117, 136	98:7	314
		98:8	314
):4–11:2	111	103:2–3	314
):4–10	113	104:7	314
):4–8	112, 113, 115, 119	106:13	127
):4–6	113	106:19	314
):7	113, 114, 115, 116, 119	107:1	314
):8	114		
):9–14	114, 117	*2 Enoch*	
):9–10	93, 112, 115, 119, 124, 127	22:8	164
0:9	113, 114	*Jubilees*	
0:11–11:2	112, 113	See above, section I	
0:11–14	113, 115, 136		
0:11–12	116	*Liber Antiquitatum Biblicarum*	
0:12	135, 139	3:2	119
0:13–15	116	6	128
0:13–14	135		
0:14	114	*Testament of Asher*	
0:15–11:2	114, 115, 116	1:8	252
0:15	113, 114, 151, 152, 153, 175	3:2	252
		6:4	252
0:16–11:2	116		
0:16	113, 155	*Testament of Benjamin*	
0:20	113	3:3–4	252
2–16	110, 114	3:3	252
4:8	164	3:4	252
5:8–11	151, 152, 153	3:5	252
5:8–9	151	3:8	252
5:8	151, 153	6:1	252
5:9	151, 152, 153	6:7	252
5:11	151	7:1	252
6:1	151, 152, 153, 175	7:2	252
9:1	151, 175		
31:1	314	*Testament of Dan*	
31:2	314	1:7	252
31:4	314	4:7	252
33–90	36	5:1	252

5:10	252	*Testament of Naphtali*	
5:11	252	2:6	252
		3:1	252
Testament of Issachar		3:2–5	303
6:1	252		
7:7	252	*Testament of Reuben*	
		1:7	76, 77
Testament of Joseph		3	82
3:3	80	3:9–15	75, 142
7:4	252	3:12–14	75–76
20:2	252	3:14	76
		3:15	76
Testament of Judah		4:7	252
1	60	4:11	252
10:1	61	6:3	252
13–14	60		
14	76	*Testament of Simeon*	
25:3	252	5:3	252
Testament of Levi		*Testament of Zebulun*	
3:3	252	9:8	252
17	7, 269		
18:12	252		
19:1	252		

V. DEAD SEA SCROLLS

1QpHab (*Pesher Habakkuk*)		VII 20	235
II 8–9	81	VII 22	235
VI 12–VII 14	284	VIII 13–15	81
VII 4–5	81	IX 13–14	236
VIII 2	174	IX 17–18	81
1QapGen ar (*Genesis Apocryphon*)		1QM (*War Scroll*)	
III 3	127	I 1	253
XII	18	I 13	253
		XIII 10–12	253
1QS (*Community Rule*)		XIV 1	212
I 8–9	243	XIV 9	253
I 18	253	XVIII 1	253
I 24	253		
II 5	253	1QH^a (*Hodayot*)	
II 18	253	IV 9	81
III 13–IV 26	100	XII 10	253
III 15–IV 26	321	XII 12–13	253
III 16	235	XIII 9	81
III 21–23	253	XIV 21–22	254
III 25	261	XV 3–4	254
V 10–11	81	XIX 9	81
VI 17–21	235		
VI 17	235	4Q37 (4QDeut^j)	
VI 18	235	XII 14	250
VI 21	235		

INDEX OF ANCIENT JEWISH SOURCES

4Q201 (4QEnᵃ ar)
1 iii 4–5   126

4Q202 (4QEnᵇ ar)
1 iii 7   112
1 iv 6–8   124
1 iv 10–11   139
1 iv 11   135

4Q204 (4QEnᶜ ar)
5 ii 17   127

4Q213a (4QLeviᵇ ar)
1–2   254

4Q216 (4QJubileesᵃ)
I 1–4   285
I 9–12   285
I 11–12   2
I 13   62
I 15–16   141
II 3–5   287
IV 1–6   285
IV 6–8   3, 6–8
IV 6   16
V 1   3
VI 8   303
VII 5–13   238–239
VII 5–10   238
VII 8–9   9
VII 9–13   6, 178, 279
VII 11–13   239
VII 11–12   258
VII 12–13   147
VII 14–16   259
VII 17   288

4Q217 (4QJubileesᵇ)
2 1–4   286

4Q219 (4QJubileesᵈ)
II 30   62
II 33   62
II 35   15, 159

4Q221 (4QJubileesᶠ)
7 4–9   80

4Q223–224 (4QpapJubileesʰ)
2 II 6   105

4Q225 (4Qpseudo-Jubileesᵃ)
1, 7   286
2 ii   206
2 ii 5–8   207

4Q228 (4QText with a Citation of Jub)
1 i 9   287

4Q252 (4QCommGen A)
I–II   107
I 1–3   120
II 1–3   53

4Q265 (4QMiscellaneous Rules)
7   57

4Q266 (4QDamascus Documentᵃ)
3 ii 5–7   253

4Q267 (4QDamascus Documentᵇ)
2, 1–3   253

4Q271 (4QDamascus Documentᶠ)
4 ii 5   287
5 i 18–19   253

4Q300 (4QMysteriesᵇ)
1a ii 2   311

4Q369 (4QPrayer of Enosh)
1 ii 6–7   258

4Q384
9, 2   287

4Q395–399 (4QMMT)
B 62–64   18, 156
C 27–32   254
C 29   254

4Q422 (4QParaphrase of Gen and Exod)
II 8   139
III 7   139

4Q495 (4QWar Scrollᵉ)
2, 3–4   253

4Q511 (4QShirᵇ)
63 iii 1–3   235

11QTempleᵃ
LX 3–4   18, 156

CD (*Damascus Document*)
I 8–11   38, 321
I 18   283
II 14–III   81, 138, 146
III 2–4   294
III 12–14   243
V 7–11   68

V 17–19	253	XVI 1–6	242
VIII 21	243	XVI 1–4	83
XII 2–3	253, 255	XVI 2–4	4, 287
XV 10	243	XVI 4–6	242
XV 13	243		

VI. Philo and Josephus

Philo
On the Life of Abraham
168   195

On the Change of Names
38   164

On the Life of Moses
2:65   132

Questions and Answers on Genesis
1:15   51

Josephus
Jewish Antiquities
I 75   119, 132
I 85   164
IV 227   17
IX 28   164
XII 241   237

VII. New Testament, Early Christian, And Classical Writings

Aeschylus, Prometheus Bound
232–233   134

Augustine, City of God
XV, 24, 24   120

Ephrem
Commentary on Genesis
49:4   77
Commentary on Exodus
II, 8   205
IV, 3   205

Epistle of Barnabas
15:4   311

Hebrews
11:5   164

Jerome, Questions on Genesis
6:3   120

Ovid, Metamorphoses
I, 250–252   134

2 Peter
3:8   311

VIII. Mishnah, Tosefta, and Talmud

Mishnah
Ma'aser Šeni
5:1–4   156
5:1   17

Nedarim
3:11   205

Niddah
3:7   50

Qiddušin
4:14   278

Šabbat
19   244
19:5   236, 242
19:6   242

Sanhedrin
4:7   79
7:4   67, 69
9:1   67, 69

Tosefta
Šabbat
8:5   69

INDEX OF ANCIENT JEWISH SOURCES

Talmud
b. ʿAbodah Zarah
4a   205
25a   53
b. Nedarim
31b–32a   205
31b   204
32a   204, 209, 210
b. Niddah
30b   50–51
b. Šabbat
133b   242
b. Sanhedrin
13a–b   303
54a   79

89b   210
108a   120
b. Soṭah
10b   71
b. Yebamot
34b   61
62b–63a   69
y. Nedarim
3:2 (37d) 63
3:11 (38b) 204, 210
y. Peʾah
7:6 (20b–c) 17
y. Soṭah
1:4 (5b)   71

IX. Targum and Midrash

Targum Onqelos
Gen 5:24   164
Gen 6:3   120
Exod 4:24 208

Targum Neofiti
Gen 6:3   120
Gen 38:26 71
Exod 4:24 208

Targum Pseudo-Jonathan
Gen 6:3   120
Gen 21:6   305
Gen 38:24 64
Exod 4:24 208
Exod 12:12 212
Lev 19:24 18
Deut 32:8 250

Genesis Rabbah
1:6   278
19:8   311
26:6   119
30:7   120
37   129
37:25   128
53:8   305
76   204
85:10   64
97   71

Exodus Rabbah
5:8   204, 205
15:11   198

41:7   209
44:8   209

Numbers Rabbah
11:3   209
14   311
21:24   307

Songs Rabbah
3   209

Qohelet Rabbah
4   209
9:2   209

Qohelet Zuṭa
4   209

Esther Rabbah
1:6   205

ʾAbot de Rabbi Nathan
A 32   120

Mekilta de-Rabbi Ishmael
Amaleq 1   210
Beshallaḥ 5 71
Pisḥa 7   212
Shirta 4   223
Shirta 5   120

Mekilta de-Rabbi Simeon b. Yoḥai
Amaleq 1   205
Pisḥa 7   198

Pesiqta de-Rab Kahana		Sifre Numbers	
28	307	6	17, 156

Pesiqta Rabbati		Sifre Deuteronomy	
40	311	306	303
		348	71

Seder 'Olam Rabbah
1	128
2	25, 85, 87
4	107
11	303
28	120

Tanḥuma (Buber)
Gen 11	273
Ki Tissa 13	209

X. Later Rabbinic and Other Jewish Texts

Abraham Ibn Ezra, Biblical Commentary
Gen 6:3	120
Gen 30:23	85
Exod 2:2	85
Exod 4:24	204
Exod 12:12	212

Maimonides, Guide to the Perplexed
III, 24	192

Nachmanides, Biblical Commentary
Gen 38:10	63
Exod 24:1	247
Exod 24:12	247

Radaq, Biblical Commentary
Gen 6:3	120
Gen 22:1–2	192

Rashi, Biblical Commentary
Gen 6:3	120
Exod 4:24	204
Exod 12:12	212
Exod 24:1	247
Exod 24:12	247
Jer 33:20	303

SUPPLEMENTS
TO THE
JOURNAL FOR THE STUDY OF JUDAISM

85. AVERY-PECK, A.J., D. HARRINGTON & J. NEUSNER. *When Judaism and Christianity Began.* Essays in Memory of Anthony J. Saldarini. 2004. ISBN 90 04 13659 2 (Set), ISBN 90 04 13660 6 (Volume I), ISBN 90 04 13661 4 (Volume II)
86. DRAWNEL, H. *An Aramaic Wisdom Text from Qumran.* A New Interpretation of the Levi Document. 2004. ISBN 90 04 13753 X
87. BERTHELOT, K. *L'«humanité de l'autre homme» dans la pensée juive ancienne.* 2004. ISBN 90 04 13797 1
88. BONS, E. (ed.) *«Car c'est l'amour qui me plaît, non le sacrifice ...».* Recherches sur Osée 6:6 et son interprétation juive et chrétienne. 2004. ISBN 90 04 13677 0
89. CHAZON, E.G., D. SATRAN & R. CLEMENTS (eds.). *Things Revealed.* Studies in Honor of Michael E. Stone. 2004. ISBN 90 04 13885 4
90. FLANNERY-DAILEY, F. *Dreamers, Scribes, and Priests.* Jewish Dreams in the Hellenistic and Roman Eras. 2004. ISBN 90 04 12367 9
91. SCOTT, J.M. *On Earth as in Heaven.* The Restoration of Sacred Time and Sacred Space in the Book of Jubilees. 2005. ISBN 90 04 13796 3
92. RICHARDSON, P. *Building Jewish in the Roman East.* 2005. ISBN 90 04 14131 6
93. BATSCH, C. *La guerre et les rites de guerre dans le judaïsme du deuxième Temple.* 2005. ISBN 90 04 13897 8
94. HACHLILI, R. *Jewish Funerary Customs, Practices and Rites in the Second Temple Period.* 2005. ISBN 90 04 12373 3
95. BAKHOS, C. *Ancient Judaism in its Hellenistic Context.* 2005. ISBN 90 04 13871 4
97. NEUSNER, J. *Contours of Coherence in Rabbinic Judaism.* 2005. ISBN 90 04 14231 2 (Set), ISBN 90 04 14436 6 (Volume I), ISBN 90 04 14437 4 (Volume II)
98. XERAVITS, G.G. & J. ZSENGELLÉR (eds.). *The Book of Tobit: Text, Tradition, Theology.* Papers of the First International Conference on the Deuterocanonical Books, Pápa, Hungary, 20-21 May, 2004. 2005. ISBN 90 04 14376 9
99. ROSENFELD, B-Z. & J. MENIRAV (Translated from the Hebrew by Chava Cassel). *Markets and Marketing in Roman Palestine.* 2005. ISBN 90 04 14049 2
100. COLLINS, J.J. *Jewish Cult and Hellenistic Culture.* Essays on the Jewish Encounter with Hellenism and Roman Rule. 2005. ISBN 90 04 14438 2

101. NEUSNER, J. *Rabbinic Categories*. Construction and Comparison. 2005. ISBN 90 04 14578 8
102. SIVERTSEV, A.M. *Households, Sects, and the Origins of Rabbinic Judaism*. 2005. ISBN 90 04 14447 1
103. BEYERLE, S. *Gottesvorstellungen in der antik-jüdischen Apokalyptik*. 2005. ISBN 90 04 13116 7
104. SIEVERS, J. & G. LEMBI (eds.). *Josephus and Jewish History in Flavian Rome and Beyond*. 2005. ISBN 90 04 14179 0
105. DAVILA, J.R. *The Provenance of the Pseudepigrapha*. Jewish, Christian, or Other? 2005. ISBN 90 04 13752 1
106. BAKHOS, C. (ed.) *Current Trends in the Study of Midrash*. 2005. ISBN 90 04 13870 6
107. FELDMAN, L.H. *Judaism and Hellenism Reconsidered*. 2006. ISBN 90 04 14906 6
108. BRUTTI, M. *The Development of the High Priesthood during the pre-Hasmonean Period*. History, Ideology, Theology. 2006. ISBN 90 04 14910 4
109. VELTRI, G. *Libraries, Translations, and "Canonic" Texts*. The Septuagint, Aquila and Ben Sira in the Jewish and Christian Traditions. 2006. ISBN 90 04 14993 7
110. RODGERS, Z. (ed.) *Making History*. Josephus and Historical Method. 2006. ISBN 90 04 15008 0
111. HEMPEL, C. & J. M. LIEU (eds.) *Biblical Traditions in Transmission*. Essays in Honour of Michael A. Knibb. 2006. ISBN 90 04 13997 4
112. GRAPPE, Ch. & J.-C. INGELAERE (éds.) *Le Temps et les Temps dans les littératures juives et chrétiennes au tournant de notre ère*. 2006. ISBN 90 04 15058 7
113. CAPPELLETTI, S. *The Jewish Community of Rome*. From the Second Century B. C. to the Third Century C.E. 2006. ISBN 90 04 15157 5
114. ORLOV, A.A. *From Apocalypticism to Merkabah Mysticism Studies in the Slavonic Pseudepigrapha*. 2007. ISBN-13: 978 90 04 15439 1, ISBN-10: 90 04 15439 6
115. MACASKILL, G. *Revealed Wisdom and Inaugurated Eschatology in Ancient Judaism and Early Christianity*. 2007. ISBN-13: 978 90 04 15582 4, ISBN-10: 90 04 15582 1
116. DVORJETSKI, E. *Leisure, Pleasure and Healing Spa Culture and Medicine in Ancient Eastern Mediterranean*. 2007. ISBN-13: 978 90 04 15681 4, ISBN-10: 90 04 15681 X
117. SEGAL, M. *The Book of Jubilees Rewritten Bible, Redaction, Ideology and Theology*. 2007. ISBN-13: 978 90 04 15057 7, ISBN-10: 90 04 15057 9
118. XERAVITS, G.G. & J. ZSENGELLÉR (eds.). *The Books of the Maccabees: History, Theology, Ideology*. Papers of the Second International Conference on the Deuterocanonical Books, Pápa, Hungary, 9-11 June, 2005. 2007. ISBN-13: 978 90 04 15700 2, ISBN-10: 90 04 15700 X

ISSN 1384-2161